NEW TESTAMENT INTRODUCTION
THE GOSPELS AND ACTS

THE GOSPELS AND ACTS

New Testament
Introduction

by

DONALD GUTHRIE, B.D., M.Th., Ph.D.

Lecturer in New Testament Language and Literature,
The London Bible College

LONDON

THE TYNDALE PRESS

39 BEDFORD SQUARE WC1

PRINTED AND BOUND IN ENGLAND BY
HAZELL WATSON AND VINEY LTD
AYLESBURY, BUCKS

CONTENTS

I THE GOSPELS   11

General Introduction (11); Their Literary Form (11); Motives for
their Production (12); The Place of the Gospels in the New Testament (15); The Best Method of Approaching the Gospels (17).

II MATTHEW'S GOSPEL   19

Characteristics (19); Purpose, Destination and Place of Origin (23);
Structure (27); Authorship (31); Date (43); Language (44);
Contents (46).

III MARK'S GOSPEL   49

Characteristics (49); Purpose and Readers (53); Structure (59);
Authorship (65); Date (68); Textual Problems (72); Language (76);
Locality, Historicity and Chronology (77); Contents (82).

IV LUKE'S GOSPEL   84

Characteristics (84); Purpose and Readers (87); Structure (90);
Authorship of the Gospel (and Acts) (92); Date (104); Language
(109); Contents (110).

V THE SYNOPTIC PROBLEM   114

The Nature of the Problem (114); A Brief Historical Survey of
Solutions (116); The Four Source Theory (124); The Marcan
Source (126); The Source Q (136); Sources Peculiar to Matthew
(150); Sources Peculiar to Luke (160).

VI FORM CRITICISM AND ITS DEVELOPMENTS   178

Reasons for the Rise of Form Criticism (178); Various Types of
Theory (181); General Criticisms of Form Criticism (189); The
Value of Form Criticism (192).

VII TOWARDS A SOLUTION   195

Guiding Principles (195); Important Factors in the Search for a
Solution (204); A Tentative Theory of Origins (209).

VIII JOHN'S GOSPEL   212

Characteristics (212); Authorship (216); Purpose (246); Date
(257); Relation to the Synoptic Gospels (262); Structure (275);
Theories of Dislocation (287); Language and Style (291); The
Background of the Gospel (294); Historicity (298); Contents (300).

IX THE ACTS OF THE APOSTLES   303
   Characteristics (303); Date (307); Purpose (316); Historicity (321);
   Sources (330); The Text (344); Language (345); Contents (347).

   GENERAL BIBLIOGRAPHY   349

   CLASSIFIED BIBLIOGRAPHY   365

   AUTHOR INDEX   369

   SUBJECT INDEX   376

ABBREVIATIONS

AbThANT	Abhandlungen zur Theologie des Alten und Neuen Testaments.
AJTh	American Journal of Theology.
ATR	Anglican Theological Review.
BC	Black's New Testament Commentary.
BJRL	Bulletin of the John Rylands Library.
CB	Century Bible.
CGT	Cambridge Greek Testament.
Clar B	Clarendon Bible.
EB	Etudes Bibliques.
EC	Epworth Preacher's Commentary.
EGT	Expositor's Greek Testament.
Enc. Bib.	Encyclopaedia Biblica.
Eng. Tr.	English Translation.
EQ	Evangelical Quarterly.
ET	Expository Times.
ETL	Ephemerides Theologica Lovanienses.
EvTh	Evangelische Theologie.
Exp.	Expositor.
Exp. Bib.	Expositor's Bible.
HDB	Hastings' Dictionary of the Bible.
HE	Eusebius' Historia Ecclesia.
HTR	Harvard Theological Review.
HTS	Harvard Theological Studies.
IB	Interpreter's Bible.
ICC	International Critical Commentary.
ILNT	Introduction to the Literature of the New Testament.
INT	Introduction to the New Testament.
JBL	Journal of Biblical Literature.
JR	Journal of Religion.
JRS	Journal of Roman Studies.
JTS	Journal of Theological Studies.
KEK	Kritisch-exegetischer Kommentar.
LHB	Lietzmann's Handbuch zum Neuen Testament.
LXX	Septuagint.

MC	Moffatt's New Testament Commentary.
NBD	New Bible Dictionary.
NkZ	Neue kirchliche Zeitschrift.
NLC	New London Commentary.
Nov. Test.	Novum Testamentum (Journal).
NTD	Neue Testament Deutsch.
NTS	New Testament Studies.
PelC	Pelican Commentary.
RB	Revue Biblique.
RGG	Die Religion in Geschichte und Gegenwart.
RHR	Revue de l'Histoire des Religions.
RSV	Revised Standard Version.
RV	Revised Version.
SJT	Scottish Journal of Theology.
StTh	Studia Theologica.
TC	Torch Commentary.
ThLZ	Theologische Literaturzeitung.
ThZ	Theologische Zeitschrift.
TNT	Tyndale New Testament Commentary.
TR	Theologische Rundschau.
TSK	Theologische Studien und Kritiken.
TU	Texte und Untersuchungen.
VC	Vigiliae Christianae.
VT	Vetus Testamentum (Journal).
WC	Westminster Commentary.
ZkT	Zeitschrift für katholische Theologie.
ZNTW	Zeitschrift für die neutestamentliche Wissenschaft.
ZTK	Zeitschrift für Theologie und Kirche.

PREFACE

In this book, which completes my series of books on New Testament Introduction, many issues are raised which are of critical importance. A true approach to the life and teaching of Jesus is essential for a right understanding of the Christian faith. Yet the Gospels and Acts have for long been under examination from a literary critical point of view and the results have not always been constructive. The various viewpoints have been discussed and special attention has been given to the problem of origins. Through lack of sufficient data much of the discussion must inevitably be no more than tentative. Fortunately, although origins are a right and proper field of enquiry, our evaluation of the Gospels and Acts does not depend on speculation regarding sources. The books have a right to exist in themselves. It is for this reason that the first three Gospels are studied individually before the Synoptic problem is discussed. This method involves several forward references to matters more fully discussed later, but it has the advantage of proceeding from the study of wholes to the study of parts. The book is so arranged, however, that those who prefer to begin with the Synoptic problem may readily reverse the order.

I am again grateful to Ralph P. Martin, M.A., Ph.D., for kindly reading the manuscript and making helpful suggestions. I am also indebted to I. Howard Marshall, M.A., B.D., Ph.D., for various constructive criticisms which have removed some, at least, of the obscurities from the original manuscript.

As this is the final volume in the series I desire to express special appreciation to the publishers whose kindness and consideration throughout the undertaking have been unsparing. The fine quality of the books is a fitting tribute to their careful attention to every detail.

I have been encouraged by the warm reception of the first two volumes and it is my earnest hope that the present one will meet a similar need.

D. G.

CHAPTER ONE

THE GOSPELS

I. GENERAL INTRODUCTION

The four Gospels have always held a place of particular interest for Christian people. They are the main source of our knowledge of our Lord's life, for without them our data would be reduced to the barest outline. It is no wonder, therefore, that scholars have concentrated such interest upon them. Yet probably no writings are more baffling for the critical investigator. Most of the problems which have arisen in the course of the history of criticism are still the subject of debate, although the more radical theories have now been largely discounted. Before dealing with these problems it is best to form some estimate of the Gospels in the form in which they have been transmitted, for there can be no doubt that they have exercised a profound influence on Christian thought quite independently of any critical assessment of them. This approach differs from that of some modern schools of criticism which begin with certain presuppositions which affect the value of the extant Gospels. The tenets of such schools of thought will be fully examined in due time, but the present treatment is based on the assumption that it is the Gospels themselves and not their sources or origins which have moulded Christian history, and that the latter must be approached by means of the former.

II. THEIR LITERARY FORM

It is customary to think of the Gospels as accounts of the life of Christ, but it is at once apparent that they are not strict biographies. This is not merely because they concentrate upon a very small part of the life of Christ. It is rather because their dominant purpose is not solely a record of facts. Whereas they are historical in form, their purpose was something more than historical. It is not, in fact, an accident that they were called 'Gospels' at an early period in Christian history. They proclaimed good news (εὐαγγέλιου), a message which was desperately needed.[1]

[1] Cf. F. F. Bruce's discussion of the true character of a gospel (*BJRL*, XLV, 1963, pp. 319–339). The use of the word εὐαγγέλιον of written records of the life and work of Jesus is testified by Justin Martyr (*Apol.* i. 66), but how long before Justin's time it was used is not known. Its basic meaning of 'good news' was used

But there were no parallels to the Gospel form which served as a pattern for the earliest writers. The literary genre arose out of the exigencies of the Gentile mission. The preachers had to stress the passion and resurrection, for these themes formed the kernel of their message. It is not surprising therefore that so much space is devoted to the narratives of these events in the written Gospels. Approximately one third of Mark's Gospel is taken up with them and the other Gospels contain proportionately only slightly less. This emphasis is in line with Paul's declaration that the tradition committed to him concerned the death and resurrection of Christ (1 Cor. xv. 3 ff.).

The accounts of our Lord's life, good deeds, miracles and teaching must have been regarded as secondary to this dominant interest, although at the same time essential to it. No mere writer of biography would ever have adopted such a perspective. The Evangelists, in short, were not literary men and were not setting out to be. They had no interest in conforming to any conventional pattern. They themselves had experienced a remarkable transformation as a result of the stupendous events they related. This at once marks out their records as set apart from other literary exercises and this fact must be constantly borne in mind when considering the critical problems of their origins. It cannot be claimed without reservation that these books should be set alongside other books on the assumption that precisely the same principles of criticism which are used in investigations of secular literary productions must necessarily be valid here also.[1] They may be so, but it is part of the problem of the literary investigation of the Gospels that no precise parallels exist by which to put this assumption to the test.[2] Such literary principles will therefore be regarded as guides rather than as criteria.

III. MOTIVES FOR THEIR PRODUCTION

The different purposes which prompted the production of the various Gospels will be dealt with when each Gospel is considered separately.

in both a secular and a sacred sense. The antecedents of the New Testament usage are to be found in the Old Testament, although it was paralleled in Emperor worship. Cf. the useful summary of the development of this word in A. Wikenhauser's *New Testament Introduction* (Eng. Tr. 1958), pp. 150–155.

[1] See p. 205 for further discussion of the uniqueness of the Gospels.

[2] The closest parallels which have been cited are Philostratus' *Life of Apollonius of Tyana* and Lucian's *False Prophet*. Cf. C. K. Barrett, *Luke the Historian in Recent Study* (1961), pp. 13–15.

But our present purpose is to deal with the general motives which led to the writing of Gospel accounts, since, as stated above, no previous patterns existed.

At first the oral apostolic testimony would possess such weight that an authenticated and consecutive Gospel in a written form may not have been conceived. There can be no denying that word of mouth carried more authority for the eastern mind than written documents, and for this reason it is generally supposed that written documents were regarded as a necessity only after the decease of the authorized eye-witnesses. In this case a period of some considerable time might well have elapsed before our earliest Gospels. The problem of the dating of the Gospels will be considered later, but it is necessary at this juncture to put in a word of caution against the too ready assumption that an extensive oral period is essential for the understanding of the origin of the Gospels. The rapid spread of Christianity may well have precipitated a need much earlier, for the apostles could not have been ubiquitous. Quite apart from the dating of the Gospels it is clear from Luke's preface that, at some undefined period before Luke himself wrote, others had produced written accounts. There is no knowing how early the earliest of these may have been and this uncertainty must condition our assessment of the view that at first no motive existed for the production of a written account.

It has often been asserted that delay was caused by the widespread belief in the imminence of the *parousia*, or return of Christ, which if taken seriously would clearly discourage any written records. What was the point if at any time the Lord might return? Records to perpetuate the story of the origin of the Church would appear relevant only when it was clear that the Church would have a continuing history. This is a reasonable conjecture and has much to commend it, but it is by no means certain that it is right. The New Testament Epistles antedate the Gospels in their canonical form. Moreover, our Lord made clear that before the *parousia* the nations must first hear the gospel. Is it then entirely unreasonable to suppose that some of the earliest preachers found use for written records? If conjecture is to be relied on, it might just as well be maintained that the production of written Gospels for propaganda purposes would have been regarded as an essential part in the Church's preparation for the *parousia*.

Other reasons which have been suggested for a delay in writing are the cost of materials and the difficulty of obtaining adequate data. The former of these cannot be lightly dismissed, for writing materials were expensive, but it is difficult to see how the problem was lessened at a later date. The view taken over the latter point will vary according to the view held regarding Gospel origins. If all the Evangelists had to go searching round for their material, some interval would probably be necessary, but this is not the only, nor is it the most reasonable, explanation of the Gospel origins, as will be seen when the Synoptic problem is dealt with later.

There were undoubtedly many motives which would have led to the production of the Gospels. The need for a historical record for catechetical purposes is at once obvious. Without minimizing the custom of oral instruction so highly esteemed among the Jews, it is questionable whether this procedure would have made so strong an appeal to Gentile converts. The Gentile mission, in fact, would have been greatly assisted by written documents for catechesis, and although the need may not have been at once recognized it must have dawned upon the missionary Church at an early stage. Closely linked with catechetical requirements would have been those of apologetics. The non-Christian world would naturally want to know what kind of person Jesus was, and the urgent need for an authoritative answer is easily recognizable. Whereas, again, an apostolic oral witness would at first suffice, the spreading work of the gospel would soon require more permanent accounts.

It has been suggested that a liturgical motive played a part in the production of some, at least, of the Gospels and those theories will be mentioned later on. Whatever decisions are reached regarding the part played by liturgical demands in prompting the production of written Gospels, it is highly probable that some account of the life, teaching, death and resurrection of Jesus would from earliest times need to be included in the forms of Christian worship. But although once again actual eyewitnesses would, at first, well supply the lack, in the Gentile regions where direct Palestinian eyewitnesses were not available the need for written records would require no time to develop.

Sufficient has been said to indicate a variety of reasons why Gospels were written. There were, on Luke's own showing, numerous attempts to meet the need, but only four of these have survived as authentic records and it will next be necessary to investigate briefly the approach of the early Church to these Gospels and its rejection of all others. The mass of apocryphal Gospels of later origin bears testimony both to the recurring fascination in filling in details which the canonical Gospels omit and to the vigilant discernment of the Christian Church in rejecting them as spurious. Some scholars have maintained that buried in the mass of fiction there may be preserved authentic sayings of the Lord.[1]

IV. THE PLACE OF THE GOSPELS IN THE NEW TESTAMENT

It is beyond the scope of our present study to investigate the growth of the Canon,[2] but a brief summary of the attitude of the early Church towards the Gospels is necessary in order to set the problems of introduction in their right perspective.

By the end of the second century it is clear from all the evidence available that our four Gospels were accepted, not only as authentic, but also as Scripture on a level with the Old Testament. Irenaeus has an illuminating passage in which he maintains that the fourfold character of the Gospel is analogous to the four quarters of the world, the four winds and the necessity for four pillars in an edifice.[3] While Irenaeus' method of reasoning may be questioned, his testimony to the exclusive use of our four Gospels is undeniable. Moreover, in the same passage he speaks of the author of each Gospel according to the traditional ascription. He goes on to adumbrate a doctrine of the inspiration of the Gospels. Admittedly Irenaeus is uncritical in his approach, but that is not to say that his testimony was not based on sound tradition. At least, it cannot be dismissed when discussing introductory questions.

Although Clement of Alexandria cites from other Gospels, as, for instance, from the *Gospel according to the Egyptians*, he carefully distinguishes them from the four canonical Gospels. Tertullian, on the other hand, exclusively cites only the four and argues strongly for the authority of those on the grounds that they were produced by apostles or by their immediate associates. None of these writers seems to have questioned the origin of these Gospels in the apostolic age, although

[1] Cf. J. Jeremias, *Unknown Sayings of Jesus* (1957).
[2] For a survey of the early approach to the Gospels, cf. A. H. McNeile, *INT*² (1953); A. Souter, *The Text and Canon of the New Testament*² (1954); Oxford Society, *The New Testament in the Apostolic Fathers* (1905); J. Knox, *Marcion and the New Testament* (1942); E. C. Blackman, *Marcion and his Influence* (1948); J. N. Sanders, *The Fourth Gospel in the Early Church* (1943); J. N. Birdsall, article 'Canon of the New Testament', *NBD*, pp. 194–199.
[3] For an English translation of Irenaeus' statement, cf. *A New Eusebius* (ed. J. Stevenson, 1957), p. 122.

their approach has been challenged by modern criticism. It may well be that these men were nearer the truth than is often allowed, a possibility which will be considered later.

Previous to AD 180 the evidence is less specific, but is nevertheless indicative of a high regard for the Gospels from the earliest times for which any data exist. Tatian's *Harmony* comprised extracts from our four Gospels[1] and is interesting as evidence of the perplexity which was then felt over the fourfold Gospel. In spite of its considerable influence in the Eastern Church, it was soon displaced by the separate Gospels, a fact which testifies to the respect with which the Synoptic Gospels were treated in spite of the large amount of common material contained in them. The Christians were less interested in a consecutive life of Christ compiled from authentic records than in the authentic records themselves. At a still earlier date Justin Martyr appears to have known and used all the Gospels, although in his case it is not possible to be certain, in view of the looseness of his citations. Of importance for our present study is his reference to the 'memoirs of the apostles' used in public services. These memoirs were elsewhere identified as 'Gospels' (εὐαγγέλια), and it is clear from this that the writings were authoritative because of their direct relationship to the apostolic recollections.

Both Clement of Rome and Ignatius made use of Gospel material, although more by way of allusion than by formal citation. All of the material, however, finds parallels in the canonical Gospels with the exception of one passage in Ignatius, which contains a Dominical saying from an extraneous source.[2] Nevertheless it has been disputed that these patristic writers were actually acquainted with the written Gospels. H. Köster,[3] for instance, speaks rather of pre-Synoptic traditions. On the other hand the *Epistle of Polycarp* contains parallels with the Gospels which reveal his undoubted acquaintance with them,[4] although in the

---

[1] Some scholars maintain that other material was also included in Tatian's *Diatessaron*. Indeed Victor of Capua called this work a *Diapente* (cf. G. Quispel, *VC*, 13, 1959, pp. 87–117; H. Montefiore and H. E. W. Turner, *Thomas and the Evangelists*, 1962, pp. 25–27) in which case it was evidently accepted that a non-canonical Gospel was drawn upon.

[2] Cf. A. Souter, *The Text and Canon of the New Testament*[2] (1954), p. 149.

[3] *Synoptische Überlieferung bei den apostolischen Vätern* (1957).

[4] Köster admits Polycarp's knowledge of Matthew and Luke, although he does not date this evidence as early as that of Ignatius, because he accepts P. N. Harrison's view that chapters i–xii of Polycarp's letter were written much later (*Polycarp's Two Epistles to the Philippians*, 1936).

case of all of these writers there has been dispute over their acquaintance with John's Gospel (see later comments, pp. 243 f.).

During the sub-apostolic period the testimony of Papias on the Gospels is highly significant, although somewhat enigmatic. As it will be considered in detail in the course of the discussions on various problems of introduction, it will be necessary here to do no more than point out that Papias says nothing which contradicts any of the patristic evidence so far cited. He made two statements about Matthew and Mark respectively, and these appear to be the earliest comments on the authorship of any of the Gospels. He believed that Mark was Peter's interpreter and that Matthew wrote in Hebrew, and although both statements have become a battleground of criticism (see pp. 31 ff., 65 f.) their evidence is of great importance because of their early date.

V. THE BEST METHOD OF APPROACHING THE GOSPELS

Before coming to the study of the separate Gospels, it may be helpful to point out some of the advantages of the method adopted in this Introduction. The first advantage is that it places the problems of sources and origins in their right perspective as subsidiary to the understanding and appreciation of the extant Gospels. However important these problems are in the study of the Gospels it is no gain to exalt them into a dominant position. The method adopted is not, however, without its difficulties, since some discussions on the separate Gospels are affected by conclusions reached regarding sources or the formation of traditions. In some cases these conclusions are anticipated, although the steps by which they are reached are postponed for later discussion. In these cases cross references will enable the reader to refer to subsequent discussions where necessary.

Another advantage is that the method chosen enables the study of each Gospel for its own sake, irrespective of the order in which it is supposed that they were actually produced. For this reason the canonical order has been retained. It will in fact be found that many important aspects of each Gospel may be discussed independently of the solution of the problem of their relationship.

Perhaps a brief reference here to the generally held theories of the origins of the first three Gospels may not, however, be amiss. The source-critical approach generally maintains that Mark was the earliest Gospel and that this was used by both Matthew and Luke, who in addition used another written source consisting mainly of sayings (Q), together with a quantity of special traditions (known respectively as M and L, irrespective of whether these were written or oral). The form-critical method of accounting for Gospel origins aims to push back the enquiry behind the sources and assumes as its guiding principle that the earliest traditions circulated as separate units, which were later edited into the sources proposed by source criticism and in this way became incorporated into our Gospels. Both source and form criticism are fully discussed in later chapters, but the work is so arranged that those who prefer to do so may study these before studying the individual Gospels.

The previous remarks have made no mention of the Gospel of John, since this is in a different category from the other three Gospels, and will be considered only after the Synoptic problem has been discussed.

CHAPTER TWO

MATTHEW'S GOSPEL

This Gospel, according to the citations found in early Christian writers, was used more than any of the other Gospels.[1] Some of the reasons for this will be seen when the purpose and structure are examined, for its adaptability to liturgical use will be especially brought out. The book has retained its appeal throughout Christian history and has exerted powerful influence, particularly through its presentation of the Sermon on the Mount.

I. CHARACTERISTICS

a. Conciseness

A feature of this Gospel as compared, for instance, with Mark is that its narratives are generally more concise. Such comparisons may be made in the account of the death of John the Baptist (Mt. xiv. 3–12; Mk. vi. 17–29) and in the incident of the healing of the epileptic child (Mt. xvii. 14–21; Mk. ix. 14–29). It may have been this feature, coupled with Matthew's general orderliness, which caused this Gospel to be so widely used for liturgical purposes in the early Church.

b. Messianic interest

It was natural for the early Christians to have an absorbing interest in the Old Testament predictions which were fulfilled in Jesus Christ, and Matthew's Gospel demonstrates this in a marked degree. There are many quotations from the Old Testament and these fall into two categories. The majority are cited from the LXX and are introduced by various formulae or else arise naturally out of the course of the narrative without special introduction. But Matthew also makes use of a group of citations from the Hebrew which are all introduced by variations of the formula—'that it might be fulfilled'. These sayings, which may have formed part of a previous collection (see later discussion on Matthew's *testimonia*, pp. 154 ff.), illustrate the deep conviction that

---

[1] Cf. E. Massaux, *Influence de l'Evangile de St. Matthieu sur la littérature chrétienne, avant St. Irenée* (1950).

there was an indisputable connection between Christianity and the Old Testament. They bear witness to a major part of the earliest creed of the Christian Church, i.e. Jesus is Messiah.[1] If it appears to modern readers that some of these 'fulfilments' are forced (e.g. Mt. ii. 15 = Ho. xi. 1), it should be remembered that for the earliest Christians who had inherited the Old Testament from Judaism and revered it as their sole Scriptures, its witness was unquestionably authoritative, and in such *testimonia* logical connection was not always looked for. In common with his Christian contemporaries Matthew in his approach to the Old Testament differed from that of the Rabbis in that he viewed it without being bound by a traditional method of interpretation. As a consequence many passages are treated as messianic which were not so treated by Jewish interpreters.[2]

c. Particularism and universalism

The Jewish interests of the author are seen in many other respects besides the appeal to the Old Testament. His Gospel often reflects the more restricted outlook of Jewish Christianity. Not one jot or tittle of the law will become invalid (v. 18 f.); the scribes and Pharisees occupy the seat of Moses and their instructions are to be observed (xxiii. 2 f.); Jesus enjoins the fulfilment of the commandments (xix. 17 ff., xxiii. 23); the Jewish temple tax is paid (xvii. 24 ff.); the disciples are expected to fast, keep the sabbath, and bring offerings as in the Jewish tradition (vi. 16 ff., xxiv. 20, v. 23 f.); Jesus Himself declares that He is sent only to the 'lost sheep of the house of Israel' (xv. 24); the genealogy of Jesus is traced from Abraham and is arranged in three groups of fourteen in rabbinic style (i. 1 ff.); and Jewish customs and phrases are included without elucidation (xv. 2, where the phrase 'tradition of the elders' occurs in the passage about handwashing scruples; xxiii. 5, where phylacteries are mentioned; and xxiii. 27, where allusion is made to whited sepulchres). In addition, the recurrent theme of Jesus as the Son of David and the triumphant entry into Jerusalem focus attention upon the Jewish Christian regard for Jesus as the Fulfiller of their national hopes.

But the significant thing about Matthew's Gospel is that universalism

[1] Cf. J. Knox, *The Early Church and the Coming Great Church* (1957), pp. 63 ff.
[2] Cf. B. F. Westcott's discussion of this in *Introduction to the Study of the Gospels*[7] (1888), pp. 159 ff. On Matthew's use of the Old Testament, cf. N. Hillyer, *EQ*, XXXVI (1964), pp. 12–26.

appears alongside this particularism. If Christianity is seen as the ideal Israel it is also seen as the New Israel, unbounded by the restricted environment out of which it emerged. At the birth of Jesus homage is offered by Gentiles according to Matthew's account (ii. 1 ff.), and when the life of Jesus is in jeopardy it is a Gentile land, Egypt, which offers asylum and protection (ii. 13 ff.). At the conclusion of the Gospel Matthew records the great commission which extends to all nations (xxviii. 18 ff.). The severe attack on the Pharisees by Jesus in xxiii. 13 ff. was called forth by a wrong emphasis on the Jewish doctrine of righteousness by works. In the parable of the vineyard (xxi. 33 ff.) Jesus suggests that another nation will supplant the original husbandmen, who clearly represent the Jewish people. This enlargement by Christianity of the narrow limits of Judaism is not a peculiarity of Matthew's Gospel, originating in a dual outlook, but belongs to the very nature of Jesus Himself.[1]

d. Ecclesiastical elements

Matthew, alone of the Gospels, records any specific teaching about the Church. Here only does the word ἐκκλησία occur attributed to Jesus. The two passages where it is used are therefore of great importance. In xvi. 18, the basis of the Church is to be Peter and his confession, and to Peter are given the keys of the kingdom, with authority to bind or loose. In the other passage (xviii. 17 f.) similar authority appears to be vested in the Church as a whole. The Church is here set forth in its disciplinary capacity. But because no other Evangelist records the use

[1] H. J. Schoeps (*Theologie und Geschichte des Judenchristentums*, 1949, p. 47), although acknowledging Matthew's Jewish-Christian emphasis, maintains that there is little Judaizing tendency. To him, however, the Gospel represents emergent Catholicity rather than the universal outlook of Jesus Himself. Cf. J. Jeremias (*Jesus' Promise to the Nations*, 1958, p. 34), who brings out Matthew's strong emphasis on the missionary activity of Jesus among the Gentiles. Cf. also K. W. Clark ('The Gentile Bias of Matthew', *JBL*, LXVI, 1947, pp. 165–172), who uses these Gentile indications to imply that the author was a Gentile Christian rather than a Jewish Christian. Another scholar who maintains a Gentile destination and who stresses the universal element is P. Nepper-Christensen, *Das Matthäusevangelium—ein judenchristliches Evangelium?* (1958). Against the latter, cf. G. Bornkamm in *Tradition and Interpretation in Matthew* (Eng. Tr. 1963), p. 51. See p. 23 n.2 for others who regard the universal aim of this Gospel as dominant. G. Strecker (*Der Weg der Gerechtigkeit*, 1962, pp. 15–35), although admitting some earlier Jewish influences in the history of the Church to which the author belonged, regards him as belonging to the dominant Gentile section.

of the word ἐκκλησία by our Lord, many scholars[1] have disputed the originality of these sayings and suggest that they arose in the ecclesiastical environment of the early communities. Yet there is no strong ground for such an assumption.[2] There is on the other hand an absence of any other explanation of the universal acceptance of the term in the primitive Church.

Two other passages may be linked with these to show Matthew's ecclesiastical interests. xviii. 20 describes the simplest form of the local church, the gathering of two or three in the name of Christ with the promise of His presence. In the concluding commission two statements are made relevant to the future Church. Its work is to consist of teaching the nations and baptizing disciples in the triune Name (xxviii. 19). The believers are moreover to be taught to observe all that Jesus had commanded (xxviii. 20), and His own presence is assured to them to the end of the age.[3]

e. Eschatological interest

Because Matthew's apocalyptic section is much longer than that of Mark, it has been supposed that his Gospel reflects a period of deepening interest in apocalyptic. Thus Streeter[4] suggested that a revival of interest might have occurred as a result of the Nero Redivivus myth[5] which expected a return of Nero at the head of a Parthian invading army. But there is no need to postulate that Matthew's more lengthy treatment of our Lord's apocalyptic teaching was determined by external influences

---

[1] Cf. A. H. McNeile, *The Gospel according to St. Matthew* (1915), pp. 241 f., for details. For recent scholars who have adopted a similar view, cf. R. Bultmann, *The History of the Synoptic Tradition* (Eng. Tr. 1963), pp. 138–140; E. Schweizer, *Church Order in the New Testament* (Eng. Tr. 1961), pp. 2b f.; G. Bornkamm, *op. cit.*, pp. 44 f., who also cites H. von Campenhausen's opinion that the statement in Mt. xvi. 17 ff. is unthinkable in the mouth of Jesus (*Kirchliches Amt und geistliche Vollmacht*, 1953, pp. 140 f.).

[2] Cf. V. Taylor, *The Gospels*[5] (1945), p. 81. Cf. also O. Cullmann, *Peter: Disciple, Apostle, and Martyr*[2] (1962), pp. 164 ff., for a discussion of Mt. xvi. 18; R. N. Flew, *Jesus and His Church* (1956), and A. Oepke, *St Th* (1948–50), pp. 110 ff.

[3] Quite apart from the ecclesiastical interests mentioned here, some scholars trace in Matthew's special emphases an echo of the ecclesiastical tensions in his own time (cf. C. W. F. Smith, *JBL*, LXXXII, 1963, pp. 149–168). But cf. C. H. Dodd's study of the similarity between Matthew's and Paul's approach to the idea of the Church and church order (*New Testament Studies*, 1953, pp. 57–62).

[4] *The Four Gospels* (1924), p. 523.

[5] Cf. R. H. Charles, *Commentary on the Revelation of St. John* (1920), II, pp. 76 ff.

in the later history of the Church. The words of Jesus cannot be divorced from eschatological interest, although there is considerable difference of opinion over the extent to which Matthew's recorded teaching (and similarly Mark's) is original to Jesus. In the absence of any positive evidence to the contrary, however, it is reasonable to conclude for the authenticity of these sayings.[1]

But Matthew does not confine his eschatological elements to the material in the great discourse of chapters xxiv, xxv, for they are apparent also in some of the parables which he alone records. The interpretation of the parable of the tares (xiii. 36 ff.) and the conclusions to both the parable of the ten virgins (xxv. 13) and the parable of the talents (xxv. 30), in all of which the end of the age is brought into sharp focus, are peculiar to Matthew.

II. PURPOSE, DESTINATION AND PLACE OF ORIGIN

It has already been shown that one of Matthew's main characteristics is the dominance, throughout his account, of Old Testament citations and allusions. This must obviously be a prime consideration in discussing the author's purpose. He writes his Gospel from a definite standpoint. He purposes to show that the major events in the life of Jesus took place in fulfilment of prophecy. In this he was not alone, for such a motive recurs frequently through the New Testament, although nowhere so clearly as in this Gospel. This feature alone would seem to indicate that the author was a Jew writing for Jews. The story begins with a genealogy intended to show our Lord's direct descent from Abraham and this gives a clear indication of what the author proposes to do. But it is significant that the book ends with a note of universalism in the sending of the disciples to preach the gospel throughout the world.[2] However Jewish many of Matthew's emphases are, his main target is to show Christianity as much more comprehensive than

[1] Cf. G. R. Beasley-Murray, *Jesus and the Future* (1954). Dodd (*op. cit.*, pp. 54–57) compares the eschatology in Matthew and Paul and considers that both reflect an early tradition.

[2] Many scholars regard this final commission as the real key to the understanding of Matthew's purpose. Cf. O. Michel, *EvTh*, x (1950–51), p. 21; G. Schille, *NTS*, 4 (1957–58), p. 113; E. P. Blair, *Jesus in the Gospel of Matthew* (1960), pp. 44 ff. C. F. D. Moule (*The Birth of the New Testament*, 1962, p. 91 n.2) cites W. Trilling (*Das wahre Israel*, 1959) for the same opinion.

Judaism.[1] Here was Old Testament fulfilment in the widest possible sense.

In all probability there was an apologetic purpose behind this Gospel. It would have answered many questions about our Lord which may well have been raised against Him by calumnists. The infancy story, for instance, would answer any charge of illegitimacy against Jesus. The descent into Egypt and the subsequent return to Nazareth would account for the residence of Jesus in Nazareth rather than Bethlehem. The same might be said of the apologetic character of some of the details in the resurrection narrative which are peculiar to Matthew (e.g. the story of the bribing of the guard, which would refute any allegation that the disciples had stolen the body of Jesus). In view of this R. V. G. Tasker[2] calls this Gospel 'an early Christian apology'.

Naturally the author's purpose needs to be interpreted in the light of the construction of the Gospel, or more precisely of the historic occasion which prompted it. Because of this, comment must be made on two recent views of the composition of the Gospel which give a new slant to considerations of purpose. The first is the community idea put forth by G. D. Kilpatrick.[3] According to this writer, the Gospel is a revision of a lectionary which grew up in answer to the liturgical needs of some Christian community. Because he maintains the documentary theory as far as Mark and Q are concerned, Kilpatrick suggests that in this particular community these two documents would have been read during worship and that other written material would have been added. In this theory, the Gospel almost becomes a community product, although it is the work of one author officially commissioned to produce it. If Kilpatrick is right, the purpose of the Gospel was to put into more permanent form the liturgical material already in use. In other words the author was really an editor who fitted the existing writings into a united whole, suitable for liturgical use. Kilpatrick[4] deduces from the Gospel several lines of evidence which he thinks support his hypothesis. (1) Many stylistic changes from Mark increase lucidity, a valuable asset in liturgy. (2) Several unnecessary details are omitted from Mark.

[1] G. Hebert (*SJT*, 14, 1961, pp. 403–413) considers that the author wrote for 'the Great Church, the Church Catholic'. He suggests that it was written after the fall of Jerusalem to preserve for a predominantly Gentile Church the teaching which Jerusalem had preserved.

[2] In his article 'Matthew, Gospel of', *NBD*, p. 796.

[3] *The Origins of the Gospel according to St. Matthew* (1946).

[4] *Op. cit.*, pp. 72 ff.

(3) When additions occur they clarify the passages. (4) Antitheses and parallelisms are frequent. (5) Formulae are repeated after the main sections. (6) Phrasing is balanced and rounded, admirably suited for liturgical use. Whereas it may be granted that all these data can be used to support the hypothesis, it cannot be said that they demand the hypothesis to account for them. In other words, an alternative explanation is possible. Lucidity, conciseness, clarity, parallelisms, balanced language and similar characteristics are not the sole possessions of liturgies. They may be accounted for by the author's natural literary skill. At the same time it is highly probable that the possession of these qualities led to the widespread use of the Gospel for liturgical purposes in the developing Church.[1]

The other recent suggestion is that of K. Stendahl,[2] who has proposed that the Gospel originated from a Matthaean school, which was designed for teachers and Church leaders. According to this theory, the author, who is conceived of as a Christian Rabbi, produced the book in the form of 'a manual for teaching and administration within the church'. Such a purpose is distinguished by Stendahl from a catechetical purpose,[3] although he does not rule out the latter. He finds such teaching as Matthew xviii to be unsuitable for general catechetical instruction and to be clearly more appropriate for Church leaders. Stendahl illustrates his thesis of a Matthaean school by a study of the author's use of the Old Testament, on the assumption that the starting-point of instruction for teachers would have been the interpretation of the Old Testament from a Christian point of view.[4] A comparison with the Habakkuk commentary from Qumran shows certain similarities between the *pesher* method of quoting Scripture favoured by the Covenanters and Matthew's method, which according to Stendahl con-

---

[1] A view similar to Kilpatrick's has been advanced by P. Carrington (*The Primitive Christian Calendar*, 1952), who regarded Matthew as an enlarged lectionary based on Mark (see pp. 62 f. for a discussion of this theory for Mark).

[2] *The School of St. Matthew and its use of the Old Testament* (1954). The idea that Matthew's Gospel was a manual of instruction for Christian churches was earlier suggested by J. H. Ropes, *The Synoptic Gospels* (1934), pp. 112 ff. Stendahl is supported by G. Schille, *NTS*, 4 (1957–58), pp. 1–24, 101–114, although the latter conceives of the Gospel as intended for catechetical purposes.

[3] For a catechetical purpose for Matthew, cf. the article of G. Schille, *NTS*, 4 (1958), pp. 101–114.

[4] Stendahl speaks of 'the rather elaborate School of Matthew with its ingenious interpretation of the Old Testament as the crown of its scholarship' (*op. cit.*, p. 34).

firms his opinion that behind Matthew's Gospel is an advanced study of Scripture.[1] This is certainly an interesting suggestion and there seems to be no intrinsic objection to it as far as the purpose of the Gospel is concerned. Yet it is strange that a Gospel which originated in such a learned school should become so popular in the second century.[2] At the same time it is not impossible, and some allowance must be made for it.

Perhaps more attention should be given, however, to the catechetical purpose of this Gospel. That there was a need for suitable material for catechetical instruction has already been mentioned.[3] The methods used in such instruction of new converts are, however, mainly a matter of conjecture. At least it may be said that Matthew's Gospel would well suit such a purpose, although this cannot establish that such a purpose is present. It may well be that the author exercised a ministry of teaching in his own church and would therefore be sensitive to the needs of his readers.

There are various suggestions regarding the precise location of the readers of this Gospel, although the available data are wholly insufficient to produce certainty. The Jewish flavouring of the Gospel would suggest a church in which this emphasis would have some point, that is, a predominantly Jewish-Christian community. The traditional view is that the Gospel originated in Palestine and this has much to commend it. But B. H. Streeter[4] rejected this because he alleged that all the patristic evidence to this effect went back to Papias, who may not have been referring to the canonical Gospel at all, and because he maintained that the original language was Greek, which would not support a

---

[1] Cf. especially, *ibid.*, pp. 35, 183–202.

[2] B. Gärtner (*Studia Theologica*, VIII, 1954, pp. 1–24) criticizes Stendahl's inferences from the Qumran evidence, and considers that the use of the Old Testament arose out of missionary preaching. C. F. D. Moule (*op. cit.*, p. 91), who is favourably disposed towards Stendahl's view, suggests that the group which collected the Matthaean traditions were obliged to defend themselves against Jewish antagonists. G. Bornkamm (*Tradition and Interpretation in Matthew* (Eng. Tr. 1963), p. 51) finds Stendahl's idea of a school of scribes convincing, but is critical of other aspects of his thesis.

[3] See p. 14.

[4] *The Four Gospels* (1924), pp. 500 ff. It should be noted that the anti-Marcionite Prologue to Luke's Gospel states that Matthew was produced in Judaea. But it is questioned what value can be attached to this prologue (cf. E. Haenchen, *Die Apostelgeschichte*,[13] *KEK*, 1961, p. 8 n.3).

Palestinian origin.[1] Accordingly he suggested Antioch. Kilpatrick[2] is more general, preferring some church in Syria, probably in Phoenicia. Streeter would have rejected the latter on the grounds that an anonymous book, as he believed the original Matthew to have been, would need the backing of an influential church to secure a place in the New Testament Canon.[3] But the suggestions of both Antioch and Phoenicia are pure conjectures and it seems best in the circumstances to leave the question open. If the theory of an Aramaic original for this Gospel is accepted, a Jerusalem origin would have as much to commend it as any, especially as the early Church seems to have assumed this without question.[4]

III. STRUCTURE

This Gospel has sometimes been described as a stately structure and the description is not inappropriate. It has more of careful design than any other of the Gospels and this fact may account for its wider use in the early Church. It shows an author with an astonishingly orderly mind, as the following details will show.

a. The five great discourse sections

The most obvious feature of Matthew's structure is the alternation of large blocks of teaching material with the narrative sections. After an

[1] This basis of argument is rightly rejected by Michaelis, *Einleitung in das Neue Testament*[3] (1961), p. 40. J. Schniewind (*Das Evangelium nach Matthäus*,[9] NTD, 1960, pp. 2, 3) points out many internal indications of a Palestinian reader-circle, the most notable of which are the ways that Matthew takes for granted his readers' knowledge of Jewish customs, such as the allusion (left unexplained) to whited sepulchres (Mt. xxiii. 27), to the Jewish garment of Jesus (ix. 20) and to the practice of presenting gifts at the altar (v. 23 f.). While these allusions would not, of course, have been unintelligible to Jews elsewhere, they would have been most meaningful to Palestinian Jews whose scruples were stricter than those of the Dispersion.

[2] *Op. cit.*, pp. 124 ff. Cf. B. W. Bacon, *Studies in Matthew* (1930), pp. 3–23 and J. S. Kennard, *ATR*, xxxi (1949), pp. 243–246, for the choice of a Syrian community.

[3] *Op. cit.*, p. 501.

[4] Streeter asserted quite categorically that all the Fathers after Irenaeus had read his works and were simply repeating his statements regarding the Palestinian origin of this Gospel, and this, he thought, went back to Papias' dictum on τὰ λόγια (*op. cit.*, p. 500). But even if a tradition can be traced back to a single root, this is no justification for assuming that it must be suspect. It may, on the contrary, be an indication of the confidence which a series of writers placed in the tradition.

initial narrative section, which includes the infancy stories, the preparation for Jesus' ministry by John the Baptist and the first incidents of
Jesus' preaching work, Matthew introduces the group of teaching
known as the Sermon on the Mount (v–vii). It is not possible to discuss
here whether our Lord spoke all this teaching on one occasion or
whether the author himself has arranged the material into a discourse,
but the former is certainly not improbable. At all events, Matthew saw
the value of including the teaching in a continuous group and this is
characteristic of his method.

Another narrative section follows, consisting mainly of a number of
miracles, after which the second discourse section is inserted (x). This
consists of the mission charge to the Twelve, again in a continuous discourse. The next descriptive sections deal with incidents which particularly illustrate growing opposition to Jesus and His method of dealing
with controversies, which form a fitting introduction to the group of
parables in xiii about the kingdom. Another narrative sequence follows
in xiv–xvii, culminating in the transfiguration and the prediction of the
passion, which prepares for another collection of sayings dealing with
the Christian community (xviii). Now the scene of the ministry is set
beyond Jordan, but rapidly moves towards Jerusalem, with our Lord's
entry into the city and the subsequent series of controversies vividly
described. Arising out of one of these controversies, Jesus pronounces a
series of woes upon the scribes and Pharisees, which serve as a prelude
to the great eschatological discourse (xxiii–xxv). The Gospel then
closes with the passion and resurrection narratives.

This alternation of narrative and discourse is clearly not accidental.[1]
A similar formula concludes all the five discourse sections, admirably
serving the purpose of linking narrative and discourse in a natural
sequence, as for instance in the first example (vii. 28), which leads into
the statement that Jesus came down from the mountain with great
crowds following Him. xi. 1 shows Jesus moving on and still addressing
crowds (xi. 7), while after the kingdom parables of xiii, the formula
shows Jesus proceeding to His own country and after xviii as moving
on into Judaea. The concluding formula (xxvi. 1) shows our Lord
anticipating the Passover and the subsequent arrest, and this is well
suited to introduce the passion narrative. Each formula is therefore a

[1] K. Stendahl (*The School of St. Matthew and its use of the Old Testament* (1954),
pp. 20 ff.) suggests that this structure is an example of the pattern—*kerygma* plus
didache (according to Dodd's theory).

literary link which helps to give continuity to the whole and illustrates the author's skill.

It has been suggested that Matthew's fivefold scheme was patterned on the fivefold character of the books of the Law, the idea being that the author was attempting to provide a 'Pentateuch', as the new law for the community of the new Israel, that is, the Christian Church.[1] The suggestion is not without some merit, but is based wholly on speculation. There is no correlation between the five divisions of Matthew's Gospel and the corresponding five books of Moses. In fact the main point of contact is the number five, which forms too slender a basis for the theory. Admittedly, in the Sermon on the Mount there are many specific references to the superiority of Christ's teaching over the Mosaic Law, but this does not throw much light on Matthew's literary structure. Although the parallelism between the Gospel and the Pentateuch cannot be entirely excluded, it would seem to be more probable that Matthew's fivefold arrangement bore no symbolic significance.[2]

The skilful planning of the book is clear in spite of the fact that the Evangelists did not belong to a literary group in the accepted sense of the word. They were men with a dominant purpose and what skill they possessed was, under the guidance of the Spirit of God, put to the fullest use.

b. Numerical groups

The author's methodical mind is also seen in the large number of times that he groups together similar sayings or events. His favourite number

---

[1] Kilpatrick (*The Origins of the Gospel according to St. Matthew*, 1946, p. 136) is quite certain that the fivefold division is modelled on the book of the Law. Cf. also B. W. Bacon, *op. cit.*, pp. 80–82; J. A. Findlay, *Exp.*, VIII, xx (1920), pp. 388–400. But against, cf. G. Barth in *Tradition and Interpretation in Matthew*, Bornkamm, Barth and Held (Eng. Tr. 1963), pp. 153–159, and P. Feine-J. Behm-W. G. Kümmel, *Einleitung*[12] (1963), p. 60. (Where the eleventh edition of this work is cited, it is noted as Feine-Behm, but where the completely revised twelfth edition is cited, it is noted as Feine-Behm-Kümmel. In many instances Kümmel takes a different line from his predecessors.)

[2] An interesting suggestion regarding Matthew's structure has been made by J. C. Fenton (*Studia Evangelica*, ed. K. Aland, W. Eltester and E. Klostermann, 1959, pp. 174–179), who finds evidence in this Gospel of the literary devices of *inclusio* and *chiasmus*, and thinks it may be possible to regard the whole book as a great *chiasmus*, chapters v–viii answering to xxii–xxv, x to xviii and xiii. 1–35 to xiii. 36–52. This sounds rather too artificial an arrangement to be convincing as an account of the disposition of Matthew's discourse material, but it may merit further investigation.

is three, although fives and sevens also occur.[1] Samples of 'three' groupings are the threefold division of the genealogy (i. 17), the three
temptations (iv. 1–11), three illustrations of righteousness, three prohibitions, three commands (vi. 1–vii. 20), three groupings of three types
of miracles—healings, power and restoration (viii. 1–ix. 34), and many
instances of three parables, questions, prayers or denials. This need not
imply that Matthew attached any symbolic importance to the number
three, but it does vividly illustrate the way in which his mind worked,
and for methodical arrangement marks him out from the other Gospel
writers. It may be that Matthew generally cited three or more instances
of a type of saying or event because he was influenced by the Mosaic
principle that evidence is established by two or three witnesses. For
him the multiplication of examples would be regarded as an authentication of the material incorporated.[2]

c. The grouping of material generally

Within both narrative and discourse Matthew aims to illustrate various
aspects of the ministry of Jesus. Thus, while v–vii illustrates His teaching,
viii–ix. 34 illustrates His work, and a similar combination is found
throughout the Gospel. In xii. 1–45 are various illustrations of His
controversies with the Pharisees, followed in xiii by illustrations of His
parabolic teaching. Behind this conscious aim there is a discernible
framework which compares with that used by both Mark and Luke.
It speaks much for the author's skill that he welds the general scheme
into the framework so well that the Gospel gives the impression of
being a united whole. Once Matthew's literary procedure is grasped, it
will be abundantly clear that he never conceived of his work as belonging to the category of biography, as at present understood. His literary
structure is, rather, designed to give, as comprehensively as possible,
the main facets of the life and character of Jesus. It is significant that it
is in the passion narratives that Matthew agrees most closely with

[1] Note, for instance, his five discourse blocks and his groupings of fourteen
in the genealogy, his seven parables in Mt. xiii and his seven woes in Mt. xxiii.
On the genealogy G. H. Box suggested that the three groups of fourteen were
governed by a numerical acrostic on the name 'David', which in Hebrew numerology totalled fourteen (*ZNTW*, 6, 1905, p. 85). But this idea seems rather far-
fetched.

[2] It has been maintained by F. V. Filson (*JBL*, LXXV, 1956, pp. 227–231), that
Matthew shows a tendency to break patterns contained in his sources and therefore it is assumed that topical arrangement took precedence for him over literary
patterns, although some of the latter are admitted.

Mark and Luke in content and sequence. There was undoubtedly at an early stage a relatively fixed structure for the relating of these solemn events.

IV. AUTHORSHIP

a. The title

The earliest description of this Gospel of which we have any evidence attributes it to Matthew (ΚΑΤΑ ΜΑΤΘΑΙΟΝ). This is testified by strong tradition. It was indisputably acknowledged before the close of the second century and there is no positive evidence that the book ever circulated without this title. Indeed it may reasonably be claimed that the title was affixed at least as early as AD 125.[1] It is, moreover, a fair inference that the form of the title would have been understood as implying authorship. Nevertheless, the title cannot without hesitation be regarded as a part of the original text. Indeed it is generally assumed that no importance can be attached to it, since it was probably acquired in the course of the early history of the document. There are no means of reaching certainty about this. Some facts, however, are clear. The author's name does not occur in the body of the text and this might suggest that the original copy was anonymous. On the other hand the absence of any parallel forms to our Gospels makes it difficult to be certain whether this literary form lent itself to the personal identification of the author. Even Luke's preface, which uses the first person singular, contains no hint of who is the writer. On the other hand the apocryphal Gospels, which are clearly imitations of the canonical Gospels, are frequently attributed to an apostolic author in the body of the text, evidently because an anonymous production was felt to be inadequate (cf. *The Gospel of Peter*).

b. Ancient tradition

But the title cannot be dismissed too lightly, for it has the support of ancient tradition and this must be the starting-point of discussion regarding authorship. The main witnesses are as follows:[2]

First: *Papias* wrote, 'Matthew composed the Logia (τὰ λογία) in the Hebrew tongue and everyone interpreted them as he was able.'[3] The

---

[1] Cf. J. H. Ropes, *The Synoptic Gospels* (1934), pp. 103 f.; N. B. Stonehouse, *Origins of the Synoptic Gospels* (1963), p. 16; G. D. Kilpatrick, op. cit., p. 4.

[2] For a full discussion of ancient tradition concerning Matthew and his Gospel, cf. P. Nepper-Christensen, *Das Matthäusevangelium—ein judenchristliches Evangelium?* (1958), pp. 37-75. [3] Cited by Eusebius, *HE*, iii. 39, 16.

relevance of this statement for our present purpose will obviously depend on the meaning of the word λογία. Its usual meaning is an oracular utterance and it is used in this sense in the New Testament to describe the Old Testament (cf. Rom. iii. 2; Heb. v. 12).[1] It clearly cannot have such a meaning in Papias, but can it describe the Gospel? Certainly the teaching of Jesus could be compared with the oracular utterances of the Old Testament, but the Gospel contains much more than the sayings of Jesus and it becomes relevant to enquire whether Papias could possibly have meant to describe our Gospel by the term λογία.

(i) *The view that* λογία *meant the Gospel.* There are various reasons which support this interpretation of Papias' words.

1. It would be in harmony with the ancient superscription, κατὰ Ματθαῖον. If this title were in use at least as early as AD 125, it must have been known to Papias. If this were so, it would be strange indeed if he had spoken of Matthew as writing anything else and yet made no allusion to the Gospel circulating under his name. Unless the superscription were added after Papias' time, it is most natural to assume that Papias was taking for granted that his use of λογία would have been identified with κατὰ Ματθαῖον.[2]

2. Moreover, Papias' own usage would support this contention, for he apparently wrote a series of books entitled *Interpretations of the Lord's Logia* (κυριακῶν λογίων ἐξηγήσεως).[3] Since Papias uses the same word here as in the Matthew statement, it is reasonable to suppose that it is used in both cases in the same sense. This suggests that Papias expounded what Matthew (and others) wrote.[4] Whereas it is possible to

---

[1] T. W. Manson (*The Sayings of Jesus*, 1949, p. 18) maintained that λογία was used, not of Scripture as a whole, but only of God's word of guidance or encouragement to Israel contained within Scripture. He considered that it must be understood in this way in Papias and could not therefore refer to Matthew's Gospel.

[2] Kilpatrick (*op.cit.*, p. 4) suggests that the form of the notices in Papias favours the inference that he knew of a κατὰ Ματθαῖον and a κατὰ Μάρκον at least.

[3] J. Quasten (*Patrology*, I, 1950, p. 82) translates the title of Papias' book as 'Explanations of the sayings of the Lord'. That sayings collections without narratives circulated is evident from such a book as the *Gospel of Thomas*, but this was, of course, a Gnostic production. For further comments on this, see pp. 145 f.

[4] This was admitted by B. W. Bacon, *The Gospel of Mark: its Composition and Date* (1925), p. 25, although he considered that Papias was wrong about Matthaean authorship.

deduce from his Matthew statement that he might have commented only on the sayings of Jesus, in which case λογία would not refer to the whole Gospel, yet such a supposition is not supported by Papias' parallel statements about Mark's Gospel, in which he not only mentions that Mark wrote down what he remembered of the words and deeds of the Lord, but implies that Mark did what Peter did not do, i.e. make a composition of Dominical oracles.[1] In that case λογία must be understood to include deeds as well as words. If this is Papias' meaning in reference to Mark it must also be so in reference to Matthew.

3. Another consideration which is not without some importance for this discussion is the fact that, whereas Papias feels it is necessary to cite his authority for his statement about Mark (i.e. the Elder), he does not do so in the case of Matthew.[2] Presumably this must mean that in Papias' time the origin of Matthew's Gospel was indisputable. An apostolic work would not require such authentication as a work by a non-apostolic author like Mark. Admittedly this argument would still obtain if λογία meant something other than the Gospel, but it is more credible if Papias is referring to a work which was generally recognized, as the Gospel is known to have been.

From these data it would seem to be a reasonable inference that Papias believed that what Matthew wrote was a Gospel.[3] And yet this has been challenged from various points of view and these objections must next be considered. The major problem is that Papias' statement would then conflict with the generally held theory regarding the origin of the Gospel, for it is generally denied that the apostle Matthew could have written it. The basis of this denial will be considered later, but for the present it should be noted that if this critical contention is correct it

---

[1] Papias uses the same expression—κυριακῶν λογίων—as is used in the title of his own book. Cf. J. Kürzinger's article in *NTS*, 10 (1963), p. 109. F. Godet (*Introduction to the New Testament: The Collection of the Four Gospels and the Gospel of St. Matthew*, 1899, p. 188) interpreted Papias' statement on Mark differently, maintaining that he is contrasting Matthew's λογία with Mark's account of both sayings *and* doings, and therefore interpreting λογία as referring to sayings only. Yet it is more probable that the contrast is over 'order' rather than content.

[2] Cf. Bacon, *op. cit.*, pp. 23 ff. For the full statement of Papias on Mark, see p. 66 f.

[3] It may be said that there are no philological grounds for arguing that λογία could not have meant the Gospel.

would clearly be necessary to suggest some other interpretation of Papias' statement.

(ii) *Alternative interpretations of Papias' λογία.* If λογία cannot on critical grounds refer to the Gospel, there are only two possible alternatives which have been suggested.

   1. λογία refers to a sayings collection. Since the current solution to the Synoptic problem posits a sayings source Q used by both Matthew and Luke, it has seemed to many scholars a reasonable assumption that Papias knew of a tradition that Matthew wrote this source. Indeed, it is claimed that the basic meaning of λογία is far better fitted to describe an authoritative sayings collection than a Gospel.[1] Although this at first sight seems plausible it is not without considerable difficulties. It would appear to involve a confusion between λογία and λόγοι, as R. M. Grant[2] has pointed out, for it is not immediately apparent why they should be identified. Moreover there is no evidence that such a document existed in Papias' time, even if it had existed at an earlier time (see discussion on the Q source on pp. 136 ff.). It is difficult, if not impossible, to imagine an apostolic sayings collection surviving well into the second century and then vanishing without trace.[3] But it is not, of course, necessary to suppose that Papias knew the document to which he refers, in which case the λογία may have vanished long before Papias' time and the report of Matthew's authorship of it alone survived. But if so, what formed the basis of Papias' own expositions? If it was the Gospel, why did he use the same word λογία to describe it? There are too many difficulties in the way of interpreting λογία as Q to make it credible.

   2. λογία refers to a *testimonia* collection. In view of the fact that λογία is used in the New Testament to describe the Old Testament, and in view of the fact that Matthew's Gospel is thought by some scholars to have drawn from a collection of *testimonia*, at least for some of the Old Testament citations (see pp. 154 ff.), it has been suggested that Papias means that Matthew was the author of such a book of λογία.[4] There is less objection to this theory than to the last, although most of the

---

[1] Cf. V. H. Stanton, *The Gospels as Historical Documents* (1923), pp. 53 ff. Stanton could not conceive that by Papias' time any Gospel could have attained such esteem as to be called 'oracles'. Cf. also T. W. Manson, *op. cit.*, pp. 18, 19.

[2] *A Historical Introduction to the New Testament* (1963), p. 117.

[3] For T. W. Manson's answer to this objection, see comment on p. 149 n.1.

[4] Cf. the strong advocacy for this interpretation by B. P. W. S. Hunt, *Primitive Gospel Sources* (1951), pp. 182 ff.

criticisms would still apply.[1] There is no certain evidence of the existence of Christian *testimonia* books as early as this, and even if the
identification were conceded, it would be extremely difficult to imagine
how Matthew's name was transferred from such a document to a
Gospel in which it formed so small a part of the author's sources.

But if neither of these alternatives is valid, are there any other possibilities? It could, of course, be maintained that Matthew's λογία is some
unknown work which has now been hopelessly lost.[2] But this is highly
improbable in view of the existence of a Gospel circulating at the same
time under the name of Matthew. Or it could be maintained that Papias
was wrong, in which case his testimony can be ignored. If λογία means
the Gospel and yet it is supposed that Matthew was not the author of
the Gospel, there is little option but to regard Papias' statement as inaccurate, unless resort is made to some such theory as Kilpatrick's,[3] in which
the ascription to Matthew is regarded as pseudonymous, in which case
Papias may be regarded as a witness to the common assumption about
the authorship of the Gospel.

(iii) *The bearing of Matthew's language on the meaning of Papias' statement.*
If it is safe, therefore, to assume that Papias' λογία meant the Gospel, a
problem immediately arises concerning the further statement about
composition in the Hebrew tongue (dialect). Almost all scholars are
agreed that Matthew's Gospel was written in Greek, not in Hebrew or
Aramaic (as Papias probably meant). This either means that Papias
made a mistake or that our interpretation of λογία is incorrect. But
since there is a strong presumption against the latter, it seems better to
prefer the former. Yet how did the mistake arise? There are several
possible suggestions. It may have been an inference from the Jewish-
Christian characteristics of the Gospel, if it was assumed that a Gospel
designed for Palestinian Jewish Christians must have been in Aramaic.
On the other hand, the tradition may have arisen through confusion
over another book, like the *Gospel according to the Hebrews*, which was

---

[1] P. Parker (*The Gospel before Mark*, 1953, pp. 153 f.) raises three objections
against this interpretation: (1) The small quantity of *testimonia* peculiar to Matthew; (2) the omission of most of the *testimonia* used elsewhere in the New
Testament; (3) the context of Papias' statement in Eusebius, who is dealing with
Gospels not *testimonia*. Parker himself identifies the λογία with a pre-Mark,
pre-Matthew Gospel, which he calls K (see p. 139).

[2] Cf. F. C. Burkitt, *The Gospel History and its Transmission*[3] (1911), p. 127.

[3] *The Origins of the Gospel according to St. Matthew* (1946), pp. 138 ff.

mixed up in the tradition with a Hebrew Matthew. Or else a Semitic translation of Matthew's Greek Gospel was known at that time.[1] None of these is particularly convincing, and all lack corroborating evidence. But even if no adequate account of the rise of the tradition can be given, it clearly cannot be correct if the Gospel of Matthew is in mind. Yet this does raise a difficulty. If the statement about language is wrong, does this not reduce the value of the statement about authorship? If the former is an inference might not the latter be also? While it is not necessary to maintain that Papias was either all right or all wrong, this objection must be faced. Could it be that Papias' statement about language has been rightly understood? It has recently been maintained by J. Kürzinger[2] that the Hebrew dialect (διάλεκτος) must be understood in a literary rather than a linguistic sense, i.e. that Matthew arranged his material in a Jewish-Christian literary form, which would naturally be dominated by Old Testament characteristics. He claims justification for this interpretation from the use of the term in Greek rhetoric. Papias' statement then ceases to be a witness to the original language of Matthew's writing and becomes a statement comparing its literary purpose with that of Mark. In further support of this hypothesis Kürzinger understands Papias' words that each interpreted as he was able as a reference to Mark and Matthew and supposes that both these writers pursued a literary purpose in accordance with their ability. If Kürzinger is right, Papias' statement would stand and his testimony to Matthaean authorship would be strengthened. But it may be questioned whether this is a very natural way to interpret Papias' use of διάλεκτος.

If the more usual interpretation of διάλεκτος is preferred there would appear to be only one alternative to assuming that Papias was wrong, and that is to assume that Matthew was not only author of the Greek Gospel but also composed something in Hebrew (Aramaic) which he incorporated into the Gospel. This would be supported by M. Black's[3] contention for Aramaic sources behind the Gospel. But it may be wondered whether Papias' testimony on this is worth defending. In any case, his testimony must be considered in the light of later testimony.

Second: *Irenaeus* wrote: 'Now Matthew published also a book of the Gospel among the Hebrews in their own dialect, while Peter and Paul

---

[1] Cf. N. B. Stonehouse, *Origins of the Synoptic Gospels* (1963), pp. 90 ff.
[2] *NTS*, 10 (1963), pp. 108 ff.   [3] Cf. the section on Matthew's language, pp. 44 f.

were preaching the gospel in Rome and founding the Church.'[1] This testimony is clearly identical with Papias' statement only if λογία is interpreted as the Gospel. Since Irenaeus was acquainted with Papias' work it may reasonably be assumed that he is here giving his own interpretation of Papias' statement and that this was in agreement with the uniform tradition of the time, since Irenaeus mentions no dissentient voices.[2]

Third: *Pantaenus*, according to Eusebius,[3] found that the Gospel according to Matthew had preceded him to India and was preserved there in Hebrew letters, having been left there by Barnabas. The veracity of this story must be doubted, but the fact remains that it bears testimony to a circulating tradition which is, at any rate, in harmony with the interpretation of Papias' λογία as Matthew's Gospel.

Fourth: *Origen*[4] similarly bears testimony to the fact that Matthew composed a Gospel in Hebrew letters.

This evidence points to an unbroken tradition that Matthew wrote his Gospel in Hebrew, and advocates of any hypothesis which disagrees with this must suggest an adequate explanation of so consistent a tradition. The usual explanation is that later Church Fathers were merely reiterating Papias' original mistake, or at least confusion, over what Matthew originally wrote in Aramaic. But since Irenaeus and Origen were both Greek-speaking and both presumably possessed Matthew's Gospel only in Greek, it is strange that neither of them considered the tradition of a Hebrew (or Aramaic) original to be at all suspicious.[5]

---

[1] *Adv. Haer.* iii. 1. 1, cited by Eusebius, *HE*, v. 8. 2. The translation cited is that of D. Theron's *Evidence of Tradition* (1957), p. 43.

[2] Since Irenaeus contains information not in the Papias tradition he may have been acquainted with other traditions besides that of Papias (cf. Nepper-Christensen, *Das Matthäusevangelium—ein judenchristliches Evangelium?* 1958, p. 56; J. Munck in *Neotestamentica et Patristica*, ed. W. C. van Unnik, 1962, p. 257). Kürzinger (*op. cit.*, pp. 110–115) interprets Irenaeus' statements in the same manner as he deals with Papias' (i.e. of Hebrew (Jewish) dialectic).

[3] *HE*, v. 10. Kürzinger considers that there is a confusion with the *Gospel to the Hebrews* in this tradition (*op. cit.*, p. 115).   [4] *Apud* Eusebius, *HE*, vi. 25.

[5] J. Munck (*op. cit.*, pp. 249–260) attaches more importance to Origen's evidence than to that of Papias or Irenaeus, since there is evidence that Origen himself knew Hebrew and would therefore be a more competent judge. Munck discusses the possibility that Papias' statement may be an indication that several

This may be put down to their uncritical approach, but the possibility must always be allowed that there was some basis for the tradition,[1] as has been mentioned also in the case of Papias.[2]

Supposing, however, that in its views on authorship the tradition is incorrect, what are the current explanations of the rise of the tradition? Scholars who identify the λογία with a sayings collection or a Testimony Book consider an adequate solution is to suppose that Matthew's name was transferred at an early stage in the tradition from one of the sources of the Gospel to the Gospel as a whole.[3] The proposition sounds reasonable, but is it really valid? If an anonymous Gospel circulated for a while and was known to have incorporated an apostolic collection of teaching or testimonies, was it natural for it to be called later by the name of the compiler of the sayings? It would be difficult to find a parallel for such a process. It is much more probable that an anonymous Gospel would circulate without anyone having the slightest knowledge of the authorship of any of its sources. One presentation of this theory is to suppose that a tradition that Matthew wrote something was preserved in the same district and at the same time as the anonymous Gospel circulated, and that it was then assumed quite uncritically that Matthew must have written the Gospel. But this still leaves unidentified what Matthew actually wrote. A third possibility is that at the time of the publication it was known as Matthew's Gospel because one of the main sources was written by Matthew. This is perhaps more probable

Greek translations of Matthew's Gospel circulated in his time. W. C. Allen (*The Gospel according to St. Matthew*, ICC, 1907, p. lxxxi) suggested that everyone knew that Matthew had written something in Hebrew, and when his name was attached to the Gospel the statement about him writing in Hebrew was also attached.

[1] C. F. D. Moule (*The Birth of the New Testament*, 1962) admits that room must be found for this persistent tradition in any account of Matthew's origin. He favours a Semitic apostolic sayings collection (i.e. a Semitic Q). Feine-Behm (*Einleitung*,[11] p. 51) conclude from the linguistic evidence that the author must have been a Greek-speaking Jewish Christian who understood Hebrew. Cf. the section on the language of this Gospel (pp. 44 f.). J. Jeremias, because of the form of Dt. vi. 5 cited in Mt. xxii. 37, maintains that the author's mother-speech was Aramaic, but that his prayer-speech was Hebrew (*ZNTW*, 50, 1959, pp. 270–274).

[2] Cf. Kürzinger's discussion, *NTS*, 10 (1963), pp. 108 ff.

[3] W. C. Allen (*op. cit.*, pp. lxxx, lxxxi) contended that if Matthew wrote the sayings collection, it would be natural for his name to be added to a Gospel two fifths of which contained sayings, especially as an apostolic name would give sanction to it. Allen describes this as 'an irresistible tendency'.

than the other two suggestions, but is still without any clear parallels to support it, and is also faced with the difficulty of explaining away the complete disappearance of the source.

c. Objections to the tradition

Since the external evidence is so embarrassing for non-Matthaean authorship, may it not be better to assume that the traditional view is correct?[1] However, certain difficulties arise which are generally considered to make this impossible.

1. The most important obstacle to the acceptance of the tradition is the generally held assumption that Matthew used Mark as his basic source, and not only used Mark but incorporated nearly all of it into his Gospel. If this is a correct assumption it would mean that an apostolic author would have used a non-apostolic source, and this is considered improbable, indeed inconceivable. Reasons will be given later to show that Marcan priority has not gone completely unchallenged in recent times and if it is a false assumption the difficulty would, of course, disappear. But since Marcan priority may be regarded as probable in spite of its difficulties, does this at once rule out apostolic authorship for Matthew's Gospel? The view that it does would seem to proceed from a particular view of apostolicity, which considers that it would have detracted from Matthew's apostolic dignity if he had quoted a non-apostolic writer.[2] It is certainly surprising to find an eyewitness making use of a secondary source, even though it is allowed that Mark preserves Peter's reminiscences.[3] But though surprising, it is not impossible. It

[1] One explanation of Papias' words is that he refers to only part of what Matthew wrote and that his comments on the rest are not preserved (cf. T. Nicklin, *Gospel Gleanings*, 1950, pp. 51–56, who suggests that Matthew wrote an Oracles book (which was referred to by Papias), Q and later the extant Gospel in Greek). F. Godet (*Introduction to the New Testament: The Collection of the Four Gospels and the Gospel of St. Matthew*, 1899, pp. 217 ff.), who also considered that Matthew compiled the 'oracles', suggested that an anonymous collaborator of his translated these λογία into Greek and added the Matthaean narratives under Matthew's direction.

[2] A similar objection has been raised over Matthew's use of Q, a non-apostolic source according to many source theories (cf. Michaelis, *Einleitung in das Neue Testament*,[3] 1961, p. 32). But see pp. 136 ff. for discussion on the Q source.

[3] Vincent Taylor calls it 'improbable in the extreme that an apostle would have used as a source the work of one who was not an eyewitness of the ministry of Jesus' (*The Gospels*, p. 81). S. Johnson (*The Gospel according to St. Matthew, IB*, 1951, p. 242) rejects apostolic authorship on the grounds that Matthew is what he calls 'a compendium of church tradition artistically edited'.

would be much more difficult to conceive if Matthew had incorporated Mark unaltered into his work, but he clearly has not done that,
since no more than fifty per cent of Mark shows verbal agreement
with Matthew (see p. 126). Moreover the ancient world's approach to
literary borrowing was different from our modern approach, and the
wholesale incorporation of another's work would not have been
regarded as impermissible, especially in view of the fact that the Gospel
traditions were common knowledge. Besides, the apostle Matthew,
being himself an eyewitness of many of the events, would be in a position to recognize the authenticity of Mark.

2. Arising, however, from the latter consideration is the contention
that Matthew could not have been written by an eyewitness since the
book is much less vivid than Mark's, and this argument must be given
full weight.[1] Yet it may be said that Matthew has had time to reflect
upon the events that he records and gives more attention to their
significance than to their vividness. But in the end this kind of consideration rarely leads to satisfactory conclusions in any direction.[2] A
more important consideration is the view that an eyewitness would not
have shown the tendencies found in this Gospel, especially ecclesiastical
and legalistic, which assume a later editorial process. This would, of
course, be a major obstacle to apostolic authorship if it were a valid
objection. But its basis needs careful investigation. If Matthew's
Gospel is more ecclesiastical than its sources, does this mean that the
author's editorial purposes belong to a time when ecclesiastical concerns were more dominant in the Church? It does not immediately
follow that this is so. Indeed, it appears to be based on the presupposition that the contemporary church situation created or at least deeply
influenced the tradition. But it is equally possible to maintain that
Matthew's editorial tendencies reflect a genuine early tradition, provided a more comprehensive picture of the teaching of Jesus is maintained.

3. Another objection of a different kind comes from Kilpatrick,[3]
who, although he accepts the view that Papias meant the Gospel in the

[1] Cf. Michaelis, *Einleitung*, pp. 31 f.; also Feine-Behm, *Einleitung*[11], pp. 49 ff.
[2] The same may be said for the view that the peculiar material in the Gospel
does not suggest the reminiscences of an apostle (cf. V. Taylor, *loc. cit.*). This
assessment depends on the assumption that the special Matthew material is
rather less historically reliable than the rest of Matthew (but see pp. 159 f. for a
discussion of this).
[3] See pp. 24 f. for Kilpatrick's theory.

statement about the λογία, and therefore accepted its ascription to Matthew, explains away the tradition as a conscious community pseudonym, purposely affixed by the church which produced the Gospel in order to commend it. By this means Kilpatrick attempts in fact to explain away the tradition. But the idea of a community pseudonym is unparalleled. Even if the idea be conceded it would be necessary to explain how any one church managed to persuade all the other churches that the book was authentically Matthaean. Moreover, Kilpatrick himself admits that pseudonymity in an individual is a problem, but considers that for a community it is less so.[1] But this supposed double standard is not supported by the evidence, and from an ethical point of view is highly doubtful. Again, if Kilpatrick's theory that apostolic authorship would have guaranteed readier acceptance is correct, why was not the same procedure followed for Mark and Luke, which were accepted without such a device?

4. A somewhat different reinterpretation of the tradition is found in Stendahl's idea of a school of Matthew,[2] for in this case the identity of the author is lost in the school out of which the Gospel grew.[3] Since the school is said to have continued the tradition of Matthew's catechesis, the ascription of the subsequently written Gospel to Matthew would have seemed natural. But on this view the knowledge that Matthew's school and not Matthew himself produced the Gospel was forgotten long before Papias, a possible but not very probable eventuality. No parallels to such a happening are extant. Nevertheless if the previous objections to Matthaean authorship are considered to be strong enough to require an alternative, this group suggestion is more satisfactory than either a community pseudonym idea or the transference of Matthew's name from a source to the whole.

---

[1] Op. cit., p. 139.   [2] See pp. 25 f. for Stendahl's theory.

[3] Op. cit. Cf. P. Gaechter's view that Matthew was trained as a Rabbi, but later became a tax collector (ZkT, 75, 1953, pp. 480 ff.). This idea is an attempt to reconcile the clear indications of Matthew's profession in the Gospel text (Mt. ix. 9, x. 3) with certain rabbinical features noted in the Gospel. Stendahl, of course, does not have this problem, for he does not identify Matthew as the author and is free to postulate an unidentified Rabbi as author.

E. P. Blair (Jesus in the Gospel of Matthew, 1960, pp. 138 ff.) regards the writer as belonging to the Hellenistic group of Christians represented by the approach of Stephen, but makes no further attempt to identify him, or to suggest why Matthew's name became attached to his work. He goes no further than to repeat the generally held hypothesis that Matthew may have written Q.

d. Incidental supports for the tradition

Supposing the tradition of Matthaean authorship to be correct, are there any incidental supporting evidences from within the Gospel itself? It must be admitted that the evidence is slight, but it may be worth mentioning. Whereas both Mark (ii. 14) and Luke (v. 27 f.) in describing the call of Matthew name him Levi, in Matthew's Gospel he is called Matthew (ix. 9). At the same time in the lists of the apostles in all the Gospels the name Matthew is used and not Levi. Could it be that for the author of this Gospel the name Matthew came to have greater significance than the name Levi, from the time of his dramatic call to follow Jesus? It is not impossible that this is a conscious personal touch.[1] Yet not all would agree with this interpretation, for it has been regarded as a device of pseudonymity,[2] but this idea is unlikely since the choice of Matthew rather than a more important apostle such as Peter would be hard to explain. Another feature is the agreement between the attention to detail essential to the tax-collector's profession and the methodical arrangement of this Gospel. It is, at least, not difficult to imagine that a former tax-collector produced it. It may be of some significance that in the dispute over paying tribute, which all the Synoptics record, it is Matthew alone who uses the more precise νόμισμα (state coin) instead of the common δηνάριον. But the variation may have nothing to do with a tax-collector's experience.

To sum up, it may be said that there is no conclusive reason for rejecting the strong external testimony regarding the authorship of Matthew, although some difficulties arise from source hypotheses. Most scholars, however, reject apostolic authorship. Yet if Matthew is not the author his identity is unknown. The idea that he was a Rabbi is purely speculative.[3]

---

[1] H. Alford (*Greek Testament*[6], 1868, I, p. 24) suggested that the author uses his apostolic name when referring to himself, in the same manner as Paul did. But Michaelis (*Einleitung*, pp. 33, 34) disputes that both names would be attached to one person, and considers that Matthew was later substituted for Levi in the tradition.

[2] Cf. G. D. Kilpatrick, *The Origins of the Gospel according to St. Matthew* (1946), p. 138. He suggests that ix. 9 and x. 3 were changed to Matthew when the title was affirmed in the original community which sanctioned the book.

[3] In addition to those mentioned on p. 41 n.3 in support of this suggestion, cf. also E. von Dobschütz, *ZNTW*, 27 (1928), pp. 338–348, and B. W. Bacon, *Studies in Matthew* (1930), pp. 131 ff.

V. DATE

It is difficult to discuss the date of any of the Synoptic Gospels without reference to the Synoptic problem, but it is valuable to enquire what possible indications may be found apart from the solution to that problem. It must be admitted that the data available are very slight. It might be argued that certain strands of Matthaean tradition are of a secondary character (see pp. 159 f.), in which case an interval of time would be required to allow for such developments,[1] but this is a judgment which lacks positive proof and is controlled largely by certain presuppositions regarding the relative values of the sources used by the Evangelists.

Similar to this line of argument is the view that Matthew's special material shows ecclesiastical and explanatory interests[2] which point to a time beyond the primitive period. But again the force of this depends on the interpretation of, and the value attached to, the passages about the Church.[3] If it be assumed that our Lord did not foresee and could not have predicted the emergence of a Church, there would be force in the argument. But the character of Jesus would lead us to expect not only that He foresaw the future Church but even prepared for it.

This predictive power of Jesus is so generally denied by Synoptic investigators that it is no wonder that the dates of Mark, Matthew and Luke are all bound up together in the dating of Mark. The argument runs as follows:[4] First, since the predictive power of Christ is denied, it is assumed that Mark was produced a few years before the fall of Jerusalem (cf. Mk. xiii. 14, and Mt. xxiv. 15). Secondly, Matthew used Mark and therefore must be dated after the fall of Jerusalem. Thirdly, both Ignatius and the *Didache* appear to have cited Matthew's Gospel and so the latter must have attained authority some time before the writings of the former. Fourthly, therefore the probable date of

---

[1] Cf. Streeter, *The Four Gospels* (1924), p. 524.

[2] Cf. V. Taylor, *The Gospels*, p. 82.

[3] It should not be forgotten in discussions of Matthew's ecclesiology that the doctrine in Matthew has certain affinities with Paul's doctrine, although differently expressed. Dodd (*New Testament Studies*, pp. 53–66) examines these points of contact and suggests that a common tradition lies behind them. In this case theological considerations are clearly unreliable indications of dating.

[4] For the generally held dating of Mark's Gospel, see the discussion on pp. 68 ff.

Matthew is AD 80–100. There is no general agreement on any more precise dating within this period.[1]

If, however, it be admitted that our Lord had power to predict the fall of Jerusalem, the main prop in the Marcan dating falls away and other data would need to be used in determining the dates of both Mark and Matthew.[2] But there is singularly little indication in either of them concerning their dates of origin and any suggestions must be largely guesswork. This is one of the problems which must therefore be left undetermined. Yet it affects our understanding of the Gospel as a whole very little, unless, of course, a purely tentative date, which can in no way be proved, is then appealed to as an indication of historical value, as has not infrequently been done. It is necessary to introduce a caution about this.

VI. LANGUAGE

There has been much discussion about the original language of the Gospels. No conclusive answer has yet been given to the question of the possible Aramaic forms from which our extant Gospels have been translated, although far less importance has been given to this than is perhaps justified by the evidence. As far as Matthew's Gospel is concerned, it has generally been held that its extant form shows no evidence of translation Greek. Moulton and Howard[3] called it 'a correct if rather colourless Greek which avoids the vulgar forms without displaying a mastery of the literary syntax'. Many scholars are strongly influenced in their estimate of Matthew's language by the assumption that the author used the Greek Mark and could not, therefore, have composed in Aramaic.[4]

There has been increasing examination of the evidence from a philo-

---

[1] Kilpatrick (*op. cit.*, pp. 124 ff.) suggests a date at the end of the first century. F. V. Filson (*The Gospel according to St. Matthew*, 1960, p. 15) prefers a date in the eighties or nineties, but declines to be more specific. Streeter (*op. cit.*, p. 524) was more precise in preferring AD 85, although he agreed it could not be mathematically demonstrated.

[2] The argument that external evidence supports the dating of Mark after Peter's death (see pp. 68 f.) would affect the dating of Matthew only on the usual assumption that Matthew used Mark. Michaelis (*Einleitung*, pp. 41, 42), who accepts Matthew's use of Mark, nevertheless suggests a date of AD 60–70 for this Gospel. For a dating a decade earlier, cf. M. Meinertz, *Einleitung in das Neue Testament*[5] (1950), pp. 176 ff.

[3] *A Grammar of New Testament Greek* (1929), II, p. 29.

[4] Cf. Streeter's statement to this effect, *op. cit.*, p. 500.

logical point of view and the idea that our Greek Gospels may go back to Aramaic originals or at least to Aramaic sources has gained some support. The main scholars who have worked in this field are Burney,[1] Torrey[2] and Matthew Black.[3] The two former, who favoured Aramaic originals, drew their arguments mainly from evidence of mistranslation, although Burney also gave attention to grammatical and syntactical considerations. Black, who maintains sources but not originals, has developed this latter approach and has attempted to prove that many grammatical peculiarities can best be explained on the assumption of Aramaic influence. It is probable that increasing weight will be given to evidence of this kind. For Matthew's Gospel it is basic to Vaganay's[4] solution to the Synoptic problem (see discussion on pp. 131 f.), which maintains an original Aramaic Matthew as the earliest Gospel, from which the canonical Greek Synoptic Gospels have all been derived.

Black's conclusion regarding sources is that there is sufficient evidence from the Gospels to point to a sayings source in Aramaic, but he does not think that Matthew's narrative sections show such Aramaic influence as Mark's sections.[5] He admits, however, that Matthew shows traces of what he calls a Jewish-Greek style.

Linguistic questions of this kind cannot be assessed in brief compass, but sufficient has been said to indicate the complicated state of the problem. It may be assumed *a priori* that since our Lord taught in Aramaic some Aramaic background would be found behind the teaching of Jesus. But it will be seen that in Matthew's case the question is really dominated by the Marcan hypothesis. It may perhaps be that this hypothesis should come to grips more effectively with linguistic considerations (see later discussion on the Synoptic problem, pp. 126 ff.).

[1] *The Poetry of our Lord* (1925); *The Aramaic Origin of the Fourth Gospel* (1922).
[2] *The Four Gospels: A New Translation* (1933).
[3] *An Aramaic Approach to the Gospels and Acts* (1946).
[4] *Le Problème synoptique* (1954). This is somewhat akin to T. Zahn's view that our Greek Matthew is a translation of an original Aramaic form of the Gospel, influenced by the Greek Mark which had previously been produced from the same Aramaic source (*INT*, 1909, II, pp. 601–617.)
[5] *Op. cit.*, pp. 206 ff.

CONTENTS

I. THE INFANCY NARRATIVES (i. 1–ii. 23)

The genealogy (i. 1–17). The birth of Jesus (i. 18–25). The Magi's visit (ii. 1–12). The flight and return (ii. 13–23).

II. THE PREPARATION FOR THE MINISTRY (iii. 1–iv. 11)

The mission of John the Baptist (iii. 1–12). Jesus' baptism (iii. 13–17). The temptation (iv. 1–11).

III. THE GALILAEAN MINISTRY (iv. 12–25)

The beginnings (iv. 12–17). Call of the first disciples (iv. 18–22). A Galilaean preaching tour (iv. 23–25).

IV. THE FIRST DISCOURSE SECTION: THE SERMON ON THE MOUNT (v. 1–vii. 29)

Introduction (v. 1, 2). The Beatitudes (v. 3–12). Illustrations from salt and light (v. 13–16). Jesus' attitude towards the ancient law (v. 17–48). His teaching on religious practices (vi. 1–vii. 27). The effect on the hearers (vii. 28, 29).

V. NARRATIVE (viii. 1–ix. 34)

Healing of the leper, the centurion's slave, Peter's mother-in-law, and others (viii. 1–17). Two disciples tested (viii. 18–22). Stilling of the waves (viii. 23–27). Healing of a demoniac and a paralytic (viii. 28–ix. 8). The call of Matthew (ix. 9–13). An enquiry about fasting (ix. 14–17). Healing of the ruler's daughter, the woman with a haemorrhage, two blind men and a dumb demoniac (ix. 18–34).

VI. THE SECOND DISCOURSE SECTION: THE MISSION DISCOURSE (ix. 35–x. 42)

Jesus' compassion (ix. 35–38). The disciples are briefed (x. 1–15), warned of future troubles (x. 16–25) and exhorted to be unafraid (x. 26–33). They are told of division within households (x. 34–39), and promised rewards (x. 40–42).

VII. NARRATIVE (xi. 1–xii. 50)

Jesus sets out to preach in Galilee (xi. 1). John the Baptist's enquiry (xi. 2–6). Jesus' testimony regarding John (xi. 7–15). His estimate of His own generation (xi. 16–19). Woes pronounced on Galilaean cities (xi. 20–24). Jesus' thanksgiving to God (xi. 25–27) and call to the weary (xi. 28–30). Sabbath in the cornfield (xii. 1–8). Healing in the synagogue (xii. 9–14). Healing of the multitude (xii. 15–21). Pharisaic criticism of Jesus, and His reply (xii. 22–37). Sign-seeking and the sign of Jonah (xii. 38–42). The return of an evil spirit (xii. 43–45). Jesus' real family (xii. 46–50).

VIII. THE THIRD DISCOURSE SECTION:
THE KINGDOM PARABLES (xiii. 1–52)

The sower and the soils (xiii. 1–9). The reason for parables (xiii. 10–15), and the privileged position of the disciples (xiii. 16, 17). The first parable interpreted (xiii. 18–23). The tares (xiii. 24–30). The mustard seed and the leaven (xiii. 31–33). Old Testament support for the use of parables (xiii. 34, 35). The tares interpreted (xiii. 36–43). Hidden treasure, the valuable pearl and the dragnet (xiii. 44–51). The trained scribe of the kingdom (xiii. 52).

IX. NARRATIVE (xiii. 53–xvii. 27)

Jesus rejected at Nazareth (xiii. 53–58). The death of John the Baptist (xiv. 1–12). Miracles: five thousand fed; the walking on the water; healings at Gennesaret (xiv. 13–36). The tradition of the elders (xv. 1–20). More miracles: the Syro-Phoenician demoniac; healings of multitudes; four thousand fed (xv. 21–39). The Pharisees demand a sign (xvi. 1–4). Discourse on leaven (xvi. 5–12). Peter's confession at Caesarea Philippi (xvi. 13–20). First prediction of the passion (xvi. 21–23) and forecast of suffering for the disciples (xvi. 24–28). The transfiguration and the saying about Elijah (xvii. 1–13). The healing of an epileptic boy (xvii. 14–21). Second prediction of the passion (xvii. 22, 23). Discussion about the temple tax (xvii. 24–27).

X. THE FOURTH DISCOURSE SECTION: VARIOUS SAYINGS
(xviii. 1–35)

An enquiry about greatness (xviii. 1–5). Responsibility for causing others to stumble (xviii. 6–10). Illustration of the lost sheep (xviii. 11–

14). Reproofs and reconciliation (xviii. 15–22). Parable of the unmerciful servant (xviii. 23–35).

XI. NARRATIVE: THE JUDAEAN PERIOD (xix. 1–xxii. 46)

Jesus goes to Perea (xix. 1, 2). Questions about marriage and divorce (xix. 3–12). Jesus blesses the little children (xix. 13–15). The rich young man comes to Jesus (xix. 16–22). Jesus' comment on riches and rewards (xix. 23–30). Parable of the labourers in the vineyard (xx. 1–16). The third prediction of the passion (xx. 17–19). Request by Zebedee's wife for places of honour for her sons (xx. 20–28). Healing of two blind men (xx. 29–34). Entry into Jerusalem (xxi. 1–11). Cleansing of the temple (xxi. 12–17). Cursing of the fig-tree (xxi. 18–22). Controversies in the temple court (xxi. 23–xxii. 46).

XII. THE FIFTH DISCOURSE SECTION: TEACHING ON ESCHATOLOGY (xxiii. 1–xxv. 46)

Pronouncement of woes against the Pharisees (xxiii. 1–36). Lament over Jerusalem (xxiii. 37–39). The apocalyptic discourse (xxiv. 1–xxv. 46).

XIII. THE PASSION AND RESURRECTION NARRATIVES (xxvi. 1–xxviii. 20)

The preparation (xxvi. 1–19). The betrayal predicted (xxvi. 20–25). The last supper (xxvi. 26–29). Peter's denial predicted (xxvi. 30–35). In Gethsemane (xxvi. 36–46). The arrest, trial and crucifixion (xxvi. 47–xxvii. 56). The burial (xxvii. 57–66). The resurrection, appearance to the eleven, and farewell commission (xxviii. 1–20).

CHAPTER THREE

MARK'S GOSPEL

Until the period of modern criticism this Gospel was the most neg-lected of all. Ancient commentaries on it are very scarce and it clearly made little appeal. It was entirely overshadowed by the more stately Matthew, and since it was commonly regarded as no more than an abstract of Matthew this is not surprising. This opinion, however, was probably not the earliest view, since tradition closely linked it with Peter's preaching. It has come into its own through the modern opinion that it is the keystone of the Synoptic problem. Reasons for this opinion will be examined later (pp. 126 ff.), but for the present all that is necessary is to recognize the importance of this Gospel in modern discussions.

I. CHARACTERISTICS

a. A Gospel of action

A glance at the contents of this Gospel at once shows that for the writer movement is more fascinating than discourse. Where the teaching of Jesus is given it is nearly always in the setting of some narrative. The vividness of the style gives the impression of a quickly moving drama with the cross as its climax.

Examples of this characteristic might be multiplied, but the following will be sufficient to illustrate it. Mark describes the breaking up of the roof of the house to let down the palsied man (Mk. ii. 4); the sleeping Jesus with His head on a pillow in the stern of the boat in a furious storm (iv. 37, 38); the arrangement of the crowds in groups like an orderly vegetable patch on the green grass (vi. 39); the process by which Jesus healed the deaf and dumb man, i.e. by putting fingers into his ears and touching his tongue (vii. 33); the gradual restoration of sight to the blind man (viii. 23 ff.); and Peter sitting with the servants warming himself by the fire in the high priest's palace (xiv. 54). Such details as these are most naturally explained as being derived from eye-witnesses, although, as will be seen later, contrary opinions have been maintained.

Mark, with the minimum of preliminaries, goes straight to the

narration of the ministry of Jesus and describes various phases of that
ministry, paying particular attention to the increasing opposition of the
Pharisees. A pivotal point in the unfolding drama is the disciple's
affirmation of faith in Jesus at Caesarea Philippi, from which point the
story moves steadily towards the passion.[1] Commenting on Mark's
outline, Vincent Taylor writes, 'That there are many gaps in this outline, and that the arrangement is often topical, cannot be denied: but
the outline itself, and the looseness with which it is drawn, suggest that
it reflects good tradition.'[2]

Mark's is an essentially factual account of the life of Jesus. It tells the
story in 'a strangely objective fashion'.[3] There is almost no emotional
content and much less of Jesus' teaching than in the other Synoptists.
What teaching there is is mostly in isolated sayings, many associated
with brief narratives. Yet in spite of the considerable number of these,
Mark's main interest appears to be more in the activity than in the
teaching of Jesus. There are consequently fewer theological implications arising from Mark than from other Gospels, although here again
contrary opinions exist over Mark's theological interests.[4]

b. A Gospel for Gentiles

There is an absence of those traces of Jewish-Christian colouring which
have been noted in Matthew's Gospel. Where Matthew records Jesus'
warning to His disciples to pray that their flight may not be in winter
or on the sabbath, Mark mentions only winter (Mk. xiii. 18). In the
story of the Syro-Phoenician woman there is no saying about Jesus'
mission to the lost sheep of the house of Israel (vii. 24 ff.). There are no
statements about the abiding validity of the law after the manner of
Matthew's jot and tittle saying (Mt. v. 18). Indeed, there are no fundamental discussions about the law as in Matthew. Furthermore, the
disciples are not in Mark forbidden to go on a mission among the
Samaritans or Gentiles, and in the eschatological discourse Jesus speci-
fies that all people must hear the gospel before the end comes (xiii.

---

[1] Cf. T. W. Manson's *The Teaching of Jesus* (1931).   [2] *The Gospels*, p. 54.
[3] Cf. T. H. Robinson, *St. Mark's Life of Jesus* (1922), p. 8.
[4] Several recent writers have placed emphasis on Mark's theologizing purpose,
notably T. A. Burkill in several articles and in his book, *Mysterious Revelation:
An examination of the Philosophy of Mark's Gospel* (1963). Cf. also W. Marxsen's
Der Evangelist Markus² (1959), and E. Schweizer's article in *Neotestamentica et
Patristica*, pp. 35–46.

10).[1] It is clear that Mark has Gentile readers in mind in writing his Gospel.[2]

c. Mark's candour

There is no attempt to cast a halo around the disciples. In fact, the writer does not hesitate to narrate their lack of understanding on many occasions (iv. 13, vi. 52, viii. 17, 21, ix. 10, 32). The attitude of Jesus' relatives is described with similar frankness; they considered Him to be mad (iii. 21). Expressions of amazement on the part of Jesus' hearers are also included (i. 27, x. 24, 32), while Jesus' inability to work mighty deeds at Nazareth is directly attributed to the unbelief of the people (vi. 5, 6).

Mark is equally unreserved in his description of the human reactions of Jesus. The emotions of compassion, severity, anger, sorrow, tenderness and love are all in turn attributed to Him (i. 41, 43, iii. 5, viii. 12, 33, x. 14, 16, 21). There is no doubt that this is the Gospel of Jesus Christ, the Son of man, as well as the Gospel of Jesus Christ the Son of God (i. 1).

d. Mark's portrait of Jesus

There has been much discussion over the extent to which Mark has overlaid his portrait of Jesus with theological interpretation, with the result that no agreement has been reached among scholars generally. But this does not mean that no clear picture can be drawn. Our purpose here is not to discuss the interpretative element, nor to consider the origins of the material, both of which will be dealt with later. Our task is but to indicate the view of our Lord which Mark in its present form contains.

(i) *Son of God*. Since the Gospel describes Jesus by means of this title in its opening words,[3] it must be assumed that it has some defining influence over the subsequent narrative, especially as the title occurs four times elsewhere in this Gospel. It is evident that this view of Christ is not developed in a doctrinal sense, but that it is worked out in His

---

[1] But cf. G. D. Kilpatrick's discussion of this verse in *Studies in the Gospels* (ed. D. E. Nineham, 1955), pp. 145 ff.

[2] For further arguments in support of this conclusion, see pp. 55 ff.

[3] Although many MSS omit the phrase τοῦ θεοῦ the weightiest evidence would appear to support its inclusion (cf. V. Taylor, *The Gospel according to St. Mark*, 1953, pp. 120–122, 152; S. Johnson, *The Gospel according to St. Mark*, BC, 1960, p. 32).

divine activity. His appeal to the multitudes is powerful. He possesses power over all types of illness and casts out evil spirits with irresistible authority. He stills storms with a word and thus shows His power over nature. When He dies, a pagan Roman centurion admits, 'Truly, this man was God's son' (xv. 39). Those who approach the Gospel with the presupposition that miracles do not happen naturally give no weight to this particular aspect of Mark's portrait. They see in it no more than the accretions of later hero-worship. The modern tendency in this direction will become clearer when certain form-critical hypotheses are discussed, but if any significance at all is to be attached to the Marcan story it is impossible to deny that the portrait it contains is of a more than human Person, although partially concealed.[1]

(ii) *Son of man.* Jesus' use of this title is especially noticeable in Mark's account, although it is frequent in the other Synoptics also. Whatever the precise significance of the title, which has been widely debated,[2] it seems clear that it contains an oblique reference to the true humanity of Jesus. Something has already been said about Mark's descriptions of the human reactions of Jesus, but this concept of our Lord's humanity is brought out in other ways. For instance, His need of prayer (i. 35, vi. 31) and His resolute steadfastness on His last journey to Jerusalem (x. 32) are both specifically mentioned. The Gospel abounds with references to the intermingling of Jesus with the common people, which

---

[1] Taylor (*op. cit.*, p. 120) considers that this title represents the most fundamental element in Mark's Christology.

[2] There has been much discussion over this term. Cf. G. Dalman, *The Words of Jesus* (1902), pp. 235–267; G. S. Duncan, *Jesus, Son of Man* (1948); R. Bultmann, *The History of the Synoptic Tradition* (translated by J. Marsh, 1963); W. L. Knox, *Sources of the Synoptic Gospels*, II (1957), pp. 140 ff.; S. Mowinckel, *He that Cometh* (1956), pp. 346 ff.; O. Cullmann, *Christology of the New Testament*[2] (1963), pp. 137–192; T. W. Manson, *BJRL*, XXXII (1950), pp. 171–193; J. W. Bowman, *ET*, LIX (1947–48), pp. 283–288; M. Black, *ET*, LX (1948–49), pp. 11–15, 32–36. Cf. also E. Sjöberg, *Der verborgene Menschensohn in den Evangelien* (1955); A. J. B. Higgins, in *New Testament Essays, Studies in Memory of T. W. Manson* (1959), pp. 119–135; H. E. Tödt, *Der Menschensohn in der synoptischen Überlieferung* (1959); E. Schweizer's article in *JBL*, LXXIX (1960), pp. 119–129. Many scholars have contended that Jesus identified the Son of man with the suffering Servant (cf. W. Manson, *Jesus the Messiah*, 1943). But this viewpoint has recently been challenged unsuccessfully by J. Knox, *The Death of Christ: The Cross in New Testament History* (1959) and M. D. Hooker, *Jesus and the Servant* (1958). Cf. the criticisms of the latter book by J. Jeremias, *JTS*, n.s., XI (1960), pp. 140–144.

strengthens the impression that He is a true representative of the people, a true Man among men.

But the title 'Son of man' must have more significance than this. A discussion of this subject belongs more to the sphere of biblical theology than to introduction, but it is not unimportant for the study of the latter. The problem whether or not Jesus intended to identify Himself with the Messiah when using this title may, for instance, affect the discussion on Mark's purpose. It may also affect the estimate of the historicity of Mark. Both these problems will be mentioned later, but for our present discussion it will be sufficient to observe that Mark presents a portrait of Jesus in which many times He urges silence upon people who have observed His works. It is at least clear that Jesus did not have as His purpose any public proclamation of His Messiahship. The most characteristic picture of the Lord in this Gospel lies elsewhere.

(iii) *The Redeemer*. In one of Mark's Son of man passages, Jesus declares that His purpose was to be a ransom for many (x. 45), and whereas this theme does not specifically recur in the Gospel, the great emphasis on the passion narrative shows the importance attached to it by the author. Mark devotes a greater proportion of space to the passion narrative than any of the other Gospels. Such an outlook is in full accord with the emphasis on the cross in primitive Christianity, as the early preaching and theology conclusively show (e.g. 1 Cor. xv. 3 ff.; Phil. ii. 5–11; 1 Pet. ii. 21 f.). Mark describes a Christ who had come to suffer.

II. PURPOSE AND READERS

In his opening sentence Mark makes clear that his intention is to write a 'Gospel', an account of the good news about Jesus Christ, the Son of God. This at once distinguishes the book from a biography[1] and explains the large proportion of space devoted to the last three weeks of the life of Jesus. The cross and resurrection were the central features of the Christian gospel. All the events and even the teaching which led up to the cross were preparatory. In this, of course, Mark's record is not unique. The same is true of all the Gospels. The movement of the narrative is dominated by the passion story, but in Mark's Gospel the

[1] Cf. A. E. J. Rawlinson's comments on this, *The Gospel according to St. Mark*[7] (1949), pp. xviii ff. He says of Mark, 'He is writing for Christians, to whom his main story, with the necessary clues for the clear understanding of the narrative, may be presumed to be familiar; and he writes in a religious, and not in a biographical interest' (p. xix).

action is heightened by the relative absence of blocks of teaching material.

This essentially evangelistic purpose should caution us against expecting too rigid a chronological framework. The purpose is to account for the historical events of the life of Jesus, who had no need to be introduced.[1] For Mark, birth-narratives and accounts of Jesus' early history were not relevant to his purpose. His narrative confronts us at once with Jesus Christ, the Son of God, as a historic fact,[2] and he assumes that his readers will know at once to whom he is referring.

Other motives undoubtedly played their part in formulating the author's purpose. It is probable that a catechetical design was in mind, especially as some at least of the material seems to have been arranged as an aid to memory.[3] A liturgical motive is less likely, for this Gospel does not seem to have been particularly adaptable for such a purpose. Its arrangement is far less symmetrical than Matthew's Gospel and its relative neglect by early writers would hardly have happened had it been widely used as a part of Christian liturgy. There was naturally an interest among the early Christians in the work of Jesus and it was part of Mark's purpose to satisfy this natural urge. It is remarkable that neither Mark nor any of the Evangelists has preserved any information about the personal appearance of our Lord, but no-one could miss the striking impression of His personality which Mark produces through his narrative.[4] Yet it was not part of his purpose to produce this im-

[1] All attempts to write an adequate life of Jesus must inevitably fail because the data are insufficient. All that can be achieved is an approximation.

[2] Some scholars have been influenced by the fact that, in Mark's Gospel, Jesus so often enjoins upon His disciples secrecy regarding His messianic claims, and have deduced from this that the author's purpose was to declare that Jesus was the Messiah and to explain why this was not generally known in Jesus' lifetime (cf. K. and S. Lake, *INT*, 1938, pp. 37, 38). For comments on Wrede's more radical deductions from the same data, see p. 179.

[3] E.g. the arrangement of material into topical groups (cf. Mk. iv for a collection of parables and Mk. x for mission instructions). Note also in Mark the arrangement according to keywords (cf. Mk. ix. 13–37). If, of course, these features are regarded as pre-Marcan, they furnish no indication of the author's purpose.

For a study of the catechetical purpose of Mark, cf. G. Schille's article in *NTS*, 4 (1957), pp. 1–24. He approaches the subject from a form-critical point of view. Even those who do not share Schille's presuppositions may grant the probability of some catechetical motive.

[4] J. Weiss (*The History of Primitive Christianity*, 1937, p. 701) refers to the unique and enigmatical greatness of the personality of Jesus.

pression. The impression itself was inescapable. Mark was no more than a channel for the tradition.

Some mention must be made of the theories of the author's purpose held by those who concentrate on the religious needs which the Gospel was intended to meet. They are connected with the form-historical method which sees in Mark an editor arranging units of material for a religious purpose; but no single motive, either theological or bio-graphical, suffices to explain the editorial process. D. E. Nineham[1] suggests several concerns which are evident in Mark's writing. (1) To show that Jesus as Messiah was innocent of Jewish charges and that His sufferings were part of God's purpose. (2) To explain why Jesus did not publicly declare Himself to be Messiah. (3) To explain why Christians have to suffer, i.e. because Jesus had to suffer. (4) To present the works of Jesus as a triumph over the forces of evil. Not all will agree with Nineham on his interpretation of these motives, but most would agree that they played some part in the writer's purpose. It is important, however, to draw a distinction between motives of selection and motives of creation. If, for instance, it is supposed that the messianic claim of Jesus was an invention of the community, the view of Mark's purpose would inevitably be affected. His aim would be to support the community tradition, and in pursuance of this aim he would create narratives which urged secrecy concerning Jesus' messianic claims, because otherwise the recollection that Jesus made no such claim would be inexplicable.[2] Reasons will be given later for questioning the validity of such form-critical presuppositions, but this example is quoted to demonstrate how ideas about an author's purpose must be affected by one's previous historical assessment of the material.

The original destination of the Gospel is impossible to decide with any certainty. Yet there are some indications which point to Gentile readers and some evidence which supports the idea that these earliest readers were located in Rome. Evidence for Gentile readers may be summarized as follows:

1. Mark explains Palestinian customs. The Pharisaic custom of hand-washing and the general traditions regarding purification are explained in vii. 3, 4 and this would not have been necessary for a Jewish audience.[3]

---

[1] *St. Mark* (Pel C, 1963), pp. 30 ff.   [2] Cf. p. 54 n.2.
[3] Cf. Vincent Taylor, *The Gospel according to St. Mark* (1953), pp. 32, 335. H. G. Wood (*Jesus in the Twentieth Century*, 1960, pp. 25 ff.) suggests that the slight emphasis on John the Baptist indicates Gentile readers.

2. Some Aramaic expressions, which are retained in the text, are interpreted into Greek and this seems to be evidence that Mark's readers would not otherwise have understood them.[1]

3. If the author belongs to the same group as his readers, the many Latinisms in Mark may point to a Gentile environment, although this is not certain since there is evidence also of some Semitisms. If, of course, the readers were in a different place from the author, this evidence would be invalid and the same applies to the next consideration.

4. It is claimed that the author was unacquainted with Palestine, since he mentions Dalmanutha (viii. 10), which is otherwise unknown.[2] But the argument is tenuous, since it is not altogether impossible that this place-name is genuine in spite of the fact that no other record of it has been preserved. Again, Mark's location of the country of the Gerasenes as extending to the Sea of Galilee (v. 1), the description of Bethsaida as a village (viii. 26), the confused references to the Herodian family (vi. 17), the assumption that the appearance of Jesus before the high priest was a 'trial', and the reference to a wife's power to divorce her husband, which was against the Jewish law (x. 12), have all been claimed to point to a non-Palestinian origin.[3] But these alleged Palestinian discrepancies are open to challenge. There may not be precise information about the Gerasene country but, unless there are data which conflict with Mark's rather vague description, the possibility of his knowledge of the area must be admitted. Vagueness of description does not necessarily imply non-acquaintance. Mark's description of Bethsaida may be claimed to be technically correct, for there were few 'cities', in the Greek sense, in that area.[4] There may be some confusion about Herodias, who according to Luke was Philip's wife, which seems to conflict with Josephus, unless there were two Philips, Philip the Tetrarch, husband of Salome, and Herod Philip, former husband of Herodias. But the confusion, if it exists, is not enough to prove Mark's lack of acquaintance with Palestinian affairs, for a glance at Josephus is enough to show the complexity of the intrigues and inter-marriage in

---

[1] Cf. S. Johnson (*The Gospel according to St. Mark*, BC, 1960, pp. 15, 16), who points out that Mark's transliterations into Greek are at best approximations. He notes that a translation is even given for Abba (xiv. 36), but it may have been a customary practice to cite both the transliterated Aramaic and Greek, since Paul does the same (Rom. viii. 15; Gal. iv. 6).

[2] Cf. *ibid.*, p. 16.   [3] Cf. *ibid.*, p. 15.

[4] Cf. A. N. Sherwin-White, *Roman Society and Roman Law in the New Testament* (1963), pp. 127 ff.

the Herod family, and it cannot be supposed that these were necessarily common knowledge to all Palestinians. The supposed vagueness of Mark about the trial scene is equally open to challenge, for it is maintained by A. N. Sherwin-White[1] that Mark's description may be substantially correct. As to the question of a wife's power to divorce her husband, it is certain that in Josephus' time it was regarded as an offence against the Jewish law, as he mentions in the case of both Salome and Herodias.[2] But the statement in x. 12 cannot be regarded as an example of Mark's ignorance of Palestinian procedure unless that statement is Mark's own invention. As a saying of Jesus it consists of a pronouncement regarding adultery, not on the custom of a wife's divorcing her husband.[3] Our Lord was not confining His teaching to Jewish custom. It will be seen therefore that these data provide no certain evidence for place of origin or for destination.

Nevertheless there is some external evidence for the Roman origin of the Gospel and this must be taken in conjunction with the internal evidence.

1. The tradition preserved by Papias[4] that Mark was Peter's interpreter, and the latter's traditional martyrdom in Rome, would support a Roman origin.

2. The anti-Marcionite Prologue[5] is more specific and adds that after Peter's death Mark wrote the Gospel in Italy.

3. Irenaeus[6] also implies that Mark wrote after the deaths of Peter and Paul in Rome. On the other hand Clement of Alexandria states that Mark wrote while Peter was still preaching the gospel at Rome. If the traditions regarding the date appear to conflict, those regarding the place of origin nevertheless coincide.

4. The reference to Mark in 1 Peter v. 13 shows Mark's connection with Rome, if 'Babylon' is to be understood in this metaphorical sense.[7]

5. The earliest testimony to the use of the Gospel comes from 1 Clement and The Shepherd of Hermas, both of which probably

[1] Op. cit., pp. 24–47. [2] Antiquities, xv. 7. 10, xviii. 5. 4.
[3] Cf. J. Murray, Divorce (1953), pp. 53 f.
[4] As quoted in Eusebius, HE, iii. 39. 15.
[5] For the Latin text of the fragment and an English translation, cf. Taylor, op. cit., p. 3.
[6] Adv. Haer. iii. 1. 2.
[7] Cf. the discussion in the writer's New Testament Introduction: Hebrews to Revelation (1962), pp. 125–127.

show acquaintance with it,[1] and both of which are associated with Rome.

6. The references to sufferings and persecutions in Mark (viii. 34–38, x. 38 f., xiii. 9–13) have been claimed as allusions to Nero's persecutions and therefore cited as evidence of the author's connection with the Roman church.[2] But this line of evidence is inconclusive, since the references to persecution are very general and could refer to any persecution.

There would seem to be considerable justification for the view that Mark is a Roman Gospel designed for a Roman audience. There is in fact only one divergent tradition, that reported by Chrysostom,[3] that the Gospel was composed in Egypt, but this is most improbable in the absence of any corroborating evidence and in view of the strength of the Roman tradition. Some have suggested Antioch,[4] but the arguments for this are not particularly strong. If the Roman tradition is wrong, the place of origin and the identity of the original recipients are anyone's guess.[5] An incidental support for the Roman location of both author and readers has been suggested in the occurrence of the many Latinisms,[6] as previously mentioned, which would at least be intelligible in a Roman environment,[7] although not much weight should be attached to this argument since Latinisms were used in various Greek-speaking parts of the Empire.[8] In view of the lack of any supported alternative, this theory must be considered to be the most probable. It should, of course, be noted that most of the evidence cited concerns the author rather than his readers, and the possibility must be allowed for that the

[1] Cf. Johnson, *op. cit.*, p. 16, for the evidence, which is not strong.

[2] Cf. V. Taylor, *op. cit.*, p. 32.   [3] *Prooem in Matt.* (cf. Taylor, *op. cit.*, p. 32).

[4] Cf. J. V. Bartlet, *St. Mark* (CB, 1922), pp. 36 f.

[5] W. C. Allen (*The Gospel according to St. Mark*, 1915, p. 6) suggested that the Gospel was first produced in Aramaic in Jerusalem and was later translated into Greek at Antioch. A Jerusalem origin was earlier suggested by J. Wellhausen, *Einleitung in die drei ersten Evangelien*[2] (1911), p. 78. A recent German writer, W. Marxsen (*op. cit.*, p. 41), has suggested Galilee.

[6] Mark uses only Roman monetary terms and not Greek terms, according to O. Roller, *Münzen, Geld und Vermögensverhältnisse in den Evangelien* (1929).

[7] Cf. Michaelis, *Einleitung*, p. 55. It should also be noted that the mention of Rufus, both in Mk. xv. 21 and in Rom. xvi. 13, has been thought to point to a Roman destination, since if Rufus were in Rome, there would be some point in Mark's incidental mention of him.

[8] Cf. S. Johnson, *op. cit.*, p. 16. Cadbury (*The Making of Luke-Acts*, pp. 88, 89) is inclined to think that the Latinisms are against, rather than for, a Roman origin.

author wrote from Rome for readers who were elsewhere, but this seems unlikely.

III. STRUCTURE

It has already been pointed out that Mark was not intending to write a consecutive biography of Jesus. A problem therefore arises concerning what principle he adopted in the structure of his Gospel. Certain form critics[1] (see pp. 178 ff.) have adopted a somewhat sceptical attitude towards this problem, maintaining that no framework is discernible. This is no doubt a logical outcome of the dissection of the Gospel into 'forms' of different kinds, provided it be conceded that the author of the whole was no more than an editor of a mass of disparate sections. But the Gospel does not read like a hotchpotch of unconnected *pericopae* (sections), for although the connecting links are often vague the over-all movement of events is clear enough.[2]

After an introduction, the Galilaean ministry is illustrated in i. 14–vi. 13, followed by an account of Jesus' work outside Galilee (vi. 14–viii. 26), the journey to Jerusalem (viii. 27–x. 52) and the final ministry with its climax in the passion and resurrection of Jesus (xi. 1–xvi). This may be called the Synoptic framework since its main pattern is followed by all the Synoptic Gospels. There seems no weighty reason to deny that this framework existed in the oral tradition. In fact, C. H. Dodd[3] has argued that Mark's framework conforms to the pattern found in Acts, particularly in x. 37 f. in the speech of Peter in Cornelius' house. From this he deduces that the framework formed part of the Christian *kerygma*. It should be noted that the skeleton framework envisaged is assumed to have been longer than the summary of Acts x. 37 f., but nevertheless no more than a skeleton. As a result the major-

---

[1] This trend was begun by K. L. Schmidt, *Der Rahmen der Geschichte Jesu* (1919). The form-critical theories of Dibelius and Bultmann result in the same scepticism (see pp. 180 ff.).

[2] It is interesting to note that F. C. Grant (*The Earliest Gospel*, 1943), although he gives credence to the general approach of form criticism nevertheless supports Dodd (see next note) on a generalized Marcan structure, which he thinks was impressed on the pre-Marcan material (cf. *op. cit.*, pp. 38 ff.). Yet Grant is not sure about the basis of Dodd's argument, especially that drawn from the Acts speeches, both because he thinks that Luke may have here been influenced by Mark and because he is uncertain about the validity of the Acts speeches.

[3] In an article in *ET*, XLIII (1932), pp. 396–400, reproduced in his *New Testament Studies* (1953), pp. 1–11.

ity of Mark's material is considered to have existed either in isolated or grouped units, which have then been fitted into the general framework. In support of his contention, Dodd further suggests that when the brief connecting summaries found in Mark are extracted and placed end to end they form a continuous narrative. If, then, a framework was part of the earliest pronouncements about Jesus, we may maintain that this framework was based on fact. We need not commit ourselves, however, to maintaining that Mark has necessarily preserved the correct order in every detail.[1]

But Dodd's arguments have been challenged by D. E. Nineham,[2] whose criticisms will be enumerated because they are representative of the form-critical school of thought which sees the Marcan material as disconnected units. (1) He complains that the proposed framework is so brief that it would have afforded little help for the fitting in of the material. (2) He suggests that few units of tradition contained hints of time or place to enable them to be fitted in with certainty. (3) Some groups, for instance the group dealing with the theme of the approaching passion, may represent our Lord's sayings on a number of occasions and have been collected into a topical group in the Gospel. (4) The comparison with the Acts speeches is invalid, since Luke would not have introduced a different summary from what he had already reproduced in his Gospel (this argument assumes that Luke composed the speeches himself). (5) There would appear to be no relevance for the life and worship of the Church in an outline of the ministry, since the Church was not interested in that kind of thing. (6) Against Dodd's argument that where topical connection is lacking in the juxtaposition of unit-traditions the connection must be historical, Nineham raises two objections: first, units may be placed in contexts to which they do not appear to belong because there was nowhere else to put them, or

---

[1] In his book on *The Origin of the Gospel of Mark* (1954), H. A. Guy devotes a chapter to what he calls 'The Disorder of Mark's Gospel'. While not all of his examples are convincing, his evidence is sufficient to show that Mark's primary concern was not 'order' (see p. 66 n.2 for a discussion of Papias' statement about Mark's order). Guy's own explanation of the structure of the Gospel is that it grew out of the repetition of the material by Christian preachers, thus accounting for several 'asides'. This suggestion of oratorical 'asides', however, would transfer some of the Lord's sayings to the preachers without sufficient warrant. Cf. the view of C. H. Turner that Mark's Gospel contains many explanatory parentheses (*JTS*, XXVI, 1925, pp. 145 ff.).

[2] Cf. his article in *Studies in the Gospels*, pp. 223–239.

else they were attached to some other unit in the tradition; and, secondly, the supposed lack of topical order may be due to a lack of understanding and would therefore be unreal.

These objections to the idea of a historical framework in the tradition vary in their validity, but are worthy of careful consideration. They will have most weight for those who accept the view that the tradition circulated in units. In fact, Nineham seems to begin with a predisposition against a skeleton outline, so that his criticisms are not unexpected. Nevertheless, when allowance is made for this, it would appear that the case against a skeleton outline is rather stronger than that for it. But is there not a third possibility? If the passion narrative was preserved in a definite historical sequence, would not the same principle have been used for other narratives? Nineham anticipates this argument, but dismisses it because of the difference of the passion material from the rest, because of its close similarities in all four Gospels, and because of the absence in it of unit-narratives similar to those which are found elsewhere. But the evidence shows the possibility of the preservation of a historical sequence and shows, moreover, the Church's interest in such a sequence. There are no grounds, therefore, for maintaining that interest was lacking merely because such a sequence held no importance for the life and worship of the Church. Would not the form of the passion narrative have led people to expect some sequence in the remainder of the material? And would not catechetical instruction have fostered such an expectation? Since one third of Mark comprises the passion and resurrection narrative, is it not reasonable to suppose that the earlier material existed in some equally connected form?[1] The sequence would have been of importance only in so far as it contributed to the main purpose, i.e. to explain the passion and resurrection narratives.[2] It is difficult to conceive that Mark did not purpose to place the recorded events in some kind of chronological

[1] W. L. Knox's theory of a number of tracts behind Mark's Gospel should be noted here. In what he calls the Twelve Source, he suggests something of the same kind of outline as in Acts x. 37 (cf. his *Sources of the Synoptic Gospels*, I, 1953, p. 28). In an article on the Marcan Framework, H. Sawyerr (*SJT*, 14, 1961, pp. 279–294) disagrees with both Dodd and Nineham, and suggests that the key to Mark's structure is to be found in his presentation of Christ's conflict with evil. He finds this as a unifying thread through the material.

[2] C. E. B. Cranfield (*The Gospel according to St. Mark*, CGT, n.s., 1959, p. 14) rightly points out that all the other sections of Mark are dominated by these narratives.

order (however loosely), for the Gospel is full of notes of time and place.[1]

Granted the broad outline of the Marcan narrative, what further indications are there to explain the arrangement of material? Leaving aside for the moment the origin of this material, which will be dealt with in the section on Mark's sources, we must ask whether it is possible to examine the principles on which Mark acted. Vincent Taylor[2] finds what he calls 'complexes' which Mark has used in his compilation. These are small groups of narratives or sayings which belong together and which Taylor thinks were received by Mark in these groupings. Mark's method, according to this theory, was to leave intact any such complexes which he took over, adding little of his own comments and stringing them together somewhat loosely with simple connecting links.[3] In other words Mark was really editing. The complexes which Taylor isolates are classified into three groups—those shaped by the writer but based on existing tradition, those based on personal testimony (probably Petrine) and those containing topical arrangements of sayings and pronouncement stories[4] (see p. 187 for an explanation of these). It may be granted that Mark's work was largely that of an arranger, although some difference of opinion may exist regarding the form of the material used.[5] Personal testimony may account for more than Taylor allows (see pp. 132 ff. on Mark's sources), but his idea of pre-Marcan complexes is not improbable.

Another explanation of Mark's structure is that of P. Carrington[6] who has suggested that the Gospel was designed for liturgical use. The

---

[1] Cf. Swete, *The Gospel according to St. Mark*[3] (1927), p. lviii, for a list of these notes.

[2] *The Gospel according to St. Mark* (1953), pp. 90–104.

[3] *Ibid.*, pp. 112, 113. In his little book in the popular World Christian Books series, E. Lohse takes it for granted that even passages that appear connected are no real unities, but are the author's attempt to create a unity (*Mark's Witness to Jesus Christ*, 1955, pp. 28, 29).

[4] *Op. cit.*, pp. 102–104.

[5] T. Nicklin (*Gospel Gleanings*, pp. 9–17) attributes the grouping of the material by similarity of subject-matter to Mark himself, and disputes that the present order is chronological. According to this view, Mark like Matthew is governed by topical considerations.

[6] *The Primitive Christian Calendar* (1952). Cf. also his article in *ET*, LXVIII (1956), pp. 100–103 and his more recent commentary *According to Mark* (1960). Cf. the strong criticism of Carrington's position by W. D. Davies in *The Background of the New Testament and its Eschatology* (1956), pp. 124–152.

basis of the arrangement was a synagogue lectionary taken over by the Christian Church. The sequence of narrative was therefore dominated by the sequence of festivals in the Jewish calendar. But in order to maintain his hypothesis Carrington, who argues for a triadic structure but admits its complicated pattern, is obliged to coax the material in a way which is not always the most natural. At the same time this theory is a serious attempt to suggest a method by which the oral teaching was transmitted in an orderly way in the Christian Church. On the other hand this theory would require even the general framework to be a production designed to meet liturgical requirements, a not very convincing proposition[1] (but cf. the similar theory for the Fourth Gospel, pp. 257, 286). If Carrington is right the Evangelist would have to be regarded as possessing superb literary skill.

A different approach to the Marcan structure is made by A. Farrer,[2] who thinks that Mark was dominated by Old Testament typology and numerical schemes. His method of argument is at times tortuous and will hardly appeal to those with a more matter-of-fact approach. This would not surprise Farrer, for he admits that his interpretation of Mark's structure is alien to our modern scientific criticism, but nevertheless maintains that it may be true. The problem with this kind of numerical theory is its highly subjective nature. What appears convincing to Farrer may well seem non-existent to others. Nevertheless, his interpretations may be a fitting reminder that the approach of the Gospel authors is not necessarily easily intelligible to modern scholars. The fact that numerology has no significance for us does not justify us

---

[1] Michaelis (*Einleitung*, p. 53) considers that this theory involves a misunderstanding and an anachronism. Cf. also E. Percy's criticisms, *Die Botschaft Jesu* (1953), pp. 227 f., cited by Michaelis. At best the amount of extant data on early Christian liturgies is very small and is quite inadequate to explain the origin of Mark with any certainty (cf. T. W. Manson's comments, *JTS*, n.s., IV, 1953, p. 78). It is at least possible that the Gospel framework influenced the form of the liturgies, not *vice versa*. V. Taylor has pointed out that the value of Mark's outline, if based on a lectionary, is likely to be depreciated (*The Life and Ministry of Jesus*, 1954, p. 32). Another comment worth noting is that of R. P. Casey who questioned whether a Gentile readership such as Mark appears to have had in mind could have been expected to have any interest in a Jewish lectionary (*Theology*, LV, 1952, pp. 362–370).

[2] *A Study in St. Mark* (1951) and *St. Matthew and St. Mark* (1953). In the latter book he changes his position somewhat and shows how Matthew sometimes breaks the numerical symbolism of Mark. Cf. the critique of Farrer's position in Helen Gardner's *The Limits of Literary Criticism* (1956).

in assuming that it had no meaning for primitive Christianity, especially in view of its undoubted occurrence in such a book as Revelation
with its undisputed frequent sevenfold structures. At the same time a
numerical basis for Mark's outline may raise the problem of its historicity (see pp. 79 ff.), for typology tends to obscure rather than clarify
history;[1] but Farrer regards Mark as a theological structure and a
lessening of its historical purpose therefore does not concern him. He
sees the book as a theological interpretation of the history of Jesus.

An interesting suggestion has recently been made by W. Marxsen[2]
to the effect that Mark composed his Gospel backwards. The earliest
part of the tradition to be written down was therefore the passion story,
out of which the rest grew. This is really a modification of what has
already been pointed out, that for Mark the passion and resurrection
story dominates the whole. It may with good reason be claimed that he
had the climax in mind before he began to write.[3]

Whatever literary technique Mark used in producing his Gospel,[4]
he achieved his obvious intention of presenting under the guidance of
the Spirit of God a picture of the Son of God in action, moving towards

---

[1] Cf. V. Taylor, *op. cit.*, pp. 29, 30.

[2] *Der Evangelist Markus*[2] (1959), pp. 18ff. Marxsen follows Schmidt's idea that
the Marcan introduction indicates Mark's method of procedure throughout the
Gospel.

[3] S. Johnson (*The Gospel according to St. Mark, BC*, 1960, p. 28) draws attention
to Mark's frequent custom of including in the earlier part of the Gospel brief anticipations of what was to be dealt with more fully later, e.g. the call of the first disciples and the subsequent call of the Twelve. But there is no reason to suppose
that these anticipations were Mark's own idea. Rather they occurred in the natural
course of events. The whole life of Jesus moved on to an inevitable climax and
Mark has fully grasped this fact.

F. C. Grant (*The Earliest Gospel*, 1943, pp. 70 ff.) suggests that the Gospel took
shape in the author's mind in the following order: passion narrative, controversies, Petrine element, Q passages, little apocalypse, current oral tradition. Some
of these supposed 'sources' or blocks of material are questionable, but few would
doubt the controlling part played by the passion narratives in the author's mind.

[4] A suggestion has been made that parts of Mark's Gospel were based on the
Greek device of *chiasmus* (according to the pattern—a b b a), cf. H. G. Wood,
Jesus in the Twentieth Century (1960), pp. 44 ff. This is a suggestion which may be
worthy of further examination.

Another feature which is evident in Mark's Gospel is the occasional insertion of
one narrative inside another where some internal connection exists (J. Schniewind, *Das Evangelium nach Markus*,[8] NTD, 1958, p. 4, points to four examples,
iii. 21–35, v. 22–43, vi. 7–33, xi. 11–25).

the cross. This was for him, as for all the Evangelists, the central theme of the Gospel.

IV. AUTHORSHIP

So strong is the early Christian testimony that Mark was the author of this Gospel that we need do little more than mention this attestation. Papias, Irenaeus, probably the Muratorian Canon, Clement of Alexandria, Origen and Jerome all refer to Mark's authorship of the Gospel. Moreover, all of them connect Mark with Peter in the production of the Gospel. Some modern criticism has challenged both of these traditional assumptions. Marcan authorship has been side-tracked by refusing to identify the Mark of the tradition with the John Mark of Acts, the companion of the apostle Paul. The Petrine witness behind the Gospel has been challenged as a result of form-critical work.

Is the Mark of the Gospel tradition the Mark of Acts? The main objections which have been raised against this identification are the non-Palestinian background of Mark's Gospel, which is said to be out of keeping with a one-time resident in Jerusalem, and the absence of any specific identification in the tradition until the time of Jerome.[1] But it has already been pointed out that the seeming indications of a non-Palestinian background may stem from our lack of data and if so the argument falls to the ground, or at least is seen to be insecurely based, while the argument from tradition is based on silence. It seems to have been assumed that Mark was John Mark.

With regard to Mark's connection with the apostle Peter, the questionings have arisen from theories which maintain that much if not all

---

[1] F. C. Grant (*op. cit.*, pp. 52 ff.) considers that Marcus was far too common a name in Rome for us to be certain that Barnabas' nephew was meant. He therefore considers that tradition mixed up the identities and that some Roman Mark, who knew Peter, was the author. Grant lets his imagination loose and visualizes a clerk in a Roman business house producing the Gospel in the evenings, much of the material coming from Peter. It is true that neither the Gospel itself nor Papias tells us which Mark was the author, but it is difficult to believe that the Roman community would have published a Gospel attributed to an unknown Christian named Mark, if it were known already that Barnabas' nephew with the same name had been a companion of both Paul and Peter. Grant queries whether Papias knew Luke-Acts and there is, of course, no means of ascertaining this, but if he did he must surely have meant John Mark in his comment on Mark's Gospel. For another recent writer who disputes the identifying of the Mark of the tradition with John Mark, cf. D. E. Nineham, *Saint Mark*, pp. 39, 40.

of Mark is composed of sections which have received their form in the life of the community. Only the more radical form critics would, however, deny all Petrine influence.[1] Many would hold that Mark was in possession of certain Petrine traditions and to this extent became Peter's interpreter. This proposition will become clearer when Mark's sources are discussed (see pp. 132 ff.), but no theory which does not adequately explain the strong tradition regarding Petrine testimony behind Mark can claim much support.[2]

[1] Cf. R. H. Lightfoot, *History and Interpretation in the Gospels* (1935), pp. 25 ff.
[2] The earliest form of this tradition is that of Papias, preserved by Eusebius, *HE*, iii. 39. 15: 'Mark indeed, since he was the interpreter (ἑρμηνευτής) of Peter, wrote accurately, but not in order (οὐ μέντοι τάξει), the things either said or done by the Lord as much as he remembered. For he neither heard the Lord nor followed Him, but afterwards, as I have said, [heard and followed] Peter, who fitted his discourses to the needs [of his hearers] but not as if making a narrative of the Lord's sayings (κυριακῶν λογίων); consequently, Mark, writing some things just as he remembered, erred in nothing; for he was careful of one thing—not to omit anything of the things he had heard or to falsify anything in them' (Eng. Tr. cited from D. Theron, *Evidence of Tradition*, p. 67). From this it will be seen that Mark's Gospel was thought to be directly related to Peter's preaching, that it was a record from memory, accurate in detail though not in order, and that Mark himself was not a hearer or a disciple of the Lord. Streeter (*The Four Gospels*, pp. 19, 20) regarded this as an apology for Mark in comparison with John. Swete (*The Gospel according to St. Mark*,[3] 1927, pp. lx, lxi) claimed that Papias' οὐ μέντοι τάξει (not in order) in this context means that Mark does not give his Gospel the kind of order belonging to an artificial treatise, and therefore that it should not be inferred from Papias' phrase that Mark had no thought for sequence. Similarly F. H. Colson (*JTS*, xiv, 1913, pp. 62 ff.) maintained that the 'order' implied was that of the rhetorical schools, but it is by no means certain that Papias is using the word in such a technical sense. For a detailed discussion of Papias' statement, with full bibliography, cf. H. A. Rigg's article, *Nov. Test.*, I (1956), pp. 161–183. He suggests an emendation to τάχει which then would mean that Mark did not write hurriedly. There is much to be said for Zahn's argument that the lack of order in Mark was due to the fact that he had to rely upon a witness, Peter, who was more concerned to adapt his teaching to his hearers' need (as Papias says) than to arrange it chronologically (*INT*, 1909, ii, p. 439).
There has been some dispute whether Papias' ἑρμηνευτής is to be rendered 'interpreter' or 'translator'. There is something to be said for the latter, since Papias may have used the corresponding verb ἑρμηνεύω in his Matthew statement in the sense of 'translating' (see pp. 31 ff.). Yet the former is the more probable, since Peter would almost certainly have been acquainted with Greek and it is not easy to see why he should have needed a translator. But cf. H. E. W. Turner's comments, *ET*, lxxi (1960), pp. 260–263.
Other patristic evidence for a connection between Mark and Peter is found in

'John Mark' is mentioned three times in the New Testament (Acts xii. 12, 25, xv. 37) and 'Mark' several times (Acts xv. 39; Col. iv. 10; 2 Tim. iv. 11; Phm. 24; 1 Pet. v. 13). In the Colossian reference he is identified as the nephew of Barnabas, which clearly equates him with the John Mark of Acts. It is very probable that his mother was a person of some substance since, according to Acts xii, her house was regarded as a *rendezvous* for many members of the primitive Church (cf. xii. 12). Mark accompanied Paul and Barnabas on part of the first missionary journey, although he drew against him Paul's anger when he forsook the party before the work was done. In spite of the fact that dissension arose between Paul and Barnabas over him, a reconciliation must have been effected later, since he was with Paul when the Epistles to the Colossians and Philemon were written (Col. iv. 10; Phm. 24).[1] At a still later date he is found in company with the apostle Peter (1 Pet. v. 13) and this association with both Peter and Paul is a most significant feature about him. Only those who are influenced by the Tübingen antithesis between Peter and Paul will consider a close connection with both apostles to be improbable. It may justifiably be claimed that all we know of Mark from the New Testament would predispose us to

Justin, *Dialogue*, 106. 3; Tertullian, *Adv. Marcion*, iv. 5; Clement of Alexandria (Eusebius, *HE*, vi. 14. 6 f.).

It has been suggested that Papias' words refer not to Mark's Gospel but to Q, which is then regarded as Mark's collection of Peter's catechetical instructions (cf. J. N. Sanders, *The Foundations of the Christian Faith*, 1950, p. 53, who consequently regarded Mark's Gospel as anonymous, and the posthumous essay of R. G. Heard, ed. C. F. D. Moule and A. M. G. Stephenson, in *NTS*, 2, 1956, pp. 114–118). But this is not the most natural interpretation of Papias' words, as is demonstrated from the subsequent strong tradition that he meant the Gospel. D. E. Nineham (*JTS*, n.s, IX, 1958, pp. 20 ff.) follows Dibelius in interposing the procedure of community tradition between Peter and Mark, which virtually nullifies Papias' statement altogether.

[1] Some earlier German scholars maintained that the Gospel of Mark was a Pauline Gospel, and from this position it was inferred that Pauline theology had influenced Marcan historicity (e.g. Volkmar, Holtzmann and Harnack). But this position has been strongly challenged. Cf. M. Werner, *Der Einfluss paulinischer Theologie im Mk-Ev* (1923; Beiheft *ZNTW*, 1). Cf. also the chapter on this subject in F. C. Grant's *The Earliest Gospel*, pp. 188–206. Both these writers tend to go to the other extreme by making almost an antithesis between Marcan and Pauline theology. Grant concludes that behind Mark there is 'common Gentile Christianity' rather than Paulinism. If Mark truly represents primitive tradition some alignment with Pauline theology is to be expected, in so far as Paul himself received the basic elements of primitive tradition, as 1 Cor. xv. 3 shows.

consider him to be a likely candidate as author of a Gospel. At any rate there is nothing which renders this impossible.[1]

V. DATE

This Gospel is the only one of the Synoptics whose date can be discussed without reference to the Synoptic problem; at least, if the current hypothesis of the priority of Mark be accepted. If on the other hand the traditional view that Mark is an abstract from Matthew had proved correct, the date of Mark would clearly have depended on the decision regarding Matthew's date. It is advisable, in any case, to deal first with all the available evidence, irrespective of Mark's connection with the other Gospels. The external evidence will be considered first.

1. It has already been noted that the early tradition is conflicting, one tradition maintaining that Mark wrote subsequent to the death of Peter and another holding that it was during Peter's lifetime that Mark's Gospel was produced (reported by Irenaeus[2] and Clement of Alexandria[3] respectively). Since both of these traditions were early and were almost contemporaneous, there must have been uncertainty about the origin of Mark, unless one of the witnesses cited can be otherwise understood. An attempt has been made, in fact, to argue that Irenaeus does not conflict with Clement, since he was not giving chronological information regarding Mark's origin but simply stating the continuity of Mark's writing with Peter's preaching.[4] Although this is a possible interpretation of Irenaeus' words, it is not the most obvious, and the majority of scholars agree that Irenaeus meant to imply that Mark wrote after Peter's death. But if this is Irenaeus' meaning it is still

---

[1] Feine-Behm-Kümmel (*Einleitung*, p. 54) consider that Marcan authorship is thoroughly possible, in spite of some difficulties. Kümmel cites four authors who have raised objections: Heard, Grant, Johnson, Beach. But the vast majority consider the author to be John Mark.

[2] *Adv. Haer.* iii. 1. 2: 'And after the death of these (Peter and Paul) Mark the disciple and interpreter (ἑρμηνευτής) of Peter, also handed down to us in writing the things preached by Peter.'

[3] According to Eusebius, *HE*, vi. 14. 6 f.: 'When Peter had preached the word publicly in Rome . . . those who were present . . . besought Mark, since he had followed him (i.e. Peter) for a long time and remembered the things that had been spoken, to write out the things that had been said; and when he had done this, he gave the Gospel to those who asked him. When Peter learned of it later, he neither obstructed nor commended' (cf. D. Theron's translation, *Evidence of Tradition*, p. 45).

[4] So Dom J. Chapman, *JTS*, VI (1905), pp. 563 ff.; A. Harnack, *The Date of Acts and the Synoptic Gospels* (1911), pp. 130 f., and W. C. Allen, *The Gospel according to St. Mark* (1915), p. 2.

necessary to decide between his statement and that of Clement. Most scholars prefer Irenaeus to Clement, but it should be observed that Irenaeus had just previously stated that Matthew was produced while Peter and Paul were still preaching, i.e. before Mark. In this case current criticism accepts one line of testimony from Irenaeus and rejects the other. It is at least a possibility that such an assessment of the evidence may be wrong. It is questionable, therefore, whether a date for Mark before Peter's death can be ruled out on the strength of Irenaeus' testimony. It is not in fact impossible to regard both Clement and Irenaeus as correct, if Mark began his Gospel before and completed it after Peter's death;[1] a suggestion which merits more consideration than it generally receives. Another possibility is that Irenaeus was not referring to Peter's death at all, but to his departure from the place where Mark was (the word ἔξοδος could clearly bear this meaning).[2] In this case it would also be possible to accept the statements of both Irenaeus and Clement, and this solution seems the more preferable.

2. The key item in the internal evidence concerns the reference in Mark xiii. 14 to the 'abomination of desolation', which was to be set up where it ought not to be, apparently an allusion to the Jerusalem temple. It is generally assumed that the event so obscurely mentioned was the siege and fall of Jerusalem in AD 70 and that Mark must have written in the period before the siege, when the political atmosphere was so tense that he or the editor of his sources here was able to foresee that the temple was likely to be defiled.[3] Some have supposed that the primary reference is to Caligula's attempt to place his own statue in the temple in AD 40, an attempt which failed because of the intervening assassination of the emperor.[4] C. C. Torrey[5] even dated Mark just after this

[1] Cf. H. A. Rigg, op. cit., p. 180 n.1.

[2] This interpretation was preferred by T. W. Manson in an essay reproduced in Studies in the Gospels and Epistles (1962), pp. 38–40.

Manson argues that a similar meaning attaches to the use of the word in the anti-Marconite Prologue to Mark's Gospel. Cf. also F. F. Bruce, The Spreading Flame (1958), p. 139 n.1.

[3] Cf. V. Taylor, The Gospel according to St. Mark, p. 511.

[4] S. G. F. Brandon ('The Date of the Markan Gospel', NTS, 7, 1961, p. 133) takes the view that Mk. xiii. 14–22 forms a pericope containing a tradition of the temple's coming desecration which is intelligible against the background of Caligula's action, but he does not regard this as furnishing any indication of the date of the Gospel as a whole.

[5] Cf. The Four Gospels, pp. 261 f.; and for a review of Torrey's arguments, cf. Bacon, The Gospel of Mark, pp. 55–63.

event, but his views have not gained much support. These two methods of using this evidence to point to the date of Mark both depend on the assumption that Mark xiii. 14, although put on the lips of Jesus, was nevertheless prophecy either after the event or else in near anticipation of it. But if it be granted that our Lord had power to predict, Mark xiii. 14 ceases to be a crux of the chronological problem. The phrase used to describe the coming event is of such vagueness that it is even more reasonable to assume that it belongs to a time well before the actual events.[1] Who would deny to Jesus the power to foresee that the seething political situation would come some day to a head,[2] with the result that some act of desecration in the temple would take place? Or, as a further possibility, if the words of Mark xiii. 14 are interpreted of the coming antichrist[3] their relevance to the date problem would be obscured.

3. Other features of the Gospel which are claimed to support a date in the decade AD 60–70 are the references to suffering and persecution (see p. 58), and the interest of the author in Gentile freedom.[4] But neither of these helps much in specifying the date, since they are both too general to tie down to any specific period. For instance, when reference is made in Mark xiii. 8 to earthquakes and famines as being the 'beginning' of sufferings, there is no reason to suppose that this must refer to the beginning of the siege. Moreover, xiii. 10, which asserts that the gospel must be preached to all nations, can hardly be cited as evidence of a date AD 60–70, any more than of an earlier date,[5] since the Gentile mission was implicit in our Lord's plans for His Church.

In spite of the confidence of the majority of scholars that Mark must be dated AD 65–70, it is by no means impossible to maintain an earlier

[1] Brandon (*op. cit.*, pp. 133, 134) regards the 'abomination' as an allusion to Titus, the emperor's son and heir, and the obscurity of the reference is because it was essential for security in Rome, especially at the time of the Flavian triumph, i.e. after AD 70, when, he believes, the Gospel was written.
[2] Cf. the further comments on this under the section dealing with the date of Luke (pp. 107ff.).
[3] Cf. Streeter, *The Four Gospels*, pp. 492, 493; E. Lohmeyer, *Das Evangelium des Markus* (1937), p. 276; A. H. McNeile, *The Gospel according to St. Matthew* (1915), p. 348.
[4] Cf. V. Taylor, *op. cit.*, p. 31. Brandon (*op. cit.*, p. 137) confidently interprets xiii. 9 as a reference to martyrdom and refers it to the Neronian persecutions But this goes beyond the text.
[5] This is one of the evidences cited by Taylor, *op. cit.*, *ad loc.*

date. In fact, Harnack[1] maintained a date before AD 60 and Allen[2] a date before AD 50. Harnack's arguments were based on an early date for Acts (i.e. AD 63) which involved a slightly earlier date for Luke, and in his view a still earlier date for Mark. Allen's theory was influenced by his contention that the original Marcan Gospel was written in Aramaic, a hypothesis which would clearly require an early date. Harnack's dating is usually rejected because his dating for Acts is not accepted (see pp. 307 ff.).[3]

Some mention must be made of theories requiring a date later than the siege of Jerusalem. One advocate of such a date was B. W. Bacon,[4] who suggested a date subsequent to AD 75—the year in which a Cynic philosopher was beheaded for denouncing Titus' immoral conduct with Bernice, sister of Agrippa II—because he saw a parallel here with the murder of John the Baptist. But such an argument is not convincing and few scholars have followed Bacon in this.

A more closely reasoned approach is that of Brandon,[5] who argues mainly from the historical situation in which the Gospel was written. He suggests that the production of such a Gospel as Mark's must have had an effective cause, and he finds this in the situation in Rome a year or so after the Flavian triumphal procession celebrating the capture of Jerusalem. His general idea is that the Roman Christians would need a Gospel which dissociated Jesus from the Jerusalem Jews, because of the odium which attached to the Jews at that time. Brandon works out his theory with great ingenuity, accounting, as he thinks, for the eschatological discourse in Mark xiii and sundry other incidental characteristics in Mark's Gospel, such as the Roman centurion's recognition of Jesus' claims (whereas His own Jewish followers failed to accept them), the account of the rending of the temple veil, the attitude of Jesus towards tribute money to Rome and the omission to call Judas 'the Zealot'. But most of Brandon's reconstruction is conjectural and the evidence he quotes could well support an earlier date. The period after

[1] *Op. cit.*, p. 126.
[2] *Op. cit.*, pp. 5 f. M. Meinertz (*op. cit.*, p. 187) suggests a date between AD 50 and 60.
[3] Cf. J. Schniewind (*Das Evangelium nach Markus*, NTD[8], 1958, p. 7) for a less precise dating. He is content to assign Mark to the first decades of the Christian Church.
[4] *Op. cit.*, pp. 73 f.
[5] *Op. cit.*, *passim*. Cf. also *idem*, *The Fall of Jerusalem and the Christian Church*[2] (1957), pp. 185 ff.

AD 70 was not the first time that odium had been attached to Jews in Roman minds. The edict of Claudius expelling Jews from Rome must have precipitated a sufficiently critical situation to provide an urge to make clear the relation of Christianity to Judaism. Moreover, Brandon's reconstruction is based on the presupposition that the author, after the fall of Jerusalem, would find it difficult to believe that Jesus had not predicted the event and thus a Dominical prediction to this effect was included.[1]

VI. TEXTUAL PROBLEMS

a. The Marcan ending

The concluding chapter of the Gospel presents a problem. The overwhelming majority of manuscripts contain the full twenty verses, and the earliest Christian writings which show acquaintance with Mark assume their genuineness. And yet there is some important evidence which suggests that the original ended at xvi. 8.

1. The two Alexandrian Uncial MSS, Vaticanus and Sinaiticus, end with ἐφοβοῦντο γάρ (xvi. 8).

2. The Sinaitic Old Syriac similarly omits the ending (i.e. xvi. 9–20).

3. Most of the Armenian MSS end at xvi. 8.

4. Some MSS contain two endings, verses 9–20 and another shorter ending (L Ψ 579 Sahidic, Ethiopic, Harklean Syriac and the earliest Bohairic versions).

5. In MS 'k' of the Old Latin the shorter ending stands alone.

6. One MS, Codex W, contains a third ending which comprises verses 9–20, plus an additional interpolation after verse 14.

7. Eusebius of Caesarea cites an apologist who appealed to 'inaccurate copies' of Mark as evidence against the genuineness of xvi. 9–20.

8. A late Armenian MS (10th century) contains a note between Mark xvi. 8 and the ending, stating 'Of the presbyter Aristion', but this note is too late to be of much value, although Swete was inclined to attach some importance to it.[2]

The following deductions may be made from this evidence: (1) the longer ending must have been attached to the Gospel at a very early

---

[1] NTS, 7 (1961), p. 135.
[2] Cf. F. C. Conybeare's advocacy of this view, Exp., IV, viii (1893), pp. 241 ff.

period in its history; (2) the shorter ending is not well attested and must have been added in an attempt to fill a gap, a testimony to the circulation of Gospels ending at xvi. 8; (3) indeed, the most satisfactory explanation of all the textual evidence is that the original ended at xvi. 8 and that the three endings were different editorial attempts to deal with verse 8.

If these deductions are correct the mass of MSS containing the longer ending must have been due to the acceptance of this ending as the most preferable. But internal evidence combines with textual evidence to raise suspicions regarding this ending. There is a difference in Greek style between xvi. 9–20 and the rest of the Gospel,[1] and while this would not of itself rule out common authorship it is difficult to believe in common authorship in face of the combination of stylistic difficulties with textual suspicions.[2] Moreover, xvi. 9 does not well follow on from xvi. 1–8 since Mary Magdalene is described as one 'from whom he had cast out seven demons' in spite of the fact that she had already been mentioned in the first part. Again verses 9–20 seem to be composed from material drawn from the other three Gospels.[3] In short this ending wears the appearance of compilation distinct from the rest of the Gospel.

The question next arises whether the present form of xvi. 8 (ἐφοβοῦντο γάρ) could conceivably have been Mark's intended ending. Many scholars have answered in the affirmative on the basis of biblical and extra-biblical parallels[4] and yet there is no other example of a book

[1] Cf. Swete, *The Gospel according to St. Mark*[3] (1927), p. cx.

[2] G. Salmon (*INT*[6], 1892, pp. 150, 151) accepted the Marcan authorship of xvi. 9–20 on the grounds that if these verses must be attributed to an early author, Mark was as good as any. Cf. also the vigorous defence of the verses by J. W. Burgon, *The Last Twelve Verses of the Gospel according to St. Mark vindicated against recent objectors and established* (1871), and F. H. A. Scrivener, *A Plain Introduction to the Criticism of the New Testament* [4] (ed. E. Millar, 1894), II, pp. 337–344.

[3] There are no resurrection appearances in Mk. xvi. 9–20, which are not related in the other Gospels.

[4] Cf. J. M. Creed, *JTS*, XXXI (1930), pp. 175–180; R. R. Otley, *JTS*, XXVII (1926), pp. 407–409; E. Lohmeyer, *Das Evangelium des Markus* (1937), pp. 356–360; R. H. Lightfoot, *The Gospel Message of St. Mark* (1950), pp. 80–97, 106–116. The latter cites some biblical parallels and one from Justin, but he admits that the parallels are not exact (*ibid.*, p. 86). Cf. idem, *Locality and Doctrine in the Gospels* (1938), pp. 1–48. Lightfoot, who regarded xvi. 1–8 as a separate narrative unit, found little difficulty in the proposed ending.

ending like this.[1] It would moreover be strange to find a Gospel, a book of good news, ending on a note of fear. To meet this objection some have understood ἐφοβοῦντο as 'reverential awe' rather than fearful apprehension.[2] On the whole it seems improbable that Mark's resurrection account would have lacked any personal appearance of the risen Lord (in verses 1–8 only the fact of His resurrection is mentioned) The author of verses 9–20 clearly recognized this. But if xvi. 8 is not likely to have been the intentional ending, could it have been accidental? It is possible to conjecture that the scroll was damaged, but if so it must have happened to the original copy, or else to a very early copy.[3] There is no means of ascertaining the correctness or otherwise of this conjecture. It has further been suggested that something happened to Mark at this point, so that he never completed the task, a suggestion which is not impossible, but which in the nature of the case cannot be confirmed.[4] Yet another idea is that Mark intended a continuation volume similar to Acts (see p. 338) and would not therefore have regarded xvi. 8 as the virtual end of his story.[5] It would seem that the only course open is to admit that we do not know the original ending.[6]

[1] W. L. Knox (HTR, 35, 1942, pp. 13–23) argued that if Mk. xvi. 8 was the original ending the *pericope* would lack a sufficient rounding off, which in his view would be not only unparalleled but incredible. Cf. also V. Taylor, *The Gospels*, pp. 49 f.

[2] Cf. N. B. Stonehouse, *The Witness of Matthew and Mark to Christ* (1944), pp. 86–118. Cf. also Lightfoot, *op. cit*. J. B. Tyson (*JBL*, LXXX, 1961, pp. 261–268), who maintains that Mark considered that the disciples had too narrow an idea of Messiah, thinks that Mk. xvi. 8 would be appropriate if Mark wished to draw attention to the disciples' failure.

[3] Cf. Streeter, *op. cit*., p. 338. He thought that this view was credible, but he strongly criticized the view that Mark's ending was intentionally suppressed (*ibid*., pp. 341 f.). F. C. Burkitt, *AJTh*, 15 (1911), maintained the accidental damage theory, but this is criticized by Lightfoot, *Locality and Doctrine*, pp. 8 ff. Cf. also C. C. McCown, *HTR*, 34 (1941), pp. 239 f.

[4] Cf. Rawlinson, *The Gospel according to St. Mark*[7] (1949), p. 270.

[5] Many scholars have maintained that such a continuation was actually written and was used by Luke for the first part of Acts (Blass, Torrey and others). Cf. W. L. Clark, *Theology*, XXIX (1934), pp. 106, 107.

[6] A. Farrer (*St. Matthew and St. Mark*, 1954, pp. 144–159) makes an attempt to suggest the form which Mark's original ending probably took. His suggestion is that after xvi. 8 there originally stood a one-sentence conclusion which Matthew later expanded. Farrer's reasoning is influenced by his symbolical interpretation of Mark's structure. In this book he takes a different view from that which he expressed in his earlier books, *The Glass of Vision* (1948), pp. 136–146 and *A*

It remains to discuss the alternative endings. The shorter may be dismissed as obviously of late origin, but the longer ending would appear to possess greater antiquity. There is attestation of xvi. 9–20 as early as the time of Irenaeus[1] who regarded the verses as part of Mark. They must have been of considerably earlier origin than this. It is not impossible, therefore, to regard them as an early independent summary used for catechetical purposes, composed from the other Gospels (especially from Luke and John).[2] The abruptness of Mark xvi. 8 as an ending caused this summary to be attached to the Gospel not later than the mid-second century. While it cannot be regarded as part of Mark's Gospel, it nevertheless represents an authentic account of resurrection appearances.

b. The beginning

Problems have also arisen about the beginning of the Gospel, but these problems are connected with interpretation rather than textual criticism, although they have led to suggestions of textual corruption. Mark i. 1 begins with a statement which comprises a subject without a predicate. This is followed by an Old Testament citation (verses 2 and 3) which refers to John the Baptist, who is not mentioned until verse 4, and this contains no grammatical connection with what precedes. Various explanations have been offered.

1. The existing beginning may be treated as non-original on the assumption that a lost ending might have been accompanied by a lost beginning.[3] This would be a plausible suggestion if the original were in codex form, for then the outer sheet containing the first two and last two pages may have been lost. But the evidence for such an early use of codices is lacking, although it cannot be said to be impossible. A difficulty would arise over the consistent textual tradition for the beginning which shows no signs, as the ending does, of ever having been in question. We should almost be driven to suppose that the mutilation

---

Study in St. Mark (1951), pp. 172–181, in which he maintained that Mark intended to end at xvi. 8. Cf. the useful survey of theories concerning the Marcan ending by F. F. Bruce, in *EQ*, xvii (1945), pp. 169 ff.

[1] *Adv. Haer.* iii. 10. 6.

[2] Cf. C. E. B. Cranfield, *St. Mark*, p. 472; F. F. Bruce, *op. cit.*, p. 180.

[3] Cf. F. Spitta, *ZNTW*, 5 (1904), pp. 305–308; T. W. Manson, *Studies in the Gospels and Epistles* (1962), pp. 30–33.

of the first part of the text must have happened to the original copy.[1] It would seem better to adopt one of the following alternative interpretations, rather than resort to such a conjecture.

2. Verse 1 may be treated as a title, in which case the Gospel begins with the Old Testament citation. This would be unusual but not impossible.[2]

3. Verses 2 and 3 may be regarded as a parenthesis and the statement in verse 1 connected with John's preaching in verse 4, a solution which makes good sense, although it is not so convincing from the point of view of the Greek.[3]

VII. LANGUAGE

The Greek of Mark's Gospel is not of a literary type. It is rather the everyday spoken language, similar to that used in the Egyptian papyrus correspondence. There is an absence of the carefully chosen periods of the classical models. Indeed, Mark's favourite construction seems to be parataxis, that is the joining of clauses with a simple conjunction (καί). It should not be assumed, however, that Mark had no concern at all for grammatical niceties, for on occasions he shows a careful use of tenses.[4]

The Latinisms of Mark, which have already been mentioned (see p. 56), are a marked characteristic of his style. It is highly unlikely, however, that they point to a Latin original as has been suggested.[5]

It should be noted that Mark's narratives are particularly striking for vividness, for fullness of detail, for use of numbers and other similar characteristics.[6] Whether these features of the Greek style are considered to be due to Mark or to his sources will be affected by the decision arrived at in the discussions on Mark's sources (see pp. 132 ff.).

Another matter of great interest is the possibility of an Aramaic

---

[1] T. W. Manson (*op. cit.*, p. 32) maintains that the loss must have been sustained at an early date since neither Matthew nor Luke appears to have known any other form of the Marcan text.

[2] In Hort's, Souter's and Nestlé's texts a full stop is inserted after verse 1, which must then be regarded as an introductory title. Cf. the discussion by V. Taylor, *St. Mark*, p. 152.

[3] Cf. C. H. Turner, in *A New Commentary on Holy Scripture*, III (1928), p. 50. Reprinted separately, *The Gospel according to St. Mark*, p. 11.

[4] Cf. Swete, *The Gospel according to St. Mark*[3] (1927), pp. xlix f.

[5] Cf. P. L. Couchard, 'Was the Gospel of Mark written in Latin?' (an article in the *Crozer Quarterly*, January 1928, cited by V. Taylor, *St. Mark*, p. 54).

[6] For a concise discussion of Mark's syntax, cf. Taylor, *op. cit.*, pp. 45–54.

original or of Aramaic sources. Most scholars are agreed that Mark's
Greek has Semitic flavouring, but the extent of it and the inferences to
be drawn from it are the subject of wide divergences of opinion. The
more thoroughgoing hypothesis that Mark's Greek is a direct translation from the Aramaic has not found complete acceptance in spite of
having some able advocates.[1] The more generally held opinion is that
Mark's Greek is 'translation Greek'[2] because he reproduces an Aramaic
κατήχησις. According to M. Black,[3] Aramaic influence in the Greek,
particularly of the sayings material, points to an Aramaic sayings
collection which was used by Mark in the production of his Gospel.
The problems involved in this discussion are highly technical, and only
Aramaic experts can decide them.[4] But the importance of the discussion must not for that reason be minimized, for it has a bearing upon
the historicity of the Gospel. According to Vincent Taylor,[5] Mark's
sympathies are Gentile, but his tradition is thoroughly Jewish Christian
and this would appear to be a fair summary of Mark's position.

VIII. LOCALITY, HISTORICITY AND CHRONOLOGY

The importance of locality in Mark has been particularly emphasized
by E. Lohmeyer,[6] who produced a theory that Galilee not Jerusalem
was the first centre of early Christianity and that Mark's Gospel is a
representative of this fact. He maintained that the ministry of Jesus in
Galilee was not a failure, as is sometimes supposed, but a success. In-

[1] Strongly maintained by Torrey, *The Four Gospels* (1933). See pp. 44 f. for
the note and bibliography on the Aramaic theory for Matthew.

[2] J. H. Moulton and W. F. Howard, *A Grammar of New Testament Greek*, II
(1929), p. 481. Howard is in agreement with M. J. Lagrange, whose opinion he
quotes.

[3] *An Aramaic Approach to the Gospels and Acts*, pp. 205 ff.

[4] F. C. Grant (*The Earliest Gospel*, pp. 89–124) examines Torrey's theory and
comes to the conclusion that Torrey overstates his case, since many of the passages to which he appeals are in no need of retranslation, or are no clearer after
retranslation, or when retranslated lack intrinsic probability. He admits some
Aramaic influence, but he attributes this to oral tradition and not to a written
document.

[5] *St. Mark*, p. 65.

[6] *Galiläa und Jerusalem* (1936). Cf. also *idem, Das Evangelium des Markus*[12] (1953).
The theory is discussed by R. H. Lightfoot, *Locality and Doctrine in the Gospels*,
pp. 124 ff., and by F. C. Grant, *The Earliest Gospel* (1943), pp. 125–147. Cf. also
L. E. Elliott-Binns, *Galilean Christianity* (1956); M. Karnetski, *ZNTW*, 52 (1961),
pp. 238 ff.; M. Black, *The Scrolls and Christian Origins* (1961), pp. 81 ff. T. A. Burkill has a critique of this theory in his *Mysterious Revelation* (1963), pp. 252–257.

deed, Galilee was considered to be *terra Christiana* in the primitive
Church, having become so as a direct result of the ministry of Jesus.
According to this theory a theological and especially eschatological
emphasis arose in Galilee, distinct from that in Jerusalem. In the former
area the Son of man Christology was dominant, but in the latter the
messianic Christology. In the resurrection narratives, Mark xvi. 7
states that the risen Christ would precede His disciples into Galilee,[1]
while the Lucan appearances are all centred in Jerusalem. This is interpreted by Lohmeyer as showing that Mark and Luke represent two
different types of primitive Christianity with the former showing the
more primitive form and the latter showing a shift of major locality
from Galilee to Jerusalem. Indeed Lohmeyer even suggested two distinct Christological creeds, 'Jesus is Lord' for Galilee and 'Jesus is
Christ' for Jerusalem. He not only appealed to the Marcan setting of
all the main action and teaching of Jesus, apart from the passion narrative, as being Galilee-centred, but also showed a lingering on in the
subsequent Church of the Galilaean type of Christianity in the sects of
the Ebionites and of the Nazarenes. He thinks that this theory accounts
for the choice of James, who was a Galilaean, as leader of the Jerusalem
church.

There are, however, several indications that this antithesis between
Galilee and Jerusalem is not supported by the facts.

1. The ministry of Jesus began with His baptism by John in the
vicinity of Jerusalem, not in Galilee.

2. Several instances of hostility to Jesus occurred in Galilee. The
series of controversies in Mark ii. 1 ff. may be cited as illustrating this,
for there is no mention of the opposition coming from Jerusalem.
Moreover, it was the people of His own country whose unbelief caused
Him to point out that a prophet is not without honour except in his
own country (vi. 4).

3. There is some evidence in this Gospel that Jesus met with favour
among certain groups in Jerusalem. The hierarchy were afraid to act
openly for fear of the people (cf. xi. 18, xii. 12, xiv. 2).

4. In the post-resurrection narrative, the prediction of an appearance
of the risen Lord in Galilee (xvi. 7) may seem to contrast with Luke's
record of Jerusalem appearances only, but the differences are rather
complementary than contradictory. Both Matthew and John record

---

[1] Cf. C. F. Evans' article on this statement, *JTS*, n.s., v (1954), pp. 3ff.

appearances in both Galilee and Jerusalem, but Mark records none. At most the evidence shows that Mark has no interest in Jerusalem appearances, whereas Luke has no interest in Galilaean appearances. But it does not necessarily follow that each represents a different type of Christianity. It would be a different matter if in the various narratives of the same event Galilee was substituted for Jerusalem or *vice versa*. The theory of divergent Christologies is, moreover, not borne out by the evidence in Acts.

It would seem that the evidence[1] is insufficient to establish such opposition between Galilee and Jerusalem as both Lohmeyer and Lightfoot claim.

The problems of historicity naturally arise for all the Gospels, but they are particularly relevant for Mark if the presupposition that Mark was the written basis of the other Gospels is correct (see pp. 126 ff.). It is for this reason that recent discussions on historicity have focused most attention on this Gospel. It has been the main field of research of form criticism, and when that method of approach to the Gospels is later explained (see pp. 178 ff.), it will become more apparent that the problem has really resolved itself into an alternative, either of accepting the Gospel narratives as presenting the historical Jesus, or of treating these narratives as the products of Christian faith and therefore historically questionable. The problem cannot here receive the full discussion that it requires, but some indication must be given of the main trends of the debate in order to assess its significance for a true approach to Mark's Gospel.

1. The main interest of Mark was not biographical but evangelistic as already mentioned (pp. 53 ff.). But this must not blind our eyes to the historical element within it. A Gospel, designed as it was to proclaim salvation to needy people, must be historically based to be valid and only the most sceptical would assume that a 'Gospel' in the true sense of the word could ever have arisen without direct relationship to the historical events recorded.

2. The view that Mark is not biographical led to the further assumption that he was not chronological either. This, of course, is supported by Papias' comment, if it is correct to understand it in this way. The various connecting links which appear to give some sequence to the narrative are consequently regarded as editorial additions with no historical value. The contents must rather be treated as a collection of

---

[1] For further considerations, see Burkill, *op. cit.*

isolated units. If this hypothesis is correct, historicity could not be determined by examining the collection as a whole. Each unit would require separate assessment. Such a procedure would shift the historical responsibility to a large extent from the Evangelist on to the communities in which the units circulated. But to offset this type of theory it is necessary to recall what has already been demonstrated, that Mark includes blocks of incidents which certainly give the impression of a historical framework.[1]

3. The close connection between the historical narrative and the primitive *kerygma* must influence any assessment of the former. As already noted in the discussion on Mark's structure,[2] the contention that the early preaching was not lacking in some kind of historical framework must be regarded as valid, in spite of criticisms of this view.[3] Since the most whole-hearted form critics usually admit that the passion narrative preserves some historical sequence, this is an admission that the primitive Church was not entirely bereft of historical interest. Before we may reject the historicity of Mark's framework it is necessary to show that the early Christians would have preferred a collection of *disjecta membra* to a formal outline. D. E. Nineham may be right in asserting that there is no convincing evidence that the early Church agreed on a formal outline,[4] but neither is there any convincing evidence that they did not. If we must resort to conjecture in order to decide the issue, that which assumes a chronological framework in the body of the Gospel similar to that in the passion narratives is more likely to be correct.

The main advocates of the theory that we find in Mark practically

---

[1] The incorporation into Mark of certain blocks of incidents would not in itself prove that the whole of the Marcan sequence is historical, but it should urge considerable caution before any assumption to the contrary is made. An example of the type of hypothesis which maintains Mark's use of some sources which contained sequences, without being committed to the historicity of the whole, is that of W. L. Knox, *Sources of the Synoptic Gospels: I St. Mark* (1953). The caution of P. Gardner-Smith might be noted here. He maintained that the Gospel as a whole tells a sober story and was thought worthy of credence by the first-century Church. The *onus probandi* must therefore rest on those regarding it 'as no more than a collection of scattered and unreliable traditions' (*The Christ of the Gospels*, 1938, p. 36).

[2] For details see pp. 59 ff.

[3] In addition to D. E. Nineham's article in *Studies in the Gospels*, pp. 223 ff., cf. also C. F. Evans, *JTS*, VII (1956), pp. 25–41.

[4] *Op. cit.*, p. 229.

no reliable data for the historical life of Jesus are Bultmann and his
associates in Germany,[1] R. H. Lightfoot and his school[2] in Britain and
J. M. Robinson[3] in America. The approach of Bultmann and Lightfoot
has been the most radical. If all the materials are community products
they are not evidence for the history of Jesus, but what T. W. Manson[4]
called 'psychological case-material concerning the early Christians'.
They inform us only about the early Christian beliefs and we are left
almost wholly in the dark about the life of Jesus. As Lightfoot puts it,
the Gospels 'yield us little more than a whisper of his voice'.[5] More
will be said about the general weakness of form criticism when that
subject is discussed later (see pp. 189 ff.), but it must be noted here that
such scepticism regarding the historicity of Mark is unavoidable if the
principle that it is a collection of community *pericopae* be accepted.
Because of this there has been a recent movement to salvage something
from the wreckage. J. M. Robinson calls for a new quest for the historical Jesus,[6] although firmly repudiating the older view that Mark in its
entirety is to be the basis of a historical account of Jesus' life. There are
signs of a shift of emphasis in the Bultmann school of thought in the
approach of both E. Käsemann[7] and G. Bornkamm.[8] The former has
focused attention on the need to maintain some kind of connection
between the message of Jesus and the proclamation of the Church,
while the latter has produced a book on the historical Jesus based on the
assumption that some such connection exists. Whereas Bultmann had
attached no importance to the events in the life of Jesus but only to His
words, his associates have shown a marked deviation from his position.
As a result even Bultmann[9] himself has somewhat modified his former
position.

[1] *The History of the Synoptic Tradition* (Eng. Tr. J. Marsh, 1963); *idem, Theology of the New Testament* (Eng. Tr. K. Grobel, 1952).

[2] *History and Interpretation in the Gospels* (1934).

[3] *The Problem of History in Mark* (1957).

[4] *Studies in the Gospels and Epistles*, p. 8.

[5] *Op. cit.*, p. 225.

[6] *A New Quest of the Historical Jesus* (1959). In this book he adopts a more thoroughgoing and theologically orientated approach.

[7] Cf. his essay in *ZTK*, 51 (1954), pp. 125–153, on the problem of the historical Jesus. Cf. also the similar approach of E. Fuchs, *ZTK*, 53 (1956), pp. 210–229.

[8] *Jesus of Nazareth* (Eng. Tr. 1960, from the German *Jesus von Nazareth*, 1956).

[9] Cf. *ZTK*, 54 (1958), pp. 244–254. Cf. also J. M. Robinson's discussion of Bultmann's shift of position (*A New Quest of the Historical Jesus*, pp. 19 ff.).

The course of the present debate illustrates a characteristic of thoroughgoing German criticism which is much less evident in British[1] and American scholarship. It is the principle of disputing everything until a query rests over all the traditionally established facts and then painfully struggling to remove at least some of the question-marks. In the case of the Gospels the validity of this procedure may be strongly challenged. The whole approach of Bultmann and his school is essentially negative; a more positive approach to the problem of Marcan historicity is to make an examination of the book itself,[2] assuming that its basis is historical until it can be proved otherwise. The theory of community invention cannot be regarded as providing such proof until evidence can be produced that the Gospel material could not have come into being in any other way—but this is an incredible suggestion.

CONTENTS

I. INTRODUCTION (i. 1–13)

Introducing John the Baptist (i. 1–8). Jesus' baptism (i. 9–11). The temptations (i. 12, 13).

II. THE GALILAEAN PERIOD: MINISTRY AROUND THE SEA OF GALILEE (i. 14–v. 43)

The first preaching (i. 14, 15). A day at Capernaum (i. 16–38): Jesus calls the first disciples, teaches in the synagogue, and heals a demoniac, Peter's mother-in-law, and others. A preaching tour (i. 39) and the healing of a leper (i. 40–45). The growth of hostility at Capernaum (ii. 1–iii. 6). Multitudes healed by the Sea of Galilee (iii. 7–12). The calling of the Twelve (iii. 13–19). The Beelzebub controversy (iii. 20–30). The real family of Jesus (iii. 31–35). A discourse section: teaching in parables (iv. 1–34)—the sower and the soils, the seed growing secretly, the mustard seed. A series of miracles (iv. 35–v. 43): the storm stilled; the Gadarene demoniac, the woman with the haemorrhage, and Jairus' daughter healed.

---

[1] For a recent British attempt to deal with the problem under discussion with an acknowledged indebtedness to the German form-critical school of thought, cf. G. Hebert's *The Christ of Faith and the Jesus of History* (1962). Cf. also the study of H. Zahrnt, *The Historical Jesus* (Eng. Tr. 1963) for a similar approach.

[2] This was well recognized by T. W. Manson, *Studies*, pp. 3 ff.

III. THE GALILAEAN PERIOD:
FURTHER JOURNEYS IN GALILEE (vi. 1–ix. 50)

Jesus is rejected at Nazareth (vi. 1–6). The sending out of the Twelve (vi. 7–13). Herod's verdict on Jesus (vi. 14–16). The execution of John the Baptist (vi. 17–29). The Twelve return and attempt to avoid the crowds (vi. 30–32). Feeding of the five thousand (vi. 33–44). The walking on the water (vi. 45–52). Multitudes healed at Gennesaret (vi. 53–56). Jesus' attitude towards the tradition (vii. 1–23). Miracles (vii. 24–viii. 10): healing of the Syro-Phoenician woman's daughter and the deaf mute; feeding of the four thousand. Further controversy with the Pharisees (viii. 11–21). A blind man healed at Bethsaida (viii. 22–26). At Caesarea Philippi (viii. 27–ix. 29): Peter's confession; the first prediction of the passion; conditions of discipleship; the transfiguration; the coming of Elijah; the healing of the epileptic boy. Concluding events in Galilee (ix. 30–50): the second prediction of the passion; the dispute over greatness; Jesus advises tolerance towards a strange exorcist; sayings about offences towards others; about salt.

IV. THE JUDAEAN PERIOD (x. 1–xiii. 37)

The journey to Jerusalem (x. 1–52): Jesus' teaching on divorce; His attitude to children; encounter with the rich young man; sayings about riches and rewards; third prediction of the passion; request of Zebedee's sons for places of honour; healing of Bartimaeus. Entry into Jerusalem (xi. 1–10). Return to Bethany, and the cursing of the fig-tree (xi. 11–14). The cleansing of the temple (xi. 15–19). The withered fig-tree explained (xi. 20–26). Further controversies (xi. 27–xii. 44). The eschatological discourse (xiii. 1–37).

V. THE PASSION AND RESURRECTION NARRATIVES
(xiv. 1–xvi. 20)

The Jews' conspiracy against Jesus (xiv. 1, 2). The anointing of Jesus at Bethany (xiv. 3–9). Judas' plan to betray Jesus (xiv. 10, 11). Preparation for the Passover (xiv. 12–16). Prediction of the betrayal (xiv. 17–21). The last supper (xiv. 22–25). Peter's denial predicted (xiv. 26–31). In Gethesemane (xiv. 32–42). The arrest, trial and crucifixion (xiv. 43–xv. 41). The burial (xv. 42–47). The resurrection, and appearances of the risen Christ (xvi. 1–20).

CHAPTER FOUR

LUKE'S GOSPEL

There is something especially attractive about this Gospel. It is full of superb stories and leaves the reader with a deep impression of the personality and teaching of Jesus. It is perhaps for this reason that for many it is their favourite Gospel. It has many characteristic features which distinguish it from the other Gospels, as will become clear from the following survey.

I. CHARACTERISTICS

a. Luke's comprehensive range

This Gospel commences with the annunciations of John the Baptist and of Jesus and includes the fullest infancy narratives. It ends with a reference to the ascension, which is absent from both Matthew and Mark. Its record is longer than its Synoptic counterparts and is especially detailed in its account of the last journey to Jerusalem. It is in fact the longest book in the New Testament.

b. Luke's universalism

There are several occasions when Luke brings out the wider implications of the gospel of Christ. (1) The angel's good-will message is directed to all men (ii. 14); (2) Simeon foretells that Jesus is to be a Light for the Gentiles (ii. 32); (3) when John the Baptist is described in the words of Isaiah as a voice crying in the wilderness, Luke continues the quotation to include the words 'all flesh shall see the salvation of God' (Is. xl. 3–5, cited in Lk. iii. 4–6); (4) the Samaritans are placed on a level with the Jews (ix. 54, x. 33, xvii. 16); (5) Luke records two illustrations which Jesus used from the Old Testament, centring on non-Israelites, the widow of Zarephath and Naaman the Syrian (iv. 25–27); (6) a significant addition appears in Luke's account of the parable of the great supper as compared with Matthew's, for he states that the servants were sent into the hedges to constrain more people to come to fill the banqueting hall (Matthew has 'highways'); (7) as in Matthew the great commission is directed to all nations (xxiv. 47).

c. Luke's interest in people

There are various ways in which Luke's interest in people manifests itself.

(i) *Focus on individuals.* Most of the parables peculiar to Luke centre attention on people, whereas Matthew's focus upon the kingdom. His portraits are incomparable. Such people as the priest Zacharias, the cousins Elizabeth and Mary, the sisters Mary and Martha, the extortionate tax-collector Zacchaeus, the mournful Cleopas and his companion, and many others spring to life through his descriptive skill. There is no doubt that Jesus' estimate of the individual greatly impressed Luke, who is obviously attracted to people himself.

(ii) *Interest in social outcasts.* In a greater measure than the other Synoptists Luke portrays our Lord's deep concern for the socially ostracized. He mentions the immoral woman in vii. 36 ff., the transformation of Zacchaeus (xix. 8 ff.), the repentance of the robber (xxiii. 39 ff.), and records three parables illustrative of the same gracious attitude—the prodigal son, the two debtors and the publican. The attitude of Jesus towards the Samaritans, nationally ostracized by the Jews, has already been referred to under the last section.

(iii) *Portrayal of women.* Luke mentions thirteen women[1] not mentioned elsewhere in the Gospels, including two who formed the subject of parables. Of particular interest is the inclusion of the story of the widow of Nain, the immoral woman, the women who supported Jesus with their gifts and those who lamented over Him on His way to the cross. Women figure prominently in both the birth and resurrection narratives (cf. xxiii. 49 (at the cross), xxiii. 55–xxiv. 11 (at the tomb)). Luke, as a Gentile, would know much of the degradation of women and would be concerned to emphasize all he had heard of the attitude of the Lord towards them.

(iv) *Interest in children.* Luke alone refers to the childhood of John the Baptist and of Jesus. On three occasions he specially mentions 'only children' (vii. 12, viii. 42, ix. 38). In the account of the children being brought to Jesus, Luke uses the word for 'infants' ($\beta\rho\acute{\epsilon}\varphi\eta$; xviii. 15), whereas both Matthew and Mark have a different word, $\pi\alpha\iota\delta\acute{\iota}\alpha$ (children).

(v) *Social relationships.* Luke records three instances of the Lord dining with Pharisees (vii. 36–50, xi. 37–44, xiv. 1–4). He mentions Jesus' social

[1] Cf. V. Taylor, *The Gospels*, p. 70.

intercourse at Bethany (x. 38–42), at Zacchaeus' house (xix. 1–10) and at Emmaus (xxiv. 13–32). He includes many of Jesus' homely illustrations, for instance, the belated traveller requiring refreshment (xi. 5–8), the lost coin (xv. 8–10), the merry-making at the prodigal's return (xv. 22 ff.) and the innkeeper tending the wounded man (x. 35).

(vi) *Poverty and wealth.* Many of Luke's special parables deal with money matters, e.g. the two debtors, the rich fool, the tower builder, the lost coin, the unjust steward, the rich man and Lazarus and the pounds. Those who are 'poor' and 'humble' are often the objects of the Saviour's mercy (vi. 20, 30, xiv. 11 ff.). The Pharisees are called 'lovers of money' (see xvi. 14). John the Baptist, in Luke's account of his ministry, warns tax-collectors against extortion and soldiers against discontent with their pay (iii. 13 ff.). At Nazareth, Jesus proclaims good tidings to the 'poor' (iv. 17–21). In the Magnificat the hungry are filled and the rich are sent away empty (i. 53). In the Sermon on the Plain the first woe is directed against the rich, who are said to have received their consolation (vi. 24), and the first beatitude is addressed to the poor, without the qualification ' in spirit' as found in Matthew (cf. Lk. vi. 20; Mt. v. 3).

d. Special emphases

There is more recorded in Luke of Jesus' teaching on the following topics than in the other Gospels.

(i) *Prayer.* Luke records nine prayers of Jesus, of which all but two are contained in no other Gospel. These prayers are associated with important events—at the baptism (iii. 21), after a day of miracles (v. 15, 16), before choosing the disciples (vi. 12), before the first prediction of the passion (ix. 18–22), at the transfiguration (ix. 29), on the return of the seventy (x. 17–21), before teaching the disciples how to pray (xi. 1), in Gethsemane (xxii. 39–46), on the cross (xxiii. 34, 46). Once He withdraws into a desert (v. 16) and once He spends a whole night in prayer (vi. 12). Two of Luke's special parables deal with prayer—the friend at midnight (xi. 5 ff.) and the unrighteous judge (xviii. 1–8) (cf. also the Pharisee and the publican (xviii. 9–14)). Luke alone relates that Jesus prayed for Peter (xxii. 31, 32), that He exhorted the disciples to pray in Gethsemane (xxii. 40), that He prayed for His enemies (xxiii. 34) and for Himself (xxii. 41). Jesus' love of quiet places is seen in iv. 42 (a lonely place), ix. 10 (apart to Bethsaida) and xxi. 37 (He went out at night and lodged on Mount Olivet).

(ii) *The Holy Spirit.* At the temptation Jesus is described as 'full of the Holy Spirit' and is led by the Spirit into the wilderness (iv. 1). He begins His ministry in the power of the Spirit (iv. 14). He rejoices in the Spirit when offering the prayer, 'Father, I thank thee', leading to the declaration of filial consciousness (x. 21, 22). The disciples are bidden to wait for the enduement of 'power from on high' (xxiv. 49), a clear allusion to the descent of the Holy Spirit at Pentecost.

(iii) *Joyfulness.* Luke uses words expressing joy or rejoicing many times (e.g. i. 14, 44, 47, x. 21), in addition to words expressing leaping for joy (vi. 23), laughter (vi. 21) and merriment (xv. 23, 32). In three of Luke's parables there is an element of rejoicing when the lost is found (xv), and also in the story of Zacchaeus. The Gospel begins and ends with rejoicing (cf. i. 47, xxiv. 52, 53). In Luke alone are the canticles recorded, Magnificat (i. 46–55), Benedictus (i. 68–79), Gloria in Excelsis (ii. 14) and Nunc Dimittis (ii. 29–32).

II. PURPOSE AND READERS

Where an author specifically states his own intention, that must always be given more weight than any scholarly conjectures. Fortunately Luke obliges us in his preface. He tells us he purposes 'to write an orderly account',[1] and while he may not mean by this a narrative in strict chronological order in every detail he is entitled to be taken seriously about his orderly intention. Moreover, he makes clear that his purpose is to be carried out after great care in ascertaining the facts.[2]

---

[1] The word καθεξῆς means 'successively' and would seem here to mean chronological and historical order (cf. J. M. Creed, *The Gospel according to St. Luke*, 1930, p. xi). H. J. Cadbury (*The Making of Luke-Acts*[2], 1958, p. 345) draws a distinction between a 'concordance between the order of events and the order of their narration' (which he thinks the words need not here imply) and 'a narrative orderly and continuous in itself' (which he prefers here).

[2] Luke's preface is illuminating in regard to his own approach to his task. He claims to have made a comprehensive and accurate survey over a considerable period, which throws a good deal of light on his seriousness of purpose. Moreover, Luke admits that others had previously attempted the same task, but his words imply that he found them unsatisfactory (cf. N. B. Stonehouse, *The Witness of Luke to Christ*, 1951, pp. 24–45, for a careful discussion of Luke's preface. Cf. also Cadbury's commentary on this section in *The Beginnings of Christianity*, II, 1922, pp. 489–510).

In short, Luke meant to write a historical account.[1]

Yet in considering this Gospel as history, an important distinction must be made between this writing and history pure and simple, either ancient or modern.[2] Because the history concerned a unique Person it would not be surprising to find no precise parallels to the form of the book. The Gospel as a literary form is in fact as unique as the Person around whom it grew. As a means of explaining the basic historic events on which the Christian faith is fashioned, it is ideal. In confirmation of this it should be noted that Luke, like his fellow Evangelists, placed the major emphasis on the passion and resurrection narratives. These were the main subjects of early Christian preaching, of which Theophilus had apparently already been informed (i. 4). But Luke aimed to describe the happenings which led up to the passion.

There have been recent attempts to claim that Luke's purpose was dominated by a theological motive.[3] In this kind of theory Luke is said to have had a different theological approach from his sources, and his own modifications are then regarded as evidence of his theology. No-one would deny that Luke's purpose is theological. But this is quite different from saying that the history has been conformed to the theology, an approach which had its origins in the Tübingen school of thought.[4] It is truer to say that Luke brings out the theological significance of the history. An interesting example of this is the prominence he gives to Jerusalem in his narrative,[5] although he does not include any

[1] H. Sahlin (*Der Messias und das Gottesvolk*, 1945, Acta Uppsala xii), who regards Luke-Acts as a whole, maintains that the author's intention was to produce a defence brief at Paul's trial and he supposed that the 'others' who had written were witnesses and minutes secretaries at the hearing of the case. But this view is criticized by Michaelis, *Einleitung*, p. 15.

[2] Any appeal to a historian such as Thucydides or any modern historian can have little relevance to Luke's work since the form of the latter's writing differs so fundamentally from theirs. See the comments on this in the section on Acts, pp. 326 ff.

[3] The most recent is H. Conzelmann, *The Theology of St. Luke* (1960), an Eng. Tr. of his *Die Mitte der Zeit*[2] (1960). Cf. E. Lohse, *EvTh*, xiv (1954), pp. 256–275.

[4] The view of this school of thought was that the purpose of Luke's writings (particularly Acts) was to reconcile antagonistic Petrine and Pauline groups. The historical account was, therefore, considered to be dominated by this 'tendency'.

[5] Conzelmann (*op. cit.*, pp. 132 ff.) makes a special point of this when discussing Luke's eschatology. Cf. Michaelis's criticisms, *Einleitung*, pp. 67–69. A. Hastings, in his book *Prophet and Witness in Jerusalem. A Study of the Teaching of St. Luke* (1958), devotes a good deal of attention to the significance of Jerusalem. For a similar phenomenon in Acts, cf. J. Cambier, *NTS*, 8 (1962), pp. 249–257.

of the special Johannine Jerusalem material. Rather he depicts the dramatic progress of Jesus from Galilee to Jerusalem. The whole movement of events had meaning for him. Jesus was moving on towards Jerusalem in order to die. That was Luke's Gospel and that was his theology. It was also the centre of the theology of the whole primitive Church. And yet there is a sense in which Luke shows his own particular theological interests, in his choice and arrangement of his material. This is revealed not only in geographical details, but also in historical details (e.g. in the greater emphasis on the universal approach of Jesus).

It should be remembered in discussions of Luke's purpose that it is impossible to treat this Gospel apart from its sequel, the book of Acts. It may reasonably be supposed that any motives which become clearly apparent in Acts had their origin in the design of the Gospel, and if this supposition is correct it is at least possible that the double work had an apologetic purpose. Hence if part of Luke's purpose in Acts was to show that Christianity was not yet subversive (see pp. 317 ff.) and that as successor to the synagogue it was entitled to the same State protection,[1] it must be assumed that the account of our Lord was written with a similar motive. But not all are agreed about the apologetic purpose of Acts, and it is even less evident in the Gospel.[2] It may at least be said that the Gospel was intended to describe the beginnings of a process which reached beyond Jerusalem to the heart of imperial Rome itself. Yet there is a sense in which the Gospel is complete in itself,[3] for it provides the substance of the preaching which forms the basis of the Acts narrative.

Luke's preface also helps us in determining the readers. There is a dedication to one man, Theophilus, who is described as 'most excellent' (κράτιστε), an expression which looks like an indication of social rank.[4] Some have supposed that Theophilus is a coined name to represent any 'lover of God', but in view of the formal character of the preface and the conventional practice of ascribing treatises to notable people, it is

[1] Cf. the views of S. M. Gilmour, *The Gospel according to St. Luke* (IB, 1952), pp. 5–7.
[2] Appeal may be made to Lk. xxiii. 4, 14, 22, where three times Pilate pronounces Jesus not guilty.
[3] Cf. Creed, *op. cit.*, p. xi.
[4] That this was a title of honour and respect cannot be doubted. W. Manson (*The Gospel of Luke, MC*, 1930, pp. 2, 3) considered that the term pointed to the holder of some procuratorial or similar office within the empire.

much more natural to regard Theophilus as a real person.[1] He was clearly a Gentile and appears already to have had some catechetical instruction, if it is correct to interpret i. 4 in this manner.[2] This suggests that the Gospel was primarily designed for all people in a similar category.

There is abundant evidence to suggest a Gentile destination, and this has already been indicated in discussing one of Luke's main characteristics, his universalism.[3] The Gospel may therefore be said to be designed for all who in the non-Christian world were not averse to Christianity and were genuinely interested in having a historical account of its origins.

Are there any indications which enable us to define more precisely the first group of readers? The anti-Marcionite Prologue states that Luke was in Achaia when he wrote his Gospel, a view which Jerome[4] also expresses in one of his books, although in another he mentions Rome as the place of origin of Acts. Since the climax of Acts is seen in the arrival of Paul at Rome, the joint work (Luke-Acts) would have been very suitable for a Roman destination. In this case it may be conjectured that Theophilus was a Roman of noble birth.

III. STRUCTURE

Since Luke states so explicitly that he purposed to arrange his narrative in an orderly account, it is of great interest to examine his structure and

---

[1] Cf. Creed, *op. cit.*, p. 5.

[2] There is difference of opinion about the interpretation of κατηχήθης. It can certainly mean definite instruction in the Christian faith (cf. Creed, *op. cit., ad loc.*), in which case Theophilus must have been a Christian. If, on the other hand, the word refers merely to information he has received, Theophilus may have been still an outsider, but interested in Christianity (so Manson, *op. cit.*, p. 3). Cadbury (*The Beginnings of Christianity*, II, pp. 508 ff.) maintained that the word could include hostile reports and that the book was written to counteract these (against this idea, cf. F. H. Colson, *JTS*, XXIV, 1923, p. 303). W. E. Bundy (*Jesus and the First Three Gospels*, 1955, p. 4) thinks that Luke's use of this title combined with his formality suggests that Theophilus was not a fellow-Christian.

[3] See p. 84. K. H. Rengstorf (*Das Evangelium nach Lukas*[8], 1958, p. 6) points out that in Luke there are few of our Lord's criticisms of the scribes and Pharisees, which would indicate a circle of readers not interested in the questions of first-century Judaism.

[4] In his commentary on Matthew he mentions parts of Achaia and Boeotia, but in *De Viris Illustribus* he maintained a Roman location. For Rome, cf. Michaelis, *Einleitung*, p. 78. Cf. also E. J. Goodspeed, *INT* (1937), p. 208.

to compare it with the other Synoptics. He uses the same general framework as Matthew and Mark, although he has many characteristic variations in his detailed structure.[1] His infancy narratives are much fuller than Matthew's and are of particular significance in the emphasis placed upon the birth of John the Baptist, to which Luke clearly attached considerable importance. This feature provides one of the main keys to Luke's structure. To him all the events are a part of a divine revelation, in a rather different sense from Matthew's viewpoint. He does not cite so specifically passages which show the fulfilment of prophecy. But to him the events themselves are significant, and John the Baptist figures prominently in the infancy stories because the public ministry of Jesus is so closely linked with John. The relevance of the birth of John for Luke lies in its miraculous character. It demonstrated that divine intervention which was operative in the history of Jesus. It is for the same reason that Luke, in giving his sixfold dating in iii. 1, connects it up with John's ministry and not with that of Jesus.

The Galilaean period of the ministry in Luke (iii. 1–ix. 50) is parallel in structure with Mark's and Matthew's, but the later period is differently arranged. Luke has what is commonly known as a travel narrative from ix. 51–xviii. 14, depicting the movement of Jesus from Galilee to Jerusalem. This is Luke's special modification of the Synoptic structure and will call for consideration later when the Synoptic problem is discussed. In this portion Luke not only includes much material which is peculiar to his Gospel, but arranges his material in such a way as to focus attention on Jerusalem as a preparation for the passion narratives. The Judaean period and passion narratives follow a pattern similar to that of the narratives in the other Synoptics, although again with some variations of detail.[2] The resurrection narratives, however, are mainly peculiar to Luke and here again one of the most striking features about

---

[1] A special feature of Luke's Gospel is the author's fondness for pairs, to which R. Morgenthaler (*Die lukanische Geschichtsschreibung als Zeugnis*, 1949) attaches considerable significance.

[2] H. Schürmann has made a very full study of the subject-matter of Lk. xxii. 7–38 (*Quellenkritische Untersuchung des lukanischen Abendmahlsberichtes*, 1953–57), in which he maintains that parts of this passage are Luke's editing of a non-Marcan source. Cf. V. Taylor's useful summary of Schürmann's views, *ET*, LXXIV (1962), pp. 77–81. Cf. J. Jeremias (*NTS*, 4, 1958, pp. 115–119), who also maintains that in the block Lk. xxii. 14 ff., Luke does not depend on Mark. For the view that Luke possibly did use Mk. xiv. 22–25, in disagreement with Jeremias, cf. H. F. D. Sparks, *NTS*, 3 (1957), pp. 219–223.

them is that the appearances of the risen Lord were all set in or near Jerusalem with no reference to any Galilaean appearances as in the other Gospels.[1]

To some scholars Luke's treatment of his material is evidence of his deliberate editorial work influenced by his theological approach.[2] The narrative ix. 51–xviii. 14 does not require a journey for its structure and this has led some to conclude that it must be historically secondary and therefore characteristically Lucan. But the journey motive may never really have been in Luke's mind. It looks as if he had collected much material which he knew belonged to the closing period of our Lord's life and he naturally fitted it in between the Galilaean and Judaean ministries. He gives little indication where the events happened, which is in striking contrast to the Acts, where place-names often occur without any events attached. It would be better to call this section simply 'From Galilee to Judaea' without using the word 'journey' which tends to suggest a detailed route.[3]

IV. AUTHORSHIP OF THE GOSPEL (AND ACTS)

a. The preface

The Gospel itself does not tell us anything specific about the identity of the author, but it does tell us about his methods. The preface to the Gospel accords with the literary customs of the period and it is the only example of a formal introduction in the New Testament. From it we

---

[1] Cf. A. R. C. Leaney (NTS, 2, 1955, pp. 110–114), who suggests that the narratives of Lk. xxiv and Jn. xx were both drawn from a common tradition. It is significant that John adds an 'appendix', including a Galilaean appearance. Cf. B. Lindars, NTS, 7 (1961), pp. 142–147, for comments on Leaney's view.

[2] This is particularly true of H. Conzelmann, The Theology of St. Luke (1960), p. 62. K. L. Schmidt (Der Rahmen der Geschichte Jesu, 1919, p. 269) did not consider that the section constituted the report of a journey, since Jesus never really makes any progress on His way to Jerusalem. Bultmann (The History of the Synoptic Tradition, pp. 25, 26) regards the journey through Samaria as Luke's own construction.

[3] See further discussion of this section on pp. 162 f. A somewhat different approach to Luke's structure is maintained by those who consider that Luke prepared an earlier draft of his Gospel (Proto-Luke) which lacked all material paralleled in Mark. This latter material was inserted later. To discover Luke's structure, the focus must be fixed on Proto-Luke rather than Luke as a whole. But even if the Proto-Luke theory could be sustained (see pp. 168 ff. for a full discussion of the theory), it tells us more about Luke's editorial processes than about the structure of the Gospel.

may make the following deductions. The author was clearly not an eyewitness, for he states that he had received information from others who were 'eyewitnesses and ministers of the word'. Moreover, he implies that he had access to earlier narratives which others had compiled, but which he seems to regard as unsatisfactory for his purpose. In addition he has himself made a thorough investigation of the facts as a result of which he claims to be able to write an orderly account. From these data, it may be inferred that the author was a cultured man in view of the style of the preface. He was also a careful writer who did not belong to the immediate circle of our Lord's followers.

For the identity of the author, reference will need to be made first to the external evidence, followed by an investigation of internal data. For this purpose it will be necessary to consider with the Gospel the authorship of the book of Acts also.

b. The testimony of tradition

The earliest witnesses to the authorship of the Gospel belong to the latter part of the second century AD, but the subsequent testimony is so fully in agreement with this that it may fairly be surmised that this tradition had already had a considerable history before its earliest witnesses. The Muratorian Canon, the anti-Marcionite Prologue to Luke, Irenaeus, Clement of Alexandria, Origen and Tertullian all specifically state that Luke was the author, not only of the Gospel, but also of the Acts of the Apostles. Moreover, at no time were any doubts raised regarding this attribution to Luke, and certainly no alternatives were mooted. The tradition could hardly be stronger, but some scholars attach little importance to it.

It is maintained by H. J. Cadbury,[1] for instance, that the earliest testimony, that of the Muratorian Canon, contains nothing that could not be inferred from the text of the New Testament itself and he, therefore, deduces that Lucan authorship was in all probability a guess based on the 'we-passages' of Acts (see pp. 334 ff.). He supports this supposition by an appeal to the uncritical approach of this Muratorian Fragment towards authorship generally, for instance, in the case of the Gospel of John (see discussion on p. 235). He is consequently not disposed to place much weight upon the tradition. It must, of course, be at once admitted that there is no certain evidence as to whether or

---

[1] Cf. his article on 'The Tradition' in Foakes Jackson-Lake's *The Beginnings of Christianity*, II, pp. 209–264. On the Muratorian Canon see pp. 255 ff.

not the whole body of external testimony was based on solid knowledge or on pure conjecture, but there is the strongest possible reason for
favouring the former. It will not be denied that an initial conjecture
may be repeated by successive witnesses until it becomes mistaken for
fact, as the history of modern criticism abundantly illustrates, but Cadbury's suggestion involves a remarkable and highly improbable process. Where various possibilities existed, what governed the choice of
Luke? Cadbury,[1] with some hesitation, suggests a process of elimination, but does not explain how it is that such a process led so inevitably
to Luke. Why not Mark or Epaphras? In any case, why did not the
second-century Church attribute both the third Gospel and Acts to an
apostolic name rather than to the insignificant Luke? And how did the
inference drawn from the books themselves gain such undisputed
sway among the Church Fathers? These questions need more concrete
answers than Cadbury gives before the tradition can so readily be set
aside as relatively unimportant in discussions of authorship.

c. The internal testimony

It is against the background of the strong external evidence that the
witness of the books themselves must be considered. Does it support
the tradition or does it cast suspicions upon it? Various opinions have
been expressed about these alternatives and it will be necessary to give
some brief indication of the arguments advanced for each view,
beginning with those in support of the tradition.

(i) *The unity of authorship of the third Gospel and Acts.* Since external
testimony assumes common authorship of the Gospel and Acts, and
since it may with good reason be maintained that the book of Acts was
accepted into the New Testament Canon without hesitation because of
its close association with the Gospel of Luke, it is of importance to
investigate the grounds on which this association may be based.
(1) Both books are dedicated to the same man, Theophilus; (2) Acts
refers to the first treatise, which is most naturally understood as the
Gospel; (3) the books contain strong similarities of language and style;
(4) both contain common interests;[2] (5) Acts naturally follows on from

---

[1] *Ibid.*, p. 261.

[2] F. F. Bruce (*The Acts of the Apostles*[2], 1952, p. 2) gives the following examples:
(1) Catholic sympathies; (2) interest in Gentiles; (3) prominence given to women;
(4) similar apologetic tendencies; (5) resurrection appearances restricted to Judaea,
and (6) Christ's appearance before Herod Antipas mentioned in both, but not
elsewhere in the New Testament.

Luke's Gospel, although many scholars have found difficulties over the connecting links.[1] It may safely be concluded that the evidence is very strong for linking the two books as the work of one man, a conclusion which few modern scholars would dispute.[2] This is helpful in supporting Lucan authorship in so far as it confirms the traditional assumption and strengthens the opinion that the tradition of authorship was also correct.

(ii) *Evidence that the author was a companion of Paul.* That there are some passages in Acts where the first person plural is used instead of the third person (xvi. 10–17, xx. 5–15, xxi. 1–18 and xxvii. 1–xxviii. 16) is strongly suggestive that the author of these sections was an eyewitness and therefore a travelling companion of the apostle Paul. If this is a fair inference it considerably narrows down the possibilities of authorship. It would mean that the author (1) first joins Paul at Philippi; (2) reappears on Paul's return visit to Philippi; (3) accompanies the apostle on the journey towards Jerusalem and stays with Philip at Caesarea, and, (4) after Paul's two years' imprisonment at Caesarea, during which time there are no definite data regarding the author's whereabouts, accompanies Paul to Rome and experiences shipwreck with him. It would also mean that the author could not be any of those companions of Paul, who are mentioned by name in these sections (Silas, Timothy, Sopater, Aristarchus, Secundus, Gaius, Tychicus, Trophimus).

Such an interpretation of the we-sections is also suggested by the use of the first person singular in the introduction to both the books (Lk. i. 1–4; Acts i. 1),[3] and it is certainly most natural to suppose that the

---

[1] Cf. P. H. Menoud's article, 'Remarques sur les textes de l'ascension dans Luc-Actes', in *Neutestamentliche Studien für Rudolf Bultmann* (1954), pp. 148–156. Cf. also W. G. Kümmel, *TR*, xxii (1954), p. 196; A. N. Wilder, *JBL*, lxii (1943), pp. 307–318; H. Conzelmann, *The Theology of St. Luke* (1960), pp. 93, 94. All these incline towards an interpolation theory involving the end of Luke or the beginning of Acts. Against, cf. P. A. van Stempvoort, *NTS*, 5 (1958–59), pp. 30–42. Cf. also Kümmel's later comments in Feine-Behm-Kümmel, *Einleitung*, pp. 99 ff.

[2] It was challenged by A. C. Clark, *The Acts of the Apostles* (1933), pp. 393 ff. Cf. the penetrating criticism of Clark's arguments in W. L. Knox's *The Acts of the Apostles* (1948), pp. 2–15.

[3] For a discussion of the bearing of the preface to Luke's Gospel on the significance of the we-sections, cf. Feine-Behm-Kümmel, *op. cit.*, p. 118; H. J. Cadbury, *NTS*, 3 (1957), pp. 128–131. The latter admits that Luke's παρηκολουθηκότι means that the author was an eyewitness of at least some of the events that he recorded. But Kümmel takes the opposite view.

author intended his readers to assume that he was himself present during the events recorded in these sections. Yet although this would seem to be natural it is by no means universally acknowledged, and other interpretations will be noted in later discussions (see pp. 334 ff.).

(iii) *Indirect evidence in support of Lucan authorship.* Since the account in Acts concludes with Paul imprisoned in Rome, it is highly probable that the author was one of those companions of Paul mentioned in the captivity Epistles, but not included in the we-sections (Mark, Jesus Justus, Epaphras, Demas, Luke and Epaphroditus). The force of this argument will naturally depend on the opinion held regarding the provenance of these Epistles,[1] but if the Roman tradition is correct there is strong probability that the author is among the above named. It would, on the other hand, not be altogether excluded if these Epistles were sent from Ephesus, although some difficulties would then arise since no we-section occurs during Paul's Ephesian ministry. However, since the probabilities that Colossians and Philemon were sent from Ephesus are slight, and an Ephesian origin of Philippians is by no means certain, the argument is at least worthy of consideration. Of those mentioned, Luke is as good as any, and since this is the traditional ascription there seems no reason to conjecture any other.

This suggestion is supported by several other more incidental considerations. In none of the Epistles written on the second and third journeys (Thessalonians, Galatians (?), Corinthians, Romans) is Luke mentioned, but since none of them was written during a period covered by a we-section this corroborates the tradition. Moreover, according to Colossians iv. 10, 14 and Philemon 24, Luke was in close touch with Mark and this may well account for the Marcan elements in the Gospel and the Marcan flavour of the first part of Acts, which has often been noted (see further discussion on sources, pp. 335 ff.). Further support has been suggested from the appropriateness of Paul's description of Luke as 'the beloved physician', not only because the author was clearly a man of some culture, but also because his vocabulary has been thought to be of a type which a physician might be expected to use. This was strongly stressed by W. K. Hobart[2] and was supported,

[1] Cf. the present writer's discussion in *New Testament Introduction: The Pauline Epistles* (1961), pp. 92–98.
[2] *The Medical Language of St. Luke* (1882).

although rather more guardedly, by A. Harnack.[1] Yet although there are remarkable parallels between Luke's vocabulary and that of such medical writers as Hippocrates, Galen and Dioscorides, H. J. Cadbury[2] has pointed out that most of the examples cited could be paralleled in other educated Greek writers of that time. In short there was nothing distinctively medical about Luke's language. As a result of Cadbury's studies less emphasis is now placed on this evidence than at one time, yet his criticisms do not exclude the argument from being used to corroborate Lucan authorship,[3] although no-one would claim that it can prove it. There are some significant instances in which Luke describes illnesses and ailments with more medical precision than his fellow Synoptists. In Luke iv. 38 Peter's mother-in-law suffers from a 'great' fever, and in v. 12 a leper is said to be 'full of leprosy'. It should also be noted that in the case of the woman suffering from haemorrhage, Luke omits the comment that she had spent her savings on doctors and was not cured (cf. Mk. v. 26; Lk. viii. 43, RSV).[4]

Beyond the fact that he was a doctor and a companion of Paul (cf. Col. iv. 14; 2 Tim. iv. 11; Phm. 24), the New Testament tells us nothing more about him, although it implies that he was a Gentile, for in the list of greetings in Colossians iv Luke is distinguished from the men of the circumcision. Certain traditions connect him with the church at Antioch;[5] while the we-sections in Acts, which start at Philippi, might perhaps suggest that that was his home town. In fact, Ramsay[6] suggested that Luke was 'the man of Macedonia', whom Paul saw in his vision beckoning him across to Europe. It is an interesting conjecture but nothing more. It may be that Luke came into contact with Paul on his missionary journeys when the apostle was in need of medical attention. It may be that Paul was responsible for his hearing

---

[1] *Lukas der Arzt* (1906; Eng. Tr. *Luke the Physician*, 1907).

[2] *Style and Literary Method of Luke* (1920).

[3] Cf. the remarks of J. M. Creed, *The Gospel according to St. Luke* (1930), pp. xviii ff.

[4] K. H. Rengstorf (*Das Evangelium nach Lukas*[8], 1958, p. 12) claims rightly that neither Luke nor Acts contains anything against the view that Luke was the author. Cf. also J. M. Creed, *op. cit.*, pp. xviii ff.

[5] E.g. the anti-Marcionite Prologue. If the Western Text of Acts xi. 28 (in Codex Bezae) is correct, the first 'we-passage' occurred in Antioch. Cf. Eusebius, *HE*, iii. 4. 6.

[6] *St. Paul the Traveller and Roman Citizen* (1920), pp. 200–203; *Luke the Physician* (1908), pp. 35 ff.

about Christianity.[1] But nothing is certain,[2] except the debt of gratitude which the Christian Church owes to him for his exquisite account of the life and passion of his Lord and of the early developments in Christian history.

The traditional view of Lucan authorship, although widely held as the view which most satisfactorily explains all the data, is nevertheless not without its challengers. Cadbury,[3] for instance, considers that the tradition was no more than an inference from the New Testament data, but if so it was remarkably consistent and widespread, and in any case may have been a perfectly true inference.

Nevertheless in spite of the weight of external and internal evidence there has been strong opposition to this tradition. A detailed statement of the case against it was made by H. Windisch[4] in 1922, and his objections, together with others more recently made, will be considered next. Most of the arguments are concerned with problems arising from the book of Acts.

(i) *Historical discrepancies.* The view that Acts conflicts with the Pauline Epistles has been a favourite argument against Lucan authorship, for it has been maintained that no companion of Paul could have made the historical blunders with which the author of Acts is charged. Among the discrepancies often mentioned are the appearance of Ananias in the story of Paul's conversion, in supposed contradiction to the fact that Paul says in Galatians that no human agent had a share in his conversion;[5] the different account of Paul's Jerusalem visits as compared with Galatians; the different attitude of Paul towards the law seen in the circumcision of Timothy and in Paul's

---

[1] Cf. S. C. Carpenter, *Christianity according to St. Luke* (1919), pp. 11, 12.

[2] The obscurity of the data led to various suppositions concerning Luke. He was supposed to have been one of the seventy since he alone records the mission charge to this group (Lk. x). Or else the unnamed companion of Cleopas on the Emmaus road (Lk. xxiv. 13 f.). Or even the well-famed, but unnamed, brother mentioned by Paul in 2 Cor. viii. 18. All of these views secured patristic support (see Michaelis, *Einleitung*, p. 61, for details), but their conjectural character will be evident. The widespread tradition that Luke was a painter is interesting, but its origin is completely unknown.

[3] In his article in *The Beginnings of Christianity*, II, pp. 250–264.

[4] In his article in *Beginnings*, II, pp. 298–348.

[5] W. Prentice (*ZNTW*, 46, 1955, pp. 250–254) goes as far as to describe Luke's account as popular legend. But for a more favourable approach to Luke's historicity, cf. H. G. Wood's article on Paul's conversion, *NTS*, I (1955), pp. 276–282.

undertaking a Jewish vow (compared with his attitude towards circumcision in the Epistles); the problem of the Council decrees, and the improbability of Paul being prepared to accept any restrictions on Gentile Christians in view of his arguments to the Galatians; and the problem of the dispute between Peter and Paul at Antioch. The whole question of Luke's reliability as a historian will be dealt with later (see pp. 321 ff.), but it must be pointed out here that these discrepancies are more apparent than real and that, although not all the difficulties may be completely removed, because of insufficient data, alternative interpretations can render the force of this argument considerably less weighty. For instance, the alleged discrepancy over Paul's conversion may at once be dismissed since Acts makes abundantly clear the superhuman character of the event; the Jerusalem visits have been discussed elsewhere[1] and may be said to confirm the independence of both accounts without making Lucan authorship impossible; the Council decrees would not have imposed an impossible burden, indeed the word 'burden' is inapplicable, for the whole account is presented as a concession on the part of the Jerusalem church, not on the part of the apostle Paul. At least, it may be said that alleged discrepancies which are capable of an alternative explanation are an insecure basis for rejecting the tradition.[2]

(ii) *Different interpretations of the we-sections.* It is further maintained that the we-sections are capable of a different interpretation from that favoured by the upholders of the traditional authorship. The first person plural, in short, need not point to an author who was a companion of Paul, but may be either a literary convention or the relic of an earlier written source (a personal diary of some kind).

The idea of a literary convention is maintained by some authors who do not deny Lucan authorship, as for instance Dibelius,[3] who considers that the we-form is used by the author to indicate his presence in all the occurrences except the shipwreck narrative, where he suggests that it

---

[1] Cf. the comments on pp. 322 f. and the writer's fuller discussion in *New Testament Introduction: The Pauline Epistles*, pp. 80 ff.

[2] Feine-Behm-Kümmel (*Einleitung*, p. 120) consider that the author shows himself to be too falsely informed to be a companion of Paul. Kümmel is particularly influenced by the references to the Jerusalem visits, the relation of Paul to the Jerusalem apostles and the Council decrees. But he gives no weight to alternative explanations of the difficulties.

[3] Cf. *Studies in the Acts of the Apostles*, pp. 104, 105, for the earlier we-forms, and for the shipwreck account, pp. 204–206.

incorporated an earlier secular account used by Luke (in this theory, Dibelius is following E. Norden).[1] The idea that Luke used the we-form to indicate that he was a companion of Paul is, therefore, in Dibelius' view, only partially true. Others assume that what has supposedly happened in the shipwreck account has happened in the other instances and the we-form may therefore be ignored for purposes of identifying the author. The most recent advocate of this type of theory is E. Haenchen,[2] to whom the 'we' is but a stylistic process to give force to the narrative and bears no historical significance. It should be noted that Haenchen on other grounds does not accept the Lucan authorship[3] and therefore is bound to suggest some alternative explanation of the we-passages.

The other possibility, which has been strongly advocated by a succession of scholars, is that the writer has used an earlier source written in the first person.[4] This source has been variously described as a diary or an itinerary (see the discussion of this idea on pp. 341 ff.). By means of such a theory some scholars have transferred the tradition of Lucan authorship from the whole book to this particular source.[5] But if this were so, two important considerations arise. Why did the author not indicate Luke's name, so as to add greater weight to his use of this eyewitness account? Or, if that were not his purpose in incorporating the source, why did he retain the first person plural? There are no satisfactory answers to these questions. The we-sections could hardly have been regarded by the uninitiated reader as an indication of an eyewitness written source without more indication of this fact. It would be more natural to suppose that he would assume that the author was himself present. Moreover, as Harnack[6] strongly maintained,

[1] *Agnostos Theos* (1913), pp. 313 f., 323 f.

[2] *Die Apostelgeschichte (KEK)*[13], (1961), pp. 428–431.

[3] Cf. especially his article, 'Tradition und Komposition in der Apostelgeschichte', *ZTK*, 52 (1955), pp. 205–225 and in his commentary *Die Apostelgeschichte*, pp. 99–103.

[4] Many of the earlier German critics maintained this view. J. Dupont, in his *Les Sources du Livre des Actes* (1960), pp. 76 ff., gives useful biographical information on this point. Not all advocates of a we-source have supposed that Luke was the author, for Timothy, Silas, Titus and even Epaphras have been proposed. Some have equated Titus with Silas as author. Yet in all these variations there is the underlying assumption that the author or redactor of the whole used someone else's personal memoirs.

[5] See especially the article by H. Windisch in *Beginnings*, II, pp. 342 ff.

[6] *Luke the Physician* (1907). pp. 1 ff.

the style and language of the we-passages agree so closely with the style and language of the rest of the book that it cannot be maintained that a separate source was used. In face of this evidence, the we-sections remain a stronger testimony to an author who was a companion of Paul than to any other.

(iii) *Theological difficulties.* The weightiest objection to Lucan author-ship, or for that matter to authorship by any of Paul's companions, has been based on the theological differences between the Acts and the Pauline Epistles.[1] It is maintained by some that Luke's record of Paul's teaching differs so radically from Paul's own presentation that it can only be concluded that the author was unacquainted with Paul. The first theological discrepancy is Paul's solution of the problem of the law.[2] In the Acts, there is no hint of the theological tension which is reflected in Paul's Galatian letter, where law is seen as leading into bondage from which Christ has freed men. Circumcision is even sup-ported by Paul in Acts (in the case of Timothy), although resisted by him in Galatians. Yet while it cannot be denied that the Lucan picture differs from Paul's, it cannot be asserted that the two pictures contra-dict one another. There is no ground for demanding that Luke must present Paul's theology in his historical book in precisely the same form as Paul presents it in his pastoral and didactic letters. The same applies to the speeches attributed to Paul in Acts, where it is maintained either that the author has composed the Pauline speeches without reference to Paul's Epistles and therefore with no attempt to make them conform to Pauline thought, or else that Luke has adapted some existing speech-form, as in the case of the Areopagus speech in Athens (Acts xvii).[3] Although it is possible to hold that the Areopagus speech was Luke's own adaptation of material in order to give an example of what a sermon to cultured people ought to be, as Dibelius,[4] in fact, maintained, it is equally possible to maintain that the speech is a faithful representa-

---

[1] Cf. Haenchen's section 'Lukas und Paulus', *Die Apostelgeschichte* (*KEK*), pp. 99–103.

[2] Haenchen, *op. cit.*, pp. 99, 100.

[3] So E. Norden, *Agnostos Theos* (1913), pp. 3–83. Cf. also A. Loisy, *Les Actes des Apôtres* (1920), pp. 660–684, and more recently H. Hommel, *ZNTW*, 46 (1955), pp. 145–178; 48 (1957), pp. 193–200. Other recent studies on this speech are those of W. Nauck, *ZTK*, 53 (1956), pp. 11–52; W. Eltester, in *N. T. Studien für R. Bultmann* (1954), pp. 202–227.

[4] *Op. cit.*, pp. 26–77.

tion of Paul's own thought on the occasion.[1] Whatever conclusions are arrived at on this score, it is clear that no argument based upon them can prove conclusive in the question of authorship. The same may be said of Paul's speech at Pisidian Antioch (Acts xiii. 16 ff.).[2] It is hardly to be expected that during a mission address the apostle would present his teaching, either in form or content, in the same manner as when writing letters to those already committed to the Christian faith.[3] For instance, a theological presentation like the Epistle to the Romans would hardly have been suited to a primary preaching of the gospel. Objections based on the un-Pauline character of this Pisidian speech which do not take into account the historical situation can have little weight (see the discussion on the speeches on pp. 326 ff.)[4]

Closely linked with the problem based on alleged differences in theology is the difference between the Paul of Acts and the Paul of the Epistles. This will be discussed when the historicity of Acts is considered (see pp. 325 f.), but if the Acts portrait is out of harmony with Paul's own self-revelation it would obviously be difficult to maintain that the author was a personal companion of the apostle. Nevertheless, it will be shown that the differences are overdrawn and that there are no proved contradictions. Differences of emphasis must be admitted, but this has no bearing on Lucan authorship. It is not so unusual for a close

[1] Cf. A. Wikenhauser, *Die Apostelgeschichte und ihr Geschichtswert* (1921), pp. 390–394; N. B. Stonehouse, *Paul before the Areopagus* (1957), pp. 1–40. For an earlier treatment, cf. F. H. Chase, *The Credibility of the Book of the Acts of the Apostles* (1902), pp. 204–234. Cf. also the detailed study by B. Gärtner, *The Areopagus Speech and Natural Revelation* (Eng. Tr. by C. H. King, 1955), who concludes for the Pauline character of the speech although admitting Lucan influence in terminology and literary form (cf. pp. 248 ff.)

[2] H. Windisch (*op. cit.*, p. 337) categorically denied that this speech could be by a companion of Paul, for three reasons: (1) it borrows from Luke's Gospel; (2) it implies that Paul was not a witness of the resurrection (verse 30); and (3) it depends on Peter's Pentecost speech (verses 34–37). This reminiscence of Peter's speech is also noted by Dibelius (*op. cit.*, pp. 105, 119), but he does not draw the same conclusion as Windisch. He sees the Petrine echoes as Luke's work.

[3] The only Acts speech which bears any analogy to the situation behind the Pauline Epistles is Paul's address to the Ephesian elders at Miletus. And it is significant that this speech approximates most closely to Paul's Epistles in language and thought (cf. F. H. Chase, *op. cit.*, pp. 234–288).

[4] Scholars who regard the speeches of Acts as Luke's work will naturally allow little weight to this consideration. Cf. U. Wilckens, *Die Missionsreden der Apostelgeschichte*[2] (1963), who regards all the speeches in Acts ii–v, x and xiii as Lucan. On Paulinisms in Acts, cf. P. Vielhauer, *Ev Th*, x (1950), pp. 1–15.

companion to paint a portrait of a person which differs from that person's self-disclosures. There is certainly insufficient ground for the conclusion that the author of Acts is a man of the sub-apostolic age.[1] There is further no theological basis for denying that the author of Luke and Acts was a companion of Paul. If Luke shows independence of Paul,[2] there is no evidence of conflicting opinion between them.

(iv) *Literary parallels.* Another type of argument has recently been advanced against Lucan authorship based on a literary comparison between Acts and the works of Justin Martyr. This is the approach of J. C. O'Neill,[3] who maintains that the two authors held common theological positions and Luke-Acts must consequently be placed well into the second century, which at once rules out Lucan authorship.[4] But this theory gives insufficient attention to the alternative explanation of the parallels, i.e. that Justin learned his theology from Luke (see further discussion of this under the Date of Acts, p. 315).

d. Conclusion

There would appear to be far stronger grounds for retaining the tradition of Lucan authorship for both the Gospel and Acts than for rejecting it. This opinion is confirmed by the fact that advocates of Lucan authorship are not only in the majority, but are also drawn from widely differing schools of theological opinion.[5]

[1] Cf. Haenchen, *op. cit.*, pp. 100–103.

[2] Cf. Creed, *The Gospel according to St. Luke* (1930), p. xviii. As R. M. Grant (*A Historical Introduction to the New Testament*, 1963, p. 135) points out, any who assume that Luke must echo Paul neglect to give sufficient weight to the variety within the unity of the early Church. The idea of Pauline influence on Luke was firmly rejected by T. E. Bleiben (*JTS*, XLV, 1944, pp. 134–140) on the grounds that Luke and Paul hold different views regarding the passion.

[3] *The Theology of Acts* (1961), pp. 10 ff., 21.

[4] There is no doubt that O'Neill comes to the study of the parallels between Acts and Justin with a strong bias against an early date, and his judgments are coloured by this disinclination to accept the primitive character of Acts (cf. *op. cit.*, pp. 4 ff.).

[5] Among those maintaining authorship by Luke the physician may be cited F. F. Bruce, *The Acts of the Apostles*[2] (1952), pp. 1–6; C. S. C. Williams, *The Acts of the Apostles* (BC, 1957), pp. 1 ff.; W. Michaelis, *Einleitung*, pp. 61–64; Bo Reicke, *Glaube und Leben der Urgemeinde* (1957), pp. 6, 7; F. V. Filson, *Three Crucial Decades* (1963), p. 10; M. Dibelius, *Studies in the Acts of the Apostles* (Eng. Tr. 1956), p. 123; R. M. Grant, *A Historical Introduction to the New Testament* (1963), pp. 134, 135 (although he does not consider the identification of the author to be

V. DATE

In some ways the date of Luke is tied up with the date of Acts, but it is advisable to begin the discussion by marshalling the evidence for the Gospel alone.

a. External evidence

This evidence suggests that in the early part of the second century the Gospel was fully recognized, and it would be a fair inference from this that it was widely known before the end of the first century. It seems to be reflected in the *Didache*[1] and in works of the Gnostics, Basilides and Valentinus,[2] while Marcion[3] used a mutilated form of this Gospel and excluded all others. Justin[4] made much use of it in the mid-second century.

b. Arguments for a second-century date

Not all scholars, however, have agreed that, if Lucan authorship is rejected, the external evidence requires a first-century dating for the Gospel. Admittedly the earlier evidence (*Didache*, Basilides and Valentinus) is not strong numerically,[5] while Marcion's and Justin's evidence, although it has generally been regarded as conclusive, has been challenged by a few scholars. The former's use of Luke has been challenged by J. Knox[6] on the supposition that he used an earlier Gospel which was later used by the writer of the canonical Gospel. But there are several reasons why this theory must be rejected. There is no doubt

as important as discussions about the purpose). B. Gärtner, *The Areopagus Speech and Natural Revelation* (1955), assumes it. Cf. also W. L. Knox, *op. cit.*; R. R. Williams, *The Acts of the Apostles* (*TC*, 1953); E. M. Blaiklock, *The Acts of the Apostles* (*TNT*, 1959), and W. Grundmann, *Das Evangelium nach Lukas*, p. 39. Feine-Behm-Kümmel (*op. cit.*, p. 123) cite the following recent scholars as rejecting Lucan authorship, Beyer, Conzelmann, Haenchen, Vielhauer, Klein, Evans and O'Neill, to whom should be added Kümmel himself. E. Trocmé, *Le 'Livre des Actes' et l'Histoire* (1957) refers throughout his book to 'l'auteur *ad Theophilum*'.

[1] Cf. Creed, *op. cit.*, pp. xxv ff., for these parallels.

[2] Cf. *ibid.*, pp. xxvii, xxviii, for details.

[3] Cf. Tertullian, *Adv. Marc.* iv.

[4] Cf. Creed, *op. cit.*, p. xxvii. J. N. Geldenhuys (*Commentary on the Gospel of Luke*, 1950, p. 30) cites especially Justin's *Dialogue*, 78, 88, 100, 103, 105, 106.

[5] To this evidence may be added that of Polycarp (see note on p. 16 n.4 on Köster's opinion on this).

[6] *Marcion and the New Testament* (1942).

that the orthodox apologists maintained that Marcion's Gospel was based on the canonical Gospel of Luke. If this had been known by Marcion's supporters to be incorrect, they could at once have countered the orthodox arguments. It is difficult to believe that the defenders of the faith would have based their attack on so insecure a foundation as the antiquity and apostolicity of the four Gospels if Knox's theory is correct. Moreover, the customary trend in Gospel editing as far as it is known suggests that editors tended to omit certain material found in their sources, while at the same time adding other material. But Marcion included no material not in Luke, although he appears to have omitted considerable portions which are present in that Gospel. A perfectly satisfactory explanation may be found in Marcion's known propensity to abbreviate, although it is not always clear why he did so in some of his omissions from Luke. It is further to be noted that the reconstructed text of Marcion's Luke made by Harnack and used as a basis for Knox's linguistic and stylistic arguments is conjectural in character and cannot for that reason form a secure foundation for challenging the general assumption that Marcion used the Gospel of Luke. Knox himself is not unmindful of this factor, but believes that the reconstructed text may in general be relied upon. The effect of his theory on the date of Luke will at once be evident, for it means that in its final form Luke must be subsequent to Marcion's adoption of its earlier form as his Gospel.

Justin's use of Luke has been challenged by J. C. O'Neill,[1] on the ground that Justin used the same special source as Luke used.[2] This common source, according to O'Neill, may have been much earlier, but the Gospel itself was not produced much before Justin's time. He tentatively suggests a date between AD 115 and 130 for Luke-Acts.[3] The fundamental weakness of this position is that it assumes that Luke, in a period of from ten to twenty years, could have gained such authority in the Christian Church that Marcion could be sure of gaining support in his exclusive choice of this Gospel. Surely such a proposition is completely incredible and must at once be abandoned. The earlier evidence for the circulation of Matthew and Mark suggests that by

[1] *Op. cit.*, pp. 28 ff.

[2] In his review of O'Neill's book, H. F. D. Sparks rejects the idea that Justin did not know Luke, which is the real basis of O'Neill's dating of Luke-Acts (*JTS*, n.s., xiv, 1963, pp. 457 ff.).

[3] *Op. cit.*, p. 25.

Marcion's time these other Gospels had been widely used and it is incredible to suppose that Marcion could have ousted these Gospels with one produced only a few years before and yet regarded as basic for his *Apostolikon*.

A date about AD 100 has sometimes been supposed on the ground that Luke knew of and consulted Josephus' *Antiquities* (published about AD 94). Part of the evidence consists of items cited in Acts, which will be mentioned later (see pp. 314 f.), but for Luke's Gospel it has been maintained that Luke iii. 1, 2 shows dependence on Josephus. The argument assumes that when Luke referred to Lysanias as tetrarch of Abilene he obtained this information from Josephus. In one passage[1] the latter refers to Abila as a place which had previously been in the tetrarchy of Lysanias and in another passage[2] he describes it simply as Abila of Lysanias. On the other hand Josephus also mentions a Lysanias who was killed by Anthony (36 BC)[3] and if Luke, as is alleged, was thinking of this man his chronology was clearly wrong. But since this Lysanias had only a brief reign and the place was named after him, it is reasonable to suppose that one of his descendants of the same name may later have been appointed tetrarch. Unless it can be established that Josephus implies only one Lysanias, and that Luke could not have obtained his information elsewhere, there is no ground for maintaining that Luke was subsequent to Josephus. Indeed, Sir William Ramsay[4] cites an inscription from ancient Abilene which refers to a Lysanias who must have been tetrarch there some time between AD 14 and 29 and this would suit Luke's reference. The Josephus theory must be as strongly discounted as the last.

c. Arguments for a late first-century date

A date in the ninth decade of the first century is favoured by most scholars on the following grounds: (1) On the basis of the theory that Luke used Mark, it is naturally required that Luke should be later than Mark. This fixes the *terminus a quo* at about AD 68 (see discussion on pp. 68 ff.). (2) A comparison of Mark xiii. 14 with Luke xxi. 20 shows that for Mark's 'abomination of desolation' which was to be set up where it ought not, Luke records that Jerusalem will be surrounded by armies. It is usually assumed that Luke has deliberately altered Mark

---

[1] *Antiquities*, xx. 7. 1.   [2] *Antiquities*, xix. 5. 1.   [3] *Antiquities*, xv. 4. 1.
[4] *The Bearing of Recent Discoveries on the Trustworthiness of the New Testament* (1915), pp. 297 f.

because by the time of writing he knew precisely what had happened.[1] In other words this is a *vaticinium ex eventu*, and would require for Luke a date subsequent to AD 70. (3) The fact that Luke wrote after many others had made the attempt is supposed by some to require an interval subsequent to AD 70, since there is no evidence of 'many' Gospels being produced before AD 70.[2] (4) It is sometimes assumed that no great interval could have separated Luke's Gospel and Matthew's,[3] and since the latter is generally dated in the ninth decade, Luke's must be also.

It is surprising that on such inconclusive evidence as the above there should be such widespread acceptance of a date between AD 75 and 85, but the insecurity of the evidence will become clear when the following considerations are weighed. No doubt the preference for this date is due to the general feeling that none of the alternatives is more convincing. Whether Luke used Mark as a written source or not, no great interval need have separated them, for if he did use Mark he may well have gained access to it very soon after it was written. After all, they were both members of Paul's group of companions. Since it has been shown that Mark need not be dated as late as the period immediately prior to the siege of Jerusalem (see pp. 69 f.), it follows that on this score Luke may also be earlier.[4]

The argument from Luke xxi. 20 is not conclusive for the following reasons: (1) It assumes that Luke's statement could have been formulated only after the event, but if the argument is valid, why is Luke's description so vague?[5] Why does not Luke give some indication of the nature of the siege to identify it more closely? (2) Moreover, is it quite

[1] Creed (*The Gospel according to St. Luke*, 1930, p. xxii) considered this to be a conclusive deduction from Lk. xxi. 20, which made it impossible to date Luke before AD 70. He admitted that taken on its own Lk. xxi might be compatible with a date in the early sixties, but claimed that when Lk. xxi was compared with Mk. xiii this was impossible. But see a criticism of this below.

[2] Geldenhuys (*Commentary on the Gospel of Luke*, 1950, p. 33) mentions this view as a secondary argument for this dating.

[3] Cf. V. Taylor, *The Gospels*, p. 73. G. D. Kilpatrick (*Origins of the Gospel according to St. Matthew*, p. 7) considers that Matthew's and Luke's independent use of two common sources, Mark and Q, requires that they be dated sufficiently near to each to avoid the possibility of one losing his independence of the other.

[4] T. W. Manson (*Studies in the Gospels and Epistles*, pp. 28 ff.), who dated Mark about AD 60, allocated Luke-Acts to the period about AD 70, somewhat earlier than the more generally held theory.

[5] Cf. S. C. Carpenter, *Christianity according to St. Luke* (1919), p. 230.

certain that Luke's statement could not have been a genuine prophecy of Jesus? Much Gospel criticism is so dominated by rigid source hypotheses that it is assumed that the only possible explanation in a case like this is that one author has modified the other for some specific motive, either theological, historical or perhaps linguistic. But it is not impossible to suppose that Mark (and Matthew) used the more obscure 'abomination of desolation' and Luke the more precise 'Jerusalem surrounded by armies' because our Lord used both expressions.[1] To Matthew the phrase at once linked the Lord's prediction with the book of Daniel, where the phrase also occurs, and would, therefore, emphasize its significance as a fulfilment of Old Testament prophecy. To Luke, on the other hand, with Gentile readers specifically in mind, the explanation regarding the surrounding armies would fit in better with his purpose.[2] That this explanation of the words of the Lord was current before AD 70 seems proved by the fact that many Jerusalem Christians fled to Pella in obedience to their Master's words when the Roman armies began to invest Jerusalem.[3] Moreover, if Luke was interpreting Mark xiii after the event, why did not Matthew do the same, since his Gospel is generally dated contemporaneously? Furthermore, history has known other instances of accurate prediction several years before the event (e.g. Savonarola's prediction of the capture of Rome[4]) and there is every indication in our Lord's character and personality to suggest that prediction of this kind should be expected from Him. No great confidence can therefore be placed in the argument from Luke xxi. 20.

The third and fourth grounds cited above are no more than doubtful inferences. There are no indications in Luke's preface as to the date when the 'many' other attempts were made and there is nothing whatever to exclude a period well before AD 70 for such literary activity. As to the relation between Matthew and Luke, more will be said in

[1] Cf. F. Blass, *Philology of the Gospels* (1898), p. 46.
[2] J. N. Geldenhuys (*op. cit.*, p. 32), who regards Luke's readers as mainly Roman Christians, suggests that Luke would never have called the Roman army or a Roman leader 'the abomination'.
[3] Reported by Eusebius, *HE*, iii. 32.
[4] Mentioned by Blass, *op.cit.*, pp. 41 f. C. H. Dodd (*JRS*, xxxvii, 1947, pp. 47–54) contends that Luke's version is not coloured by the events of AD 66–70. It is coloured, in fact, by Old Testament references to the fall of Jerusalem in 586 BC. R. M. Grant (*A Historical Introduction to the New Testament*, 1963, p. 69) refers to Dodd's argument with some favour.

discussing the Synoptic problem (see pp. 136 ff.), but for the purpose of dating it must be noted that no confidence can be placed on relative dating of the Gospels until their literary relationships can be determined in a manner independent of pure conjecture.

d. Arguments for a date prior to AD 70

The remaining possibility is a date prior to AD 70, and those favouring this dating generally fix upon a date about AD 60–61.[1] The supporting arguments for this are closely tied up with the date of Acts, but if the latter may reasonably be dated about AD 63 (see pp. 307 ff. for the discussion of this) Luke must clearly be before that. Moreover, Luke had spent some time in Palestine while Paul was imprisoned at Caesarea. There is indeed a we-passage which suggests that Luke was with Paul when he visited Philip the Evangelist (see pp. 335 f.). It is a reasonable conjecture (although no more than a conjecture) that Luke collected up much of his own special material while at Caesarea, and it is an equally reasonable conjecture that he would have proceeded to write his Gospel soon after.[2] If these conjectures are correct they would support the date mentioned above.

Once the argument from Luke xxi. 20 is dismissed, there is really little tangible data to enable the date of the Gospel to be specifically fixed.

VI. LANGUAGE

Luke's Greek is remarkable for its adaptability. The preface is modelled on classical patterns, which gives some insight into his cultural background. But after writing i. 1–4, he drops the literary style for a type of Greek strongly flavoured with Semitisms, which he uses for the infancy narratives. Subsequent to this he generally uses what may be

[1] Harnack (*The Date of Acts and the Synoptic Gospels*, 1911, pp. 90 ff.) was a notable advocate for an early date for Luke on the strength of an early date for Acts.

[2] Those who accept Lucan authorship, but who date the Gospel about AD 80, must suppose that Luke was several years collecting his own information. It is difficult to believe that he would have made notes of the testimony he received before AD 60 and have done nothing about it for another twenty years. The Proto-Luke hypothesis (see pp. 168 ff.) does nothing to alleviate the difficulty, for under this theory the first draft of Luke must have been carried about for a similar period. Cf. Streeter (*The Four Gospels*, pp. 217–221) and V. Taylor (*Behind the Third Gospel*, 1926, pp. 202–215) who both regard Proto-Luke as having been written soon after Luke left Caesarea.

described as a good literary *Koiné* Greek,[1] although even here some Semitisms are found. Clearly Luke did not consider that the literary style of the preface was at all suitable for the narration of the life and teaching of Jesus. But in his choice of suitable literary styles he shows himself to be a considerable literary artist.

Particularly noticeable is the type of Septuagint Greek used for the infancy narratives which seems to have been strongly influenced by the style of the canticles which he includes in his narratives.[2] The strongly Hebraistic character of Luke's Greek in this section is admirably adapted to link the incarnation of Jesus with the Old Testament history and that may well be the effect that Luke wished to create. By his obvious familiarity with the Septuagint, which he often cites throughout the Gospel, Luke's Greek has become strongly coloured with Hebraisms. At the same time Luke's vocabulary is unusually rich and varied for a New Testament writer, for he uses several hundred words[3] which no other New Testament writer uses.

CONTENTS

I. THE PROLOGUE (i. 1–4)

II. THE INFANCY NARRATIVES (i. 5–ii. 52)

The foretelling of John the Baptist's birth (i. 5–25). The annunciation to Mary (i. 26–38). Mary visits Elizabeth (i. 39–56). John's birth (i. 57–80). Jesus' birth (ii. 1–20). The circumcision and presentation of Christ (ii. 21–40). Jesus in Jerusalem when twelve years old (ii. 41–52).

[1] That Luke was acquainted with good literary style is apparent in the main body of the Gospel, when he uses certain idioms which are relatively absent from the other New Testament writers, e.g. the optative, the articular infinitive, the use of the article in indirect questions, the use of πρίν with the subjunctive or optative (cf. Creed, *The Gospel according to St. Luke*, 1930, p. lxxxii, for details and examples).

[2] For a fuller discussion of the linguistic characteristics of the infancy narratives, see pp. 163 ff.

[3] Sir J. C. Hawkins (*Horae Synopticae*[2], 1909, pp. 201–207) gives a list of 261 words peculiar to this Gospel, 58 shared by Luke and Acts only, and 413 peculiar to Acts. R. Morgenthaler (*Statistik des Neutestamentlichen Wortschatzes*, 1958, p. 170) gives the numbers as 266, 60 and 415 respectively, excluding proper names.

III. THE PREPARATION FOR THE MINISTRY (iii. 1–iv. 13)

The mission of John the Baptist (iii. 1–20). The baptism of Jesus (iii. 21, 22). The genealogy of Jesus (iii. 23–38). The temptation (iv. 1–13).

IV. THE GALILAEAN MINISTRY (iv. 14–ix. 50)

a. The beginnings (iv. 14–44)

Jesus rejected at Nazareth (iv. 16–30); a miracle in the synagogue at Capernaum (iv. 31–37); Peter's mother-in-law healed (iv. 38, 39); other healings in the evening (iv. 40, 41); Jesus' withdrawal to a lonely place, followed by further preaching (iv. 42–44).

b. The call of the disciples (v. 1–vi. 16)

The miraculous draught of fishes, and Simon's call (v. 1–11); a leper and a paralytic healed (v. 12–26); the call of Levi (v. 27–32); an enquiry about fasting (v. 33–39); controversies over the sabbath (vi. 1–11); the appointment of the Twelve (vi. 12–16).

c. The Sermon on the Plain (vi. 17–49)

Introduction (vi. 17–19); Beatitudes (vi. 20–23); woes (vi. 24–26); other sayings (vi. 27–49).

d. At Capernaum and the surrounding district (vii. 1–viii. 56)

The healing of the centurion's slave (vii. 1–10); the raising of the widow's son at Nain (vii. 11–17); John the Baptist's enquiry about Jesus (vii. 18–23); Jesus' testimony about John (vii. 24–30); His estimate of His own generation (vii. 31–35); the anointing by the sinful woman (vii. 36–50); the women disciples of Jesus (viii. 1–3).

The parable of the sower and the soils, and its interpretation; the reason for parables, and their right use (viii. 4–18).

Jesus' true family relationships (viii. 19–21).

A series of miracles (viii. 22–56): the stilling of the storm, and healing of the Gerasene demoniac, the woman with the haemorrhage and Jairus' daughter.

e. Incidents centring on the Twelve (ix. 1–50)

Their mission (ix. 1–6); Herod's reaction to Jesus (ix. 7–9); the return of the Twelve and the feeding of the five thousand (ix. 10–17); Peter's confession at Caesarea Philippi (ix. 18–21); first prediction of the passion (ix. 22); conditions for discipleship (ix. 23–27); the transfiguration (ix. 28–36); healing of the epileptic boy (ix. 37–43); second prediction of the passion (ix. 44, 45); a dispute about greatness (ix. 46–48); Jesus' attitude towards the strange exorcist (ix. 49, 50).

v. FROM GALILEE TO JERUSALEM (ix. 51–xix. 27)

a. Jesus and the Samaritans (ix. 51–x. 37)

A Samaritan village unwilling to receive Jesus (ix. 51–56); tests for aspiring disciples (ix. 57–62); the mission of the seventy (x. 1–20); Jesus' thanksgiving and pronouncement of blessing on the disciples (x. 21–24); the lawyer's enquiries and the parable of the good Samaritan (x. 25–37).

b. On the value of meditation and prayer (x. 38–xi. 13)

Mary and Martha (x. 38–42); the Lord's prayer (xi. 1–4); the friend at midnight (xi. 5–13).

c. Jesus and the Pharisees (xi. 14–54)

The Beelzebub controversy (xi. 14–23); the return of the evil spirit (xi. 24–26); a blessing pronounced on Jesus' mother (xi. 27, 28); Jesus condemns His contemporaries for sign-seeking (xi. 29–32); sayings about light (xi. 33–36); criticism of the Pharisees and the lawyers (xi. 37–54).

d. Jesus' advice to His disciples (xii. 1–53)

Exhortations to fearless witness (xii. 1–12); parable of the rich fool (xii. 13–21); about anxiety (xii. 22–34); about watchfulness and responsibility (xii. 35–48); warnings about the repercussions of Jesus' mission on family life (xii. 49–53).

e. Various sayings and events (xii. 54–xix. 27)

On interpreting signs (xii. 54–56); on settling legal disputes (xii. 57–59); examples of catastrophes cited to press the need for repentance (xiii. 1–9); the crippled woman healed, and consequent sabbath controversy (xiii. 10–17); parables of the mustard seed and the leaven (xiii. 18–21); sayings about the coming kingdom (xiii. 22–30); Jesus leaves Galilee (xiii. 31–33); lament over Jerusalem (xiii. 34, 35).

Jesus dines out (xiv. 1–24): sabbath healing of a man with dropsy (xiv. 1–6); saying about choosing the lowest places (xiv. 7–14); parable of the great supper (xiv. 15–24).

Sayings on discipleship (xiv. 25–35): cost of discipleship (xiv. 25–33); saying about savourless salt (xiv. 34, 35).

The parables of the lost sheep, lost coin, prodigal son and unjust steward (xv. 1–xvi. 13). Warnings against Pharisaic hypocrisy (xvi. 14–18). Dives and Lazarus (xvi. 19–31). Teaching about offences, forgiveness, faith and rewards (xvii. 1–10).

The healing of ten lepers (xvii. 11–19). Teaching about the end of the age (xvii. 20–37). Parables of the unjust judge, and the Pharisee and the tax-collector (xviii. 1–14). Young children blessed (xviii. 15–17). The rich young man (xviii. 18–30). The third prediction of the passion (xviii. 31–34). Events in Jericho (xviii. 35–xix. 27): a blind man healed; Zacchaeus entertains Jesus; the parable of the pounds.

VI. IN JERUSALEM (xix. 28–xxi. 38)

The entry (xix. 28–38). Prediction of destruction of Jerusalem (xix. 39–44). Cleansing of, and daily teaching in, the temple (xix. 45–48). Jesus' authority challenged (xx. 1–8). The parable of the wicked husbandmen (xx. 9–19) and questions on tribute, the resurrection and the son of David (xx. 20–44). Warnings and commendations (xx. 45–xxi. 4). The eschatological discourse (xxi. 5–36). Summary of the Jerusalem ministry (xxi. 37, 38).

VII. THE PASSION AND RESURRECTION NARRATIVES
(xxii. 1–xxiv. 53)

The preparation (xxii. 1–13). The institution of the last supper (xxii. 14–20). The betrayal predicted (xxii. 21–23). The disciples' dispute over greatness (xxii. 24–30). Peter's denial predicted (xxii. 31–34). The incident of the two swords (xxii. 35–38). In Gethsemane (xxii. 39–46). The arrest, trial and crucifixion (xxii. 47–xxiii. 49). The burial (xxiii. 50–56). The resurrection, the appearances on the Emmaus road and in Jerusalem (xxiv. 1–49). The ascension (xxiv. 50–53).

CHAPTER FIVE

THE SYNOPTIC PROBLEM

I. THE NATURE OF THE PROBLEM

Arising out of a detailed study of the three Synoptic Gospels is the important question of their relationship to each other, and this is affected by the following main considerations.

a. Similarity of arrangement

All these Gospels are based on the same general historical structure. They begin with the baptism and temptation of Jesus; they deal in varying detail with the public ministry in Galilee; they all portray Peter's confession at Caesarea Philippi as the turning-point in the ministry; they all describe the last journey to Jerusalem, the trial, the crucifixion and resurrection. Moreover, there is a high proportion of the Gospel material common to all three Gospels.[1]

b. Similarity of style and wording

In many sections of the Gospels not only is there similarity of contents but also of vocabulary. Examples of such close verbal agreements may be seen in the following incidents—the healing of the leper (Mt. viii. 1 ff.; Mk. i. 40 ff.; Lk. v. 12 ff.), the question of Jesus' authority (Mt. xxi. 23 ff.; Mk. xi. 27 ff.; Lk. xx. 1 ff.), portions of the eschatological discourse (Mt. xxiv. 4 ff., 15 ff.; Mk. xiii. 5 ff., 14 ff.; Lk. xxi. 8 ff., 20 ff.), and the request of Joseph of Arimathaea for the body of Jesus (Mt. xxvii. 58; Mk. xv. 43; Lk. xxiii. 52).[2]

c. Similarities in two Gospels only

(1) There are some cases where sections recorded in all three Gospels agree more closely in style and wording in two as compared with the

[1] For further details, cf. p. 126.

[2] These parallels are best studied in a synopsis of the Gospels in the Greek text. The most convenient is that of A. Huck, *Synopsis of the First Three Gospels*[9] (ed. H. Lietzmann, English edition by F. L. Cross, 1949).

Cf. B. de Solages, *A Greek Synopsis of the Gospels* (1959), for a mathematical comparison. For an English Harmony, cf. J. M. Thompson, *The Synoptic Gospels* (1910) and H. F. D. Sparks, *A Synopsis of the Gospels* (1964).

third, and this phenomenon is not without some significance in determining their origins and relationships. (2) But the more important data
under this heading relate to Matthew and Luke, which contain a considerable amount of material common to both but omitted from Mark.
Most of this material comprises the teaching of Jesus, with very little
narrative and no part of the passion story. As with the material common to all three, the similarity in this Matthew–Luke material often
extends to the wording (cf. Mt. iii. 7–10; Lk. iii. 7–9, relating to the
preaching of John the Baptist; Mt. vi. 24; Lk. xvi. 13, on serving two
masters; Mt. xi. 4 ff.; Lk. vii. 22 ff., containing Jesus' answer to John
the Baptist's question; Mt. xxiii. 37–39; Lk. xiii. 34, 35, recording
Jesus' lament over Jerusalem).

d. Divergences

The problem would be less difficult to solve were it not for the considerable differences both in arrangement and vocabulary over many
points of detail. Some sections of common material have little verbal
similarity, while others are placed in different historical settings. The
healing of the centurion's servant, for instance (Mt. viii. 5 ff.; Lk. vii.
1 ff.), is not only placed in a different order in the two Gospels, but
differs widely in its narration. The passion narratives of the three
Gospels, while conforming fairly closely to a similar sequence, nevertheless contain many differences of detail and wording.

In addition to the difference just mentioned, each of the three
Synoptics has certain sections peculiar to it. This is particularly so in
the cases of Matthew and Luke. The birth narratives of the first and
third Gospels are quite different and bear very little relationship to each
other, while Luke has a long section, commonly known as the 'travel'
narrative (ix. 51–xviii. 14), which largely comprises his own material.
Matthew records such stories as Peter's walking on the water and the
coin in the fish's mouth, which neither of the others contains. Matthew's Sermon on the Mount is related only loosely to Luke's Sermon
on the Plain, which is much shorter, although some of the omitted
material occurs elsewhere in Luke in scattered contexts. Other details
will be given later, when source theories are discussed.

Whereas the three Synoptics often agree in sections common to
them all, Matthew and Mark often agree against Luke, and Luke and
Mark against Matthew, and sometimes, though more rarely, Matthew
and Luke against Mark.

These are the basic details which constitute the problem. A brief historical summary will now be given of the various solutions which have been proposed.

II. A BRIEF HISTORICAL SURVEY OF SOLUTIONS

Little attention was given to this problem until the eighteenth century, although its existence had been obvious from earliest times. The widespread influence of Tatian's *Diatessaron* is sufficient evidence of the desire for the removal of the difficulties by means of harmonization. Even when the separate Gospels displaced Tatian's harmony in the Eastern Church and were indisputably established in the West, the difficulties were resolved by harmonization without any attempt being made to settle the problem of origins or relationship. Indeed, these questions were not seriously considered until they were forced to the forefront by the upsurge of rationalism in the eighteenth century.[1]

a. The original Gospel hypothesis

The first solution suggested was that of G. E. Lessing,[2] who postulated that our Gospels were different translations or abstracts from an old Aramaic *Gospel of the Nazarenes*, which Jerome mentions as still being current among the sect of the Nazarenes in the fourth century. This was further elaborated in a complicated and rather artificial manner by J. G. Eichhorn,[3] who not only proposed that nine different Gospels issued from the original Aramaic (which he considered to have been an apostolic rough draft for use in the instruction of teachers) but that the Synoptics were the concluding phenomena of this literary process.

b. The fragment theory

The unsatisfactory character of Eichhorn's solution led F. Schleiermacher[4] to produce a different, though no more satisfactory, suggestion. He postulated that the apostles wrote down records of the words of Jesus as they were known to witnesses. These were later required

---

[1] It is interesting to note that John Calvin, who wrote a commentary on *A Harmonie upon the three Evangelistes, Matthewe, Marke and Luke* (Eng. Tr. by E. Paget, 1584), chose this form for convenience and not because he was seriously concerned about the Synoptic problem.

[2] *Neue Hypothese über die Evangelisten als bloss menschliche Geschichtsschreiber* (1778).

[3] *Historische-kritische Einleitung in das Neue Testament* (1812).

[4] *A critical Essay on the Gospel of St. Luke* (Eng. Tr. 1825).

for use beyond the borders of Palestine and various collections were made. One teacher might have collected miracle-stories, another sayings, a third passion narratives, and so on. Luke's Prologue was appealed to in support of this hypothesis, and the collected records were then held to have been used in the production of the canonical Gospels. The major weaknesses of this hypothesis are the absence of any traces of such early records and the inability of the theory to account for the remarkable similarities in the Synoptic Gospels, not only in vocabulary but in the sequence of events. Its importance, however, cannot be lightly dismissed since it has much in common with certain types of form criticism. It may also be said to have set the stage for the appearance of various other fragment hypotheses in attempted solutions of other New Testament problems.[1]

c. The oral theory

In view of the lack of sufficient data on the state of Gospel traditions prior to our written Gospels, it is natural to investigate the possibility that similarities and divergences arose in the course of a period of oral transmission. Even if the theory can claim no notable recent supporters, it merits careful consideration because it has at least some affinity with form criticism.

In the era during which the first indications of the urge towards a scientific study of the New Testament arose, the idea that oral tradition lay at the base of the Synoptic material was mooted by G. Herder.[2] Soon after this, in 1818, J. K. L. Gieseler,[3] produced what might be called the prototype of the oral theory, maintaining that the apostolic preaching would form itself into similar oral traditions which would then form a kind of basic oral Gospel. This oral Gospel was preserved in the original Aramaic, but the needs of the Gentile mission would give rise to the demand for a Greek translation. This basic Aramaic and the Greek translation later became the main source for the three Evangelists, being used differently according to the different approach of each writer. Thus Matthew produced a genuine Palestinian Gospel,

---

[1] The theory of W. L. Knox that various 'tracts' lay behind Mark is similar to Schleiermacher's theory. Cf. his *Sources of the Synoptic Gospels: I St. Mark* (1953).

[2] *Von der Regel der Zustimmung unserer Evangelien* (1797), reproduced in *Werke zur Religion und Theologie*, 12 (1810).

[3] *Historisch-kritischer Versuch über die Entstehung und die frühesten Schicksale der schriftlichen Evangelien* (1818).

Mark a modified Palestinian and Luke a Pauline Gospel. The literary differences between them were conditioned by the respective authors' training and ability. There are some similarities between this and later oral theories, but one significant difference should be noted. Gieseler disputed the possibility of any systematic learning by heart, on which Westcott, for instance, placed such stress.

Westcott's presentation of the oral theory may be regarded as its classic formulation,[1] which for a time secured many adherents, particularly among those who rejected the German source theories dominant in his day. The main idea of his theory may be briefly summarized as follows.

1. Since the Jews would not commit to writing their mass of oral traditions, it is improbable that the first Christian leaders would have entertained doing so.[2] The literary traditions of the Jews, with their great emphasis on oral transmission as the main educative medium, would encourage the Church to prefer oral rather than written teaching. This would mean a considerable period during which the traditions would be floating in an oral form.

2. Since the apostolic circle was primarily composed of preachers and not writers, literary enterprises would not at once have occurred to them.[3] Here Westcott assumed that, on the one hand, the work of preaching would occupy the apostles to such an extent that literary methods of propaganda would be ruled out, and, on the other hand, that these men by education and culture would have been unfitted for the task, even if its possibilities had been recognized. Nevertheless, he maintained that this disinclination towards an immediate reduction of the Gospel material to writing was later invaluable since 'the very form of the Gospels was only determined by the experience of teaching'.[4]

3. Since the Gospels arose out of the recurring needs of the community, the most attention would naturally be given to those narratives which were most used in the apostolic preaching, and this would admirably account for the space devoted to the passion and resurrection narratives.[5] Such a feature accords with the testimony of the Acts and the Epistles.

4. Westcott claimed that the testimony of the Apostolic Fathers, in so far as they bear any witness to the origin of the Gospels, supports an

[1] B. F. Westcott, *An Introduction to the Study of the Gospels*[7] (1888, first published in 1851).

[2] *Ibid.*, p. 167.   [3] *Ibid.*, pp. 168 ff.   [4] *Ibid.*, p. 170.   [5] *Ibid.*, pp. 174 ff.

oral theory.[1] Papias, for instance, expressed a definite preference for oral testimony himself and may be reflecting a much earlier tendency. Moreover the same writer implies that Mark wrote down some of the things he had heard Peter narrate.

5. Assuming that Mark's Gospel, by reason of its 'vivid simplicity', was the 'most direct representation of the Evangelic tradition', which was the common foundation on which the others were reared, West-cott[2] regarded Matthew's and Luke's Gospels as types of recension of the simple narrative. Matthew preserves the Hebraic form of the tradition while Luke presents the Greek form.[3]

Subsequent to Westcott's formulation of the theory, two other writers introduced significant modifications. G. Wetzel[4] evolved the theory that one apostle (Matthew) was specially assigned to oral instruction. As a result of constant repetition of the instruction the tradition would acquire fixation. The hearers would pass on the tradition in the form taught and would often make notes to aid their memories. Such notes would later have been used to compile the accounts to which Luke makes reference in his preface, and the use of such notes by the writers of the Synoptic Gospels would, in Wetzel's view, account for the similarities and differences in their accounts.

A different modification of the theory was proposed by A. Wright.[5] In his opinion Peter, in Jerusalem, gave Aramaic oral instruction, while Mark acted as his interpreter for Greek-speaking people. Those so instructed became catechists to other churches.[6] At the same time in Jerusalem another collection of material arose, which Wright called by the name Logia. In order to account for the common structure of the narratives, he further postulated that the order became fixed as an aid to the memory.[7] He also suggested that the oral Gospel may have been divided into weekly church lessons,[8] an idea which may find some

---

[1] Ibid., pp. 184 ff.   [2] Ibid., pp. 209 f.

[3] Westcott (op. cit., pp. 192 f.) maintained that the oral Gospel originally existed in both Aramaic and Greek.

[4] Die synoptischen Evangelien (1883).

[5] Synopsis of the Gospels in Greek (1896); The Composition of the Four Gospels (1890); Some New Testament Problems (1898); St. Luke in Greek (1900).

[6] Wright insisted that some form of definite catechizing which involved committing the teaching to memory was essential for any soundly based oral theory (cf. his Synopsis, p. xiv).

[7] Ibid., p. xvii.

[8] St. Luke in Greek, p. xi.

support from recent suggestions which have been made about the relation between the Gospels and Jewish lectionaries.[1]

But the majority of scholars have discounted the oral theory and their main objections will need to be mentioned.

1. The first difficulty concerns the narrative sequence. Most scholars find it hard to believe that both the precise order of events and in many cases the precise words could have been orally preserved in the forms in which they are recorded in the canonical Gospels. Westcott had maintained that 'the whole period was one in essence, undivided by years or festivals and the record would be marked not so much by divisions of time as by groups of events'.[2] But it is generally felt that this does not adequately account for the variations as well as the similarities occurring in the Gospels. It must not, however, be overlooked that there is little material available for deciding this issue conclusively, and the fact that careful memory work was certainly widely known among the Jews should make the investigator cautious about too much dogmatism regarding it.[3]

2. In view of the fact that both Matthew and Luke always return to Mark's order after deviation from it, it is considered much more reasonable to suppose that they worked from a written rather than from an oral tradition. This is a more weighty objection than the last, for it may be maintained that the Evangelists would not revert to their original sequence so readily after a break if they were relying on memory alone. But again a caution is necessary, since the dominant sequence might have become deeply imprinted through constant repetition, and have reasserted itself almost subconsciously without the intervention of a written reminder. Yet this is pure conjecture and all that can safely be said is that it is possible.[4] It is not surprising that those

[1] Cf. especially the work of A. Farrer and P. Carrington on Mark and A. Guilding on John. For comments on these theories see pp. 62 ff., 286 f.

[2] *Op. cit.*, p. 208.

[3] B. Gerhardsson (*Memory and Manuscript*, 1961) gives a thorough and illuminating study of the methods of oral transmission in rabbinic Judaism and suggests that similar methods would have been adopted among Christians. See pp. 197 ff. for further discussion of Gerhardsson's ideas.

[4] Westcott accounted for the phenomenon by maintaining that Mark's account was the earliest and therefore 'represents most closely the original form' from which the Gospel started (*op. cit.*, p. 211). In this case the dominance of Mark's order would not be surprising. The real crux seems to be whether an extensive Gospel framework could have been transmitted by oral methods. Form criticism is against the possibility, but it cannot be said to be entirely out of the ques-

committed to source criticism rejected the oral solution on this score.

3. A more perplexing difficulty for the oral theory is the omission from Mark of the mass of teaching material incorporated by Matthew and Luke in different ways. If, as Westcott maintained, Mark's Gospel was the first to be produced, why was so little of the teaching incorporated in it? This is by no means an unanswerable objection to the oral theory, for on any theory which assumes Marcan priority the difficulty exists. The postulation of a sayings source 'Q' (see pp. 136 ff.) does little to remove this difficulty unless it can be shown that Mark knew of the existence of Q, but this is open to question. Also, it is not entirely improbable that Mark, if he were the first to produce a written Gospel, preferred narrative material to discourse material and for that reason left the latter for others to reduce to writing. In other words, his omission of the discourse material would be damaging to the oral theory only in so far as it is assumed that he must have reduced to writing at least some samples of all the material in the oral tradition. But this condition is not so evident if his purpose was to highlight the narrative, which he has certainly done with considerable vividness.

The above reasons are nevertheless considered by most scholars to be sufficient to dispense with the oral hypothesis in favour of a source solution. But the shift of emphasis in recent times from the minutiae of source analysis to form criticism has once again brought the oral phase of Gospel transmission into focus and the relationship between the oral theory and form criticism therefore warrants some comment.

As form criticism is fully discussed later, all that is here intended is to give some indication of its points of contact and contrast with the oral theory. These may be summarized as follows.

1. Both emphasize the importance of the pre-literary period of the tradition. It is significant that after a century of source criticism which led, in its extreme forms, to too great a bondage to written origins, the critical pendulum has swung towards the oral tradition, although with a vital difference.

2. Whereas the oral theory denies the use of written sources by the Gospel writers, form criticism generally accepts the documentary framework but pushes the investigation behind those sources. In this

tion in view of the contemporary Jewish procedure in the transmission of rabbinic traditions, although these are mainly didactic. Modern criticism tends to place too much emphasis on editorial practices which were alien to the first-century outlook. It is a danger that must constantly be borne in mind.

way form criticism allows an additional factor (intermediary sources) which the oral theory saw no need to postulate. Nevertheless it must be admitted that focus upon the pre-literary stage cannot fail in some degree to lessen complete confidence in the adequacy of the source hypotheses. This will become clearer later, but if different literary forms could arise from the oral tradition it is perhaps not unreasonable to suggest that each Evangelist may have drawn material from such oral forms, especially if he had had any hand in the shaping of the forms through catechetical instruction. But this latter possibility is generally ruled out by both source and form critics.

3. The oral theory contrasts with the form-critical approach in leaving the oral tradition in a somewhat nebulous state, whereas the latter attempts to classify the various materials into precise literary categories and then proceeds to investigate their *Sitz im Leben* (the life-situation in which they arose). On the face of it the latter method has the appearance of being more scientific and, in so far as it confines itself to classification of literary forms, this may well be justified. Yet it may be said from the side of the less precise oral theory that scientific investigation cannot be based on insufficient data, and no-one can deny that the data available for pre-literary study are not particularly weighty.

d. The mutual dependence hypothesis

Another eighteenth-century proposal which has been subject to many variations is the idea of literary dependence one upon another. J. J. Griesbach,[1] following the suggestion of Augustine, considered Mark as an epitomizer of Matthew, while even Luke was considered to be earlier than Mark. Mark i. 32 became a celebrated illustration of this process, since it appears to conflate the accounts of the other Synoptic Gospels. But this theory, although embraced by the Tübingen school of critics, has been discounted because it fails to do justice to the literary characteristics of Mark.[2] The theory that Mark was basic, followed by

---

[1] *Commentatio qua Marci evangelium totum e Matthaei et Lucae commentariis decerptum esse demonstratur* (1789).

[2] H. G. Jameson (*The Origin of the Synoptic Gospels*, 1922) maintained a theory similar to Griesbach's but he considered that Matthew was basic to Mark and that both Matthew and Mark were used by Luke. It should be noted that the order Matthew–Mark–Luke appears to have been assumed in the second century *milieu* to which the anti-Marcionite Prologue to Luke belonged. Another modification is that of W. Lockton (*Church Quarterly Review*, July, 1922), who suggested that Luke was basic to Mark and that both these were used by Matthew.

Matthew and Luke in that order, was propounded by C. Lachmann.[1]
Although not now acceptable in the form originally suggested, it undoubtedly prepared the way for the source hypothesis, which we shall
consider next.[2]

e. The documentary hypothesis

The basic form of this theory is that the similarities and divergences
can be accounted for by the postulation of two written sources, one
of which was the canonical Mark or an earlier written form of it, and
the other a common source used by Matthew and Luke in different
ways. This latter source was named Q, probably after the German
Quelle (source). The Mark-Q theory may be regarded as the basic
element in modern source criticism of the Synoptic Gospels. But many
of the variations between Matthew and Luke are difficult to account
for adequately under this theory and this has led to a number of proposed modifications. In many hypotheses Q became not a single source
but a multiplication of sources,[3] and this understandably tended to
weaken confidence in the hypothesis.

Owing to the cosmopolitan characteristics of the so-called Q-docu-
ment under the two document theory, B. H. Streeter[4] posited a four
source hypothesis which has won wide support and will merit detailed
examination. For the purpose of the present survey, it may be said that
Streeter's solution supplied two new developments in the study of the
Synoptic problem. In the first place, he strictly limited the source Q
to that material which was used by both Matthew and Luke but not
Mark, and two other sources were proposed for Matthew's (M) and
Luke's (L) special sayings material. This meant that Matthew used
Mark, Q and M as his main sources, and Luke used Mark, Q and L. In
the second place Streeter called attention to the need for noting the
locality from which the different earlier sources originated. Mark was
the Roman Gospel, Q was probably based on Antioch, M represented

[1] 'De ordine narrationum in evangeliis synopticis', *TSK*, 8 (1835), pp. 570 ff.
[2] The view that Luke used Matthew was held by E. Simons, *Hat der dritte
Evangelist den kanonischen Matthäus benutzt?* (1880; cited by Stanton, *The Gospels
as Historical Documents*, II, p. 30). Most recently this has been advocated by A.
Farrer in *Studies in the Gospels* (ed. D. E. Nineham, 1955), pp. 55 ff.
[3] J. Moffatt (*ILNT*³, 1918, pp. 197 ff.) gives sixteen reconstructions of Q,
none of which agrees with any other in detail. See the later discussion on Q on
pp. 136 ff.
[4] *The Four Gospels* (1924).

a Jerusalem sayings-document and L represented the Caesarean tradition, probably oral in character.[1] These proposals were admittedly
conjectural, but Streeter considered that the association of sources with
important centres guaranteed their authority, but when the Gospels
became accepted the preservation of these earlier sources, with the exception of Mark, was rendered unnecessary. While there have been
many modifications of this type of four document theory and a decided lessening of emphasis upon a multiplication of written sources
due largely to the influence of form criticism, it is still widely regarded,
at least among British scholars, as the most workable hypothesis of
Gospel origins.[2]

f. The form-historical method

In reaction to the multiplicity of written sources which had been
postulated and the minute attention which had been devoted to source
analysis, a movement sprang up to investigate more closely the manner
in which these sources had themselves been codified from the oral
tradition. This movement, called in Germany *Die formgeschichtliche
Methode* but generally known in England as form criticism, had as its
aim not only to classify the material into 'forms' of tradition, but also
to attempt to discover the historical situation (*Sitz im Leben*) in which
they grew. This type of approach will require detailed examination in
a separate chapter, for it has had considerable influence in recent New
Testament criticism. Its chief advocates have been M. Dibelius, R.
Bultmann, M. Albertz in Germany, B. S. Easton, W. E. Bundy and
F. C. Grant in America, and E. B. Redlich, R. H. Lightfoot, V. Taylor
and D. E. Nineham in this country.[3]

III. THE FOUR SOURCE THEORY

It has already been shown that the four source theory is really a modification of the two source theory. Still fundamental to it is the assumption that the basic sources of Matthew and Luke were Mark and Q.

[1] Vincent Taylor, who accepts much of Streeter's theory, in his recent *The Life
and Ministry of Jesus* (1954), p. 14, maintains only Mark, Q and M as written sources
and this approach is representative of a wide circle of scholars committed to
the four source theory.

[2] Cf. F. C. Grant, *The Gospels, their origin and growth* (1957), pp. 50, 51, who
holds to a multiple source theory, which is essentially based on Streeter's
proposals.

[3] See pp. 178 ff. for a full discussion of form criticism.

In other words it preserves what has become a basic principle of Synoptic criticism, i.e. that the similarities observable in the Synoptic Gospels can be accounted for only on the basis of literary dependence. The king-pin of the whole hypothesis is Marcan priority, which has become an almost undisputed canon of criticism. The reasons for this are discussed in the next section, but it should be noted that however strong these reasons appear to be, the inferences drawn from them can never be finally conclusive. It may be the best explanation of the phenomena, but it cannot be proved because the data available for tracing the processes of early Christian transmission are too limited.

As far as Q is concerned its postulation is much more hypothetical, and this is clear from Streeter's plea that it should be limited to the material common to Matthew and Luke, but excluded from Mark. As will be seen later the delineation and even the very existence of Q has been much discussed, particularly in recent years, and Streeter's conception of it cannot be regarded as unchallengeable. Nevertheless the assumption that it is basic to Synoptic criticism is still generally dominant. Modern criticism finds it difficult to conceive that the common teaching material in Matthew and Luke could have come about in any other way than by their respective authors both using an earlier source. But the New Testament investigator must guard against the fallacious assumption that what is inconceivable to him must be false. It may have happened in a manner alien to twentieth-century experience of the transmission of ideas. Q may after all be no more than the creation of modern imagination. As to Streeter's other sources, M and L, the postulation of these was just as logical as the postulation of various recensions of Q, but little more so. The theory is more realistic in allowing that L may be oral tradition rather than a written source, but this concession to oral transmission is made only because this material exists in a single tradition instead of a double or triple tradition.[1]

Our next task will be to examine the evidence for the four source hypothesis.

---

[1] Although this concession to oral tradition is made for L, it is maintained that it was probably reduced to writing before Luke left Caesarea. This assumption has led H. Montefiore to question whether the L hypothesis, in the form in which it is generally held, is tenable since the document would not have survived the shipwreck in which Luke was involved (Acts xxvii; cf. his article, 'Does "L" hold water?', *JTS*, n.s., XII, 1961, pp. 59, 60). He thinks L cannot represent pure Caesarean tradition.

IV. THE MARCAN SOURCE

a. Reasons for its priority

Augustine's opinion that Mark was an abstract of Matthew was generally held until the early part of the nineteenth century, but with the exception of certain recent Roman Catholic scholars this opinion is now almost wholly discounted. The reasons for this change of outlook may be summarized as follows.

(i) *The proportion of Mark reproduced.* Almost the whole of Mark is paralleled in Matthew (about 90 per cent). There are, in fact, only seven short passages which do not appear. About half of Mark also appears in Luke. In Matthew and Luke combined all but four paragraphs of Mark are paralleled.[1] In just over half of the common material which Matthew and Luke respectively share with Mark, there is more or less verbal agreement.

(ii) *The primary order of Mark.* In the main the three Gospels keep to the same general outline, but where they diverge in matters of detail it is more rare for Matthew and Luke to agree against Mark, than for Mark to be in the majority.[2] In the case of Matthew the transpositions may generally be accounted for satisfactorily by the editor's desire to group his material into series.

(iii) *The literary characteristics.* There are a number of ways in which Mark's language and style appear to give a more primitive account.[3] First, Mark's amplifications of details and even of whole sections are made more concise in Matthew and Luke. For Mark's details, absent from Matthew and Luke, compare the following examples—'when the sun did set' (i. 32; Mt. viii. 16), the 'green' grass (vi. 39; Mt. xiv. 19; Lk. ix. 14), the 'three hundred pence' (xiv. 5; Mt. xxvi. 9). An example of the shortening of a whole narrative may be seen in the account of the healing of the multitudes (iii. 7–12; Mt. xii. 15, 16; Lk. vi. 17–19). Secondly, Mark's style is polished by Matthew and Luke. His vivid historic presents (151 times) are rarely paralleled in Matthew (21 times)

---

[1] Cf. H. B. Swete, *Mark,* p. lxiii.

[2] Cf. Feine-Behm-Kümmel's tabulated comparisons (*Einleitung,* pp. 28, 29). These comparisons show how Mark's order is dominant in both Matthew and Luke.

[3] W. C. Allen (*The Gospel according to St. Matthew,* pp. xix ff.) gives a very useful list of instances where he considers Matthew has changed Mark's language. Cf. also V. H. Stanton, *The Gospels as Historical Documents* (1923), pp. 51–53.

and only once in Luke, in passages common to all three. It should be noted, however, that Matthew uses historic presents 72 times in his non-Marcan material and this must be taken into account in assessing this evidence for priority. In many cases grammatical improvements are observed when Matthew and Luke are compared with the parallel passage in Mark, e.g. redundant negatives, unusual words and difficult constructions are removed. Thirdly, some weight has also been placed on Mark's inclusion of eight Aramaic words of Jesus as compared with one in Matthew and none in Luke. It is contended that Aramaic words would be more readily omitted from, rather than added to, an existing source.

(iv) *The greater historical candour*. Because Mark often records evidences of Jesus' human emotions (see p. 51 for details) where Matthew and Luke in parallel passages either omit or modify, it is supposed that he must represent an earlier tradition. The modifications are regarded as signs of increasing reverence. Of a similar character are those passages in which the other Synoptics appear to tone down statements which in Mark might be thought to give Jesus' limitations too great a prominence. A well-known case of such modification is found in Mark vi. 5; Matthew xiii. 58, where Mark states that Jesus could not do any mighty work in Nazareth, whereas Matthew has 'not many' and Luke omits the episode altogether. But it should be noted that Mark refers to a few sick people who were healed, which somewhat lessens the alleged modification. In the account of the cursing of the fig-tree the withering is more protracted in Mark than in Matthew (Mk. xi. 12 ff.; Mt. xxi. 18 ff.), while the words in Mark which might suggest that Jesus expected to find figs on the tree but was disappointed are lacking in Matthew, although the idea is implied. Although it is quite intelligible to explain these as reverential modifications, it is not impossible to give a different explanation. It may be a case of different emphases in parallel traditions, in which event it would cease to be evidence of later modifications of Mark. All that can safely be said is that if literary dependence is accepted it is more reasonable to suppose that Mark has been modified by Matthew and Luke than *vice versa*.

The greater candour of Mark is also said to be reflected in the portrayal of the disciples. The implied rebuke of Mark iv. 13 because of the disciples' failure to understand the parable of the sower is absent from both Matthew and Luke (Mt. xiii. 18; Lk. viii. 11). In the account of the stilling of the storm Mark records Jesus' question, 'How is it that you have no faith?' but Luke has 'Where is your faith?' and Matthew uses the word 'of small faith' (ὀλιγόπιστοι) (Mk. iv. 40; Mt. viii. 26; Lk. viii. 25). In the same incident Mark's 'Carest thou not that we perish?' appears in both Matthew and Luke as a statement, 'we perish'.

(v) *The least explicit account.* In the narrative of Peter's confession at Caesarea Philippi Mark has only 'Thou art the Christ', but both Matthew and Luke add further descriptions (Mk. viii. 29; Mt. xvi. 16; Lk. ix. 20). In referring to Herod, Mark calls him a king but the other two use the more precise 'tetrarch' (Mk. vi. 14; Mt. xiv. 1; Lk. ix. 7). On the occasion of the third prediction of the passion, Mark's 'kill' appears in Matthew as 'crucify', although Luke has the same as Mark (Mk. x. 34; Mt. xx. 19; Lk. xviii. 33).

These differences in Matthew and Luke when compared with Mark are considered by the majority of scholars[1] to be of sufficient weight to establish the priority of Mark. The contrary hypothesis that Mark is dependent on either one or both of the others raises more problems. Even if the Marcan hypothesis is not without its own problems, it is generally maintained to be most probable on the grounds that the theory which solves a greater number of the difficulties is more likely to be correct. Another subsidiary consideration in favour of the Marcan hypothesis is the claim that the most vivid Gospel is more likely to be prior, since vividness is not likely to have been impressed upon an existing source.

b. Problems arising from the theory of Marcan priority

(i) The first problem arises from the agreements of Matthew and Luke against Mark.[2] These agreements were at one time made the basis of a theory that an earlier source of Mark's Gospel existed (Ur-Markus) from which both Matthew and Luke copied their records. But these

---

[1] Cf. the full discussion in Streeter's *The Four Gospels*, pp. 151–168, and the concise summary in V. Taylor, *The Gospels*, pp. 44 ff.; cf. also Feine-Behm-Kümmel, *op. cit.*, pp. 27 ff.

[2] E. A. Abbott's *Corrections of Mark* (1901) contains a full list of the coincidences of Matthew and Luke against Mark. Cf. also J. C. Hawkins, *Horae Synopticae*, pp. 174 ff.; F. C. Burkitt, *The Gospel History and its Transmission*[3] (1911), pp. 42–58; L. Vaganay, *Le Problème synoptique* (1954), pp. 319 ff.

agreements have been variously assessed by different scholars. Streeter[1] claimed that they could mostly be eliminated by means of textual criticism, being explained as scribal corruptions. But others who have not been impressed by Streeter's solution have maintained that Matthew and Luke have independently corrected Mark and that their agreements are due to the 'naturalness' of these editorial corrections.[2] Another suggestion is that at these points Q may have overlapped Mark and that Matthew and Luke preferred the Q version to Mark, while yet another is that Matthew and Luke knew Mark in an Aramaic and a Greek form and that they corrected the Greek by means of the Aramaic.[3] The conjectural character of most of these reasons will be readily apparent and will lead cautious minds to recognize that the Marcan hypothesis is still not without its difficulties.[4] At the same time it must be recognized that the agreements under discussion form only a small percentage of the common material.[5]

(ii) The second problem concerns the great omission, the name given to that section in the middle of Mark (vi. 45–viii. 26) which Luke entirely omits. So striking is this omission that some satisfactory reason is demanded, and four types of solution have been proposed.

1. That an editor has added it to the original Mark after Luke had used Mark as the basis for his Gospel. This requires the acceptance of the Ur-Markus hypothesis already mentioned, but there seems to be no adequate motive for a later editor inserting this section if it did not exist in the original copy. In any case Matthew has used much of this material, which makes the above explanation more difficult, for it

[1] *The Four Gospels*, pp. 293–331. W. Sanday (*Oxford Studies*, p. 21) suggested that Matthew and Luke used a different recension of Mark from that from which the extant MSS are descended. Quite recently a similar theory has been advanced by J. P. Brown(*JBL*, LXXVIII, 1959, pp. 215–227), who maintains that the Caesarean text is the best witness to the recension of Mark which was used by Matthew and Luke.

[2] K. and S. Lake (*An Introduction to the New Testament*, 1938, pp. 6, 7), who regard textual corruption as responsible for only a few of the agreements, explain the rest as natural editorial corrections by Matthew and Luke. C. H. Turner (*JTS*, X, 1909, pp. 175 ff.) considered our knowledge of the original text of the Gospels to be insufficient to enable the textual critical argument to be used with certainty.

[3] Cf. the theory of C. C. Torrey, *The Four Gospels: A New Translation*, 1933.

[4] Cf. W. Sanday, in *Oxford Studies in the Synoptic Problem* (1911), p. 20.

[5] Cf. N. B. Stonehouse, *Origins of the Synoptic Gospels* (1963), p. 63.

would necessitate the assumption that Matthew used the edited form of Mark and not Ur-Markus.

2. That Luke accidentally omitted this section by passing from the feeding of the crowds in Mark vi. 42–44 to the similar incident in viii. 19–21. Sanday[1] pointed out that ancient writers had much greater difficulties in composing documents than modern writers especially when using other written sources, since it was no easy process to verify material from cumbrous rolls. A mistake of this kind is therefore by no means improbable.

3. That Luke deliberately omitted the section. This may have been either because it did not suit his purpose or because he preferred his alternative source and limits of space prevented him from making use of all his material. Hawkins[2] suggested that the solution might lie in a combination of accident and intention if Luke first accidentally omitted it and later realized that its inclusion would add nothing to his narrative. But Vincent Taylor,[3] who advocates an original draft of Luke (see the discussion on Proto-Luke, pp. 168 ff.), thinks that this section is not the kind that Luke would have selected when expanding his original draft by means of Mark.[4]

4. That Luke used a mutilated copy of Mark. This view, put forward by Streeter,[5] postulates that Luke's copy contained only the commencement of the section, and that he had to patch together the mutilated portions. Streeter admitted that this was merely a tentative suggestion and it has not commended itself to other scholars.[6]

[1] Op. cit., pp. 16, 17.   [2] Op. cit., p. 74.   [3] Op. cit., p. 48.

[4] Many scholars have considered that Luke's omission of this material may have been due to his desire to avoid 'doublets'. W. Bussmann (Synoptische Studien, I, 1925, pp. 1–66) gives detailed attention to these so-called 'doublets'. But W. Grundmann (Das Evangelium nach Lukas, p. 8) rightly points out that Luke does in fact include many examples of duplicated material (e.g. the double mission passages and the double apocalyptic sections). It is reasonable to conclude therefore that this duplicated material was included because Luke assumed that both accounts were relevant.

[5] Op. cit., pp. 176 ff.

[6] A modification of this view is that of T. Nicklin (Gospel Gleanings, 1950, pp. 3 ff.) who maintains that Mk. vi. 47–viii. 27a occupied twelve pages (three complete sheets) of Mark's original and that these pages formed the middle portion of a quire which would readily account for their being detached. In this theory there are two assumptions: one that the Gospel was originally written in codex form, which although not altogether improbable lacks proof, and the other that Luke's copy of Mark was the only copy to suffer mutilation in this way and that Luke did not suspect it.

There seems to be no need, in order to maintain the theory of Marcan priority and the use of it in the production of Luke's Gospel, to postulate any other reason than Luke's individual choice. Only those not satisfied with anything less than a minute analysis of the author's mind will feel confident when pushing the enquiry further. Those who challenge the literary dependence altogether will not, of course, regard the problem as a relevant one.

c. Alternatives to Marcan priority

The foregoing considerations have been regarded by the great majority of scholars as sufficient to establish the theory. In fact, it is generally treated as the one assured result of criticism. It is certainly the foundation-stone of most Synoptic literary criticism. Hypotheses regarding Matthew's and Luke's Gospels almost invariably proceed from the assumption that both have used Mark as a source.

There have been, nevertheless, some recent attempts to solve the Synoptic problem apart from the Marcan hypothesis. The most thoroughgoing of these attempts is that of B. C. Butler[1] who maintains the priority of Matthew over against Mark. By postulating such a theory, Butler also dispenses with Q, and much of the force of his arguments against Marcan priority depends on the inadmissibility of appealing to Q as an explanation of cases where Matthew appears to be the more original. The records of the preaching of John the Baptist may be quoted as an example. But since most source critics maintain the Q hypothesis, Butler's arguments are generally regarded as unconvincing. Although he has found few supporters for his contentions, he has drawn attention to difficulties in the Marcan hypothesis which would be obviated if Matthew were the first Gospel. Other Roman Catholic writers have maintained a modified form of Matthaean priority, suggesting the use by Mark of an earlier and shorter edition of Matthew as the basic Gospel. This view has been maintained by L. Vaganay,[2] who claims to be able to account for the various phenomena more adequately by postulating two main sources from which the

---

[1] The Originality of Matthew (1951). Cf. the criticisms of H. G. Wood (ET, LXV, 1953–54, pp. 17–19), who maintained that the order and arrangement of incidents in Matthew and Mark exclude Butler's view. Another careful critique of Butler may be found in G. M. Styler's 'Excursus on the Priority of Mark' in C. F. D. Moule's The Birth of the New Testament, pp. 223–232.

[2] Op. cit. See further comment on pp. 138 f.

three Synoptic Gospels were derived, a Greek translation of an original Aramaic Matthew and a sayings source used in Greek by Matthew and Luke. If this is correct neither Matthew nor Luke need have used Mark as a basic source, although Vaganay supposed that Luke did in fact use Mark. A rather similar theory has been maintained by L. Cerfaux[1] in that he too postulates a Proto-Matthew, and at the same time retains the current view that our present Greek Matthew and Luke depend on Mark.

Dissatisfaction with the Marcan hypothesis has also led to a modification of it by the postulation of various sources of which Matthew had access to only a part.[2] This is really a revised version of the earlier Ur-Markus theory, but is rather more thoroughgoing in its scope. None of these challenges to the established theory of Marcan priority has received much support, and yet they are significant reminders that the theory may not be as assured as it has been alleged to be.[3] All that can be said is that the theory may be regarded as the most probable basic source hypothesis yet proposed.

d. Sources of the Marcan source

Generally speaking source criticism has been content to treat Mark as a basic source without enquiring too specifically into its origins. One exception to this attitude has been the suggestion first proposed by T. Colani[4] in 1864 that Mark has incorporated a previously existing Jewish Christian apocalypse (Mk. xiii). There has been considerable support for this theory, so much so that it has come to be regarded almost as a fact of Synoptic criticism.[5] The main basis for the theory is the

[1] Cf. *Recueil Lucien Cerfaux*, I (1954), pp. 399–469.

[2] Cf. D. F. Robinson's suggestion that Matthew used a shorter form of Mark, which was later enlarged from additional sources (*JBL*, LXVI, 1947, pp. 153 ff.). He based his suggestions on a comparative study of the arrangement of the common material in Matthew and Mark.

[3] In his recent article on the alleged Matthaean errata, N. Walker (*NTS*, 9, 1963, pp. 391–394) suggests that a study of the passages which are supposed to show Matthew's inaccuracies not only shows that such allegations are unjustified but casts doubt on Marcan priority. He speaks of Mark reducing Matthew.

[4] *Jésus Christ et les croyances messianiques de son temps*[2] (1864).

[5] Cf. Moffatt, *ILNT*, p. 209; Stanton, *The Gospels as Historical Documents* 1923), pp. 115–121; Streeter, *The Four Gospels*, pp. 491–494; Rawlinson, *The Gospel according to St. Mark*, pp. 177–182, 187 ff.; T. W. Manson, *The Teaching of Jesus* (1931), pp. 260–263; V. Taylor, *The Gospels*, p. 50; *idem, The Gospel*

alleged inconsistencies within the passage as it stands, inconsistencies with the teaching of Jesus elsewhere and incongruities between the passage and its immediate context. But the hypothesis has not gone without its challengers. G. R. Beasley-Murray[1] has traced the development of the theory from its origins and has pointed out the insecurity of its foundations. His work may pave the way for a more traditional approach to the acceptance of the fact that Jesus Himself used apocalyptic language. It may be shown also that the alleged inconsistencies are capable of intelligible interpretations without recourse to this theory. In spite of the fact that many still regard some earlier source as practically certain, there are signs that the theory may be loosening its grip. C. E. B. Cranfield[2] concludes his investigation of Mark xiii. 5–37 with the opinion that it gives substantially our Lord's teaching.

Some attention has been paid to the special sources of Mark's passion narrative. It has recently been maintained that Mark has used two main sources for his account, one of which was non-Semitic, containing a straightforward narrative, and the other a strongly Semitic collection of self-contained narratives.[3] The two sources were, of course, parallel but independent[4] and Mark has merged the two together in his account. The basis of this theory is mainly linguistic and stylistic and depends on the general source-critical presupposition that similarities in language denote a similar source, and dissimilarities indicate dissimilar sources. Provided this principle of criticism is accepted there is some support for the two source theory for Mark's passion narrative. It is not impossible, in fact, on this basis to suppose that Mark has here drawn from different strata of the tradition. Taylor suggests that Mark found a passion narrative at Rome and expanded it by means of Petrine tradi-

---

according to St. Mark, ad loc. E. Klostermann (Das Markusevangelium[4], 1950, pp. 131, 132) accepts with very little discussion or comment the view that Mk. xiii consists of a Jewish apocalyptic document with Christian editorial additions.

[1] Jesus and the Future (1954). Cf. idem, A Commentary on Mark Thirteen (1957). For a criticism of this author's arguments, cf. S. G. F. Brandon, The Fall of Jerusalem and the Christian Church, Note III, pp. 270 ff., and H. Conzelmann, ZNTW, 50 (1959), pp. 210–221.

[2] The Gospel according to St. Mark (CGT, n.s., 1959), p. 390. Cf. also his articles in SJT, 6 (1953), pp. 189–196, 287–303, 7 (1954), pp. 284–303.

[3] Cf. V. Taylor, The Gospel according to St. Mark, pp. 653–664. Cf. also his articles in NTS, 4 (1958), pp. 215 ff.

[4] Cf. the further study of S. Temple, NTS, 7 (1960), pp. 77–85.

tion. But the main weakness of Taylor's linguistic analysis is its complicated character. His A source is divided into eighteen sections in order to be combined with seventeen sections of the B source, many of which sections are exceedingly brief.[1] It would seem better to speak of an editorial process rather than a source, at least for his B material. It must also be noted that this analysis is based mainly on the presence or absence of Semitisms (A mainly lacking them), but it is difficult to be sure of the Semitic character of all the evidence Taylor cites.

Although the earlier Ur-Markus theory[2] is now out of favour, there are some recent theories which are closely akin to it. One such complicated theory[3] proposes an original form of the Gospel (Mk. I) which existed in Aramaic and was used by a later editor with the help of another source to become eventually our Gospel of Mark. This is not likely to win support, but there are other less radical propositions which are based on the groupings of pre-Marcan material.[4] But although groupings within the oral tradition are highly probable, it cannot be excluded that Mark himself was the collector and arranger. It makes little difference who grouped the material provided its origin can be traced in some way (as in the Papias tradition) to an apostolic, and therefore authoritative, source.

There have been different opinions about Mark's use of Q (see next section), but the discussion has not been profitable.[5] Reasons will be given for regarding Q as no more than a convenient symbol for the material common to Matthew and Luke and lacking from Mark, in which case Mark's use of Q cannot arise. Even if a specific written

[1] Taylor (*St. Mark*, p. 658) gives the following list for source A, the rest being attributed to B: xiv. 1, 2, 10, 11 (12–16), 17–21, 26–31, 43–46 (53, 55–64), xv. 1, 3–5, 15, 21–24, 26, 29 f., 34–37, 39, 42–46 (xvi. 1–8).

[2] Cf. E. Wendling, *Ur-Marcus* (1905). Cf. also J. Jeremias (*ZNTW*, 35, 1936, pp. 280–282), who revives a kind of Ur-Markus theory based on textual criticism.

[3] So E. Hirsch, whose theory is summarized by Michaelis (*Einleitung*, p. 49), who cites from Hirsch's *Frühgeschichte des Ev: I. Das Werden des Mk-Ev*[2] (1951). Cf. also W. Eltester's critique, *ZNTW*, 44 (1952–53), pp. 265 ff.

[4] See p. 62 for comments on V. Taylor's theory of Marcan complexes. Cf. W. L. Knox's *Sources of the Synoptic Gospels: I St Mark* (1953). Cf. also J. Jeremias, *The Eucharistic Words of Jesus* (1955), pp. 132 ff., for the suggestion of a pre-Marcan form of the account of the last supper.

[5] B. H. Throckmorton (*JBL*, LXVII, 1948, pp. 319–329) rightly pointed out the futility of discussing Mark's use of Q until the latter has been more clearly defined.

document existed which was wider than the common material of
Matthew and Luke, there is no means of identifying any of this additional material in Mark. Where similarities between Mark and Q exist
it is much more credible to postulate an oral basis for this common
material.[1]

If the tradition is correct that the apostle Peter is behind this Gospel,
we possess most valuable information about the author's sources. We
need not, of course, assume that all Mark's information came *via* Peter,
but there is nothing to exclude the idea that much of it did.[2] If Mark
was the young man who fled from the garden, it may be that he was
personally acquainted with some of the events of passion week. This
is no more than a conjecture. Some scholars have found difficulty in
this interpretation because of their acceptance of the Johannine chronology, the assumption being that the young man must surely have
known the precise day of those momentous happenings. If the chronology of John and of the Synoptists can be reconciled (see discussion on
pp. 268 ff.), or if Mark's chronology is preferred to John's, this difficulty would not arise.

Some attempt has been made to isolate parts of the Gospel which may
be traced to Peter. C. H. Turner appealed to a number of passages in
which Mark's third person plural could quite easily be changed into the
first person plural and these passages, he maintained, could be assumed
to be Petrine eyewitness reminiscences.[3] T. W. Manson took the process
further and included many of the passages adjacent to Turner's pass-

---

[1] For an advocacy of Mark's use of Q, cf. F. C. Grant, *The Gospels, their origin
and growth* (1957), pp. 108, 109. S. Johnson (*The Gospel according to St. Matthew*,
IB, 1951, p. 237) seems favourable to the view that Mark may have heard Q
read and have remembered some sayings from it.

[2] F. C. Burkitt (*The Earliest Sources for the Life of Jesus*, 1922, pp. 77 ff.) accepted
a general Petrine source, but considered that some portions were independent of
such a source (as for instance the incident of the demoniac and the swine). Burkitt,
however, did not favour the view that the general plan of the work was traceable to Peter (*ibid.*, p. 93). In support of the Petrine tradition, cf. H. E. W. Turner,
ET, LXXI (1960), pp. 260–263. Against the tradition, cf. D. E. Nineham (*Saint
Mark*, Pelican Gospel Commentaries, 1963, p. 27), who argues that since *some*
Marcan material is non-Petrine (because he considers it to be community products), therefore it is logical to suppose that *none* of the material is Petrine because
all could be understood as community products.

[3] Cf. C. H. Turner, in *A New Commentary on Holy Scripture*, III, p. 54. His
passages are i. 21, 29, v. 1, 38, vi. 53, 54, viii. 22, ix. 14, 30, 33, x. 32, 46, xi. 1, 12,
15, 20, 27, xiv. 18, 22, 26, 32.

ages, because there were clear connections between them.[1] In this way a considerable proportion of the Marcan material may be traceable to Peter. Of the remaining material it has been suggested that much of this consisted of well-defined blocks, which may indicate some already arranged pre-Marcan material. It must also not be lost sight of that if the tradition of Marcan authorship is correct, he would have been in touch with a large number of eyewitnesses in his Jerusalem days and this must have contributed much to the composition of his Gospel.

V. THE SOURCE Q

a. Reasons for alleging its existence

Because of the large amount of non-Marcan material which is found in both Matthew and Luke it has been presumed by many scholars that these Evangelists must both have used a common source. This follows from the rejection of any possibility that one used the other or that both could have drawn so much common material, often closely related verbally, from oral tradition. The common source Q, if it existed, would have contained mainly the teaching of Jesus with only a few narrative sections. It is this feature that has led to the use of the description 'Logia', after the allusion in the report of Papias that Matthew wrote such *logia*.

Once New Testament scholarship was committed to the pursuit of written documents behind the Gospels, the postulation of Q as a written source was considered most reasonable and in fact almost inevitable. The data upon which this hypothesis was founded are as follows.

1. The large amount of common material in Matthew and Luke only (up to 250 verses), much of it possessing a considerable measure of verbal agreement, was felt to be impossible on any theory but a common written source.[2]

---

[1] *Studies in the Gospels and Epistles*, p. 42. Manson's list is as follows: Mk. i. 16–39, ii. 1–14, iii. 13–19, iv. 35–v. 43, vi. 7–13, 50–56, viii. 14–ix. 48, x. 32–52, xi. 1–33, xiii. 3,4, 32–37, xiv. 17–50, 53, 54, 66–72. This totals almost half the Gospel.

[2] For a rejection of the oral hypothesis as an adequate account of this phenomenon, cf. J. C. Hawkins' study in *Oxford Studies in the Synoptic Problem* (1911), pp. 98 ff.

2. The order in which both Matthew and Luke have used their common material is roughly similar. Yet the variations in order are not inconsiderable and the question naturally arises whether Matthew or Luke is closer to the original order of Q. There are differing opinions on this matter. Those who prefer Matthew's order claim that his literary method would not lead him to treat his sources with the same artistic freedom as Luke may have done.[1] But this seems to be contradicted by Matthew's acknowledged habit of conflating his sources. Luke, inclined generally to incorporate his sources in 'blocks', would probably see less reason than Matthew for changing the order.[2] While a common order, therefore, must be regarded with some reserve, most advocates of the Q hypothesis consider it to be strong enough to suggest the use of a common source.

3. The existence of so-called doublets in Matthew and Luke is also claimed to support the Q hypothesis. These are sayings which occur twice, in which one comes from Mark and the other, because of some variations, apparently does not and this requires the postulation of another source which contained some parallel traditions.[3]

4. Another consideration is that sometimes the agreements in Matthew and Luke reach to unusual words and phrases and also to grammatical peculiarities.[4]

The conclusion of Vincent Taylor is that 'these considerations justify us in believing that a written source lay before Matthew and Luke, containing sayings of Jesus'.[5] But not all scholars have been so certain that Q was a single source. W. Bussmann,[6] for example, split it

---

[1] C. F. Burney (*The Poetry of our Lord*, 1925, pp. 87 f.) suggested that Matthew more often preserves the poetical pattern.

[2] B. H. Streeter (*The Four Gospels*, p. 275) maintained that Luke's order was plainly more original because of Matthew's disposition towards topical arrangement and the inappropriateness of certain sayings in their Matthaean context. Against this view, cf. A. Farrer, *Studies in the Gospels* (ed. D. E. Nineham, 1955), pp. 62 ff. E. Nestlé (*ZNTW*, I, 1900, pp. 252 ff.) suggested that the original collection of sayings may have been arranged in five books, as Papias so arranged his expositions and as was common among the Jews after the pattern of the Pentateuch.

[3] Cf. Hawkins, *Horae Synopticae*[2] (1909), pp. 80 ff.

[4] Cf. Hawkins, *Oxford Studies*, p. 99.

[5] *The Gospels*, p. 22. B. de Solages, *A Greek Synopsis of the Gospels* (1959), claims to reach the same conclusion by mathematical demonstration.

[6] *Synoptische Studien*, II (1929).

into two sources, an Aramaic source R and a Greek source T. The latter was used with a large measure of agreement by Matthew and Luke, but the former with considerable variations. This hypothesis, however, has not commended itself.[1] W. L. Knox[2] suggested that some of the Q material originally existed in the form of tracts, the whole falling into two sections which roughly corresponded with Bussmann's sources. The single source idea has been further weakened by the tendency to regard Q as the stratum of common material used by Matthew and Luke without specifying whether it was one source or many.[3]

Owing to the problems of the Q sources (see below), Vaganay[4] has dispensed with Q altogether, but has substituted for it another source (Sg) which he thinks more adequately accounts for the double tradition. This source differs from Q both in its character and extent. It consists mainly of sayings of the kind Luke includes in his 'travel' document (ix. 51–xviii. 14), mostly common to Matthew but with many verses which Matthew and Luke individually include. This source, like Vaganay's Proto-Matthew, is supposed to have existed in the form of five books. It was not homogeneous either in vocabulary or style. This theory was prompted by Vaganay's assumption that the earliest writing was an Aramaic Proto-Matthew, which necessitated the postulation of another source which lay behind the canonical Gospels. Both these earlier sources, he thinks, were used by the Evangelists in a Greek form. But Vaganay's Sg source is no more certain in its

---

[1] Cf. the criticism of T. W. Manson, *The Sayings of Jesus* (1949), p. 20. An Aramaic Q has been suggested quite apart from Bussmann's theory of dual sources (cf. P. Bussby, *ET*, LXV, 1954, pp. 272–275). M. Black (*An Aramaic Approach to the Gospels and Acts*, 1954, pp. 270 ff.) criticizes Bussmann's theory, but considers that Q was originally in Aramaic. He nevertheless feels that the presence of non-translation Greek in the Q material shows that we cannot speak without qualification of a translation from Aramaic. He further suggests that Matthew's Q is a Greek literary composition, while Luke's Q, although it shows evidence of having been edited to remove Jewish materials for the benefit of Gentile readers, is nevertheless the more primitive translation from Aramaic. On the strength of the postulation of this Aramaic source, Black believes that in a limited number of cases the presence of some Synoptic variants can be explained. But his list of thirteen examples shows a drastic reduction from Bussmann's list of more than one hundred.

[2] *Sources of the Synoptic Gospels*, II (1957), pp. 3 ff., 45–47.

[3] E.g. C. K. Barrett, 'Q: A re-examination', *ET*, LIV (1943), pp. 320–323.

[4] *Le Problème synoptique* (1954).

content than the Q source which it displaces, for it must unavoidably be a matter of the proposer's own selection.[1]

Another recent hypothesis is that of P. Parker,[2] who calls the original document K (virtually a Proto-Matthew) and admits a second source Q, which nevertheless differs from former proposals regarding the Q source. His main idea is that Matthew and Mark used K, but that Luke knew it only through Mark. But he thinks that both Matthew and Luke used Q.[3]

b. The contents of Q

There is considerable difference of opinion among scholars who postulate a Q source as to the precise details of contents, but there is general agreement about the major sections. The following outline gives the main features which are assumed to have belonged to Q, although many scholars would add other passages where verbal agreement is more slight or where only one of the Evangelists has used the material. These latter details must necessarily be speculative.

(i) *The preparation*
John's preaching of repentance (Lk. iii. 7–9; Mt. iii. 7–10).
The temptation of Jesus (Lk. iv. 1–13; Mt. iv. 1–11).

(ii) *Sayings* (Sermon on the Mount)
Beatitudes (Lk. vi. 20–23; Mt. v. 3, 4, 6, 11, 12).
Love to one's enemies (Lk. vi. 27–36; Mt. v. 39–42, 44–48, vii. 12).
On judging (Lk. vi. 37–42; Mt. vii. 1–5, x. 24, 25, xv. 14).
Hearers and doers of the Word (Lk. vi. 47–49; Mt. vii. 24–27).

---

[1] X. Léon-Dufour points out this weakness in his article on 'Le fait synoptique', *Introduction à la Bible* (ed. A. Robert-A. Feuillet), II (1959), p. 291. For a concise résumé and critique of Vaganay's theory, cf. A. Wikenhauser, *New Testament Introduction*, pp. 235–239.

[2] *The Gospel before Mark* (1953).

[3] For yet another theory, cf. A. M. Perry's suggestion that Luke used a Jewish-Christian source, which he called N, in Lk. xi. 33–xii. 46, which consisted mainly of Q materials (*JBL*, LXIX, 1930, pp. 181–194). The many modifications and complications of the Q theory raise doubts regarding its validity, as J. H. Ropes (*The Synoptic Gospels*, 1934, p. 93) noted long before the theory met its more serious challengers. Cf. also P. Gardner-Smith (*The Christ of the Gospels*, 1938, p. 39), who thought that some of the common material of Matthew and Luke differed so much as to be best explained on the basis of oral teaching.

(iii) *Narratives*

The centurion's servant (Lk. vii. 1–10; Mt. vii. 28a, viii. 5–10, 13).

The Baptist's question (Lk. vii. 18–20; Mt. xi. 2, 3).

The Lord's answer (Lk. vii. 22–35; Mt. xi. 4–19).

(iv) *On discipleship*

Its cost (Lk. ix. 57–60; Mt. viii. 19–22).

The mission charge (Lk. x. 2–12; Mt. ix. 37, 38, x. 9–15).

Woes on recalcitrant Galilaean cities (Lk. x. 13–15; Mt. xi. 20–24).

(v) *Various sayings*

The pattern prayer (Lk. xi. 2–4; Mt. vi. 9–13).

On answers to prayer (Lk. xi. 9–13; Mt. vii. 7–11).

About the Beelzebub controversy (Lk. xi. 14–22; Mt. xii. 12–32).

About unclean spirits (Lk. xi. 24–26; Mt. xii. 43–45).

The sign of the prophet Jonah (Lk. xi. 29–32; Mt. xii. 38–42).

About light (Lk. xi. 33–36; Mt. v. 15, vi. 22, 23).

(vi) *Discourse*

Warnings against the Pharisees (Lk. xi. 37–xii. 1; Mt. xxiii. 1–36).

(vii) *Further sayings*

About fearless confession (Lk. xii. 2–12; Mt. x. 19, 26–33).

On cares about earthly things (Lk. xii. 22–34; Mt. vi. 19–21, 25–33).

On faithfulness (Lk. xii. 39–46; Mt. xxiv. 43–51).

On signs for this age (Lk. xii. 51–56; Mt. x. 34–36, xvi. 2, 3).

On agreeing with one's adversaries (Lk. xii. 57–59; Mt. v. 25, 26).

(viii) *Parables*

The mustard seed and the leaven (Lk. xiii. 18–21; Mt. xiii. 31–33).

(ix) *Other sayings*

Condemnation of Israel (Lk. xiii. 23–30; Mt. vii. 13, 14, viii. 11, 12, xxv. 10–12).

Lament over Jerusalem (Lk. xiii. 34, 35; Mt. xxiii. 37–39).

Cost of discipleship (Lk. xiv. 26–35; Mt. x. 37, 38, v. 13).

On serving two masters (Lk. xvi. 13; Mt. vi. 24).

On law and divorce (Lk. xvi. 16–18; Mt. xi. 12, 13, v. 18, 32).

On offences, forgiveness and faith (Lk. xvii. 1–6; Mt. xviii. 6, 7, 15, 21, 22).

The day of the Son of man (Lk. xvii. 22–27, 33–37; Mt. xxiv. 26–28, 37–39).

Although this list would be regarded as tentative by most advocates of the two basic source theory, there are many modifications proposed by different scholars. Nevertheless these modifications do not materially alter the essential character of the document. The most important question is whether or not it included any passion narratives, although most source critics tend to deny this.

It will be seen that the above reconstruction of Q presents a document with little apparent cohesion and with an extraordinary paucity of narrative material. The inclusion of the healing of the centurion's servant is certainly mystifying. Moreover there appears to be a preponderance of isolated sayings with no evident framework to hold them together.

The order given is that in which the material is used by Luke, following the generally accepted opinion that his order is more original than Matthew's.[1] But if Luke's order is that of the original certain problems arise. It would be clear that the compiler of Q had little conception of chronological or topical arrangement and that his primary purpose was the preservation of the teaching of Jesus without much regard for sequence. It would also appear that he had no reason to record the passion narratives. It is not easy to believe that an original document existed in this form, but the difficulties are certainly lessened if the theory of various tracts comprising Q material is maintained. Yet, as mentioned previously, a multiplication of Q sources goes far to weaken the whole hypothesis. It may be more reasonable to maintain that part only of the Q source has been preserved by Matthew and Luke between them, on the analogy of the use of Mark by both these Evangelists. Since it is possible to reconstruct with certainty the whole of Mark from Matthew and Luke[2] it may reasonably be expected that the same will apply to Q.

[1] V. Taylor (*JTS*, n.s., IV, 1953, pp. 27–31) has defended the Lucan order by maintaining that the difficulties in this hypothesis vanish if the parallel Matthaean material is arranged in six columns, corresponding to the five great discourses and an additional column for the rest. In each column occur many sequences in the same order as Luke, which is then claimed as evidence of a common documentary source, since the theory that one used the other is unacceptable to Taylor. Commenting on the data given in the above article, O. E. Evans (*ET*, LXXII, 1960–61, pp. 295–299) regards the Q hypothesis as the only reasonable explanation. In an article in *New Testament Essays* (ed. A. J. B. Higgins, 1959), pp. 246–269, V. Taylor has further developed the argument of the previously mentioned article, and again firmly asserts that Luke has followed the order of Q with great fidelity.

[2] F. C. Burkitt (*The Gospel History and its Transmission*, p. 17) considered the attempt to reconstruct Mark from Matthew and Luke to be futile, and argued that the same applies to the contents of Q. K. and S. Lake (*INT*, pp. 12, 13) speak of such attempts as miserable failures.

The different ways in which the Q material was used by Matthew and Luke are striking, particularly the highly selective method employed by Matthew. It is also noticeable that in the outline given above only one section of considerable length runs parallel in order in Matthew and Luke, i.e. the sayings from the Sermon on the Mount, which according to Hawkins[1] formed the basic structure on which the teaching of Jesus was moulded. But it is here that it is most noticeable that according to the generally held source theory Matthew has not only grouped this material into topics but has drawn other material into his discourse section from other contexts in Q and from his own special sources.

There have been different explanations of the fact that in some Q passages there are close agreements while in others there are wide divergences. V. Taylor[2] lists four proposals: (1) editorial modifications;[3] (2) different recensions;[4] (3) parallel versions;[5] and (4) composite theories of Q.[6] He considers that the choice must rest between (3) and (4), and in common with most source critics he prefers (3), in which, according to Streeter, Q and M overlapped. In these cases Luke

[1] In *Oxford Studies*, p. 121. W. L. Knox (*Sources of the Synoptic Gospels*, II, 1957, pp. 7 ff.) strongly maintained the greater originality of Luke's version of the Sermon on the Mount. W. Grundmann ('Die Bergpredigt nach der Lukasfassung', *Studia Evangelica*, pp. 180–189) finds an earlier theology in Luke's version as compared with Matthew's, but this view assumes that the theology of each author has affected his reconstruction of the Sermon. Yet the notion that Matthew's theology differs from Luke's is not the only possible explanation. The view that Jesus repeated this sermon material on many occasions with varying emphases cannot be dismissed without consideration. If Luke's and Matthew's versions relate to different events, the evidence of this material for the order of Q is at once nullified.

J. Schniewind (*Das Evangelium nach Matthäus*, p. 4) makes much of the differences between Matthew's and Luke's Sermon on the Mount material (and other discourse material) as a reason for rejecting the hypothesis that Luke used Matthew, a factor which counts strongly with many scholars.

[2] Cf. his article on 'The Elusive Q', in *ET*, XLVI (1934), pp. 68 ff.
[3] Cf. A. Harnack's *The Sayings of Jesus* (1908), pp. 1 ff.
[4] Cf. C. S. Patten (*Sources of the Synoptic Gospels*, 1915), who argued for an Aramaic document behind Q, which was translated into two Greek recensions. G. Bornkamm, who maintains a two recension theory, is content to explain this by the continuing influence of oral tradition, a significant concession (*Jesus o Nazareth*, 1960, p. 217).
[5] As proposed by Streeter in his four source theory.
[6] As Bussmann; see pp. 137 f. for details.

followed Q and Matthew M. But the existence of these variations emphasizes the fact that Q is not without its problems.

If a written source is felt necessary, the idea of different recensions must result in a weakening of the evidence, since the main prop of the theory is that too much verbal similarity exists for anything but a written basis to be envisaged. This merely pushes the problem one stage further back. If Luke used Q1 and Matthew used Q2, it is then necessary to postulate an Ur-Q from which both recensions developed, unless Q2 is an edited form of Q1. This latter proposition has recently been strongly maintained by J. P. Brown[1] who regards Matthew's source Q as an ecclesiastically revised form of Luke's Q material. It is difficult to see how this recension theory avoids the problems which are alleged to belong to any theory that Luke used Matthew or *vice versa*.

c. Problems of the Q source

Mention has already been made of the existence of passages where Matthew and Luke agree against Mark, and this was cited as a difficulty in the theory of Marcan priority. But the evidence could be regarded as a support for the theory that Luke used Matthew (or *vice versa*), in which case the reason for Q's existence vanishes.[2] Nevertheless it is generally felt to be difficult to hold such a theory because Luke's change of order of the sayings in Matthew would become incomprehensible. But the change of order may have been occasioned by Luke's greater desire to preserve the historical framework of the sayings as compared with Matthew's topical arrangement, although under this theory it would be necessary to assume that Luke had access to other

[1] Cf. *NTS*, 8 (1961–62), pp. 27–42. In a further article in *NTS*, 10 (1963), Brown examines the Synoptic parallels in the Epistles and suggests that most of the sayings echoed in the Epistles are derived from Q. The Epistles, according to him, have modified the original sayings of Jesus into something more useful for their immediate situation, and Matthew's Q approximates to this. But all Brown has really succeeded in doing is to demonstrate the flexible character which any theory of Q must have to be tenable at all.

[2] W. C. Allen (*St. Matthew*, pp. xlvii ff.) admitted this as a possibility more credible than the Q source. It has recently been strongly proposed by Austin Farrer in his article in *Studies in the Gospels* (ed. D. E. Nineham), p. 62. R. McL. Wilson, in *Studia Evangelica*, pp. 254–257, is critical of Farrer's methods of disposing of Streeter's arguments. E. L. Bradby (*ET*, LXVIII, 1956–57, pp. 315–318) has argued from some passages common to the three Synoptics that Luke is closer to Mark than to Matthew, which suggests to him Luke's ignorance of Matthew and therefore in his opinion supports the Q hypothesis. But does it?

information about the framework. Indeed, the basis of the difficulty over the order of Luke's Q material is the assumption that Luke's order is more natural than Matthew's. Or to put it in another way, a topical arrangement, being less natural, must be secondary and therefore Matthew cannot be basic to Luke. Clearly the original order of Q is of paramount importance. Once admit the originality of Matthew's arrangement and the *raison d'être* for Q's existence is virtually at an end. Another solution would be to regard the Q material as oral rather than written,[1] but in this case also the existence of Q as a self-contained entity becomes more difficult to maintain, and indeed hardly remains necessary.

But the classical source structure with Mark and Q as its foundation-stones strongly excludes the idea of Luke's use of Matthew on yet other grounds. We need not take seriously the argument that Luke would not have omitted so much of Matthew had he known it,[2] for Luke was clearly writing for a specific purpose and must surely be allowed the liberty of leaving out from his source anything he wished. Another argument is that some of Luke's sayings look more primitive in form than the parallel sayings in Matthew,[3] but the weakness in the argument is the difficulty in defining primitiveness. Indeed, it may equally well be maintained that on the whole Matthew looks more primitive than Luke, as for instance in its Jewish-Christian emphases. A further consideration arises from Luke's use of Mark. It can be demonstrated that he used Mark in roughly the same order as the material appears in that Gospel. If he used Matthew it is maintained that with this source he followed a quite different method. But it is not clear why he should not have adapted his method to his purpose. The amount of data available for determining Luke's literary methods is too slight to carry

---

[1] Cf. J. Jeremias, *ZNTW*, 29 (1930), pp. 147–149. R. H. Fuller (*The New Testament in Current Study*, 1962, p. 74) approves of E. Fascher's description of the Q material as 'a layer of tradition'.

[2] Cf. A. Wikenhauser, *New Testament Introduction*, p. 251.

[3] It is generally maintained that Matthew's topical arrangement of the discourses shows a more developed stage in the transmission of the tradition than Luke's more isolated sayings (cf. Schniewind, *Das Evangelium nach Matthäus*, p. 5). This view assumes that our Lord never delivered connected discourses of the type found, for instance, in Mt. v–vii, but this assumption may be challenged. As pointed out elsewhere (see pp. 192, 199) there is no logical reason why Jesus should not have repeated the same material on different occasions and in different contexts.

conviction.[1] Moreover, under the hypothesis being reviewed Luke would have incorporated more of Matthew than of Mark, if the passion narratives are disregarded. The concluding consideration is that whereas Matthew places some of his common sayings material in Marcan contexts, Luke places them in non-Marcan contexts. But the argument could be used in two ways. It could mean that both have used Q but have chosen different contexts for it, or that Luke has used Matthew and has rearranged the material. Is it certain that the former is more credible than the latter? It needs to be demonstrable if it is to serve as a support for the Q hypothesis.

Another consideration which presents a problem for the Q theory is the lack of any contemporary literature parallel to the type of document which Q is supposed to be.[2] It was clearly not a Gospel, for it lacked the most essential feature of the Gospel-form, the passion narrative. A document consisting mainly of teaching is not, of course, impossible to conceive, as the Gnostic *Gospel of Thomas* shows.[3]

The teaching of Jesus would naturally have been of surpassing interest to the early Christians as it was to the Gnostics, and it may at first seem that the analogous form of the Gnostic *Thomas* and the proposed Q source is a strong argument in favour of the latter. But is the analogy sufficiently close? If, as seems most likely, the *Gospel of Thomas* consists mainly of extracts from our written Gospels, it becomes at once distinguished from Q which *ex hypothesi* clearly had no such origin. This means that the form of *Thomas* was dictated by a principle of selection, which did not obtain in the same way for Q. The Gnostic compiler of the former has no interest in the historical context and for this reason excludes all narrative material.[4] But Q not only contains a few narrative sections, but lacks the dogmatic purpose of *Thomas*.

---

[1] This has been recognized by the advocates of the Proto-Luke hypothesis in which it is denied that Luke based his structure on Mark. Cf. V. Taylor, *op. cit.*, p. 37, and *idem, Behind the Third Gospel*. See pp. 168 ff. for a further discussion of Proto-Luke.

[2] Farrer (*Studies in the Gospels*, pp. 58 ff.) makes a strong point of this.

[3] It should be noted, however, that the extant evidence belongs to a later period than the formative period of the Synoptic Gospels. Cf. R. McL. Wilson, *HTR*, 53 (1960), pp. 231–250; H. Montefiore and H. E. W. Turner, *Thomas and the Evangelists* (1962).

[4] H. E. W. Turner (*op. cit.*, p. 114) says of Thomas, 'The principle of selection is itself evidence of intention and gives no indication that the compiler assigned any real place to history in his economy of salvation.'

The most that the evidence demonstrates is that a sayings collection was not considered incongruous in Gnostic circles and may not therefore have been regarded as unsuitable among the orthodox Christians.[1] At the same time, the existence of a document like Q during the first century AD must be considered to be unparalleled. The uniqueness of Q would not, of course, be damaging to the hypothesis, if there were such convincing grounds for it that a new type of literature could be confidently assumed. But it is otherwise with Q. It is hypothetical, unsupported by any external evidence—a precarious basis for a unique document.

Some scholars who admit difficulties in supposing that Luke used Matthew dispense with Q by maintaining that he used an Aramaic Proto-Matthew, as for instance in the theory of Vaganay already mentioned. But, increasingly, many who still retain the Q hypothesis in name are disinclined to regard it any more definitely than as a convenient symbol of Matthaean-Lucan common material.[2]

d. The probable purpose of Q

It is essential for the proposers of Q to suggest an adequate motive for its production and this is usually done by appealing to the catechetical demands of the early Church. It is not difficult to imagine the usefulness of a collection of the sayings of Jesus in the primitive communities. The majority of those assigned to Q deal with practical questions of Christian discipleship. Thus Q, if it existed, would have formed a kind

---

[1] Feine-Behm-Kümmel (*Einleitung*, p. 41) do not regard this Gnostic Gospel as belonging to the same kind (*Gattung*) as Q.

[2] This has been trenchantly emphasized by Stewart Petrie in an article in which he maintains that Q is what you make it (*Nov. Test.*, 3, 1959, pp. 28–33). He suggestively points out that so varied have been the hypotheses concerning Q that the value of the theory may be questioned. Another who has called for a greater precision among scholars in the use of the symbol Q is T. R. Rosché (*JBL*, 79, 1960, pp. 210–220). He draws attention to the fact that both Matthew and Luke, where they parallel Marcan sayings material, reproduce it with a high percentage of verbal agreement, although not quite so high in the narrative portions. The agreement reached also to the order of the contents. But these two factors are absent from Matthew's and Luke's alleged use of Q sayings material, where differences of order are clear enough. Unless it can be shown that the authors of Matthew and Luke differed widely when using sources, the source Q becomes suspect. There is much that is suggestive in Rosché's article. R. M. Grant (*A Historical Introduction to the New Testament*, 1963, p. 116) regards Q as no more than a symbol of material which was partly written and partly oral.

of primitive manual of discipline, backed by the authority of the Lord Himself. It would presumably have helped in the solving of many problems which became living issues as Christianity spread into Gentile lands.[1] There are passages in Q, for instance, which deal with John the Baptist, his preaching of repentance, his question to Jesus about His messianic office and Jesus' own testimony to John. It is conceivable that this material would have been useful in dealing with the problem of the relationship of John's disciples to the Christian Church. Similarly the passages giving our Lord's teaching about taxes would have had an obviously practical application in settling Christian obligation towards the State.

While these probable purposes may be admitted, they could, of course, have been met in other ways. Teaching on these important questions may have been part of the process of oral catechesis rather than incorporated in a written document. On the other hand, the finished Gospels would have performed the same purpose, and this leads to the enquiry whether the Q source, if substantiated, could possess any greater value than Matthew's and Luke's Gospels.

e. The value of the Q hypothesis

The most obvious value may be said to be for Christian evidences, since, if true, Q would push the written records nearer to the time of Jesus. Vincent Taylor[2] suggests the following particular values which can be attached to it. (1) It is the most valuable source of the teaching of Jesus, although it should be noted that other teaching was recorded elsewhere. (2) It gives insight into the character of Jesus. Many sayings are autobiographical in character, illuminating the inner consciousness of Jesus (cf. Mt. xi. 27; Lk. x. 22). There are abundant references to nature, showing a real appreciation of it. Many of the sayings are in poetic form.[3] There are allusions to the healing ministry, to lack of mighty works done and to unrecorded visits to Jerusalem culminating in the lament. (3) It shows our Lord's interest in common life, particularly in the countryside. So much so that J. M. C. Crum[4] maintained that Q must have had a country origin.

[1] Cf. R. V. G. Tasker, *The Nature and Purpose of the Gospels* (1944), p. 23. Streeter, in *Oxford Studies*, pp. 209 ff., and F. B. Clogg, *INT*[3] (1948), p. 190, considered that Q was intended to supplement oral tradition.

[2] *The Gospels*, pp. 24 ff.

[3] Cf. C. F. Burney, *The Poetry of our Lord* (1925), pp. 87 ff.

[4] Cf. J. M. C. Crum, *The Original Jerusalem Gospel* (1927), pp. 49–63.

Although Vincent Taylor himself warns against over-emphasizing the value of Q, there is a tendency among many source critics to attach higher value to this hypothetical source than to the two canonical Gospels which incorporate the material. But it must never be overlooked that these Gospels were accorded a status which was never attained by the source Q, or, if it was, this was not of sufficient weight to prevent it from being entirely superseded. If the Gospels are dated much later than Q (i.e. twenty-five to thirty years, as is generally maintained), then the advocates of the latter can reasonably claim to have pushed back the evidence to a significantly earlier time. But if the dating of the Gospels is considerably brought forward it is more difficult to attach any significant value to Q.[1]

f. Date and place of origin

Because of its hypothetical character it is clearly not possible to specify with any exactness either the date or provenance of Q. Streeter[2] suggested (and T. W. Manson[3] concurred) that it was written about AD 50, probably at Antioch. This is, of course, a guess, and since there are no data to lead to greater certainty it is probably as good a guess as any. In any case it is generally admitted that it could not have been much later than AD 60.[4]

g. The authorship of Q

It is difficult enough to establish authorship of some of the extant New Testament writings, but it is doubly difficult to discuss the author of a hypothetical source. The suggestions which have been made have been mainly influenced by the statement of Papias, recorded by Eusebius (see pp. 31 ff. for a discussion of the statement). Traditionally it was assumed that Papias was asserting that Matthew wrote his Gospel

---

[1] R. M. Grant (*op. cit.*, p. 116) warns against treating Q as a written source in any way comparable to Mark. An important suggestion has recently been made by H. Schürmann, in *Der historische Jesus und der kerygmatische Christus* (ed. H. Ristow and K. Matthiae, 1962, pp. 342–370), who believes that some of the Q materials were not only collected in the time of Jesus but were also used by the disciples. If the suggestion is valid, it would support the authenticity of these sayings materials in the Gospels.

[2] *The Four Gospels*, p. 150.

[3] *The Sayings of Jesus* (1949), p. 20.

[4] Feine–Behm–Kümmel (*op. cit.*, p. 38) say vaguely that it is improbable that Q was later than AD 50–70.

(τὰ λογία) in the Hebrew dialect, but with the postulation of a source Q it was only natural that Papias' λογία would be identified with this source. If this identification is correct it would be very early evidence not only for the authorship of Q, but for its very existence. If, then, it be supposed that Matthew did not write his Gospel and if it be further supposed that the writer of that Gospel used Q, it would clearly be a useful explanation of the attachment of Matthew's name to the whole Gospel if he were known to have been the author of one of its sources. But apart from Papias' ambiguous statement there is no other hint in early Christian history that anyone ever suspected that Matthew wrote only a portion of the Gospel attributed to him. Moreover, some explanation would need to be given of the complete disappearance of an apostolic source such as Q in favour of two presumably non-apostolic Gospels.[1] If Papias meant our canonical Gospel and not Q, the quest for the author of the hypothetical Q must be regarded as hopeless. He must remain one of the early Christian unknowns, perhaps even the greatest. It may be that this is a further reason, although by no means conclusive, for questioning the validity of the hypothesis of a written source Q.

h. Conclusion

It will be apparent from the preceding discussion that there is no unanimity about the Q source. It would be fair to say, however, that the great majority of scholars still regard it, in spite of its inherent difficulties, as the most reasonable explanation of the origin of the double tradition (Mt./Lk.). Between this full source theory and the other extreme of supposing that both authors have drawn material from oral tradition lie various other possibilities. Luke's use of Matthew cannot be pronounced impossible, although it is not without special difficulties of its own. It is perhaps preferable to suppose that early catechetical instruction included much of the teaching of Jesus and this would be

---

[1] Cf. Kilpatrick, *The Origins of the Gospel according to St. Matthew* (1946), p. 4. T. W. Manson (*op. cit.*, pp. 19, 20) explains the disappearance on the following grounds: the primitive Church was not interested in archives, especially in view of the end-expectation, and an Aramaic document (as he held Q to be) would have held interest for few at the turn of the century. Moreover, Manson tries to find an analogy in the disappearance of Shakespeare's autographs. But none of these reasons really explains the disappearance of an *apostolic* source of such importance, which must have been treasured from more than mere interest in archaic things.

imparted according to a fixed pattern. Hence the Q material may well have existed in an oral form of a sufficiently fixed character to account for both the verbal similarities and differences. Alternatively it may be conjectured that part of the sayings material was reduced to writing in the form of brief notes and that these were used by Matthew and Luke and supplemented by other oral traditions. One advantage of both these proposals is that they obviate the need for differentiating too sharply between Q and the special material of Matthew and Luke. In a field of study in which there is so much which must be considered conjectural, it would be foolish to be dogmatic. The symbol Q may still be used as a convenient description of the common material, while each investigator must be left to make clear whether he is thinking of written or oral material or a mixture of both.

VI. SOURCES PECULIAR TO MATTHEW

According to the four source hypothesis Matthew used in addition to Mark and Q other sources of information either unknown to or unused by the other Evangelists.[1] It is this unique material which gives the Gospel its distinctive characteristics and which has also been determinative in discussions of the historical value of the Gospel as a whole. The material may conveniently be studied under the following subdivisions: (a) sayings collection;[2] (b) *testimonia*; (c) birth narratives; (d) other narratives.

a. Sayings collection (M)

Streeter's postulated M source[3] for Matthew consisted of a certain amount of sayings material which could not readily be assigned to Q because of the lack of any close parallels between Matthew and Luke. This M source, he thought, was based on Jerusalem, largely because of

---

[1] It should be noted that continental scholars have been less inclined than British scholars to follow Streeter's M hypothesis. A recent writer, G. Strecker (*Der Weg der Gerechtigkeit*, 1962, pp. 12, 13), considers it to be basically unnecessary so long as Q material is not tied too rigidly to the double tradition of Matthew and Luke. Strecker does not accept Streeter's distinction between a Judaistic M and a Hellenistic-Christian Q.

[2] W. C. Allen (*Oxford Studies*, pp. 233–286) argued for a Book of Sayings used by the First Gospel, but far more comprehensive than Streeter's M source, because he did not admit Matthew's use of Q.

[3] *The Four Gospels*, pp. 254 ff.

its predominantly Jewish tone. The following suggestions may be noted about this material.

(i) *Reasons for the postulation of this source.* (1) In view of the similarity of subject-matter in Matthew and Luke, combined with many instances of dissimilarity of verbal forms, it is suggested that a source which overlapped the Q source in these cases would account for both. In other words these sections cannot with confidence be assigned to Q and must therefore have been derived from another parallel source which Matthew alone has used. (2) This theory is said by some scholars to be supported by Matthew's method of conflating his Marcan source with Q, thus providing an assumption that he did the same thing with M and Q. Vincent Taylor[1] cites Matthew iv. 11, x. 9–15, xii. 22–32, xiii. 31, 32 as illustrations of this process. (3) If Matthew conflates M and Q, Luke, in accordance with his usual practice of using one source at a time, is thought to have preferred Q. It is then suggested that this would account for the differences as well as the principles of selection used by the two Evangelists.[2] (4) Various data are thought to distinguish the M sayings from the Q sayings, such as evidence from structure and stereotyped explanations.[3]

Whether these reasons are sufficient for the postulation of a special M source will appear differently to different minds, depending largely on the presuppositions with which the problem is approached. For instance, if the priority of Matthew to Luke can be maintained, much of the justification for M vanishes, at least in the form in which Streeter proposed it. It would then be more difficult to distinguish Matthew's unique sayings from those of the double tradition (i.e. Q). Indeed, there would be no motive for doing so. Consequently those who would dispense with Q generally also dispense with M, at least as a written source,[4] although the symbol may still be used to denote the material peculiar to Matthew. It is moreover difficult to decide to what extent the interplay of oral tradition and written sources may have produced

[1] *The Gospels*, p. 30. In the parallel passages Mt. iv. 11; Lk. iv. 13, ὁ διάβολος is the only word in common.

[2] Hawkins (*Oxford Studies*, pp. 29–59) strongly maintained that Luke did not use Mark in his 'travel' narrative (ix. 51–xviii. 14) but alternates Q with his own special material. Such a phenomenon does not occur in Matthew. Cf. on this point the discussions of the Proto-Luke theory, pp. 168 ff.

[3] See G. D. Kilpatrick's discussion of this material, *The Origins of the Gospel according to St. Matthew* (1946), pp. 8 ff.

[4] As for instance in A. Farrer's theory (see p. 143 n.2).

the parallel traditions, with their similarities and differences, which the Q and M hypothesis is intended to explain.[1] At best the M source, in any of its proposed forms, lacks much connection of thought[2] and it is not easy therefore to conceive how it was originally compiled.

(ii) *The main characteristics of the source.* The Jewish character of Matthew's Gospel has already been indicated (see pp. 19 ff.), but it is necessary here to point out that some of this Jewish emphasis appears in passages which are paralleled in Luke, although mostly it occurs in the material peculiar to Matthew. An example of the former may be seen in the statement about the Law and the Prophets (Mt. v. 17–19; Lk. xvi. 17). Matthew has, 'Think not that I have come to abolish the law and the prophets; I have come not to abolish them but to fulfil them. For truly, I say to you, till heaven and earth pass away, not an iota, not a dot, will pass from the law until all is accomplished. Whoever then relaxes one of the least of these commandments and teaches men so, shall be called least in the kingdom of heaven; but he who does them and teaches them shall be called great in the kingdom of heaven' (RSV). Luke much more briefly and in a quite different context has, 'But it is easier for heaven and earth to pass away, than for one dot of the law to become void' (RSV). In a later context Luke has, 'Heaven and earth will pass away, but my words will not pass away' (xxi. 33, RSV; cf. Mt. xxiv. 35; Mk. xiii. 31). It will be seen that what is explicit in Matthew is nevertheless implicit in Luke, although by treating it less emphatically Luke would have had in mind his predominantly Gentile readership.

Examples of Judaistic emphasis in Matthew's own material may be seen in isolated sayings in Q contexts, such as the passage about the lost sheep of the house of Israel (x. 6), and in Matthew's sayings collection, such as the statement about things old and new at the close of the parable section (xiii. 52) and the later parables of the wedding garment, the virgins, and the sheep and the goats (xxii, xxv). The sayings about Moses' seat (xxiii. 2) and the twelve thrones of Israel (xix. 28) come under the same category.

If M existed as a source its most dominant feature was, therefore, its Jewish flavouring.

(iii) *The probable contents of the source.* Since the existence of M is even

---

[1] H. E. W. Turner (*Jesus, Master and Lord*[2], 1954, pp. 51, 52) is very doubtful whether the lack of homogeneity in this material warrants the postulation of a written source. He prefers to regard it as due to editorial modifications and oral tradition.

[2] Kilpatrick, *op. cit.*, p. 36, admits this.

more hypothetical than Q, and is admitted to be so even by its own advocates, it is impossible to define its original contents.[1] Any suggestions will amount to little more than that it was a collection of the sayings material peculiar to Matthew. As in the case of Q, however, it cannot be assumed that all the material which originally belonged to M has been preserved in Matthew's Gospel. The following contents list must, even from the source-critical point of view, be regarded as highly tentative.

1. A discourse containing material which was mainly anti-Pharisaical and which was incorporated in Matthew's Sermon on the Mount. McNeile[2] suggested that two sermons originally existed in written form, the Lucan form and this Matthaean discourse.[3] Matthew is then supposed to have conflated the two.

2. A similar anti-Pharisaic discourse, incorporated in Matthew xxiii, which is also thought to have been conflated.

3. Parts of the mission charge absent from Q, or in other words absent from Luke.

4. A collection of parables, comprising the tares, hidden treasure, merchant, dragnet (Mt. xiii), the debtor (Mt. xviii. 23–35), the labourers (xx. 1–16), the two sons (xxi. 28–32), wedding garment (xxii. 11–14), virgins (xxv. 1–13) and the sheep and the goats (xxv. 31–33). Streeter also added three parables with parallels in Luke, the lost sheep (xviii. 10–14), marriage feast (xxii. 1–10) and talents (xxv. 14–30).

In addition to these main features many other isolated sayings are assigned to Matthew's special source (e.g. xii. 11, 12, xiii. 52).

(iv) *The value of M*. Advocates of the four source theory have usually claimed to be able to pronounce on the comparative value of the various sources. These are arranged in descending order of importance and it is only natural that Mark and Q have been accorded first place and all other source material tends to be regarded as correspondingly less original. It is no surprise, therefore, that traces of what are presumed

[1] E. B. Redlich (*The Student's Introduction to the Synoptic Gospels*, 1936, pp. 203–218) attempted a reconstruction of M but, as S. Johnson (*The Gospel according to St. Matthew*, IB, 1951, p. 238) pointed out, if this is correct, the author of Matthew's Gospel must have used a scissors and paste method. The Gospel as a whole does not give such an impression.

[2] *St. Matthew*, p. 86.

[3] W. E. Bundy (*Jesus and the First Three Gospels*, 1955, pp. 93, 94) regards Matthew's Sermon as primarily an early Christian tract. He holds, however, that the original source of this Sermon was identical with the source of Luke's because of its similar beginning and ending and its seven common discourse units.

to be later Jewish-Christian influences are found in the source M, especially in view of its distinctively Jewish tone, together with other influences such as the teaching of John the Baptist.[1] But this method of assessment depends for its validity on the acceptance of the view that Mark and Q are sufficient criteria for measuring primitive documents. But this virtually means that all material which differs from these tends to be regarded with preliminary suspicion. This tendency in its developed form leads to suspicion being cast on any facts or sayings which are not witnessed to by more than one author.

Vincent Taylor,[2] in claiming justification for the existence of M, at least as a body of oral tradition if not as a written source, maintains that it does justice to the Judaic character of the tradition. But if this Jewish colouring was due to Matthew's own selection it would be more adequately explained. The author or 'editor' of the Gospel must be allowed more personal initiative than many source critics are prepared to assign to him. Those who regard M as a symbol for a body of oral tradition are, of course, not so open to this criticism, and for this reason there is a preference among many scholars for using the term 'strata' rather than written 'sources'.[3]

(v) *Date and place of origin.* Any scholar who attempts to define either the date or place of origin of M knows only too well that he has no data to rely upon other than his own speculations. Streeter[4] suggested a date about AD 65 and located it in Jerusalem. The date must clearly be arbitrary, although it must have preceded the publication of the Gospel, and is naturally dated after Mark and Q. The location may be indicated by its Jewish characteristics, although Jerusalem was not the only place where Jewish influences were strong. The matter is of slight importance in the study of Gospel origins, because of its wholly conjectural character.

b. The book of testimonies

The many citations from the Old Testament in Matthew's Gospel fall into two distinct groups. The majority conform more or less precisely

[1] T. W. Manson (*The Sayings of Jesus*, p. 25) regards M with some suspicion, owing to these two influences.

[2] *The Gospels*, p. 32.

[3] Cf. V. Taylor, *op. cit.*, p. 34. Bornkamm (*Jesus of Nazareth*, 1960, p. 216), like most German scholars, rejects the idea of a special Matthew source (and a special Luke source) because of the widely varied character of the material.

[4] *The Four Gospels*, pp. 500–524.

to the text of the LXX, or at least to a Greek translation of the Hebrew
text.[1] A small group of citations, twelve in number, is apparently
derived direct from the Hebrew text. This latter group is exclusive to
Matthew with the exception of one quotation which occurs also in
Mark and Luke (i.e. the passage about the voice crying in the wilderness applied to John the Baptist—Mt. iii. 3; Mk. i. 2, 3; Lk. iii. 4–6).
The others are: the virgin passage (i. 23), the ruler from Bethlehem
(ii. 6), the call out of Egypt (ii. 15), the voice in Ramah applied to the
incident of the slaughter of the innocents (ii. 18), the Nazarene statement (ii. 23), the people in darkness see a great light (iv. 15, 16), 'He
took our infirmities' applied to the healing ministry (viii. 17), the Servant passage illustrating the non-belligerent attitude of Jesus (xii.
18–21), the statement about parables (xiii. 35), the king riding upon an
ass (xxi. 5), and the thirty pieces of silver (xxvii. 9).

Since each of these citations is introduced by a similar formula
('that it might be fulfilled which was spoken through . . .') it has been
suggested that an independent collection of Old Testament citations
existed[2] distinct from those used elsewhere in the Gospel. F. C. Burkitt[2]
and J. Rendel Harris[3] argued that this type of collection was in existence
in the contemporary Jewish world.[4] These scholars postulated an Aramaic collection of testimonies as the source of Matthew's citations. In
some cases (e.g. i. 23) the citation differs from both the LXX and Hebrew
texts and may perhaps be explained by Aramaic influence, in which
case it would be support for an Aramaic original. McNeile[5] suggested
on the contrary that this source may have been translated into Greek
before Matthew used it.

The idea of a collection of *testimonia* is supported by what is known
of early Christian interest in the Old Testament witness to Christ. It

---

[1] Cf. Feine-Behm-Kümmel, *Einleitung*, p. 64, for the view that some of Matthew's citations could be from another translation of the Hebrew text rather than
from the LXX.

[2] *The Gospel History and its Transmission*[3] (1911), p. 127.

[3] *Testimonies*, I (1916). Cf. also D. Plooij's monograph *Studies in the Testimony
Book* (1932).

[4] It should be noted that some support may be found for this contention in the
Qumran *testimonia* document (4 Q Test), in which three sections consist wholly
of biblical quotations of messianic expectations and the fourth is from the apocryphal *Psalms of Joshua*. For a translation of the complete text cf. A. Dupont-
Sommer, *The Essene Writings from Qumran* (1961), pp. 315 ff.

[5] *INT*, p. 85.

is not, therefore, intrinsically improbable that such Christian collections existed. Yet certain features of this hypothesis cannot be substantiated.

1. Both Burkitt and Harris maintained, on the basis of Papias' reference to Matthew's λογία, that Matthew was the author of such a book of *testimonia*, but this is improbable because Papias uses the word in relation to Jesus but not, it would seem, of Old Testament proof-texts.[1]

2. The theory moreover lacks primitive Christian parallels, although it is known that similar *testimonia* existed in the time of Tertullian and Cyprian. Moreover, these later testimony books do not follow Matthew's model in sequence or in language.[2]

3. Some at least of these proof-texts would certainly have been unintelligible if they had existed in isolation from any context, although the possibility that a tradition of interpretation may have accompanied such a list cannot be ruled out. Christian interest in Old Testament *testimonia* is more likely to have been centred in important passages than in proof-texts, as C. H. Dodd[3] has pointed out.

4. Insufficient attention has been given by the advocates of the theory to the connection which the citations have with their Matthaean contexts. Are they perhaps proof-texts which suggested themselves to the mind of the author in the course of his compilation? Some of them may be more reasonably accounted for in this manner, as for instance the citing of Hosea xi. 1 ('out of Egypt have I called my son') to demonstrate that the descent into Egypt was a divinely foreshadowed event.[4] However strange the exegesis may appear to modern standards it is reasonable to suppose that the writer recalled the Hosea passage as he meditated on the event itself. The alternative would appear to be that the author selected his events to illustrate the *testimonia*, but this is less likely.[5]

[1] See comments on pp. 31 ff.

[2] Cf. J. A. Findlay, *The First Gospel and the Book of Testimonies* (1933), pp. 57–71.

[3] *According to the Scriptures* (1952).

[4] Cf. N. Walker (*NTS*, 9, 1963, p. 393) who suggests that Matthew's intention was to find Old Testament texts to fit the events of the story, not *vice versa*. For a full examination of Matthew's use of these passages from the point of view that they reveal Matthew's theologizing purpose, cf. G. Strecker, *Der Weg der Gerechtigkeit* (1962), pp. 49–85.

[5] S. V. McCasland (*JBL*, LXXX, 1961, pp. 143–148) charges Matthew with twisting the Scriptures. His views are answered by Walker.

W. L. Knox[1] maintained that the *testimonia* did not all belong to one source. The first five of those unique in Matthew occur in the birth narratives and were part of that source (see next section). Of the remaining six, four formed part of another source consisting of *testimonia* and the remaining two were added from yet another source, possibly oral.[2] But such a multiplication of *testimonia* sources makes the whole hypothesis less credible.[3] Even if all the relevant passages were originally in a testimony source there are hardly sufficient to have formed a book, and to split them still further would require the postulation of testimony fly-sheets, which is possible but improbable.

The idea of a Matthaean school, which has already been mentioned in the discussion over the purpose of the Gospel,[4] has been mainly based on Matthew's use of the Old Testament. Exegesis of selected *testimonia* would have been a major method in New Testament apologetics,[5] and to this extent Matthew's concentration upon proof-texts is not surprising. But the school idea is not the most probable explanation of the origin of these *testimonia* texts which are cited by Matthew, although it may explain the author's interest in exegesis. If Matthew belonged to a group which, like the men of Qumran, were devoted to such exegesis, it is easy to see how many of the texts would spring naturally to his mind when he was writing his narrative.[6] But why did he use a special formula for one group of citations and not for the rest? It would seem that this was specifically used to draw attention to the fulfilment of prophecies which were being interpreted in a messianic way by Christian apologists.

c. Matthew's birth narratives

Although these will be dealt with under a separate sub-heading, they are sometimes regarded as part of the larger cycle of narratives peculiar

---

[1] *Sources of the Synoptic Gospels*, II, pp. 121 ff.

[2] G. D. Kilpatrick, *The Origins of the Gospel according to St. Matthew* (1946), p. 46. Cf. also p. 66, where Kilpatrick expresses his doubts about the existence of a testimony book.

[3] Cf. A. M. Hunter, *Paul and his Predecessors*[2] (1961), pp. 58 ff.

[4] Cf. pp. 25 f. for comments on K. Stendahl's book, *The School of Matthew and its use of the Old Testament* (1954).

[5] B. Lindars' book on *New Testament Apologetic* (1961) makes a great deal of this.

[6] Lindars (*op. cit.*, p. 265) suggests that the school's stock of quotations which were used orally in catechetical work would have been known to Matthew.

to Matthew.[1] It is useful, however, to consider these narratives separately.

1. Matthew's birth narratives are quite different from Luke's and clearly came from a different source. The interest in Joseph's part of the story is significant when compared with Luke's greater interest in Mary.

2. There is an absorbing interest in the Old Testament to such an extent that Knox maintained that 'each story is woven round a *testimonium* from the Old Testament'.[2] This goes too far, but there is no doubt that the primitive Church was particularly concerned to demonstrate the Old Testament predictions of Christ's advent, and this concern would have affected the form in which the tradition was preserved. It is equally possible, however, that the author himself was the first to reduce these particular traditions to writing and has himself introduced the relevant *testimonia* as suggested in the last section.

3. It has been further proposed that these stories arose from a Christianizing of the story of Moses and Israel,[3] forming a kind of commentary on them. But although Old Testament interest is undeniable, this is very different from maintaining that the Old Testament formed the motif for the formation of the stories. It is reasonable to suppose that a close check would have been kept on such compilations.

4. It has often been maintained that Matthew's birth narratives cannot be considered historical, but that they arose at a later period prompted by dogmatic concern to embellish the coming of Jesus. Yet such a view springs all too often more from a dislike of the supernatural and a disbelief in the virgin birth than from a historical appraisal of the data.[4]

---

[1] Cf. Streeter, *The Four Gospels*, pp. 266, 502 f.

[2] *Op. cit.*, p. 121.

[3] Cf. A. H. McNeile, *St. Matthew*, p. 23; W. C. Allen, *St. Matthew*, p. 18. A rather different, although allied, theory is that of C. H. Cave (*NTS*, 9, 1963, pp. 382–390) who develops the view of D. Daube (*The New Testament and Rabbinic Judaism*, 1955, pp. 158 ff.) that the background of the Matthaean birth narratives is to be found in the Passover Midrash and the synagogue lections.

[4] It should be noted that Matthew does not actually describe the birth of Jesus. His name and its significance is more important in Matthew's narrative than the event itself. Cf. K. Stendahl's study, 'Quis et unde?' in *Judentum, Urchristentum, Kirche* (ed. W. Eltester, 1960), pp. 94–105. He rightly points out that Matthew's narrative not only shows the author's knowledge of the virgin birth, but also the slanders which it had occasioned.

d. Matthew's other narratives

The main narratives which are found in no other source are: (1) the
hesitation of John the Baptist at the baptism of Jesus (iii. 14 f.); (2)
the account of Peter walking on the water (xiv. 28–31); (3) the coin
in the fish's mouth (xvii. 24–27); (4) several stories in the passion narratives, such as Judas' bargain with the priests (xxvi. 14–16), Pilate's hand-
washing (xxvii. 24 f.), the earthquake and the resurrection of certain
saints (xxvii. 51–53), and, in the concluding section, the reference
to the watch, the angel rolling away the stone and the bribing of
the guard (xxvii. 62–xxviii. 15). Kilpatrick[1] divides the material
into three sections, Petrine stories (xiv. 28–31, xvi. 17–19, xvii.
24–27, xviii. 15–22), passion and resurrection stories (xxvi. 52–54,
xxvii. 3–10, 19, 24 f., 51–53, 62–66, xxviii. 2–4, 9–20) and miscel-
laneous narratives (iii. 14 f., iv. 23, ix. 35, xv. 22–24, xvii. 6 f., xxi. 10 f.,
14–16).

Many scholars have found some homogeneity in these sections and
have suggested a common source with the birth narratives. The characteristic features which are said to unite this material are: (1) stylistic
features; (2) references to angels and prophecy; (3) an emphasis upon
the miraculous, and (4) a dogmatic purpose to support primitive tradition.[2] Not much value can be attached to the first point since there are
few distinctive features to mark these narratives as stylistically different
from the rest of the Gospel, but the other three points, if valid, may
certainly suggest a common origin for these narratives. Interest in
angels, however, is not confined to this special source, except the
expression 'angel of the Lord'. Moreover, both Mark and Luke
contain references to angels and this must therefore be considered to
be a common feature in the primitive tradition. Admittedly the
prophetic element is more dominant in Matthew than in the
other Synoptic Gospels, which is no doubt mainly due to the purpose of the Gospel. It is probably true that the miraculous element
is more emphasized in Matthew's narratives than elsewhere, but
Matthew's treatment seems highly restrained when compared with
the supernatural embellishments of apocryphal Gospels. It is mis-

---

[1] *Op. cit.*, p. 37. Sometimes the symbol N has been used to denote the
source of Matthew's special narratives, but Kilpatrick rejects this because he
regards the material as derived from oral tradition.

[2] Cf. V. Taylor, *The Gospels*, p. 65.

leading, therefore, to describe Matthew's special material as 'apocryphal'.[1]

Peter's attempt to walk on the water is no more improbable than Jesus' own action as far as the physical aspect of it is concerned, and the latter event is not confined to Matthew's record. Indeed the sequel rather suggests a quite different motive from embellishment, for Peter cannot be said to come out of the story particularly enhanced. Vincent Taylor[2] finds dogmatic purpose in John's hesitation, in the story of the coin in the fish's mouth and in the account of the resurrection guard, all of which are supposed to answer difficulties currently felt. The second, for example, is claimed to offer a solution to the problem whether or not Christians should pay taxes.[3] But though this suggestion *may* explain the origin of these stories, the narratives themselves do not necessarily *require* such an explanation. If they had historical validity, which is denied by many scholars, they would still be answers to the same problems. It is often assumed that the difficulties created the narratives to solve them, but it is surely more reasonable to suppose that the problems themselves were a dominant factor in the processes of selection and preservation of already existing material.

Vincent Taylor's conclusion that this cycle of tradition is the least valuable of the Gospel traditions is prompted by his low estimate of the influences described above. If this assessment is correct, the conclusion must be allowed. Yet reasons have been given which suggest the advisability of great caution in assessing historical value by this means.

VII. SOURCES PECULIAR TO LUKE

The amount of material not found elsewhere which has been incorporated in Luke is even greater than that in Matthew. Streeter suggested that this special Lucan material L was based on Caesarea. It is not generally supposed that it existed in a written form and the symbol

---

[1] F. C. Grant (*The Gospels, their origin and growth*, p. 147) unhesitatingly describes this material as 'apocryphal'. Cf. also A. J. B. Higgins (*The Reliability of the Gospels*, 1952, pp. 22 ff.) who makes a comparison with the type of development found in the *Gospel of Peter*. But there is an obvious difference between this material in the canonical and apocryphal Gospels.

[2] *Op. cit.*, p. 65.

[3] Both G. Bornkamm and G. Barth regard this story as evidence that at the time when Matthew's Gospel was issued the congregation represented by Matthew still regarded itself as a part of Judaism, liable for the temple tax (*Tradition and Interpretation in Matthew*, pp. 19 f., 90).

L may therefore be regarded as representative of the oral tradition,[1] probably collected by Luke while he was at Caesarea.

a. General contents

Within this L material there are fourteen parables: the two debtors (Lk. vii. 41–43), the good Samaritan (x. 29–37), the friend at midnight (xi. 5–8), the rich fool (xii. 13–21), the fig-tree (xiii. 6–9), the tower builder (xiv. 28–30), the rash king (xiv. 31–33), the lost coin (xv. 8–10), the prodigal son (xv. 11–32), the dishonest steward (xvi. 1–9), the rich man and Lazarus (xvi. 19–31), the servant's duty (xvii. 7–10), the unjust judge (xviii. 1–8), the Pharisee and the tax collector (xviii. 9–14). If the parable of the pounds (xix. 11–27) is considered separate from the parable of the talents this too must be added, but many scholars think them to be variants of the same parable. The differences are, however, sufficient to justify treating them separately.

In addition to these parables there are also a number of isolated sayings such as the dispute about the inheritance (xii. 13–15), statements on the disaster which overtook the Galilaeans at Siloam (xiii. 1–5) and sayings about humility (xiv. 7–14) and hypocrisy (xvi. 14, 15).

A large amount of narrative material is also peculiar to this L-stratum, and this may be summarized as follows:

(i) *During the Galilaean period*
The rejection at Nazareth (iv. 16–30).
The miraculous draught of fishes (v. 1–11).
The widow's son at Nain (vii. 11–17).
The sinful woman (vii. 36–50).
The ministering women (viii. 1–3).

(ii) *In the 'travel' narrative*
The Samaritan villages (ix. 51–56).
The mission of the seventy (x. 1–16).
Mary and Martha (x. 38–42).
The woman who declared the blessedness of Christ's mother (xi. 27, 28).
The woman with the spirit of infirmity (xiii. 10–17).
The man with the dropsy (xiv. 1–6).

[1] Some scholars have sought evidence for pre-Lucan structural forms. Cf. W. R. Farmer's discussion of the parallel groupings of materials in Lk. xiii. 1–9 and xv. 1–32 and their comparison with the Greek rhetorical form of *chreia*, with concise introduction, two brief parables and a third parable to illustrate the point of the former (*NTS*, 8, 1962, pp. 301–316).

The ten lepers (xvii. 11–19).
Zacchaeus (xix. 1–10).

(iii) *The passion narratives*

Differences in the account of the institution of the last supper (xxii. 15–30).
The sweat of blood (xxii. 40–46).
The arrest (xxii. 47–53).
The triple trial (xxii. 54–xxiii. 16).
The weeping women (xxiii. 26–31).
The penitent thief at the cross (xxiii. 39–43).

(iv) *The resurrection narratives*

The women at the tomb (xxiv. 1–12).
The Emmaus walk (xxiv. 13–35).
The appearance at Jerusalem (xxiv. 36–49).
The departure of Jesus (xxiv. 50–53).

This list must be regarded as tentative,[1] as some of the accounts overlap narratives in the other Gospels (e.g. xxiv. 1–12), but there are significant differences which have been thought sufficient to suggest a different source.

It is noteworthy that most of Luke's special parables and sayings material occurs in his 'travel' narrative, together with many of his special narratives. This will have a bearing on our consideration of the Proto-Luke hypothesis (see pp. 168 ff.). From the material detailed above certain characteristic features of Luke's special source may be noted. (1) The parables are not, as so often in Matthew, called kingdom parables, although, according to Jeremias, they are equally full of the secret of the kingdom. Interest in people is particularly evident. (2) The narratives contain a number of miracles, some of them very striking, but they are not generally classed by source critics in the same category as those of Matthew's special source. (3) There is a marked interest in women.

It has already been noted that the description of Luke ix. 51–xviii. 14 as a 'travel' narrative is not altogether apt (see p. 92). It certainly fills in the gap between the Galilaean and Judaean ministries left by the other Synoptics, but there are in fact very few references to a journey.

---

[1] The list given follows V. Taylor's list (*The Gospels*, pp. 32 f.), but Streeter allowed more material in L (*The Four Gospels*, p. 198). McNeile-Williams (*INT*, pp. 87 ff.) adhere to Streeter's list.

At its commencement Jesus is in Galilee with His face set towards Jerusalem (ix. 51) and just after its ending He is near Jerusalem (xix. 28), but the progress of any journey in the body of the section is vague.[1] This has led to the view that Luke has himself filled the gap mainly with a mixture of his own special material and Q with little attention to geographical detail.[2] Indeed it is maintained that xiii. 31–33 is inconsistent with ix. 51 since it implies that Jesus is only just about to leave Galilee.[3] But Galilee is not mentioned, only Herod's territory (which included a part of Perea), and the alleged inconsistency would vanish if Jesus was then in Perea. Again xvii. 11, which states that Jesus journeyed to Jerusalem between Samaria and Galilee, is considered to be geographically difficult. It would certainly be strange if xiii. 31–33 had earlier placed Jesus in Perea. The explanation may be that xvii. 11 is reminiscent of an earlier incident, but if so Luke's attention to the journey sequence was overshadowed by his greater interest in the character of the contents. It has been suggested[4] that the dominating feature of the material as Luke has arranged it is an alternation between instruction and discussion, designed especially for the training of preachers and missionaries. It has also been proposed that in this material is a higher proportion of polemical matter than elsewhere.[5]

b. Luke's nativity narratives

There is much discussion over Luke's infancy stories. It is generally supposed that he possessed a special source for this material, in which

---

[1] Jerusalem itself is mentioned only at xiii. 22, 33 and xvii. 11, while the movements of Jesus and His disciples are elsewhere described in very general terms.

[2] Cf. H. Conzelmann, *The Theology of St. Luke* (1960), pp. 60 ff., for the view that in parts Luke's topography is unreliable, since geographical elements are introduced for a theological purpose.

[3] Cf. Bo Reicke's article in *Studia Evangelica*, p. 214. He cites J. Schneider's article in *Synoptische Studien für A. Wikenhauser* (1935), pp. 215 ff., for this view, and from it deduces that chapter xiv marks a new part of the narrative distinct from the opening section.

[4] Cf. Bo Reicke, *op. cit.*, pp. 206–216.

[5] Cf. Manson, *The Sayings of Jesus*, p. 28. Yet another, but less likely, explanation is the typological theory suggested by C. F. Evans, who wonders whether there are parallels between Luke's central section and Dt. i–xxvi. The idea that Luke presents a kind of Christian 'Deuteronomy' requires more convincing evidence than Evans is able to give (cf. his article, 'The Central Section of St. Luke's Gospel', in *Studies in the Gospels*, ed. D. E. Nineham, 1955, pp. 37–53). He attempts to establish a coincidence of order in the parallel material, but many of his parallels are very strained.

case it may have been distinct from the general L material. If L consisted of oral tradition it is easier to believe that such oral tradition included the nativity narratives than that a written source included them. This is due to the marked linguistic differences between Luke i and ii and the rest of the special Lucan material. The special characteristics of these stories may be briefly summarized as follows.

1. Their language and style are distinctive. After his literary preface (i. 1–4), Luke's style in the next section (i. 5–ii. 52) drops into what W. L. Knox[1] calls 'an orgy of Hebraic Greek with occasional improvements'. McNeile[2] called the language 'translation Greek'. Whatever its description the Greek of this part of Luke differs markedly from the Greek before and after, for from iii. 1 ff. the style lacks the strong Hebraic features of the infancy stories and may generally be regarded as literary *Koiné* Greek. This linguistic peculiarity clearly requires some explanation.

2. Their contents are also unusual. It is remarkable that it is in this section alone that Luke includes canticles and these are written in a form which appears to be modelled on the more poetic portions of the LXX. They are all saturated with Old Testament allusions.

3. They are independent of Matthew's stories.[3] Luke's interest centres on Nazareth rather than on Judaea, on Mary more than on Joseph, on the relationship between John the Baptist and Jesus, and on the childhood of Jesus.

Various explanations of the origin of these narratives have been proposed, but it is not possible to give more than the briefest mention of them here.

(i) *The theory of a Hebrew source.* The idea that Luke has used an older Hebrew source has often been proposed. It was strongly maintained by C. C. Torrey[4] and was regarded by McNeile[5] as a 'certain' conclusion. More recently it has been advocated from various points of view, one suggestion being that it originated in a John the Baptist sect,[6] while yet another basis for this contention has been the occurrence

---

[1] *Sources of the Synoptic Gospels*, II, p. 40.   [2] *INT*, p. 88.

[3] For an attempt to show that Luke's narrative was composed with Matthew's infancy stories in view, cf. P. J. Thompson, *Studia Evangelica* (1959), pp. 217–222, but his arguments are not convincing.

[4] *The Four Gospels*, p. 266.   [5] *INT*, p. 88.

[6] Cf. P. Vielhauer, *ZTK*, 49 (1952), pp. 255 ff.; P. Winter, *Nov. Test.*, I (1956), pp. 184–199. Cf. also H. Sahlin, *Der Messias und das Gottesvolk* (1945), cited by Feine-Behm, *Einleitung*, p. 45.

in these narratives of features similar to the word-plays which were so characteristic in Hebrew literature, since this is apparent only if an underlying Hebrew text is presupposed.[1] P. Winter[2] has an involved theory for the origin of Luke's material, including the suggestion that the Magnificat and part of the Benedictus were originally Maccabean battle hymns, while part of the narrative sections (Lk. i. 5–80, ii. 1–21) was from a 'baptist' document and another part was associated with James the Just (ii. 22–39, 41–51a). It is, however, highly doubtful whether Luke would have so radically adapted a John the Baptist source as this theory supposes, in view of his tendency to retain his sources with as little alteration as possible.[3]

Even if an original Hebrew source were admitted there would still remain the question of whether Luke himself translated it into Greek or already possessed a Greek translation of it.[4] It makes little difference to the general theory, however, whether Luke or someone else translated the Hebrew, as long as it is recognized that he retained much evidence of Semitisms.

(ii) *The theory of an Aramaic source.* This was favoured by certain older scholars,[5] but it is not now in such wide favour.[6] McNeile[7] remarked that the absence of distinctive Aramaisms in this section would involve for this theory the notion that the Aramaic was rendered into Greek,

---

[1] Cf. R. Laurentin's articles in *Biblica*, 37 (1956), pp. 435 ff.; 38 (1957), pp. 1 ff. He has fully treated the whole subject in his *Structure et Théologie de Luc I–II* (1957). In the first article mentioned, Laurentin gives a useful summary of arguments for a Hebrew source (pp. 454–456).

[2] Winter has discussed these chapters in a number of articles (*NTS*, 1, 1955, pp. 111 ff.; *ZNTW*, 45, 1954, pp. 145–179; 46, 1955, pp. 261–263; 47, 1956, pp. 217–242; *HTR*, 48, 1955, pp. 213 ff.; *BJRL*, xxxvii, 1954, p. 328). His general position is concisely summarized by R. McL. Wilson in his article in *Studia Evangelica*, pp. 242–248. Winter speaks of a Baptist document, of temple *pericopae* and of a Nazarene adaptation. As a basis for his Baptist document, Winter appeals to Pseudo-Philo's *Liber Antiquitatum Biblicarum* (cf. *Nov.Test.*, 1956, 1, pp. 186 ff.).

[3] Cf. Wilson's criticisms, *op. cit.*, p. 248. Cf. also P. Benoit, *NTS*, 3 (1957), pp. 169–194.

[4] W. L. Knox suggested that Luke tried to reduce his source to tolerable Greek, but abandoned the attempt (*op. cit.*, p. 41).

[5] Cf. A. Plummer, *St. Luke* (ICC, 1896), p. xxvi; C. A. Briggs, *The Messiah of the Gospels* (1895); F. Spitta, *ZNTW*, 7 (1906), p. 294.

[6] But cf. Feine-Behm, *op. cit.*, p. 45. However, the influence of the LXX on Luke's treatment of his source is admitted.

[7] *Op. cit.*, p. 89.

modelled after the LXX, but with a skilful avoidance of Aramaisms. This he thought to be improbable.

(iii) *The theory of Luke's free composition.* A widely advocated hypothesis is that these narratives are Luke's own work. Howard,[1] for instance, considered that Luke was so steeped in the diction of the LXX and especially of the Psalter that this might well account for the Hebraisms. Harnack[2] went further and suggested that the Hebraisms were intentional, but this suggestion was dismissed by Torrey[3] because it would involve 'a grotesque performance' on Luke's part for which there was no apparent motive. But if Luke intentionally composed his infancy stories in imitation of the LXX, why did he do it? It has been suggested with some plausibility that Luke's intention was to show the close connection between the birth events and the Old Testament.[4] In this case he would have followed Old Testament (LXX) models and the presence of Hebraisms would at once be accounted for, unless of course there was enough evidence to show that the Hebrew text and not the LXX could best account for his style. In the latter event a Hebrew original would be more probable, but the evidence is not sufficient to dispose of the LXX as the main influence on Luke's Greek.[5] If he did base his language on LXX models the result bears eloquent testimony to his literary artistry.[6]

There are various forms in which the hypothesis of Luke's combining oral traditional material with Old Testament models can be presented.[7] It can be maintained that Luke selected biblical material to combine with and illustrate the oral traditions in his possession.[8] Or it can be suggested that the oral tradition was itself strongly influenced by biblical models because the canticles, if any authenticity is to be attached to

[1] In Moulton and Howard, *Grammar of New Testament Greek*, II, p. 483. Cf. also N. Turner's article, *NTS*, 2 (1956), pp. 100 ff.

[2] *Luke the Physician* (1907), pp. 96–105, 190–218.

[3] Cf. his article in *C. H. Toy Studies*, pp. 286 ff., cited by Howard, *op. cit.*, p. 482.

[4] Cf. W. L. Knox, *op. cit.*, p. 39.

[5] Cf. P. Benoit's article in *NTS*, 3 (1957), pp. 169 ff. It may be, as R. McL. Wilson suggests, that Luke used a Hebrew source but was naturally influenced by his strong liking for LXX Greek (*op. cit.*, pp. 252, 253).

[6] Cf. V. Taylor, *The Gospels*, p. 63.

[7] The idea that Luke's work in these narratives consisted largely of accommodating two sources has recently been suggested by A. R. C. Leaney (*NTS*, 8, 1962, pp. 158–166), who does not, however, discuss their probable language.

[8] So P. Benoit, *op. cit.*

them, must by their very character have influenced the form of the narrative. Another, but very radical, view is that Luke ignored oral tradition altogether and composed his infancy stories as pious fictions after the manner of the rabbinic Haggadists.[1] Of these views, the second would seem the most probable, particularly if Luke had personal acquaintance with Mary the mother of our Lord, which is not at all improbable. The first is conceivable, but makes much greater demands on Luke's artistry. The third must be dismissed, for it is inconceivable that these priceless stories had no basis in fact, nor is it credible that they are the products of the author's imagination playing upon Old Testament typologies.

(iv) *The historical value of these narratives.* The assessment of historical worth is inevitably affected by views regarding the origin of the material. If the whole is a fiction there is no point in discussing historicity. But if sources, either written or oral, were used the value of Luke's record will depend on their reliability. Many scholars have impugned Luke's historicity on the grounds that he made an error over the enrolment under Quirinius (Lk. ii. 3), but the evidence from archaeology has helped to restore more confidence in Luke's veracity.[2] Nevertheless there have been theories of pagan influences[3] which have seriously called in question Luke's historicity. Yet, as Taylor has pointed out, the narratives are as a whole free from mythological colouring and are Jewish Christian in theology and spirit.[4] It is of course necessary

---

[1] Cf. M. D. Goulder and M. L. Sanderson, *JTS*, n.s., VIII (1957), pp. 12 ff.

[2] Cf. the discussion on this point in E. Stauffer, *Jesus and His Story* (1960), pp. 27 ff. The theory is here advanced that Quirinius was appointed Governor of the East and that he held this office from 12 BC to AD 16, together with the office of Governor of Judaea from AD 6. Unfortunately, Stauffer cites no specific supporting evidence, although if his theory is true it would remove all the difficulties. A. N. Sherwin-White (*Roman Society and Roman Law in the New Testament*, 1963, pp. 162–171) has a note about Quirinius in which he maintains the accuracy of Luke's dating of the census in AD 6 but considers Matthew to be incorrect.

[3] Cf. J. M. Creed, *The Gospel according to St. Luke* (1930), pp. 30–32. Cf. also the study of M. Dibelius from a form-critical point of view, *Jungfrauensohn und Krippenkind* (1932).

[4] *Op. cit.*, p. 64. Yet H. K. Luce (*St. Luke*, CGT, 1949, p. 84) calls these stories 'the imaginative poetry of devotion rather than the sober prose of history', but their poetic form need not imply non-historicity. Cf. G. H. Box (*ZNTW*, 6, 1905, pp. 80–101), against the view that Luke (or Matthew) shows the influence of heathen ideas. Cf. J. G. Machen, *The Virgin Birth* (1930), for a full discussion of

here to be clear what is meant by Jewish Christian. It must be understood in the broadest sense, in a manner which would be true of our Lord Himself, for these narratives transcend all narrowness and contain more than one indication of His universal mission (cf. Simeon's song, Lk. ii. 29–32).

Those who connect up one of the sources with the Baptist sect tend to see these narratives as an attempt to link the movement of John the Baptist with Jewish Christianity.[1] But this seems most improbable in view of the smallness of the Baptist's group of adherents.[2] Luke's purpose as a whole is much larger than this. Quite apart from the birth narratives he shows an impressive sense of John's importance in the scheme of things, marking the commencement of his ministry with an elaborate dating (iii. 1). This dating suggests that the preceding narratives were not originally attached (see next section on the Proto-Luke hypothesis). But it cannot be entirely ruled out that Luke intentionally regarded the birth narratives as a kind of prelude to the formal announcement of the commencement of the public ministry of Jesus.

c. The Proto-Luke hypothesis

The theory that Luke put together a draft of his Gospel before he became acquainted with Mark and later inserted some Marcan material before publishing the Gospel was first seriously proposed by Streeter.[3] Many other scholars had, however, prepared the way by various studies which focused attention on the difficulties in the established hypothesis that Luke's Gospel was built on a Marcan framework.[4] Streeter found a staunch ally in Vincent Taylor, whose admirable presentation of the theory has done much to commend it to many scholars. He proposes that Luke came into possession of a copy of Q

Lk. i and ii. On the subject of the virgin birth, cf. also D. Edwards (*The Virgin Birth in History and Faith*, 1941), who adopts a similar line to Machen, and T. Boslooper (*The Virgin Birth*, 1962), who regards the nativity narratives as mythological and opposes the literal historical interpretation.

[1] Cf. H. L. MacNeill, *JBL*, lxv (1946), pp. 123–130. W. L. Knox (*Sources of the Synoptic Gospels*, II, p. 41) partly favours the idea.

[2] The precise origin and extent of the Baptist sect is not known, but it is doubtful whether it was widespread (see p. 255 n.3).

[3] Cf. *The Four Gospels*, pp. 199 ff.

[4] V. Taylor (*Behind the Third Gospel*, 1926, pp. 2 ff.) traces the development of the idea in the works of Feine, Weiss (B. and J.), Burkitt, Stanton, Hawkins, Bartlet, Sanday and Perry.

and while at Caesarea collected information (L) which he then combined with Q. This combination was called Proto-Luke, but it was not
suggested that this was any more than a rough draft. It was not a published Gospel. According to Vincent Taylor it 'was not, and could not,
be published until Luke was able to expand it by drawing upon Mark'.[1]
It is important for this to be borne in mind when assessing the value of
the hypothesis.

(i) *The grounds for the hypothesis.* The basis cannot be better presented
than by using Vincent Taylor's own summary.[2]

1. The passion narrative. By a careful comparison of Luke's narrative of the passion with Mark's, Taylor comes to the conclusion that
Luke's version is not a recasting of Mark, but is based on an independent
narrative.[3] It is claimed that the Marcan material has been added, because when it is extracted the residue is a continuous narrative. This
view is further supported by the numerous occasions when Luke
changes the Marcan order in this section.[4] Hence the Proto-Luke theory
is claimed to account satisfactorily for this phenomenon.[5]

2. The eschatological discourse. Luke xxi shows the same characteristics as the passion narrative and this has led to the suggestion that part
at least (verses 20–34) 'rests on a non-Markan source supplemented by
Markan insertions'.[6] Vincent Taylor did not include this in Proto-

[1] *ET*, LXVII (1955), p. 15.   [2] Cf. *ibid.*, p. 12.

[3] R. Bultmann thought it most probable that Luke used an older redaction
of the passion narrative used by Mark, a view which focuses attention upon the
differences between the two narratives (cf. *The History of the Synoptic Tradition*,
pp. 262 ff.). In his recent book on *Historical Tradition in the Fourth Gospel* (1963),
p. 52, C. H. Dodd regards any theory that Luke is editing Mark's passion narrative
as having no plausibility. G. B. Caird (*Saint Luke, The Pelican Gospel Commentaries*, 1963, p. 25) maintains that in these narratives verbal similarity amounts
to only 20 per cent, compared with 53 per cent elsewhere when Luke uses Mark.

[4] Cf. J. C. Hawkins in *Oxford Studies*, pp. 80–84, who mentions twelve instances between Lk. xxii. 14 and xxiv. 11.

[5] There has been much recent discussion over Luke's passion narrative, but
agreement has not been reached over Luke's relation to Mark. Cf. S. I. Buse's
articles in *NTS*, 1 (1954), pp. 29–41; 7 (1960), pp. 65–76. Cf. also P. Borgen,
NTS, 5 (1959), pp. 249 ff.; C. E. Osty, *Recherches de Science religieuse*, XXXIX
(1951). Buse's suggestion is that behind Luke's narrative is a passion source which
was known to Luke before he knew Mark, and if this is established it would lend
support to the Proto-Luke hypothesis. Cf. also S. Temple's study, *NTS*, 7 (1960),
pp. 77–85. An earlier advocate for an independent source for Luke's passion
narrative was A. M. Perry, *ET*, XLVI (1935), pp. 256–260.

[6] V. Taylor, *ET*, LXVII (1955), p. 16.

Luke, but considered that its structure illustrated the literary processes behind the Gospel.

3. The main narrative section. In those parts which deal with the public ministry and the travel narrative, the Marcan material exists in blocks alternating with blocks of non-Marcan material. When the Marcan material is extracted the remainder possesses 'a relative continuity'. On the contrary, the Marcan sections are claimed to be 'topical panels' lacking any connection between them.

4. The treatment of Q. It is claimed that Luke's use of Q shows a tendency to expansion by the addition of the L material. In other words the Q material is always combined with the L material and never inserted into the Marcan material. It is then presumed that Q and L must have been combined together before the insertion of the Marcan material. If this claim could be substantiated it would be a strong argument for the hypothesis. It is certainly evident that Luke has left his Marcan material in blocks and it has accordingly been supposed that the only satisfactory explanation of this is that the rest of the material was already fused.[1]

5. The omission of Marcan material. Altogether about half of Mark's Gospel is paralleled in Luke. The omitted material according to this theory may be explained by supposing that Luke preferred a parallel tradition or else had no need for the material in his expansion of QL.[2] The strength of this factor must be gauged by the fact that a similar explanation could apply without recourse to the Proto-Luke theory.

6. The use of Marcan material. The Proto-Luke draft had deficiencies regarding Galilaean material, nature miracles and kingdom parables. Luke therefore supplied this lack from Marcan material.

---

[1] Cf. G. B. Caird, op. cit., p. 26. Caird argues that the only alternative is to suppose that Luke had so high an opinion of Mark that he determined to keep it distinct, which he rightly dismisses as less satisfactory. But he does not take into account the possibility that Luke may have decided on a scheme which involved the alternation of non-Marcan and Marcan material. Cf. R. M. Grant's scheme of Luke's use of Mark, A Historical Introduction to the New Testament (1963), p. 136. He apparently does not consider this to be a possible procedure.

[2] Where sayings are duplicated and one comes from Mark and the other from another source (of which there are eleven instances in Luke), the author had overlapping sources. (Cf. Caird, op. cit., p. 24.) The overlapping of Mark and Q is also said to be supported by several occasions where Luke diverges from Mark's order (Caird, op. cit., pp. 24, 25).

Vincent Taylor calls Mark a 'quarry' from which stone is obtained to enlarge an existing building.[1] The difficulty with this line of argument is that the deficiencies are laid bare only because the 'quarried stone' has already been removed.[2] It may quite well have been part of the original design.

7. Luke's literary method. The elaborate dating in iii. 1 certainly looks like a beginning, and if this is so it would support the contention that Proto-Luke began at this point. This is also supported by the position of the genealogy, which unlike that of Matthew appears after the birth narratives, and indeed after the first mention of the ministry of Jesus. This is undoubtedly one of the strongest arguments in favour of Proto-Luke.[3] To this may be added the indication of Luke's method which may be inferred from his preface and his use of the we-sections of Acts, both of which are claimed to show that the manner in which Luke treats his sources is in full accord with the Proto-Luke hypothesis.[4]

Certain other considerations have been brought forward in support of the theory. Luke refers to Jesus as Lord on fourteen occasions, whereas Mark and Matthew never do, which supports the contention that this feature is editorial. Similarly a different word is used for the exponents of the Jewish law in passages derived from Mark (γραμματός) as compared with those derived from Q (νομικοί). Both these features are said to be intelligible if Luke composed the Gospel in two stages.

[1] Op. cit., p. 39.

[2] R. M. Grant (op. cit., p. 118) considers that the Proto-Luke theory carries no more conviction than any theory which is based on an analysis of the remainder of a book after a portion has been removed.

[3] M. Goguel (HTR, 26, 1933, p. 12) maintained that Luke's position for the genealogy between the baptism and the temptation 'suggests that he found it as a separate piece, not as part of a general account'. But Goguel did not support the Proto-Luke hypothesis.

[4] Goguel disputed the validity of this point on the grounds that literary analysis in Acts is uncertain (yet see pp. 330 ff. for discussion of this) and on the further grounds that Acts is not a fair subject for comparison since no parallel existed as a model as in the case of the Gospels (op. cit., pp. 8, 9 n.). In a recent book A. Q. Morton and G. H. C. Macgregor (The Structure of Luke and Acts, 1964) have claimed to show by statistical methods that Luke and Acts are closely parallel in literary structure, which is in turn controlled by what they call the 'physical structure', i.e. the need to arrange the material to fit in with a predetermined number of a specified size of papyrus. In their opinion this lends support to the Proto-Luke hypothesis. Yet mathematical considerations cannot prove the theory although they may have some bearing on Luke's method once the theory has been adopted on other grounds.

Another consideration is the echo of the phrase from the mission charge to the seventy (Lk. x. 4) in a reminder by Jesus to the Twelve (Lk. xxii. 35), which is felt to be best explained by supposing that at the time of composing xxii. 35, Luke did not possess the mission charge to the Twelve (ix. 3), which expresses the phrase in a different way.[1] Such an argument would naturally have force only if it were accepted that in Luke xxii the author had no dependable tradition on which to rely.

The above-mentioned arguments are considered by the advocates of the hypothesis to constitute a sound basis, provided the evidence is considered cumulatively. Nevertheless there have been many criticisms levelled against the theory, often against single issues, admittedly, but this is unavoidable. It is important, however, when considering these to keep in mind the contribution which the issue being discussed makes to the cumulative whole, to keep the matter in true perspective.

(ii) *Criticisms of the hypothesis.* 1. The non-Marcan character of the passion narratives has been challenged, particularly by G. D. Kilpatrick,[2] who maintains that the Evangelist has so modified the Marcan material that the basis for a continuous non-Marcan passion narrative vanishes. His arguments are based mainly on linguistic considerations, but Vincent Taylor has replied that such considerations afford 'too slender a ground for the total rejection of a Lukan passion narrative'.[3]

The narrative runs from xxii. 14 to xxiv. 11 and is preceded, in Vincent Taylor's reconstruction, by xix. 47, 48, which describes the daily teaching of Jesus in the temple and the determination of the chief priests to destroy Him. But it is difficult to imagine, even in a rough draft, that Luke would have proposed so abrupt a transference of thought as to make the immediate sequel of this plot the scene in the upper room with the passover meal about to begin. The Marcan section, Luke xx. 1–8, in which the previously mentioned plot begins to be implemented, links so naturally with the context that it is difficult to believe that it was missing from Luke's original draft. The dramatic suspense of the repeated mention of the plot in xxii. 1 ff. would entirely vanish if the Marcan sections were withdrawn, and without them Luke's passion narratives would be robbed of some of their signifi-

---

[1] All these considerations are listed by Caird, *op. cit.*, p. 26.

[2] *JTS*, XLIII (1942), pp. 34–36; n.s., I (1950), pp. 56–60. Kilpatrick thinks that there are suggestions that Luke has modified Mark in order to portray the trial of Jesus as a miscarriage of justice.

[3] *ET*, LXVII (1955), p. 15.

cance.[1] The question resolves itself into which it seems more reasonable to suppose: that the non-Proto-Luke elements (xx–xxii. 13) were added as an explanatory suture between xix. 48 and xxii. 14; or that Luke originally planned his material in such a way as to show the development of the final plot as the background against which he sets the institution of the Lord's supper. It is admittedly not easy to decide, but the latter seems to accord best with the historical and literary sense of Luke.[2] Some scholars find linguistic justification for maintaining that even in the Marcan part of Luke there is evidence that Luke has used his own source for part of the narrative and has enriched it from Marcan material.[3] Although such a theory could fit into the Proto-Luke hypothesis, it does not require it, for Luke might have drawn from his two sources at the time of the composition of the whole book.

The appeal to Luke's twelve changes in the Marcan order as pointed out by Hawkins is differently used by him and Taylor. The former considered that these possibly occurred in oral rather than written transmission, and he therefore contended that Luke did not use Mark in this section. Although Taylor accepts a similar position, he uses it to support his Proto-Luke hypothesis by claiming that elsewhere when the order is the same as Mark's the sections may be regarded as insertions. In other words Luke used oral tradition for most of the passion narratives, but imposed upon it certain snippets of written material culled from Mark. But in this case it would be simpler to suppose that the Marcan 'insertions' were also preserved in oral tradition.

2. Little need be said about the eschatological discourse (which if it

[1] V. Taylor tries to lessen this difficulty by postulating that the section xxii. 1–13 (Marcan) replaced Proto-Luke's original introduction to the passion narratives (*Behind the Third Gospel*, pp. 177–181).

[2] S. M. Gilmour contends that Taylor has underrated the Marcan material in the passion narrative (*JBL*, LXVII, 1948, pp. 143–152). Cf. the same writer's arguments against Proto-Luke in *The Gospel according to St. Luke* (IB, 1952), pp. 16–18. Gilmour thinks that the difficulty of the 'gap' would disappear if Proto-Luke is abandoned (*JBL*, LXVII, p. 147). Cf. also J. M. Creed's contentions along the same line (*St. Luke*, p. lviii). For the view that Luke re-wrote Mark's passion narratives, see Creed's articles, *ET*, XLVI (1934), pp. 101 ff., 378 f. and cf. also A. Barr's article, *ET*, LV (1944), pp. 227–231. For Taylor's reply to Creed, *ET*, XLVI (1934), pp. 236 ff.

[3] Cf. F. Rehkopf's examination of two passages in Lk. xxii, *Die lukanische Sonderquelle* (1959), and H. Schürmann's studies on the same chapter, *Quellenkritische Untersuchung des lukanischen Abendmahlsberichtes* (1953–57).

is an independent narrative would support the Proto-Luke theory), apart from the fact that it is not universally agreed that Luke xxi was from an entirely independent source.

3. There have been criticisms of the continuity of the narrative in the Proto-Lucan sections. Creed called it an 'amorphous collection'[1] and this description is not without some weight. An analysis of Proto-Luke[2] shows that it contains 706 verses, of which no fewer than 556 are concerned with the concluding journey to Jerusalem and the passion narratives. It is, of course, possible that such a lop-sided arrangement existed in Luke's original draft,[3] but it is difficult to believe that he was so limited in his description of the early ministry merely because he did not know Mark, whereas he had succeeded in collecting a particularly varied body of tradition for the later ministry. A major difficulty is caused by the assumption that the Marcan material existed *only* in the form of Mark's Gospel, but it may be questioned whether this makes sufficient allowance for the possibility of some oral transmission of this material.

4. The occurrence in Luke iii. 1–iv. 30 of some phrases identical with Mark is admitted by Vincent Taylor,[4] but he does not attach much importance to it. C. S. Petrie[5] further pointed out that half the section from Luke iii. 1 to ix. 50 is Marcan, but Taylor does not consider this is sufficient to disprove his own theory that this Marcan material was an addition to the original draft.[6] Questions of this kind are notoriously difficult to decide on any objective basis. An alterna-

---

[1] *Op. cit.*, p. lviii n. Bundy (*Jesus and the First Three Gospels*, pp. 328, 329) considers that this section of Luke contains a 'formless mass of matter'.

[2] Based on the details given by V. Taylor, *The Gospels*, p. 41. The following will serve as a brief résumé:

The opening portion of the ministry: Lk. iii. 1–iv. 30, v. 1–11, vi. 12–viii. 3.

The 'travel' narrative: ix. 51–xviii. 14.

Judaean events: xix. 1–28, 37–44, 47, 48.

Passion narratives: xxii. 14–xxiv.

An analysis of the number of verses shows 170 in the first section, 334 in the 'travel' section and 202 in the rest.

[3] The lack of clear sequence in the material in this 'travel' narrative may possibly be explained by the absence of chronological or geographical data in Luke's sources (cf. Michaelis, *Einleitung*, p. 67). If this is a true supposition it may account for Luke's grouping of this material between the Galilaean and Judaean work of Jesus.

[4] *Loc. cit.*   [5] *ET*, LIV (1943), pp. 172–177.

[6] Cf. his reply to Petrie in *ET*, LIV (1943), pp. 219–222.

tive explanation of these Marcan sections is that they formed part of Q.[1]

5. Another difficulty is the awkward gap in the section viii. 3–ix. 51, when the Marcan material is removed. An attempt by Vincent Taylor to find non-Marcan traces in this section in order to postulate their probable inclusion in Proto-Luke is not self-evidently convincing.

In assessing the *pros* and *cons* of this theory it must be admitted that many of the supporting arguments contain considerable weaknesses when submitted to detailed analysis. Yet in fairness to the advocates of the theory the evidence must also be considered in its cumulative effect. However, although the hypothesis *may* explain certain features in the literary construction of Luke, it cannot be said that these features *demand* the hypothesis.

If Conzelmann's theory of Luke's free editing of Mark is correct, the Proto-Luke theory would at once be ruled out. But it must not be imagined that the only alternative to the acceptance of the theory is to postulate a wholesale rewriting of sources from Luke's own theological standpoint, for if more allowance is made for Luke's own industry in the collection of authentic information a two-stage production of his Gospel becomes equally unnecessary. Supposing that Luke had at his disposal Mark, the Q material and the L material, the fact that he prefers to use his material in blocks and prefers to combine Q with L material does not necessarily mean that he must have done this before incorporating the Marcan material. But the Proto-Luke hypothesis would have little point if it merely consisted of a suggestion regarding the manner in which Luke went to work. This leads to the enquiry as to its positive value.

(iii) *The value of the hypothesis.* It is a relevant question whether the theory, if proved, would have any value. There are four main claims in this direction: (1) the existence of an authority comparable to Mark (Streeter stressed the importance of this); (2) a corroboration of the Johannine tradition; (3) a basis for the traditional ideas characteristic of Paul; (4) a confirmation of the early character of the Lucan portraiture of Jesus. The first of these features has validity only within the framework of a rigid source criticism, which not only makes Mark early but the canonical Luke late. The second loses its value if the Johannine tradition is shown to be early, as is being increasingly recognized. The

---

[1] This is substantially Caird's solution, *Saint Luke*, p. 24.

third point is by no means clear, since Paul's close association with Luke would equally well account for any similarity of emphasis which may be observed in their writings. The final point is singularly inconclusive since the Lucan portraiture of Jesus is no clearer in Proto-Luke than in the Gospel, and if the latter is early the postulation of an earlier draft does not seem to be required. Since these values all depend on the assumption that Proto-Luke is rightly dated about AD 60–65,[1] they become less weighty if the canonical Luke is placed much earlier than is generally proposed under the four source theory. In proportion as the interval between Proto-Luke and the Gospel becomes less, so the value of the hypothesis necessarily weakens.

Nevertheless there are a number of scholars who would maintain that, however early Luke might be, Proto-Luke is a valuable witness to an earlier fixation of the tradition. But it is still questionable how Proto-Luke could be regarded as a fixation of the tradition until it was published, which does not appear to have happened until it was expanded into Luke's Gospel.

The theory of Streeter and Vincent Taylor has been given at some length because it has exerted most influence, but there have been other types of Proto-Luke theories. H. Sahlin's theory,[2] although called by the same name, is a very different proposition, in that he supposes that Luke i. 5–Acts xv. 35 was written in Aramaic by one author. This Proto-Luke was later translated and supplemented (Lk. i. 1–4; Acts xv. 36 ff.) by Luke, who is to be distinguished from the author of Proto-Luke, said to have been a Jewish Christian of Syria. Another theory is that of E. Schweizer,[3] who suggests an original source consisting of Wonder-stories (W) and an additional Hebraistic source for Luke's special narratives, these two sources being combined into one by Luke's predecessor, whom he calls H. Still later, Luke edits this combination with the aid of Mark. It will be seen that Schweizer's theory bears closer resemblance to Streeter's than Sahlin's does, although it differs from Streeter's theory in that Schweizer does not regard Luke as author of his Proto-Luke.

---

[1] Cf. V. Taylor, *op. cit.*, p. 40.

[2] *Der Messias und das Gottesvolk* (1945) and *Studien zum dritten Kapitel des Lukasevangeliums* (1949).

[3] E. Schweizer, *ThZ*, IV (1949), pp. 469–471; V (1949), pp. 228–231. For a summary of Sahlin's and Schweizer's views, cf. Michaelis, *Einleitung*, pp. 71–74; W. Grundmann, *Das Evangelium nach Lukas*, p. 16.

VIII. CONCLUSION

This survey of the various source theories has shown that the Synoptic problem still remains, and it will therefore be necessary to discuss possible avenues along which further investigations may be made. Before doing this, a survey of form-critical studies will be made in order to discern whether these studies have in any way modified the generally maintained source hypotheses.

CHAPTER SIX

FORM CRITICISM AND ITS DEVELOPMENTS

The most significant development in Gospel criticism in the twentieth century has been the rise of form criticism (in Germany, its home of origin, it is generally known as *Formgeschichte* (form history)). To appreciate its significance it is necessary to survey its historical setting and to study the reasons for its rise.

I. REASONS FOR THE RISE OF FORM CRITICISM

Many influences converged to produce this movement, and the main ones may fairly easily be discerned.

1. The first is the weakness of source criticism. Although form criticism is not an alternative for, but a supplement to, source criticism, it owed much of its origin to certain basic weaknesses in current source-critical speculations. Source criticism claimed to be a literary discipline and accordingly confined itself to the documents to hand. In the case of Matthew and Luke, the basic assumptions, as has been shown, centred around the use of Mark and Q. But source criticism could not push the study behind these documents. The most it could do was to suggest an earlier form of Mark (Ur-Markus) which proved unsatisfactory, or a multiplication of Q's which increasingly weakened the whole structure of the hypothesis. The form critic, however, proposed to study the origins of both Mark and Q and this appeared to be a laudable objective. The fact that the source critic could produce no documentary theory of Mark's origin offered a *carte blanche* to the form critic to suggest methods by which the original tradition was fixed.

The source critic had left a gap of some twenty to thirty years after the death of Jesus before any written documents had appeared and it was only natural that some attempt should be made to fill in the deficiency. However speculative the attempt, it must be made, and form criticism is the result. In some respects form criticism was traversing the same tracks as the earlier oral tradition theory, although there was little recognition of this fact, for the methods employed were very different, as indeed were the results.

The very fact that our historical data for the first thirty years of

Christian history are so limited means that form critics inevitably had to draw a good deal on imagination, although not all of them were conscious of doing so. Indeed, the attempt to classify the Gospel material into various literary forms was considered to be wholly scientific in scope and in fact a continuation of the best traditions of source criticism. But the large measure of conjecture will become apparent when the various types of theory are outlined.

2. Secondly, form criticism resulted from the challenge to the historicity of the Marcan account of Jesus. The way was prepared by W. Wrede's[1] theory that the framework of Mark's Gospel was the author's own creation in the interests of what he called 'the Messianic Secret'. He maintained that Jesus did not reveal His Messiahship until the resurrection, which meant that Mark's account of Peter's confession was not historical. The author of Mark, according to this view, has imposed his own framework on what were previously independently circulating units. In spite of the fact that Wrede's theory was strongly criticized,[2] it undoubtedly exerted a powerful influence on early form critics who turned their attention to the units of tradition and assumed as a valid presupposition that the framework of the Gospel narrative was suspect and the context of stories and sayings consequently of little importance.

Akin to Wrede's view was that of Wellhausen,[3] who claimed that the primitive tradition was overlaid with editorial additions which were influenced by contemporary Christian theology. This theory gave impetus to those form-critical theories which attribute much of the shaping of the material, and even its origin, to the Christian community (see discussion below).

A later writer, K. L. Schmidt,[4] examined the framework of Mark more thoroughly and concluded that the Gospel is chronologically and also geographically unreliable. No biographical reconstruction of the life of Jesus is now possible, on this theory.

Such challenges to the historicity of Mark drew attention to the need for a careful sifting of the evidence for the reliability of Mark's material, and this need the form critics claimed to meet. Nevertheless some of the theories proposed actually undermined still further the historical

[1] *Das Messiasgeheimnis in den Evangelien* (1901; reprinted Göttingen, 1963).
[2] Cf. J. Weiss, *Das älteste Evangelium* (1903); A. E. J. Rawlinson, *The Gospel according to St. Mark*[7] (1949), pp. 258–262.
[3] *Das Evangelium Marci* (1903).
[4] *Der Rahmen der Geschichte Jesu* (1919).

veracity of the Gospel narratives as a whole (see comments on Bultmann's theories below).[1]

3. Another factor which helped to promote form criticism was the
desire to modernize the Gospels. The assumption that much of the
material in the canonical Gospels was couched in first-century conceptions of the world of nature and of men which are quite outdated by
modern scientific knowledge gave birth to the movement for restating
the Gospel in concepts acceptable to twentieth-century thought. This
naturally focused attention upon the original literary forms and led,
among some form critics, to the quest for the essence of the Gospel
apart from these 'forms' (e.g. miracle stories). In other words, interest
in the forms was mainly in order to reinterpret them, and to recast in
modern dress the material which could be salvaged from them. This
was the approach of Bultmann, in particular, whose purpose was
governed by his philosophical presuppositions. The movement to
which it led, known as 'demythologization',[2] is the attempt to interpret
the Gospels stripped of all elements which form analysis have shown to
belong to the first-century environment of the early Church. Not sur-
prisingly the movement reached its climax in historical scepticism.[3] It
would be wrong however to suppose that all form criticism was
motivated by such apologetic considerations.

4. A further reason for form criticism was the urge to place the
literary materials in the Gospels in their historical situation, i.e. the *Sitz
im Leben*, or life-situation. This historical quest appealed strongly to
the modern tendency to emphasize the background of the Gospels. It
was a legitimate quest, but it contained within it a hidden snare. It was
inclined to assume without adequate proof that the material owed its
present shape to the practical needs of the community. A good deal of

---

[1] That the views of Wrede and Wellhausen exercised a powerful influence
on Bultmann is clear from his own works; cf. 'The Study of the Synoptic Gospels'
in *Form Criticism* (two essays by R. Bultmann and K. Kundsin, 1962), pp. 22 ff.
Cf. also *idem, The History of the Synoptic Tradition*, pp. 1 ff. A useful brief critique
of Bultmann's position and an assessment of the influence of the work of Wrede
and others upon him can be found in H. G. Wood's *Jesus in the Twentieth Century*
(1960), pp. 78 ff. Cf. also T. W. Manson's essay in *The Background of the New
Testament and its Eschatology* (ed. Davies and Daube), pp. 211–221.

[2] For a discussion of this movement, cf. I. Henderson, *Myth in the New Testament* (1952); P. E. Hughes, *Scripture and Myth* (1956); D. M. Baillie, *God was in
Christ*[2] (1955), pp. 211–227.

[3] Bultmann himself denies that complete scepticism is the result, although he
admits 'considerable uncertainty' (cf. his essay in *Form Criticism*, p. 60).

the life-situations proposed for isolated units of tradition is purely speculative. This important factor must not be lost sight of when assessing the rise and achievements of form criticism. What began with a perfectly legitimate historical motive has tended to develop along un-historical lines.[1]

This latter tendency arises very largely from the basic assumption of most form criticism that the *Sitz im Leben* must be found in the post-Easter period and could not have existed in the pre-Easter period. Such an assumption excludes any possibility of a continuation between the two periods, and leads to the inevitable concentration of attention on the Christ of faith rather than the Jesus of history. But, as has recently been argued by H. Schürmann,[2] form-critical enquiries need not and should not be confined to the post-Easter *Sitz im Leben*. The recognition of this fact puts the *Sitz im Leben* motive on a firmer footing.

II. VARIOUS TYPES OF THEORY

Before a general critique of form criticism is given, a summary of the main theories, arranged according to their chief advocates, will be made. Only the broadest outline will be possible, but with sufficient illustrations in detail to make the outline intelligible. Particular criti-cisms of individual theories will also be added.

a. The missionary preaching theory

M. Dibelius[3] began by assuming that traditions in the early Church were conditioned by missionary needs. This meant that he proceeded

[1] E. Fascher (*Die formgeschichtliche Methode*, 1924), in his survey and criticism o various form-critical theories (those of Dibelius, Bultmann, Albertz and Bertram), points out that all the theories under review postulate at times a different *Sitz im Leben* for the same form, which shows that form and history are distinct and that the latter cannot be safely inferred from the former (cf. especially pp. 212 ff.). It is signi-ficant that all the scholars mentioned were desirous of making such an inference.

[2] Cf. his essay in *Der historische Jesus und der kerygmatische Christus* (ed. H. Ristow and K. Matthiae, 1962), pp. 342–370. Schürmann maintains that since Jesus sent out His disciples to preach during His own ministry, this would have provided a *Sitz im Leben* for many of the sayings preserved in the Gospels, since the disciples would have needed teaching materials themselves and would also have required instruction for the undertaking of the task.

[3] *From Tradition to Gospel* (translated by B. Lee Woolf[2], 1934, from *Die Form-geschichte des Evangeliums*, first published in 1919). Cf. also *idem, A Fresh Approach to the New Testament and Early Christian Literature* (1936), pp. 27 ff., for further comments on his classification, and his article in *TR*, n.f., 1 (1929), pp. 185–216, for an assessment of form-critical trends up to that date.

from what he conceived to have been the early Christian method to an analysis of the text of the Gospels. According to him the traditions existed first of all in sermons and the earliest forms were therefore imposed by the demands of the *kerygma* to be added to later by more developed forms adaptable to other practical needs.

(i) *Paradigms*. These were short narratives which ended with a saying and which were designed mainly to bring out the importance of the saying. Examples of these are the healing of the sick of the palsy and the incident of the ears of corn.

(ii) *Novellen or tales*. These were narratives which aimed to show Jesus as a wonder-worker. According to Dibelius these are differentiated from the former by having no saying attached to them and by having a more secular tone. Moreover, while the paradigms were used by preachers, *Novellen* were created by story-tellers. Examples are the cleansing of the leper and the stilling of the storm.

(iii) *Sayings*. For the purpose of catechesis there would be collections of sayings, distinct from those in the paradigms because unattached to any narratives.

(iv) *Legends*. The name is unfortunate for it at once suggests something unhistorical. Under it Dibelius classed narratives relating extraordinary things about holy people. As an example, the infancy stories may be mentioned.

(v) *Myths*. Under this classification, Dibelius included the baptism, temptation and transfiguration, in each of which he found an inter-action between what he called mythological persons.

Because of the varied character of the forms thus classified, Dibelius supposed that there were at least three different types of Christian workers involved—preachers, teachers and narrators. But the distinction seems to have been created by Dibelius' analysis rather than being vouched for by independent historical testimony. In fact, it is difficult to conceive of any certain method of defining the difference between the various functions, while there is no evidence at all for a class of people wholly devoted to telling stories about Jesus without preaching the gospel.[1]

[1] It should be noted that many scholars who do not accept Dibelius' categories nevertheless maintain that mission work exerted a formative influence on the tradition. In a study of a portion of Luke's special material, W. R. Farmer (*NTS*, 8, 1962, pp. 301–316), suggests that a certain Greek rhetorical form (*Chreia*) is

b. The Christian imagination theory

More radical in its conception is Bultmann's theory,[1] for he traces the majority of the material to the imagination of early Christian communities. His classification of forms, however, is very similar to that of Dibelius. Instead of paradigms, Bultmann speaks of apophthegms, but he means almost the same thing. He has a sayings category comprised of various types (wisdom words, 'I' words, prophetic words, law words and rules and parables), but he has a poor opinion of much of this material and supposes only about forty sayings to be genuine. Two other groups proposed by him—miracle stories and legends—contain nothing of historical value. By the time Bultmann has finished with the Gospel material there is little genuine content left and it is certainly impossible to reconstruct anything remotely resembling a historical sequence. Clearly he attaches little importance to the history of Jesus.

What he does not explain is how the community imagination developed. It needs some convincing parallels to make credible the idea that the vast majority of Christian traditions were formed by the community and then implicitly believed by them to be historically true. In cases where Bultmann admits genuine material (mostly in the sayings of Jesus) he attributes their context to the creation of later tradition, especially to the Evangelists themselves.[2] He attempts to salvage something by admitting that even sayings which may have originated in the community may show in them the spirit of Jesus.[3]

discernible in the introductory material to some of Luke's parables, and this leads him to suppose that Christian preachers and teachers often conformed to this contemporary method of presenting material. Cf. M. Dibelius, *From Tradition to Gospel* (1934), pp. 152 ff., for a similar line of argument. Farmer does not hold that the preachers created the material, but only that they selected the form in which to present it, and there is clearly less objection to this view than to that of Dibelius. It is by no means evident, however, that the 'form' could not have been part of our Lord's own presentation.

[1] *The History of the Synoptic Tradition.* For a concise summary of his position, cf. E. B. Redlich, *Form Criticism* (1939), pp. 30 ff., and more recently R. H. Fuller, *The New Testament in Current Study* (1962), pp. 9 ff.

[2] Cf., e.g., his *Form Criticism*, p. 55.

[3] *Ibid.*, p. 58. F. C. Grant, in *N. T. Studien für R. Bultmann* (1954), pp. 137–143, in an attempt to maintain some authenticity for the sayings of Jesus within the framework of Bultmann's general approach, includes in his notion of authenticity both 'historical authenticity' and 'veracious representation'—a highly dubious distinction, for under the latter category he could then include material which was regarded by him as non-historical!

He considers that his method can be scientifically demonstrated, for instance, where material exists in the triple tradition. Here he assumes that variations must be due to editorial processes and this forms the basis of his stripping procedure. In the end his criterion is what he conceives must have happened in the transmission of Christian tradition and not what is known to have happened. His theory takes insufficient account of the presence of eyewitnesses and earwitnesses who might at least be expected to have exerted some restraining influence on the creative ingenuity of the Christian community as a whole.[1] Moreover, no importance is attached to the fact that communities lean on their leaders,[2] and in the case of the early Church these would have been apostolic men who would have been too close in time to the dominating influence of Jesus to have given free rein to their imagination. It is quite unconvincing to attribute such key narratives as the resurrection and the institution of the Lord's supper to the 'cultic motive' behind Christian imagination.[3] It is inconceivable that these narratives grew up because Christians wished to establish a historical basis for their faith. Such a reconstruction of early traditions is wholly inadequate to explain the growth and development of the early Church.[4] It might

[1] Cf. V. Taylor, *Formation of the Gospel Tradition* (1935), pp. 41–43, 107. He maintains that if this theory is correct all the disciples must have been translated to heaven after the resurrection. H. E. W. Turner (*Jesus, Master and Lord*, p. 81) points out that the Christian preacher always faced the risk of an eyewitness being in his audience to challenge him. Acts i. 21, 22; Lk. i. 2 and the whole conception of the apostolate show the importance of eyewitness testimony. Cf. also P. Benoit, *RB*, LIII (1946), pp. 504, 505. See pp. 189 f. for a criticism of D. E. Nineham's dismissal of eyewitnesses.

[2] W. Manson, in his brief but incisive comments on the presuppositions of form criticism in his *Jesus the Messiah* (1943), pp. 24 ff., places emphasis upon this. He draws attention to the fact that the tradition of Peter's influence behind Mark is contrary to the community hypothesis of Mark's origin and cannot be discredited as easily as most form critics suppose. Moreover, why did the communities from which the authors of Matthew and Luke drew their traditions not create enough material to render it unnecessary for both authors to use Mark, supposed to be the product of another community? Thus Manson suggests that if Matthew was connected with Antioch, 'the rich communal tradition' of that church would lead us to expect much greater independence of Mark.

[3] Bultmann, *op. cit.*, pp. 66 f.

[4] Turner (*op. cit.*, p. 84) rightly draws attention to the urgent need for advocates of this type of theory to account for the origin of the community. Moreover, if the communities 'created' the Gospel material to lend support to their own doctrinal bent or to help to solve ecclesiastical problems, why is there no reflection

have happened in the case of one or two individuals, but could not have commended itself to whole communities, still less to groups of communities, with any degree of unanimity. The quest for the *Sitz im Leben* along this track would lead to a *Sitz im Leben* which seems to be far removed from real life.

Moreover, this type of form criticism is based on a definite presupposition regarding the earliest Christian period. It first is assumed that all the Synoptic Gospel records are community products and it then follows automatically that they become witnesses to the actual life and teaching of the Church rather than to the life and teaching of Jesus. Thus Kundsin[1] can reconstruct the main steps of sub-apostolic development from the Synoptic material itself, dividing it into three stages, the Son of man approach, the ecstatic spiritual approach and the ecclesiastical approach.[2] The supporters of each of these groups are represented as attributing to Jesus statements which uphold their own particular point of view.[3] But the superstructure so ingeniously worked out collapses if the presupposition is proved to be invalid. And this is where the Bultmann school of form criticism has conspicuously failed. It is not enough to conceive what might have happened. No theory can have a solid foundation on such a basis. It amounts to taking traditionally attested sayings of Jesus and asserting without warrant, apart from the proposer's imagination, that these cannot be 'uncoloured' tradition. But what Bultmann and his followers cannot explain is how the original Jesus became so 'coloured' or adapted to their own point of view by the later Christian community.[4] Is it not much more credible

of spiritual gifts, circumcision and the Gentile problem, all of which were pressing issues in primitive Church history? P. Benoit (*op. cit.*, pp. 505, 506) points out that Christians did not survive opposition and persecution by the inventions of an anonymous crowd.

[1] 'Primitive Christianity in the light of Gospel research', in *Form Criticism*, pp. 79 ff.

[2] Cf. especially *ibid.*, pp. 96 ff.

[3] To illustrate, Kundsin speaks of Luke retouching the picture of Jesus' life in view of the Hellenistic conception of the Spirit (*op. cit.*, p. 127), and of Matthew tracing back the Church idea to Jesus (p. 143). This kind of approach is fundamental to his whole interpretation of the Gospels.

[4] H. E. W. Turner, in his *Historicity and the Gospels* (1963), has some acute comments on Bultmann's approach to history. He particularly challenges the validity of Bultmann's appeal to a distinction between *Geschichte* and *Historie*. The latter term is reserved for events which can be scientifically proved, the former for what has arisen from faith. This means for Bultmann that little relevant

to believe that the Christian community was 'coloured' by the authentic teaching of Jesus?

c. The theory of purely literary analysis

Several form critics have recognized the largely subjective character of the two views already mentioned and prefer to limit the movement to a study of literary forms, without claiming that such study can conclusively give the relative ages of the forms (as Dibelius believed) or their historical value. One of the leading representatives of this approach was B. S. Easton,[1] who, although he did not exclude all legendary elements and did not regard all the material as historical, nevertheless claimed that the study of forms is no guide to historical reliability.[2] Although he is much more reserved in his conclusions than Dibelius or Bultmann, Easton allows for apologetic and ecclesiastical influences having affected the tradition. For instance, in the case of Luke xi. 42b, Matthew xxiii. 23b, he considers the statement about tithing mint, anise and cummin to be impossible in Jesus' mouth.[3] At the same time his examination of the different forms is more literary and less dogmatic than the two others mentioned.

In contrast to the scepticism of Bultmann, Easton compares the teaching of the various forms with what is known to have been the teaching of the early Church, a sure safeguard against the unrestrained imagination. His conclusion is that 'where beliefs of the Synoptic period can be distinguished with certainty from the teachings of Jesus, we find the former most scantily supported by sayings placed in his mouth'.[4] This shows a rather more realistic approach to the sayings than Bultmann's, although it is disputable with what certainty, if any, the beliefs of the period when the Synoptic Gospels were produced can be distinguished from the teachings of our Lord.

data about the historical Jesus remains. Turner (*op. cit.*, pp. 61 ff.) rightly points out that those who wrote early Christian records could not detach themselves from the history they wrote. To this extent all Christian history must in a measure be 'coloured' by the standpoint of the writer, but this does not make it unhistorical, as Bultmann seems to take for granted.

[1] *The Gospel before the Gospels* (1928), pp. 80, 81.

[2] F. C. Grant (*The Earliest Gospel*, 1943, p. 41) maintains that it is an impossible position to suppose that form criticism has nothing to do with the historicity of the events, but only with the tradition's outward form. But surely Easton is nearer the truth when he claims that 'forms' give no indication of historicity. Both truth and error can be expressed in the same literary form.

[3] *Ibid.*, p. 107.   [4] *Ibid.*, p. 109.

d. Theories of limited value

Two English writers on form criticism may be cited as representing a view of its value in much more restricted terms. Vincent Taylor[1] takes the view that much of form criticism is open to question, particularly those theories which take no account of the influence of eyewitnesses during the formative period of the tradition. And yet he does not class all form criticism as valueless. He himself examines the forms under the following categories—passion narratives, pronouncement stories, sayings and parables, miracle stories and stories about Jesus. His pronouncement stories roughly correspond with Dibelius' paradigms and Bultmann's apophthegms, but he strongly rejects the historical scepticism of the latter. Moreover, in discussing the miracle stories he admits that form criticism cannot solve the problem of the miracles. It cannot reject them as worthless. It can only place them in the best position for the historical critic to decide. Such temperate claims have done much to rescue form criticism from the vagaries of mere speculation and to set it in its place, subsidiary to historical criticism.

Basil Redlich[2] has taken up a similar position and before considering the apophthegm stories (as he prefers to call the pronouncement stories of Taylor), the miracle stories, sayings and parables and the passion narrative, together with material which he classes as 'formless stories', he gives a concise critique of the assumptions of form criticism. Some of his points will be mentioned in the next section, but the reserve with which he approaches the subject will be seen from the fact that he categorically claims that a mass of stories in the Gospels are beyond the province of form criticism (hence his classification of 'formless stories'). Redlich rightly rejected such classifications as legends and myths, favoured by Dibelius and Bultmann, because they are dictated not by literary form but by content. After a careful examination of these, he concludes, 'The Form-less stories, even those called myths, bear their witness to the reality of the Cross and of the Personality of Jesus.'[3]

Another scholar who has claimed certain historical values for form criticism and who does not support the German sceptical schools of thought is C. H. Dodd,[4] who regards the form-critical method as

---

[1] *Formation of the Gospel Tradition* (1935), pp. 41 ff.
[2] *Form Criticism* (1939), pp. 34 ff.   [3] *Ibid.*, p. 196.
[4] Cf. his *History and the Gospel* (1938), pp. 86–110. In his article on 'The Appearances of the Risen Christ', in *Studies in the Gospels* (ed. D. E. Nineham, 1955), pp. 9–35, Dodd applies the form-critical method to the resurrection narratives.

valuable for demonstrating the substantial historicity of some, at least, of the traditions. His method of procedure is to select certain themes and then to show that these themes recur in different strains of the tradition such as aphorisms, parables, poetical sayings, dialogues and various story forms. He has contended that such analysis enables comparisons to be made between the various types of tradition, by which means he claims to be able more easily to check on the historicity of the material. While he admits that such a method of approach shows the influence of the interpretative element in Gospel tradition, yet he maintains that the Gospels represent a substantially true memory of the facts. The difference between this approach and Bultmann's will be readily apparent.

e. Theories of theological editing

The most recent trend in form criticism is the study of the editing of the forms of the tradition as it is seen in our extant Gospels. Such a method of approach (*Redaktionsgeschichte*) is adopted, for example, by Conzelmann[1] in dealing with Luke's treatment, Marxsen[2] with Mark's, Bornkamm[3] with Matthew's and Haenchen[4] with Acts'. This means that the Evangelists are being regarded as theologians rather than as historians. Such an approach presupposes that the materials which the Evangelists used had not already attained fixation and could be shaped even at a late stage in the history of the primitive Church. Strictly this is a development which has a negative as well as a positive aspect. It is certainly more valuable to concentrate on the part played by the Evangelists than to speculate on the productive ingenuities of primitive communities, but the study of editorial processes is nevertheless not free from the danger of speculative influences. It must never be forgotten that no Evangelist would have been able to impose upon his material a theological slant which was alien to the outlook of the primitive communities generally. Theories which depend on a distinctive interpretation of the interpretative element in the work of the Evangelists are, moreover, open to dispute on the part of those who prefer a different interpretation. An example will elucidate this point. Bornkamm considers that the account of the stilling of the storm in

---

[1] *The Theology of St. Luke* (Eng. Tr. 1960).   [2] *Der Evangelist Markus*[2] (1959).
[3] *Tradition and Interpretation in Matthew* (Eng. Tr. 1963), in conjunction with G. Barth and H. J. Held, who adopt a similar view.
[4] *Die Apostelgeschichte*[13] (*KEK*, 1961).

Matthew shows a large amount of interpretation and is intended to show the danger and glory of discipleship.[1] But the incident is capable of a more historical explanation which the form critic cannot dispense with on the prior assumption that it does not exist. In so far as *Redaktionsgeschichte* is governed by form-critical principles it is open to the same criticisms as the older movements, which will be summarized next.

III. GENERAL CRITICISMS OF FORM CRITICISM

It will now be valuable to summarize the most important criticisms of form criticism in order to get the whole movement into perspective and to assess its value. According to Redlich[2] there are six assumptions made by the thoroughgoing form critics:

1. That before the written Gospels there was a period of oral tradition.

2. That during this period, narratives and sayings (except the passion narrative) circulated as separate self-contained units.

3. That the Gospel material can be classified according to literary form.

4. That the vital factors which produced and preserved these forms are to be found in the practical interests of the Christian community.

5. That the traditions have no chronological or geographical value.

6. That the original form of the traditions may be recovered by studying the laws of the tradition.

Very few of these assumptions can be considered valid, at least in the form in which form critics generally accept them. Even the first must be qualified by the recognition of eyewitnesses who would have exercised some constraining influence on the tradition. But it is a basic assumption of form criticism that eyewitness testimony had no influence upon the development of community products. This has recently been vigorously maintained by D. E. Nineham,[3] who considers the community argument to be *a posteriori* and the eyewitness point of view to be *a priori*. This is because he regards the Gospels as no more than collections of 'units', and from this deduces that eyewitnesses could have had nothing to do with the preservation of the material. But in rejecting the *a priori* view in favour of the *a posteriori* he comes

---

[1] *Op. cit.*, p. 57.   [2] *Op. cit.*, pp. 34 ff.
[3] *JTS*, n.s., IX (1958), pp. 13–25, 243–252; XI (1960), pp. 253–264.

very near to arguing in a circle. Since he accepts as the basic article of
form criticism the virtual exclusion of eyewitness influence he is bound
to explain away all eyewitness traces. The fallacy of his method is
clearly seen when, in order to dispute Petrine recollections behind
Mark, he enquires why Mark did not make more use of these (if he
had access to them) in preference to community traditions.[1] As a concluding justification for the form-critical approach he appeals to the
fact that the modern approach to history puts less value on eyewitness
attestation than on later assessment. But it is difficult to suppose, for
instance, that a Christian some thirty or forty years after the incident
of, let us say, the coin and the tribute problem, would have been in a
better position to assess its validity than an eyewitness who not only
saw the coin and heard the conversation, but was himself under obligation to pay tribute. This method of making the alleged absence of eyewitness attestation into a virtue must be rejected.

The idea of detached units may be true of some of the material, but
the Gospels themselves bear testimony to many connected sequences
(e.g. Mk. i. 21–39, ii. 1–iii. 6). If the passion narrative existed in continuous form, as is generally conceded, why not other narratives? The
fallacy of supposing that the Christian community was wholly responsible for the origin of the different forms has already been exposed
when criticizing Bultmann. As far as the sayings material is concerned it
may just as well be assumed that the originator of the forms was our
Lord Himself. Moreover, to maintain that the traditional materials
have no chronological or geographical value is a value judgment
which is not borne out by the evidence of the New Testament as a
whole. The resemblance of the general outline of Mark's Gospel to
the summary of Peter's proclamation in Cornelius' house (Acts x.
38 f.) has been shown to point to some sequence. Moreover, the tradition that behind Mark may be traced the reminiscences of Peter has
too much to commend it to be lightly dismissed (see pp. 135 f.) and it
is impossible to suppose that an eyewitness would be entirely bereft of
chronological or geographical sense.[2] Again, since the events contained
in the Gospels present a reasonably intelligible sequence and location, it
is unreasonable to deny this impression or to attribute it to later influences without the strongest possible justification; but this would

[1] *JTS*, IX, p. 22.
[2] Form critics would not, of course, admit the validity of this argument since
eyewitness testimony is *ex hypothesi* excluded.

seem to be lacking.[1] The idea of laws of the traditions is misleading, for it suggests a rigidity which is not only most unlikely, but definitely unsupported by other evidence. When dealing with human minds, through whom the tradition was passed on, it is difficult to speak of laws. Moreover, if the proposed laws are deduced from a wide range of folk material stretching over centuries it could not be assumed that oral traditions must always conform to these.[2] There are too many unpredictable factors. Moreover, the controlling influence of the Holy Spirit over the tradition finds no place in this conception.

The limits of form criticism

But in spite of the very considerable modifications which need to be made to the assumptions just considered, is there not some ground for maintaining that the Gospels material can be classified according to literary form? The form critics would, of course, reply in the affirmative although, as already mentioned, with various emphases. The obvious danger of classifying the material according to content rather than literary form is well illustrated in the hypotheses of Dibelius and Bultmann, but such procedure ceases to be form criticism, in the strict sense of the word.

Any assessment of form criticism must take into account the following limits.

1. Only materials with recognized forms may be included and classification according to contents must be excluded.

2. It must be remembered that Christ the Teacher was greater than the Christian community which He founded and it must be expected that He left His stamp on the form as well as the content of the oral tradition of His teaching.

[1] Conzelmann's carefully reasoned arguments that Luke's geographical allusions are dictated by his theological purpose, if valid, would supply such justification, but his arguments are too often dominated by his form-critical method to be convincing. To cite one example, in discussing the passage Lk. vi. 1–vii. 50, he sees the references to some places (mountain, lake) as symbolic or where specific, as in vi. 17, as being more significant for omissions (Galilee, Idumaea, Peraea) than inclusions (*The Theology of St. Luke*, pp. 44 ff.). Yet he gives no serious consideration to the references to Capernaum and Nain in this passage. It is difficult to escape the impression that much of the symbolism is Conzelmann's rather than Luke's. But these arguments warrant a fuller and more detailed critique than is possible here.

[2] C. H. Dodd, in his *Historical Tradition in the Fourth Gospel* (1963), p. 6, cautions against such an assumption.

3. Variations in the tradition may not be assumed on that account to be unhistorical, since Jesus may Himself have repeated some of His teachings on different occasions and in different forms.

4. No form-critical hypotheses are justified which ignore the presence of eyewitnesses during the oral period.

5. Form criticism cannot assume that a study of non-Christian forms such as legends and myths must supply sufficient parallels without regard to the uniqueness of content of the Gospel material.

6. The uniqueness of the material is because of the uniqueness of the Person in whom it is centred and for whom the early Christians were prepared to suffer even death. Any form criticism which loses sight of this becomes at once divorced from reality. The Christians would not have been prepared to die in order to defend the products of their own imaginations.

When all the limitations are taken into account the scope of a true form-critical approach will be seen to be severely restricted. Yet with such restrictions it may well be asked whether such a movement can really make any effective contribution to Gospel criticism. Some indication of the claims made for it by the more moderate form critics may consequently be given.

IV. THE VALUE OF FORM CRITICISM

1. It has been claimed to be an indispensable adjunct to source criticism because it draws attention to problems with which the latter does not and cannot deal. In so far as it focuses attention on certain pressing problems, which would not otherwise have been brought to notice, such a claim is justified.

2. It has been said that form criticism plunges us into the twilight period of the Christian Church and directly connects up the formation of the oral tradition with the life of the early communities. Inasmuch as source criticism had tended to obscure this fact, form criticism has performed a useful service. But it should be noted that to account for the Synoptic problem, the advocates of the theory of oral tradition had earlier called attention to the many-sided aspects of early Christian traditions, although they did not tackle the problem from quite the same point of view nor in the same detail.

3. It has been suggested that form criticism has pointed to the possibility of collections of the *ipsissima verba* of our Lord. This claim is obviously not true for so radical a form critic as Bultmann, except

in a severely restricted sense. But there is a greater tendency among less radical critics to recognize that much care would have been exercised by the primitive communities in the transmission of the words of the Lord.

4. The idea that the Gospels contain insertions added by the Christian community has been claimed as a fruitful product of form-critical research. In other words an analysis of literary form is said to reveal extraneous material. But the source critics had always claimed to make similar discoveries and this can hardly be regarded, therefore, as a form-critical achievement, if achievement it is. And where there is the possibility of accepting the documents as they stand, as preserving reliable tradition, this must be preferable to the speculations of form-critics.[1]

5. Some value must be attached to the failure of much form criticism, for the quest for Gospel origins has at least been stimulated, even if it has not achieved much success. It should mean that more reserve will be exercised by all Gospel critics before asserting that any assured results have been secured.[2] If this is a negative value it is nevertheless a factor which it is hoped will exert increasing influence on future Gospel criticism.

6. The important question remaining is whether form criticism has contributed anything valuable to the interpretation of the Gospels, and if so to what extent. This question will naturally be answered in different ways according to the weight attached to the preceding values. If, for instance, the form of the interpretation of the parable of the sower be considered secondary, it may be claimed that the true interpretation of the parable may be independent of that preserved in the tradition.[3]

[1] In referring to what they call the 'most solid and undoubtedly permanent achievement' of form criticism, K. and S. Lake (*INT*, p. 20) paradoxically state this to be the bringing of more imagination into the question. But when investigators have to rely on imagination the results can never be solid and permanent. Had the movement brought to bear less imagination and more historical data its achievements would have been considerably greater.

[2] When discussing the methods of Gospel criticism, V. Taylor admits that none of the current methods—statistical, literary and stylistic or form-critical—can lead to absolute certainty, but he pleads for what he calls 'moral certainty' (*ET*, LXXI, 1959, pp. 68–72).

[3] J. Jeremias, *The Parables of Jesus*[2] (Eng. Tr. 1963), claims by form-critical methods to have cleared away several alterations which have occurred in the transmission of the parables, and therefore to have made possible a more adequate exegesis. Such alterations he attributes to translation, to embellishments, to change

But if it be considered that a parabolic interpretation may require a different form from the parable itself, form criticism would contribute nothing. Perhaps the most significant way in which Gospel interpretation has been affected is in the lessening of dependence on parallel sources. Source criticism has all too often tended to assume that double or triple traditions (as in most of Mark and in Q) are more reliable than single traditions (as in M and L materials), but since form criticism concentrates on units of material this tendency has diminished. Another factor which has come to the fore is the ability more readily to explain gaps in the material. It can no longer be assumed that absence of any major theme in parts of the tradition means that it was unknown in the area where that tradition was preserved. The paucity of references to the Holy Spirit in Mark and Matthew may be a case in point, for the traditions, according to form criticism, were formulated under the influence of the needs of the community. It could be argued that in a society under the conscious guidance of the Spirit there would be no need for catechetical instruction regarding His activity, and hence material about the Spirit would tend to be less repeated. Whether or not this is a valid approach may be worth considering.[1]

What gains there have been have not been spectacular and form criticism can hardly be said to have advanced very far the cause of Gospel understanding. But we should be grateful for any movement which assists in freeing criticism from excessive confidence in and multiplication of sources, which in the nature of the case must remain hypothetical, and form criticism has certainly done that. In spite of its extravagances, it has begun a new era in the approach to the Synoptic problem, an era in which oral tradition is justly receiving attention.

of audience, to new situations to which the parables were applied, to the fusing of parables and to the influence of their present contexts. But although much of his evidence may be otherwise explained, his treatment at least provides a warning against both a moralizing and an allegorizing interpretation. For a critique of modern approaches to the parables, cf. I. H. Marshall, *Eschatology and the Parables* (1963).

[1] For an advocacy of this, cf. V. Taylor, *The Holy Spirit* (1937), pp. 53–55, and for a criticism, cf. C. K. Barrett, *The Holy Spirit and the Gospel Tradition* (1947), pp. 140 ff.

CHAPTER SEVEN

TOWARDS A SOLUTION

It would be foolish to affirm that the last word has yet been said about the Synoptic problem. The variety of theories, together with the evident inadequacies of each, is a sufficient incentive to continue the quest, although there may be a feeling that the impossible is being attempted. Even confident critics are generally wary of adopting an attitude of finality in respect of proposed hypotheses. The following comments may be regarded as no more than an assessment of the present position and an attempt to indicate possible avenues which may yet need to be more fully explored.

I. GUIDING PRINCIPLES

a. The need to account for external testimony

One of the most difficult problems to settle in Gospel criticism is the place of tradition. Some schools of criticism play down external evidence as a datum for scientific criticism on the grounds that the witnesses were not scientific in their approach and cannot be relied upon to preserve authentic traditions. On the other extreme is that school of thought which almost regards ancient testimony as sacrosanct and therefore unquestionably true. Neither of these approaches is satisfactory. The former is guilty of over-modernization in assuming that only testimony presented in accordance with modern scientific formulae can be valid. In spite of the fact that the early Christians were men of their own age, a largely non-critical and non-scientific age, it does not follow that they were credulous over matters vitally affecting their faith when they knew that at any time they might be called upon to defend their position. As to the view which regards tradition as being as important as internal evidence, this is indefensible since some traditions are manifestly inaccurate. No-one would take too seriously, for example, the part that Andrew is supposed to have played in the production of John's Gospel according to the Muratorian Canon (see p. 235). Clearly traditions must be carefully weighed.

Where there is a strongly attested ancient tradition, it is a fair approach to suppose that this tradition is probably correct, until it can be proved wrong. In other words, where tradition and internal considerations conflict, the interpretation of the latter must be beyond challenge before it may be confidently assumed that the traditional view must be wrong. Where the internal testimony clearly and indisputably contradicts the tradition, the latter must certainly be rejected. To cite a case in which internal considerations are by no means unanimous against the tradition, reference may be made to the relationship between Peter and Mark's Gospel.

Although it is possible to make out a case for disputing any connection between the two, as certain form critics have done, yet probability is strongly in support of some connection, since there is a known association of Peter with Mark. In other words, the general agreement of all the extant early traditions on this matter establishes a strong probability that it is based on fact, which requires more than a mere possibility to dislodge. Suggestions as to how something *could* have happened may be very far removed from what actually *did* happen. Where tradition asserts the latter with reasonable unanimity and clarity, criticism must prove first that this could *not* have happened, before producing any evidence in support of an alternative. In other words, possibilities cannot oust probabilities.

Another factor in assessing the value of traditions regarding authorship and kindred factors of Gospel criticism is the need for furnishing some adequate account of the origin of a rejected tradition. Too often scholars have resorted to the 'guesswork' method. If a tradition does not accord with modern theories about any Gospel, the ancient witness is supposed to be propagating his own guess. It is not, of course, impossible that some traditions had their origin in this way. But this kind of thing is very difficult to track down. For instance, did Papias guess at the Hebrew origin of Matthew's Gospel, or is he merely reflecting an earlier tradition? If the latter, which seems highly probable, where did the guess enter the stream of tradition? The fact that no-one can answer this question does not necessarily mean that the 'guess' could not have happened, but it does mean that considerable reserve should be exercised over such a theory. Probability is against the Christians of the first century being left to their unguided imaginations to decide the not unimportant issue of the origins of their treasured literature about Jesus Christ.

In considering any possible solution to the Synoptic problem, therefore, due attention must be paid to ancient traditions. The task will be to disentangle what is true from what is false. It may be assumed as a starting-point that most of the well-attested traditions were based, at least partially, on fact. After eliminating any which are clearly and conclusively wrong, the rest must be regarded as part of the data on the basis of which a solution is proposed.

b. The place of personal reminiscence in theories of development

It has already been pointed out that the most important service rendered by form criticism has been to concentrate interest once more on the oral period and there can be no question but that any real advance in solving the Synoptic problem must be located in this period. Is it possible, however, to define more closely what is meant by the oral period? Vagueness over this issue may well lead to confusion over the whole solution proposed. The existence of such an oral period immediately subsequent to the events recorded in the Gospels is undeniable. But the terminus of this period is much less easy to fix, for it depends on the dating of the Gospels and on the view held regarding intermediate written sources. It is generally assumed that the oral period stretched over about thirty years, i.e. across the life-span of the first generation of Christians. But it should be noted that this need not exclude the parallel development of written sources. It would seem reasonable to suppose, without fixing too rigidly a thirty-year oral period, that for a time oral teaching was the main means of communicating the Christian traditions, but that it was supplemented by some literary productions. Although few data are available for this primitive period, there are certain lines of investigation which throw some light upon it.

The starting-point may be found in a closer examination of the Jewish oral tradition and its methods of transmission. The careful study of B. Gerhardsson[1] and the earlier suggestions of H. Riesenfeld[2] have provided an impetus in this direction. Gerhardsson's main contention is that rabbinical teachers not only taught traditional material, but taught it in set forms and vocabulary which the pupils were expected to learn by heart. There were various mnemonic devices to help them in this task. Since the earliest Christian preachers were Jews, Gerhardsson

---

[1] *Memory and Manuscript* (1961).
[2] In his article, 'The Gospel Tradition and its Beginnings', in *Studia Evangelica* (1959), pp. 43–65.

envisages that they would have followed the rabbinical practice. He also supposes that our Lord instructed His disciples in the same manner. From this it follows that a basic oral tradition would be formulated which could be transmitted through catechesis. But there are some basic assumptions in Gerhardsson's theory which require careful consideration.

To begin with, it needs to be demonstrated that our Lord's teaching was similar in kind to that of the Rabbis, if similar teaching methods are supposed. But this has been challenged. For instance, E. Fuchs[1] has claimed that the early Christian speech was creative and therefore novel. A. N. Wilder[2] takes this up as a basis for criticising Gerhardsson, maintaining that the Gospel material was too novel for conventional methods of transmission. Moreover the novelty of Jesus' speech-forms is linked with the novelty of His mode of life, which differed so radically from that of the conventional Rabbi. He established no catechetical school and His method of instruction must, therefore, have differed from the regular memorization methods of the Jewish teachers. Moreover, W. D. Davies[3] draws attention to the vital difference between Judaism and Christianity in its centre of gravity. In the former it was the Torah, in the latter it was Jesus Christ Himself. This shift of emphasis makes it more dubious to assume that Jesus taught His disciples in a manner similar to the Rabbis.[4]

Yet if Gerhardsson's propositions need modification they are invaluable in drawing attention to various factors in the background of

---

[1] 'Die Sprache im Neuen Testament', in *Das Problem der Sprache in Theologie und Kirche* (ed. W. Schneemelcher, 1959), pp. 21–55.

[2] 'Form-history and the oldest tradition', in *Neotestamentica et Patristica* (ed. W. C. van Unnik, 1962), pp. 3–13.

[3] 'The Gospel Tradition' in *Neotestamentica et Patristica*, pp. 14–34.

[4] Morton Smith (*JBL*, LXXXII, 1963, pp. 169–176) strongly criticizes Gerhardsson for misrepresenting both the rabbinic and Christian tradition. He maintains that no evidence exists for the memory techniques of Judaism before AD 70 and further complains that Gerhardsson pays no attention to other Jewish groups outside Pharisaism. He claims that those parts of the Mishnah dealing with daily life (as distinct from historical tractates) were created by the second-century Rabbis. There are, moreover, marked differences between rabbinic and New Testament material and this must clearly be taken into account, although it need not altogether, as Morton Smith claims, refute Gerhardsson's hypothesis. It is possible that different types of material required different memory techniques, but evidence on this subject during the first century is too scanty for any fixed opinion to be formed about it.

early Christian tradition. Memorization was a cardinal principle in religious education and it is impossible to suppose that no use was made of it in Christian catechesis. Even if our Lord was not a conventional Rabbi, which very clearly He was not, it does not automatically follow that He would have refused to use any memory techniques. The probability that He repeated His teaching material many times would in itself account for some of the differences in the Synoptic records. But if the Jewish educative procedure had had any influence upon our Lord and upon the apostolic circle, it would also go far to explain many of the similarities, particularly in language.

Another important consideration arises from the thesis of J. W. Doeve[1] that the Gospel material was taught, rabbinic fashion, as a commentary upon various Old Testament passages. The preoccupation of the early Christian preachers with Old Testament *testimonia* strongly supports this point of view, which had been adumbrated by Rendel Harris,[2] advocated by Stather Hunt[3] and modified by C. H. Dodd.[4] It would be claiming too much to maintain that a theory of Old Testament exegesis accounts for the majority of the material incorporated in the Gospels. But it was undoubtedly a contributory factor in recalling to the minds of eyewitnesses events which they recognized as being in fulfilment of Old Testament prophecy. Because of the conviction that there was a continuity between the Old and New, the early Christians sought out the incidents which emphasized fulfilment. This was not merely for apologetic purposes, but primarily for theological reasons. The Old Testament Scriptures took on a new meaning because of the close connection between event and fulfilment. Recognition of this fact enables the student of Gospel origins to postulate regulative influences in the oral period. The tradition was partially controlled by means of Scripture, but there were other constraining influences.

The words of Jesus would be regarded as sacred and committed to memory because of their intrinsic worth and because of the regard in which the Christians held their Lord. This surpassed any rabbinical

---

[1] 'Le Rôle de la Tradition orale dans la composition des Evangiles synoptiques', in *La Formation des Evangiles* (ed. J. Heuschen, 1957), pp. 70–84. Cf. also *idem*, *Jewish Hermeneutics in the Synoptic Gospels and Acts* (1954), pp. 177 ff.

[2] *Testimonies*, I (1916).   [3] *Primitive Gospel Sources* (1951).

[4] *According to the Scriptures* (1952).

teacher–pupil relationship.[1] They recognized His divine nature which invested His words with such authority that every effort would be made to retain as far as possible the very words in which He taught. This accounts for the significant fact that fewer deviations occur in parallel accounts of His sayings than in the narratives of His doings. When it is remembered that Jesus was acknowledged as Lord, it is difficult to conceive that the primitive communities would have 'created' in His honour Gospel material which could be placed on a level with His own authentic teaching. This would appear to make the Christians as great or greater than Christ Himself, a presupposition which is impossible. Oral tradition for this reason could never run riot. Moreover, as men of the Spirit the Gospel writers were sensitive to the quality of the tradition,[2] a fact to which the more extreme form critics have paid no attention.

Another factor which needs serious consideration in any tentative solution of the Synoptic problem is the possibility of the use of written notes as aids to memory. Gerhardsson[3] produces some evidence which suggests that such notes were used in Jewish oral tradition and it seems quite natural to suppose that Christian tradition would not have neglected to use aids of this kind. Admittedly this is conjectural, but it is based on some probability. If this happened the tradition may have reached a stage of partial fixation long before the written Gospels were produced.[4] The conjectural character of this suggestion will render it improbable for some, but there is no evidence which makes it impossible. Eyewitnesses may well have considered it worth while to jot down reminiscences, especially of the sayings of Jesus, and these jottings would have proved invaluable when the Gospels came to be written. It is not impossible that some of Luke's predecessors may have used written notes. It may be so, but there is no means of being certain about this.

The real problem is to determine the degree in which oral tradition

---

[1] For a presentation of Jesus as Teacher, cf. W. A. Curtis' book *Jesus Christ the Teacher* (1943). He brings out the parallels between the teaching methods of Jesus and the methods of the Rabbis, but also shows the superiority of Jesus.

[2] For further discussion on this, see pp. 206 ff.

[3] *Memory and Manuscript* (1961), pp. 157 ff.

[4] Gerhardsson (*op. cit.*, p. 335) considers that the Evangelists 'worked on a basis of a fixed, distinct tradition from, and about, Jesus—a tradition which was partly memorized and partly written down in notebooks and private scrolls, but invariably isolated from the teachings of other doctrinal authorities'.

could account for the similarities in the Synoptic Gospels. It is almost an axiom of New Testament criticism that, at most, oral tradition could account for differences but not similarities.[1] But where can the justification for this point of view be found? It assumes that divergences must occur in oral transmission. But whereas full allowance must be made for such divergences, a study of the place of memory in ancient catechesis, especially Jewish, as outlined above, shows that a far greater measure of agreement might be achieved in oral tradition than is generally conceded. In fact the proportion of similarity was very much greater than the divergence and it is to be expected that the degree of accuracy was certainly no less, probably very much more than this, in Christian tradition.

In the final analysis, however, it is not the methods of transmission which are the determining factors in the Synoptic problem, but the proximity of the writers to the sources of those traditions. This leads to our next important consideration. Were the writers authors in the fullest sense of the word, or were they no more than editors or arrangers of a conglomerate of existing traditions, whether floating or fixed, oral or written?

c. The distinction between authorship and editorship in New Testament criticism

It would not be realistic to attempt to draw too fine a distinction between authorship and editorship, and yet some differentiation is essential if a true picture of the Synoptic literature is to be sketched. Theories which suppose a direct eyewitness account to be behind any of the Gospels (as for instance Mark's reliance on Peter's personal testimony) are here faced with no difficulty. In such cases it is proper to speak of an author rather than an editor. But is this to be regarded as an indication of what might be expected as a norm? There is strong corroborating evidence that this is so.

Luke's preface is invaluable for ascertaining the method used by

---

[1] Artificial methods of testing the processes of oral tradition such as the classroom experiments of Vincent Taylor, reported in his *Formation of the Gospel Tradition* (1935), pp. 202–209, must be rejected. To be valid the experiment would need to be conducted among students whose mental processes were thoroughly conditioned by oral transmission methods. The method was severely criticized by K. Grobel (*Formgeschichte und synoptische Quellenanalyse*, 1937, p. 111) who called it absurd because an academic atmosphere could not reproduce the right conditions for ancient oral transmission.

Gospel writers, although some reserve is necessary before concluding that all the Gospel writers necessarily followed a similar course. Compilation of written narratives was evidently common in Luke's time. It is equally evident that these writings were based on reports of eyewitnesses and ministers of the word. There seems to be little room here for the idea of an editor in the narrower sense of an arranger of tractates of disconnected narratives and sayings. Each writer would choose from eyewitness accounts material that was most relevant to his own particular purpose. But it is impossible to say what measure of agreement would have been achieved by Luke's many predecessors. It is at least a reasonable assumption that had these attempts remained extant they would have shown the same phenomena of similarities and divergences as are visible in our Synoptic Gospels. In other words, if two authors recorded the same incident from the same eyewitness (or group of eyewitnesses) a large measure of agreement would be expected, even in the verbal expressions of the narrative.

Luke seems to suggest that he is writing an independent account, for although he mentions the earlier attempts he does not say that he used them. In fact, as mentioned in discussing Luke's Gospel, he claims quite specifically to have made a thorough investigation himself on the same basis of reliable personal sources as his predecessors. Yet according to the generally assumed theory of Lucan origin, this search for authentic material on Luke's part was confined largely to his own peculiar material (L). There is, of course, no need to exclude from Luke's statement the use of written sources. It may be that among the predecessors to whom Luke refers was Mark, perhaps even Matthew. But the fact remains that Luke puts most emphasis upon his own careful investigations.

One question of great importance in this discussion is the meaning of ὑπηρέται τοῦ λόγου in Luke's preface. Did these 'ministers of the word' have any special function as tradition-bearers? Since Luke specifically states that these, together with eyewitnesses, delivered (παρέδοσαν) the material to him and to others, it is highly probable that this special function was not only recognized but was officially controlled. Such a factor can be regarded as only hypothetical, but it has strong probability on its side. It has been noted in connection with the position of elders, but has been allowed little part in considerations of the Synoptic problem. Form criticism has tended to over-emphasize the part played by the community, without giving sufficient attention to the possible part played by official 'tradition-bearers'. If the probability of these be admitted it is not difficult to imagine that the tradition would have been handed on in set forms which met with the approval of the apostolic circle. It is far more difficult to imagine that the transmission of the traditions of the life and teaching of our Lord would have been left to chance, to be hammered out in the experience of the early Church. Were no discussions held among the early Christian leaders to decide on the best method of spreading the news, and would not the content of the teaching have been of vital concern to them?

There is much to be said for the view that the 'eyewitnesses' and 'ministers of the word' in Luke i were the same group and that this group consisted mainly of apostles or apostolic men. If this is correct it means that the tradition was apostolically authenticated in its basic form, and would have become modified only if the apostles had relaxed their careful surveillance, which they would surely not have done while they were capable of exerting any influence over it.

d. The value of simplification

In view of the variety of complicated source theories it is relevant to ask whether the Synoptic problem cannot be solved in a simpler manner. There is a tendency in scholastic circles to eschew simple solutions, but these may often be nearer the truth than proposals involving multiple sources. For instance, an appeal to an eyewitness account in discussing the origin of a Gospel narrative is clearly a simpler proposition than an appeal to underlying units of tradition preserved in the course of catechetical instruction in the community. The former introduces less 'unknowns' and is therefore definitely preferable. But is it an over-simplification?

It has already been shown that the older presentation of the oral theory was criticized because it was thought to leave unanswered too many phenomena in the Synoptic Gospels (see pp. 120 ff.). But the same charge may be made against source criticism and form criticism. The simple two source theory had become a conglomerate of many sources before it developed into a more specific four source theory, which in turn has never been quite convincing. Indeed most scholars would admit that no thoroughgoing source theory has yet been produced which answers all the major problems in these Gospels. It is even more noticeable that form criticism has been obliged to resort to many questionable propositions in an endeavour to account for the variety of forms observed—and thus the initial urge towards greater simplicity becomes lost. At the same time it would be idle to expect a simple answer to a very complex problem. It may reasonably be assumed, however, that the simplest answer with the fewest 'unknowns' is probably nearer the truth than more complicated theories.

II. IMPORTANT FACTORS IN THE SEARCH FOR A SOLUTION

Owing to lack of sufficient data the Synoptic problem must very largely remain unsolved. Yet this does not mean that there can be no certainty anywhere in this field, for there are some propositions which, in spite of the variety of Gospel hypotheses, remain valid, and it is as well for these to be asserted even if the details of Gospel origins continue in a state of uncertainty.

1. The written Gospels were accepted at a very early period as authoritative. Their authority was inherent and nót imposed upon them from without. Their claims to authenticity must, therefore, have been beyond dispute. By the first half of the second century they were so widely esteemed that heretical groups such as the Gnostics had taken them over and had even considered it worth while to produce commentaries upon them. But was there a period before the end of the first century when they were not regarded as authoritative? Since this is the twilight period of Christian development as far as our information is concerned, it is impossible to be dogmatic, but probability is against the notion of non-authoritative initial circulation. For if this had been the case, it would involve the assumption that at some stage in its primitive history each Gospel acquired an authority which it did not previously possess, and while this is not intrinsically impossible it is difficult to imagine how such a process could so soon have led to unanimity. It may be questioned, however, why the attempts of Luke's predecessors, who must have written at an early stage in Christian history, were not similarly accorded an authoritative position. The only possible answer to this question seems to be that these previous attempts evidently did not possess an inherent authority, however authentic their contents may have been. If Mark was included among Luke's predecessors, it would mean that the distinction between Mark and the rest was so obvious that no-one confused the issue. This may, of course, have been brought about by the known connection of Mark with Peter. But it is unprofitable to speculate further. All that is known for certain is that the Gospels now extant were alone regarded as

authoritative and that there is no evidence (except in the case of the Fourth Gospel among the small group known as the Alogi, see pp. 245 f.) that their authority was ever challenged.

2. The Gospels concern a unique Person and must therefore themselves be in some measure unique. Comparative studies in Jewish and Hellenistic oral and literary procedures may throw much valuable light upon the background of the Gospels but they cannot produce exact parallels, for the Gospels are essentially Christocentric and there are no parallels to this. The very uniqueness of Christ demands the possibility that the records of His life and teaching will possess unique characteristics. Some differences must therefore be anticipated between Synoptic criticism and general literary methods.[1] It is reasonable to suppose that the originality of our Lord's teaching and the originality of the influence of His actions upon His followers produced a unique situation for the germination of unique records of His life and teaching.[2] Had this not been so the Synoptic problem would never have arisen, for there must have been a unique regard for the records for three so similar and yet divergent records to have been retained with equal authority. Recognition of this uniqueness will promote caution in appealing too readily to non-Christian parallels. Too often Gospel criticism has begun from some point outside the phenomena of the Gospels themselves and the latter have been forced into a mould that they were never meant to fill. One of the major contributory factors in Bultmann's scepticism is a failure to recognize the literary uniqueness of the Gospels.

3. Arising directly out of the previous consideration is the fact that

[1] Many scholars maintain as a fundamental presupposition that the Gospels must be regarded on the same footing as any other books (cf. V. Taylor, *The Gospels*, p. 11; T. Henshaw, *New Testament Literature*, 1952, p. 63). But this presupposition may be strongly challenged on the grounds of the uniqueness of the subject-matter of the Gospels. At the same time their unique theme does not exempt them from all critical examination. It does mean, however, that what is valid for other writings may not necessarily be valid for these.

[2] H. G. Wood(*Jesus in the Twentieth Century*, 1960, p. 80), in emphasizing the uniqueness of the Gospels, drew attention to the lack of any exact parallels. Cf. also H. E. W. Turner, *Jesus, Master and Lord*[2] (1954), pp. 29 ff. There is no doubt that where this fact has been recognized, it has restrained the critic from many speculations based on doubtful parallels. Whatever may have been the custom in contemporary literary practice, it cannot be accepted *a priori* that a similar process must have taken place in the development of such unique documents as the Gospels.

the Gospel material formed the basis of Christian preaching and teaching and was not the consequence of those Christian activities. The *Sitz im Leben* school of thought has tended to reverse this procedure. But the early missionaries must have possessed certain Christian traditions which were agreed upon and which they were able to impart to others. Indeed few scholars would deny this, although there are wide differences over the extent of the authentic traditions. It is not enough to claim that each preacher and teacher exercised a charismatic ministry and that catechetical material was spontaneously passed on. This was undoubtedly true in the application of the Christian message, but is it necessary to suppose that every one who proclaimed the facts of Christ's life and teaching relied wholly on independent charismatic prompting? Our Lord promised such prompting when His disciples were confronted with magisterial inquisitors, but this cannot be regarded as a normal procedure whenever and in whatever circumstances the disciples might be placed. Nor can it have any direct relation to the transmission of the authentic Gospel material.

It seems most natural to assume that the Christian traditions were transmitted because they were believed to be authentic and were most probably regarded as authentic in the form in which they were transmitted. This means that the 'forms' were essential parts of the tradition and were not, as some form-critics have maintained, the productions of the community. Whatever part the community played in the process of transmission, it is inconceivable that the community created either the sayings of Jesus or the narratives about Him. The Christian communities were groups of people who had 'received' Christian traditions, and had believed them to be true and on the basis of them had made personal committal of themselves to Christ.[1] No other explanation can make early Christian development intelligible. The future of form criticism will largely depend on the degree to which this fact is recognized.

4. The final consideration is the impossibility of explaining the origins of the Gospels apart from the activity of the Holy Spirit. This consideration rarely finds a place in discussions on the Synoptic pro-

---

[1] S. H. Hooke (*Alpha and Omega*, 1961, p. 137) points out that behind all textual criticism, source criticism and form criticism lies the fact that the Gospels were the products of minds dedicated to making known the pattern of redemption. He agrees with Austin Farrer's strictures against theories which make the authors 'colourless disciples'.

blem, because it is thought to belong to dogmatics rather than to historical criticism. But in this case no divorce can be allowed, for the operation of the Spirit in Gospel origins is a vital factor, indeed *the* vital factor, in the historical situation. The clear promise of Jesus that the Spirit would teach the disciples all things and bring to their remembrance all that He had said to them (Jn. xiv. 26) cannot be dismissed simply because it does not fit into the normal categories of literary criticism. Whatever view is adopted regarding John's Gospel, it cannot be denied that this is testimony that the immediate disciples of Jesus were to receive special help of the Spirit in recalling what Jesus had said and that this help was directly promised by Jesus Himself. The only alternative would be to suppose that the Johannine account was an attempt to justify the self-claims of the disciples, but this would make unintelligible the teaching about the Spirit found elsewhere in the New Testament.

In the light of our Lord's promise certain propositions may be made which have a direct bearing on the Synoptic problem. It may first be asserted that the Holy Spirit controlled the traditions. However transmission was made during the preliterary period, it cannot be supposed that the Holy Spirit would leave this to chance procedures. The tradition-bearers were men of the Spirit, sensitive to the promptings of the Spirit and anxious to maintain the honour of Christ in accordance with the purpose of the Spirit (Jn. xv. 26, xvi. 13, 14). The Gospel writers come under the same category. Literary and historical criticism may throw light on the external circumstances and conditions of the oral period, but cannot pronounce upon the psychological and spiritual factors which led to the preservation of the Gospel traditions during this period.

The next proposition affects the selective processes of the separate authors. If the Spirit aided memory it is inconceivable that He did not also control selection. There were clearly more traditions than could be incorporated, as John xx. 30, xxi. 25 show. There was need therefore for the authors to select, whether from eyewitness oral accounts or written sources or perhaps their own personal observations. In this they would have submitted themselves as fully to the guidance of the Spirit as in the collection of the data. This view need not exclude the personal contribution of each. Matthew's Gospel, for example, was clearly written by a man whose mind was deeply impressed by the royal dignity of Jesus and by His fulfilment of Old Testament prophecy.

This was one of the controlling principles in his selection and arrangement of material. Yet it was mediated to him through the Spirit. The different emphases of the four Evangelists resulting in different methods of presentation may be more adequately explained by the controlling influence of the same Spirit than by the natural theological bent of the individual authors. Whatever the psychological motives which prompted each author to write, the evident spiritual power and general harmony of their presentations is unaccountable apart from the acceptance of a more than normal intuition. Whereas such a conception does not rule out the source hypotheses for Gospel origins, it is one of the fundamental weaknesses of all thoroughgoing source criticism that little room is left for the dynamic operation of the Spirit of God in the final writers of the canonical Gospels. It invariably leads to too mechanical and rigid an interpretation of the psychology of Gospel authorship. It tends to tie down the authors so closely to their sources that it becomes a matter of great importance to postulate why they modify them as they do. Yet very often no satisfactory answers can be given and the barrenness of much thoroughgoing source criticism bears witness to a lack of fluidity in the fundamental premises. A more moderate approach to source criticism, in which the author is allowed more freedom to draw where necessary from oral traditions, is more in keeping with the New Testament conception of the early Christians as men of the Spirit.

It is furthermore difficult to envisage a Spirit-controlled development of unitary literary forms as posited by form criticism, for it is a tacit assumption of that method that various church conditions have been the dominant factors in the shaping of the material. It would be nearer the truth to maintain that the Gospel material was found to be ideally suited to the needs of the communities because of the sovereign direction of the Spirit in the selection of the material. Or, on the other hand, the Spirit may have used the interaction between the oral tradition and the Church's needs as the controlling factor. It is unimportant so long as it is recognized that the Gospels were the result, not of editorial ingenuity in creating a continuous narrative out of a mass of disconnected units, but of a purposive selective process in keeping with the Spirit's control. The Gospel writers were men of the Spirit whose purpose was to produce documents which would be spiritually useful in the ministry of the Church, and any theory of origins must accord with this fact.

III. A TENTATIVE THEORY OF ORIGINS

In the light of the considerations just enumerated, a tentative hypothesis may be proposed, taking into account all that may be regarded as solid contributions of New Testament scholarship.

Stage 1. The apostolic preachers gave most prominence to the passion material, but they could not present this narrative in isolation. Hence Peter in his preaching gave connected accounts of the events of Jesus (cf. his discourse recorded in Acts x. 39 ff.) and this may well have been the standard pattern.

Stage 2. At the same time catechetical instruction was being given to the new converts and this would most certainly have required some careful arrangements. The major content of the catechesis would most probably have been the sayings of Jesus, especially chosen under the guidance of the Spirit to meet the needs of the communities. Such catechesis may have been entirely in oral form, or entirely written (Q?), or a mixture of both. The latter suggestion has much to commend it and, if valid, may lead us to suppose that certain tracts were officially produced to assist the catechetical teachers. The methods used by the early Church in this process are unfortunately impossible to ascertain. It is possible that this early catechesis was closely connected with Matthew and that it existed in its earliest form in Aramaic.

Stage 3. Mark, who had had close contact with Peter and had many times heard Peter preach, reduced the content of Peter's preaching to writing. The result was a Gospel with more action than discourse. It is not impossible to suppose that Mark made notes in the course of his association with Peter and later used these when writing his Gospel. If the external tradition is correct, Mark and Peter were together at Rome and after Peter's departure Mark wrote down his recollections.

Stage 4. After the production of Mark's Gospel, probably at Rome, Matthew may have come into possession of a copy of it and have been led to expand it by the addition of a considerable amount of teaching material from the catechesis and other material, some of which was drawn from personal reminiscences. Much of the sayings material was preserved in discourses and these were utilized by Matthew to dovetail the teaching material into Mark's framework.

Stage 5. Luke, who was personally acquainted with Mark, conceived a plan to write a careful account of the course of events from the beginning (i.e. from the advent of Jesus). He studied all the material he could lay his hands upon and all the reports given to him orally by eyewitnesses. He appears to have had a copy of Mark, although he may not have come into possession of this until after making an initial draft consisting of teaching material plus much narrative material (if some form of Proto-Luke theory is valid). The bulk of the teaching material was transmitted to him through catechesis, picked up mainly when Luke was at Caesarea, where he probably stayed for some time. He may have had access to some written tracts. He may even have had a copy of Matthew. It is impossible to be certain. But if he did use Matthew he supplemented Matthew from the oral tradition which by this time was well fixed. The catechesis to which Luke had access tended to preserve shorter discourses of Jesus than those preserved in Matthew. This may account for the differences between the arrangement of the sayings material in Matthew and Luke. On the whole it would seem easier to account for the peculiarities of each if Luke did not use Matthew as a source, but if both drew independently from the catechesis material.

Stage 6. It is probable that at first the tendency was for churches to use one only of the three Gospels as authoritative, because all would not necessarily circulate in the same areas. How long an interval elapsed before all three became widely known cannot now be ascertained, but the interchange which took place over Paul's Epistles would lead us to expect a similar process over the Gospels. Ease of communication in the ancient world would greatly facilitate this. But why were all three preserved? Variations of emphasis and content were evidently no barrier to the eventual acceptance of the three. Were the early Christians unaware of the problems, or did they consider that these were insignificant when set over against the immeasurable advantage of having a multiple witness to the life and teaching of Jesus? Here again it must not be forgotten that they were men of the Spirit who would recognize at once those literary productions which were authentically Spirit-directed, in which case the variations in the narratives would themselves be regarded as a part of the revelatory character of the records.

Through these various stages the Synoptic Gospels may have reached the forms in which we now know them. But the tentative character of these suggestions must not be lost sight of, for in the ultimate analysis our data are insufficient to lead to definite conclusions. We are dealing at best with probabilities. We cannot be certain, but we can affirm the powerful influence that these Gospels exerted at an early stage in their history. If the last word has not yet been said about their origins, their importance throughout Christian history cannot be disputed.

CHAPTER EIGHT

JOHN'S GOSPEL

It is obvious to the most casual reader that John has features which are strikingly different from the Synoptic Gospels. The problems which this creates will be considered later, but for the present it will be valuable to mention some of the dominating characteristics of this Gospel.

I. CHARACTERISTICS

a. The place of the Old Testament

So much emphasis has been placed on Hellenistic influences on John's Gospel (see later discussion, pp. 256 f., 296 f.) that the part played by Old Testament ideas has not always been fully realized. There is much which bears on Jewish history. The Gospel shows that Jesus was a part of that history, and that the Jews, in rejecting Christ, were rejecting One who belonged to them (cf. Jn. i. 11). When He came to the temple He claimed a rightful authority over it (Jn. ii. 16). The Jewish leader Nicodemus recognized Jesus' authority as a teacher (iii. 2), while Jesus classed Himself among the Jews as possessing the secret of salvation (iv. 22).

It is against this background that our Lord's own appeal to Scripture in this Gospel must be measured. He charged His hearers with searching Scripture and yet not recognizing that it testified to Him (v. 39). Moreover, He maintained that those who believed Moses would believe Him (v. 45 f.), implying that there was a clear continuity between them. The Old Testament colouring in the bread discourse is unmistakable, with its allusions to the manna in the wilderness (vi). When referring to the coming of the Spirit (vii. 38), Jesus appeals again to Scripture, even though the precise passage in mind cannot be identified with certainty. Old Testament shepherd-imagery lay behind the discourse on the shepherd and sheep in chapter x. As in the Synoptics the entry into Jerusalem on an ass is viewed as a fulfilment of Old Testament prophecy (xii. 14), while the unbelief of the Jews is illustrated from Isaiah (xii. 38, 39). John alone records that at the crucifixion Jesus' legs were not broken, as a fulfilment of Scripture, and in this case the inviolability of Scripture is particularly stressed (xix. 36).

In addition, Jesus several times refers to Old Testament figures, particularly Abraham. Appeal to Abrahamic descent forms the theme of the dialogue in chapter viii, reaching its climax in the claim that Abraham saw Christ's day (viii. 56). Nothing could express more clearly that there was a direct continuity between the Old and the New. Another link with the patriarchal age is found in the vision of Jacob cited by Jesus to Nathanael as being fulfilled in the Son of man (i. 50, 51). Jesus, speaking to Nicodemus, makes a comparison between a typical act of Moses and its counterpart in the Son of man, thus expressing His death in Old Testament terminology (iii. 14, 15). Jesus, moreover, claims the support of Moses in His approach to the sabbath (vii. 22). The prophet Isaiah is said to have seen the glory of Christ (xii. 41). The same prophet predicted the forerunner (i. 23), a fact mentioned in all the Gospels.

It is significant that Jesus appealed to the Scriptures on occasions when dealing with opponents, as in x. 34 where He brings out an interpretation which is regarded as authoritative. It will be seen, therefore, that both our Lord's use of the Old Testament and the Evangelist's own comments assume that all Scripture points to Christ. He is the fulfilment of the Old, and this fact must guide us in interpreting the concepts of the Gospel.

b. Teaching on the Spirit

There is more of our Lord's teaching about the Spirit in this Gospel than in any other.

In the Nicodemus discourse, the work of the Spirit in regeneration is clearly brought out (Jn. iii). A distinction is made between natural and spiritual birth which focuses attention on one of the major antitheses of this Gospel. Our Lord's teaching is frequently misunderstood because its spiritual character has not been apprehended. It is as impossible to predict the operation of the Spirit as that of the wind (Jn. iii. 8), which leads Jesus to point out that heavenly things need a different method of apprehension from earthly things. The mission of Jesus must be spiritually interpreted.

In harmony with this is our Lord's insistence on the spiritual nature of God (iv. 24), which requires therefore a spiritual method of worship. This was a definite advance on the limited conception of Judaism which itself had nobler notions than its pagan contemporaries. The Spirit of God was promised after the glorification of Jesus (vii. 39), when He would come as streams of refreshing water on those who believe in Christ.

It is in the farewell discourses (xiv–xvi) that the fullest exposition of the Spirit's work is found. His names, Paraclete and Spirit of truth, reveal His character, the former meaning Counsellor or Advocate or Comforter.[1] xiv. 16, 17 shows Him as representative of Christ indwelling the believer. In xiv. 26, Jesus assures the disciples that the Holy Spirit will teach all things, recalling to their minds what Jesus had said. He will be a witness to Christ, which is to be His main function (xv. 26, xvi. 14). He it is who will convince the world of sin, righteousness and judgment (xvi. 8–11), and who will guide His own people into all the truth (xvi. 13). It is evident that on the eve of His death Jesus' thoughts were much concentrated on the Spirit's work, but John's Gospel alone focuses attention upon this.

c. Prevalence of great themes

Unlike the teaching in the Synoptic Gospels the teaching in John tends to present abstract themes such as light, life, love, truth, abiding, which recur at intervals throughout the book. Some of these occur first in the Prologue (i. 1–18), which may be regarded as introductory to the whole, giving some indication of the type of themes to be presented in the following discourses. For instance i. 4 states that in Him was life and the life was the light of men. This verse combines two themes which find several later echoes. Christ came to give eternal life (iii. 15, 16, 36, vi. 47, 54, xvii. 2). Indeed, He describes Himself as the 'bread of life' (vi. 35), offers water which wells up to eternal life (iv. 14), declares His purpose is to confer abundant life on others (x. 10), to mention only a few of the references to life in this Gospel. It is not surprising to find the theme often recurring, in view of the Evangelist's expressly stated purpose in xx. 31, i.e. that his readers might believe and have life. Similarly the idea of light recurs in viii. 12 where another of Jesus' great 'I am' statements is found, reiterated again in ix. 5 and illustrated in the subsequent healing of the blind man. But there are many other echoes of the light theme (see, for example, iii. 19 ff., v. 35, xi. 9, xii. 46).

The theme of love is no less dominant, although most pronounced in the farewell discourses. The Father's love of the Son is often stressed

---

[1] Cf. S. Mowinckel, *ZNTW*, 32 (1933), pp. 97–130, for a full discussion of this.

(cf. iii. 35, v. 20, x. 17), as is also His love towards men (iii. 16, xiv. 23, xvi. 27). In fact the whole mission of Jesus has its basis in the love of God. In the concluding chapter love forms the key to Peter's reconciliation. While the theme occurs in the Synoptics it is nowhere so clearly expressed as here.

It is unnecessary to cite further instances to illustrate the characteristic recurrence of these abstract themes.

d. The comparative lack of movement

It has often been noted that John's record tends to be static, although this is largely due to the amount of discourse material. The proportion of narrative to discourse is much less in this Gospel than in the Synoptic Gospels. Nevertheless movement is not entirely absent. In i. 19–ii. 11 a whole week's events seem to be in mind, and several journeys are mentioned (e.g. ii. 12, iii. 22, iv. 3 f., 43 f., v. 1, vi. 1, vii. 1, x. 40). At the same time the Evangelist is not primarily interested in movements, nor for that matter in events, at least, not for their own sake. He concentrated on their significance. Thus in chapter iii Nicodemus fades out, and in the bread discourse the audience seems to alternate between the disciples and the hostile Jews. This characteristic of John's Gospel emphasizes the weakness of attempting to regard the book as in any sense biographical. The same is true, of course, of the Synoptics, but not to the same extent as here. This absorbing interest in discourse material has, in fact, given a particular colouring to the Gospel as a whole. It is reflective in mood.

e. The portrait of Jesus

Since the problems raised by the Johannine portrait of Jesus will be discussed later, it will be necessary here only to give an account of the positive emphasis made by John. The title Son of man is more sparingly found than in the Synoptics, although where it does occur it is significant (cf. for instance, i. 51, iii. 13, 14). More often the title Son of God is used, or else the unqualified 'Son'. There is much stress on the filial relationship of Jesus to God and its significance for His relationship to believers.

Nevertheless, the humanity of Jesus is not lacking and is in fact brought out with almost greater clarity than in the Synoptics. The wedding at Cana shows Jesus in an essentially domestic scene and in fact in a domestic capacity. At the well at Sychar He is seen as tired and thirsty. At the grave of Lazarus He is deeply moved and then weeps. In the upper room He washes the disciples' feet, and on the cross He thirsts.

More of the inner consciousness of Jesus is revealed in this Gospel than in the others and this reaches its climax in xvii where He prays aloud. It is this special characteristic of the portrait which is deeply impressive and which makes the reader realize that the Person of Christ is beyond comprehension in its depth.

It is easier to trace the messianic idea in this Gospel. Right at its commencement Christ's messianic office is recognized by some of His disciples (i. 41). Moreover, at an early stage it is also recognized by the Samaritan woman following a direct claim to this effect by Jesus Himself. This differs from the Synoptic Gospels and has been considered a contradiction (see later discussion). But John clearly brings out our Lord's willingness to admit His messianic office to a Samaritan, although He may well have hesitated to do so to the Jews because of their erroneous ideas about the function of the coming Messiah. It is significant that in John alone is it recorded that the multitude which Jesus had fed desired to make Him king (vi. 15), but Jesus at once thwarted this intention.

Perhaps the most characteristic feature in John's Gospel regarding the Person of Christ is the Logos doctrine which serves as an introduction to this Gospel. Whatever the background of the Prologue (see later discussion), it is evident that the Jesus to be presented in the body of the Gospel is first portrayed not only as pre-existent but as possessing the nature of God Himself.

II. AUTHORSHIP

The problem of the authorship of this Gospel has been so widely and so thoroughly discussed that it is not easy to express with any conciseness all the ramifications of the different hypotheses which have been proposed.[1] Moreover it is difficult to approach the problem without preconceptions. In the following summary the evidence from within the Gospel will be considered first, as it is recognized that this may be an important factor in examining the external evidence.

---

[1] The recent literature on this and kindred Johannine critical problems is summarized by E. Haenchen(TR, n.f., 23, 1955, pp. 295–335), who discusses the position since 1929.

a. Personal allusions in the Gospel

Nowhere in the Gospel does the author state his name, and yet he has not left his work without any traces of his own hand. These must be carefully considered and assessed in the light of the author's obvious desire to obscure his own identity as much as possible.

(i) *Self-indications in the Gospel.* In the Prologue of the Gospel the author states 'We beheld his glory' (i. 14), and it is natural to suppose that this is an indication of eyewitnesses among whom the author is himself included. This interpretation is confirmed by 1 John i. 1–4 where the first person plural performs a similar function. Some have interpreted the 'we' of the Epistle as referring to Christians generally,[1] but the statement in the Gospel would lose much of its point unless understood as an eyewitness claim. The author is not merely asserting that the Word became flesh in a general sense, but that in a particular sense the Word dwelt among us (ἐν ἡμῖν). While it is no doubt possible to regard ἐν ἡμῖν as referring to humanity in general, the subsequent verb (ἐθεασάμεθα) must clearly be restricted to Christians. Moreover the New Testament use of this verb suggests that the 'seeing' is physical and not spiritual sight,[2] in spite of the fact that many have interpreted it in the latter sense.[3]

Whatever conclusion is reached regarding the meaning of the word 'glory', which is here said to be the content of what was seen, it seems most reasonable to suppose that the author intended his readers to

---

[1] See the discussion of this interpretation in the author's *New Testament Introduction: Hebrews to Revelation* (1962), pp. 187, 188. It is maintained by C. H. Dodd, *The Johannine Epistles* (1946), p. 12.

[2] Cf. the discussion of J. H. Bernard, *Gospel according to St. John*, 1 (1928), pp. 19 ff.

[3] C. K. Barrett (*The Gospel according to St. John*, 1956, p. 138) states categorically that it is not an eyewitness but the apostolic Church which speaks in Jn. i. 14, but his reason for excluding apostolic witnesses is that he had already concluded that the author was not an apostle (cf. p. 119). Whereas it is not impossible to interpret Jn. i. 14 in this way, it involves an assumption—i.e. that the author speaks on behalf of the apostolic Church. It would have had considerably more point, however, if the spokesman had been an eyewitness. Feine-Behm-Kümmel (*Einleitung*, p. 160) agree with Barrett here. Bultmann (*Das Evangelium des Johannes*,[11] 1950, pp. 45 f.) steers between the bare alternative of an historical or spiritual interpretation, although he interprets i. 14 in the light of i. 16 as the 'sight' of faith. He admits that such 'sight' must be connected, however, with the event (ὁ λόγος σάρξ ἐγένετο) as well as its consequences (δόξα).

understand that the facts of the Gospel could be authenticated by visual witnesses and that some at least had been seen by himself.

Another passage which bears directly on the question of authorship is xix. 35 where the words occur, 'He who saw it has borne witness—his testimony is true, and he (ἐκεῖνος) knows that he tells the truth' (RSV). The immediate context is the piercing of our Lord's side and the initial reference must be to this. But since in the next verse the plural ταῦτα is used, the reference may be intended to indicate the whole content of our Lord's ministry of which this special phenomenon accompanying His death was the climax (cf. the use of ταῦτα in xxi. 24, which is discussed below). The problem here is whether the writer is referring to himself or to someone else bearing witness. If he does not intend his readers to understand himself as an eyewitness, the statement must have been added to make clear that the source of the narrative was an eyewitness. The ἐκεῖνος is somewhat ambiguous, for this could refer to the witness distinct from the author, the witness identified with the author, or to God as the witness's Authenticator. The third suggestion is least probable since the context contains no hint that ἐκεῖνος is to be understood as referring to God. The other two suggestions are equally possible, although some scholars maintain that it is less natural for the author to use ἐκεῖνος of himself than for another to use it of him and they consequently prefer the first interpretation. On the other hand the elusive character of the statement is more probable if the witness is the author than if he is another person, for in that case the testimony would have been more weighty if the author had named his source. But the matter cannot be pressed. It is sufficient to note that the author may be making a reference to himself as an eyewitness, although this is perhaps not conclusive.

The remaining passage is xxi. 24, 25, although this is more problematic because of the dispute whether these words are the author's own work or are editorial. At the same time there is no evidence that this statement was not an original part of the Gospel and it must therefore be regarded as a valuable witness on the matter of authorship. Verse 24 states, 'This is the disciple who is bearing witness to these things, and who has written these things; and we know that his testimony is true' (RSV). It is most natural to interpret the οὗτος of the subject of the preceding statement, i.e. the beloved disciple who leaned on Jesus' breast (verse 20). If this is correct the statement appears to assert that this disciple was not only the witness but also the author. Some have

avoided this conclusion by stressing that the witnessing is mentioned
before the writing and was, therefore, considered to be of greater
importance and may indicate that the author of the appendix was not
sure about the authorship.[1] But the order of verbs is perfectly natural to
express the idea of a writing based on personal testimony, since the
testimony existed before the writing. It may be possible to maintain
that the 'writing' could have been done through another as no doubt
happened when, as John records, Pilate 'wrote' the superscription over
the cross (xix. 19–22). But this is a strained interpretation, for since
μαρτυρῶν can be understood only of personal witness it is most natural
to suppose that γράψας should be taken in the same way. If, then, this
verse claims that the beloved disciple was the author,[2] what has led to
so many alternative interpretations? The fact is that advocates of
theories of authorship which deny an eyewitness author treat the clear
testimony of this verse as a redactional device. C. K. Barrett[3] considers
that those who published the Gospel modelled this statement on xix. 35
and claimed for it by this means the authority of the beloved disciple.[4]
Although Barrett considers that this was done in all good faith, it is an
unsatisfactory method of dealing with internal evidence. By such a
method any embarrassing evidence can be disposed of. Unless there are
convincing grounds for maintaining a contrary opinion (and they are yet
to be produced) the words of verse 24 must be taken with full seriousness as an indication of an author who claims to be an eyewitness.[5]

[1] A view mentioned by Redlich (*Form Criticism*, 1939, p. 43).

[2] C. H. Dodd (*Historical Tradition in the Fourth Gospel*, p. 12, and *JTS*, n.s., IV,
1953, pp. 212, 213) understands ταῦτα in xxi. 24 as a reference to the preceding
pericope, or at most to the whole appendix only, and he therefore disputes this
verse as evidence for the authorship of the whole Gospel.

[3] *Op. cit.*, p. 489.

[4] Cf. also A. Harnack (*Die Chronologie der altchristlichen Literatur bis Eusebius*,
1897, pp. 678 ff.), who maintained that this Gospel was attributed to John the
apostle by a legend purposely set on foot. But cf. W. Sanday's criticisms, *The
Criticism of the Fourth Gospel* (1905), pp. 63 ff.

[5] It should be noted that if these verses are regarded as an appendage made by
someone belonging to the apostle's own circle they would still be a very early
testimony to apostolic authorship (cf. Meinertz, *Einleitung*, p. 232, on Jn. xxi.
25; Tasker, *The Gospel according to St. John*, TNT, 1960, pp. 13 f.).

In addition to the specific statements made in the Gospel it is necessary to take
account of the general impression of the whole. As A. C. Headlam (*The Fourth
Gospel as History*, 1948, p. 44) pointed out, the Gospel demands as its author one
who had a close intimacy with Jesus. Cf. also Sir F. Kenyon, *The Bible and Modern
Scholarship* (1948), pp. 24, 25.

(ii) *The problem of the 'beloved disciple'*. The expression 'the disciple whom Jesus loved' has just been considered in the context of the Appendix (xxi) where it was shown that xxi. 24 seems intended to identify this disciple as the author of the Gospel. His name is not given, but he was among the group mentioned in xxi. 2, comprising Peter, Thomas, Nathanael, the sons of Zebedee and two others. The 'beloved disciple' who is unnamed must be among the last four. Other details concerning him, recorded in chapter xxi, are firstly, that he leaned on Jesus' breast at the last supper and asked about the betrayer, and secondly, that he appears to have had close association with Peter. Both facts are closely linked in xiii. 23, 24, the first occasion on which this disciple is so described. The echo of xiii. 23 f. in xxi shows how vividly the writer recalls the incident, which is most intelligible if the writer was himself that beloved disciple.[1]

It is significant that when earlier in chapter xxi 'the beloved disciple' is introduced he addresses himself to Simon Peter (verse 7) and announces the presence of the Lord. He was evidently in close contact with Peter. These two are found in each other's company by Mary Magdalene when she rushes to tell them of the disappearance of the body of Jesus (xx. 2). Moreover, the writer mentions that the beloved disciple when he saw the empty tomb believed (xx. 8), which is again highly intelligible if the author were that disciple, who would not easily forget the precise moment when faith took possession of him. Such a detail might, of course, have been passed on by the beloved disciple to the author, but the narrative is so natural that the former interpretation is preferable.

The remaining reference to the beloved disciple is in the account of the crucifixion, where Jesus commends His mother to the care of this disciple, who at once took her to his own home (xix. 26). This is the only occasion when he is mentioned apart from Peter.

It is reasonable to suppose, therefore, that the beloved disciple was an associate of Peter and that there was a particular reason for his being introduced in this oblique way in the passion narratives and not in the earlier part of the Gospel. The obvious choice in fulfilment of the former of these conditions is John, son of Zebedee. He and Peter belonged to the inner circle of disciples and were present, together with

---

[1] Michaelis (*Einleitung*, pp. 98 f.) argues firmly for the identification of the beloved disciple with John the son of Zebedee, particularly on the strength of the evidence of xxi. 2.

James, on three occasions when the others were absent (cf. Mk. v. 37, ix. 2, xiv. 33). Moreover, Peter and John were selected by Jesus to prepare the Passover for Himself and His disciples (Lk. xxii. 8). They were still closely associated together after the resurrection, as Acts iii. 1, 11, iv. 13 show. They are mentioned together again in Acts viii. 14 as delegates sent from Jerusalem to Samaria. The same association is found in Paul's reference to the 'pillar apostles', James, Cephas and John (Gal. ii. 9). All this evidence suggests a strong probability that the 'beloved disciple' was intended to describe the son of Zebedee.[1] This supposition is strengthened by the fact that nowhere in the Gospel is the apostle John mentioned by name, although he is mentioned twenty times (including parallels) in the Synoptic Gospels. Moreover, John the Baptist is described as 'John' without further qualification, which strongly suggests that the writer intended the apostle John to be understood under another title. It cannot be denied that absence of specific reference to him creates a definite predisposition towards Johannine authorship and any alternative views must reckon with this peculiarity and provide an adequate explanation.

Yet some consideration must be given to the delayed appearance of the 'beloved disciple' in the Gospel narrative. Why does he not appear until the events in the upper room? When Matthew's references to John are examined it is found that John comes into the story only in the narrative of his call, in the names of the Twelve and in the transfiguration account. In Mark he is also mentioned as being in the house when Peter's mother-in-law was healed (i. 29), as being taken with Peter and James into Jairus' house (v. 37), as reporting to Jesus his well-intentioned but officious action in forbidding an exorcist who was casting out demons in Jesus' name (ix. 38), as requesting the place of honour in the kingdom with James (x. 35 ff.), as being among the small group of disciples who asked for a sign (xiii. 3 f.), and as being with Jesus in the Garden of Gethsemane (xiv. 32 f.). On the whole Mark's picture does not flatter John. Nor in fact does Luke's, for he has only two references not in the other Synoptics, his part in the preparation of the Passover

---

[1] It is significant that this identification was assumed without question by patristic writers, who regarded the apostle John as the author of the Gospel (cf. M. F. Wiles, *The Spiritual Gospel*, 1960, pp. 9 f.). This writer notes that Origen and Chrysostom regarded the description 'the beloved disciple' as furnishing the key to the purpose of the Gospel. The author's own exalted position tallies with the exalted character of the Gospel.

(Matthew refers vaguely to 'disciples', Mark to 'two of the disciples', but Luke alone names them), and his desire with James to call down heavenly fire on an unreceptive Samaritan village. Supposing John to have been the beloved disciple and the writer of the Gospel, which of these Synoptic incidents would we have expected him to relate? Those which illustrated his fiery nature? Since the stories of his weakness were no doubt already well known and his triumph over these weaknesses was abundantly manifest in his life, he would reserve his personal appearances in his own story of Jesus for those hours during which he had learned in a special measure to draw closer to the heart and mind of Jesus than others had done.

But a problem arises at this juncture. Is it conceivable that any man would have described himself as 'the disciple whom Jesus loved'? Some scholars are so convinced that such a process is highly improbable that they feel obliged, in spite of the strength of the evidence just quoted, either to find some other identification for the beloved disciple, or to draw a distinction between that disciple and the writer of the Gospel.[1]

The difficulty must be admitted, but is it entirely improbable for John to have called himself the disciple ὃν ἠγάπα ὁ Ἰησοῦς?[2] If the phrase means any preferential love on Jesus' part towards this disciple it would certainly be difficult to conceive. Yet John, as his First Epistle shows,[3] had grasped something of the significance of God's love in Christ and the phrase may have sprung out of his wonder that Jesus should fasten His love upon him. It must not be overlooked that it would be almost as difficult for someone else to single out one of the

[1] R. H. Strachan (*The Fourth Evangelist, Dramatist or Historian?*, 1925), who fully accepted the identification of the beloved disciple as John, son of Zebedee, considered that the Evangelist was one of John's closest disciples who had imbibed so much of his leader's spiritual experience that it had become his own. According to this theory the Evangelist called upon his dramatic imagination for the eyewitness touches, in which case these touches would give no support to apostolic authorship. Even the Evangelist's picture of the beloved disciple was considered to be idealized (cf. *op. cit.*, pp. 49 ff., 73 ff.). Yet the unpretentious manner in which the beloved disciple is introduced does not at once suggest any desire for dramatic effect. If this is dramatic skill, it is so superbly executed as to be almost completely unselfconscious.

[2] The phrase is identical in xiii. 23, xix. 26, xxi. 7, 20, but in xx. 2 the verb ἐφίλει is substituted for ἠγάπα.

[3] The verb ἀγαπάω occurs twenty-one times in I John alone, more times than any other New Testament book except John's Gospel.

disciples as the special object of Jesus' love as for the beloved disciple himself. It might, of course, be that this was the familiar description of the aged apostle in Asia, in which case the original readers would at once identify him and would not misunderstand the motives for its use. Far from being an evidence of arrogance, as is so often suggested, it may perhaps be regarded as a sign of modesty. John will not mention his name but will rather draw attention to what he owes to the love of Jesus.

Nevertheless, those who deny the identity of the beloved disciple with the apostle John claim to avoid this difficulty by suggesting a different identity. The rich young ruler has been suggested because Mark x. 21 states that Jesus, looking upon him, loved him. But since we do not even know whether this man became a believer the suggestion is precarious. Another suggestion is Nathanael, but this, in the nature of the case, is conjectural since we know so little about him and in any case he is named in John xxi in such a way as to suggest that he is distinct from the beloved disciple. A more widely held theory is that the disciple was Lazarus and there is rather more to be said for this.[1] He first appears after Lazarus is introduced into the narrative in chapters xi and xii. Moreover in xi. 3 Lazarus is described by his sisters as 'he whom you love' (RSV; ὃν φιλεῖς). The suggestion is interesting, but was Lazarus in the upper room, and would he especially have reclined on Jesus' breast? It is highly improbable. The Synoptic Gospels, at any rate, make it clear that only the apostles were with Jesus on the Passover night. But if the possibility be admitted it would still be necessary to explain why Lazarus is mentioned by name in xi and xii and then by a descriptive phrase in xiii ff., a difficulty which is obviated if the beloved disciple remains anonymous throughout.

Yet another interpretation of the beloved disciple is to regard him as an ideal figure.[2] His anonymity is then interpreted as indicating that

[1] For a recent advocacy of this view, cf. J. N. Sanders' article 'Who was the disciple whom Jesus loved?' in *Studies in the Fourth Gospel* (ed. F. L. Cross, 1957), pp. 72–82. Cf. also F. V. Filson's article in *JBL*, LXVIII (1949), pp. 83–88, and his exposition of the same view in his article on John in *Current Issues in New Testament Interpretation* (ed. W. Klassen and G. F. Snyder, 1962), pp. 111–123, in which he argues that this view best fits into the theme of life, which is so dominant in the Gospel. Another suggestion, Matthias, is proposed by E. L. Titus, *JBL*, LXIX (1950), pp. 323–328, based on the symbolism of Judas as a type of the Jews being replaced by a man who was a representative Christian, but the connection of Acts i with John's Gospel is not at all apparent.

[2] Cf. A. Correll's *Consummatum Est* (1958), pp. 204 ff.

the Gospel is not the work of a single individual but of the Church. The presentation of the life and teaching of Jesus becomes in this view the Church's own testimony to itself and to its Lord.[1] But this is a most unsatisfactory interpretation because it involves treating the beloved disciple as unhistorical in spite of the contrary impression in the narrative, and because it assumes that any community could create such an idealization to represent its collective experience of Jesus. Yet the almost incidental allusions to the beloved disciple in the Gospel do not read like symbolic allusions. It is a fair principle of criticism that if a figure can reasonably be regarded as historical it should not be turned into a symbol which can mean anything the interpreter cares to read into it. It may further be questioned whether any of the allusions to the beloved disciple would make any sense in the context if considered as no more than fictitious idealizations.

It would seem at least a reasonable conclusion to maintain that there are no irrefutable historical grounds for rejecting the identification of the beloved disciple as John the son of Zebedee.[2]

b. Palestinian background

The preceding discussion has shown that the writer intended his readers to recognize that the events were related from first-hand witnesses, and the next consideration is whether there are indirect confirmations of this from the way in which he refers to Palestinian affairs. Is he thoroughly acquainted with them or does he introduce improbabilities or inaccuracies? If the latter, an eyewitness behind the Gospel would clearly be excluded.

(i) *Knowledge of Jewish customs.* Several times in the course of the Gospel the writer displays accurate and detailed knowledge of Jewish

---

[1] E. F. Scott (*The Fourth Gospel, its Purpose and Theology*, 1906, p. 144) suggested that the beloved disciple was 'the prototype of the future Church'. R. M. Grant (*HTR*, 35, 1942, p. 116) regards him as symbolic and non-historical. On this, cf. also H. Lietzmann, *The Beginnings of the Christian Church* (Eng. Tr. 1937), p. 311. E. Käsemann (*Exegetische Versüche und Besinnungen*, I, 1960, p. 180) suggests that he was the ideal bearer of apostolic testimony. R. Bultmann (*Das Evangelium des Johannes*, pp. 369 f.) regards him as an ideal figure representative of Gentile Christianity, and finds significance in his close association with Peter, the representative of Jewish Christianity (xiii. 21–30, xx. 2–10).

[2] Another proposed solution of the beloved disciple problem is to treat all the allusions as interpolations (cf. A. Kragerud, *Der Lieblingsjünger im Joh.*, 1959, cited by Feine-Behm-Kümmel, *Einleitung*, p. 165).

life in the period before the fall of Jerusalem. He knows about Jewish ritual scruples, as is plain from ii. 6 (purification rites), vii. 37, viii. 12 (libation and illumination ritual at the Feast of Tabernacles), and xviii. 28, xix. 31–42 (pollution regulations regarding the Passover). He mentions several Jewish feasts (e.g. Passover, Tabernacles, Dedication). He is acquainted with specific Jewish doctrines, as for instance the inferiority of women (iv. 27), the laws concerning the sabbath (v. 10, vii. 21–23, ix. 14 ff.), and ideas of hereditary sin (ix. 2).[1]

(ii) *Knowledge of Jewish history.* The author possessed detailed knowledge about the time taken to build the temple up to the time of Jesus' cleansing of it, and as far as can be ascertained his knowledge appears to be accurate. He is aware, moreover, of the political attitudes of the Jewish people seen especially in their enmity against the Samaritans (iv. 9). He knows of the Palestinian contempt for the Jews of the Dispersion (vii. 35). He is acquainted with the history of the hierarchy, mentioning both Annas and Caiaphas as high priests and yet describing Caiaphas as *the* high priest in that fateful year (xi. 49, xviii. 13 ff.).

(iii) *Knowledge of Palestinian geography.* The writer has clearly had some first-hand acquaintance with Jerusalem, for he knows the Hebrew name of a pool near the Sheep Gate and knows that it had five porches. This detail is strikingly confirmed by recent excavations near the temple revealing a pool with five porticos with inscriptions suggesting the healing properties of the water.[2] He similarly knows the Hebrew name (*Gabbatha*) of a paved area outside the Praetorium, another detail confirmed by archaeological discovery near the tower of Antonia, which overlooked the temple area. Since this pavement stood on a

[1] Some scholars discount the strength of this evidence by maintaining that it shows only a general knowledge of Judaism and need not point to an author who was a native of Palestine. C. K. Barrett, for instance, takes the view that any material connected with Jesus would be expected to show traces of Palestinian origin (*The Gospel according to St. John*, 1956, p. 104), but this really evades the issue. It may as confidently be said that such traces would be expected in an apostolic work, and if there are other internal considerations which point in the same direction it is unsatisfactory to claim that a non-Palestinian Jew *could* have possessed such knowledge. The more relevant enquiry is whether a Palestinian Jew *must* have had more detailed knowledge, but this surely cannot be answered in the affirmative.

[2] Cf. J. Jeremias, *Die Wiederentdeckung von Bethesda* (1949) and W. F. Howard, *Commentary on John* (IB, 1952), pp. 539 f. Cf. also R. D. Potter's article on the Johannine topography in *Studia Evangelica*, pp. 329–337.

rocky ledge, the Hebrew name, which means 'ridge', would be descriptive of its position.[1] He also knows about the pool of Siloam (ix. 7) and the brook Kidron (xviii. 1).

On numerous occasions topographical details are given in this Gospel, sometimes in narratives where the Synoptic parallels lack them.[2] There is mention of two Bethanys (i. 28, RV, RSV, xii. 1), of Aenon near to Salim (iii. 23),[3] of Cana in Galilee (ii. 1, iv. 46, xxi. 2), of Tiberias as an alternative name for the Sea of Galilee (vi. 1, xxi. 1), of Sychar near Shechem (iv. 5), Mt. Gerizim near a well (iv. 21), and of Ephraim near the wilderness (xi. 54).[4]

It seems impossible to deny that the author was either himself a

[1] Cf. A. J. B. Higgins, *The Historicity of the Fourth Gospel* (1960), pp. 81, 82.

[2] E.g. Philip, Andrew and Peter are all said to come from Bethsaida (or Bethzatha).

[3] Archaeologists have recently claimed to have identified this place as the modern *Ainun* (cf. W. F. Albright, 'Recent Discoveries in Palestine and the Gospel of St. John', *The Background of the New Testament and its Eschatology*, ed. W. D. Davies and D. Daube, 1956, pp. 158–160).

[4] Barrett's approach to this topographical evidence is that John's special knowledge refers to the south rather than the north of Palestine, which does not suggest a close dependence on John, son of Zebedee (*op. cit.*, p. 102). But this cannot be taken seriously since the bulk of the Gospel deals with our Lord's ministry in the south, which gives no indication at all of the author's place of origin. It is possible, for instance, for a Scotsman to give accurate topographical descriptions of an English scene without it being assumed that he could not have been a Scotsman. More serious, and yet equally unsupportable, is Barrett's observation that tradition tends to add names of places, with the inference, presumably, that the Johannine topographical details may be traditional accretions. An examination of the allusions to the Gospels in the Apostolic Fathers and in the apocryphal literature does not support this view of tradition. Rather the reverse seems to be true. Names of persons and places tend to give way to much vaguer or more muddled allusions. In the *Protevangelium of James*, for instance, names from the canonical Gospels are used, but mostly in a different context (e.g. Simeon becomes high priest). In the *Acts of Paul* no fewer than fifty-six persons are named, but there is no instance of a person mentioned anonymously in the canonical Acts reappearing in the apocryphal *Acts* with an identity attached. Topographical details in the latter are extraordinarily vague compared with the canonical book. For a study of the topographical details in John's Gospel which are claimed to possess special significance, cf. K. Kundsin's *Topologische Überlieferungsstücke im Joh.* (1925). Bultmann (*The History of the Synoptic Tradition*, pp. 67 f.) argues that with the development of the tradition there was a tendency to add more precise details, including the addition of names to previously anonymous speakers. This tendency may be found in later apocryphal literature, but Bultmann cites no first-century parallels.

native of Palestine or else in very close touch with someone who was.[1] The former alternative seems the more likely since in many cases there appears to be no reason for the inclusion of topographical details if personal reminiscence is not responsible.

c. Details which suggest an eyewitness

Any such emphasis on detail, however, inevitably raises the question of John's historical accuracy. For if the Gospel is no more than an imaginative writing-up of narrative and discourse based on a genuine core of tradition, or if, as some maintain, it is pure fiction, there is clearly little value in appealing to those touches which serve to point to an eyewitness.[2] The general question of historicity will be discussed later, but for our present purpose it must be noted that it is highly improbable that some of the details should have been created as pure fiction. What purpose would be served by the mention of six waterpots at Cana (ii. 6), of the twenty-five or thirty stadia as the distance rowed by the disciples across the Sea of Galilee (vi. 19), or of the number of fish caught, and the distance the boat was from the land, on the occasion of the post-resurrection appearance of Jesus to His disciples (xxi. 8, 11)? It is not convincing to regard these details as possessing symbolical rather than historical significance, unless there is clear indication that they were intended so to be understood. C. K. Barrett,[3] for instance, on ii. 6 admits the possibility of a symbolic interpretation, but agrees that such a suggestion is not entirely satisfactory, although he favours an allegorical treatment of xxi. 11, representing the full total of the catholic Church. Those for whom this method of approach appears fanciful may prefer to regard the 153 fish as the vivid recollection of an eyewitness. Had the author intended an allegorical meaning, surely he would have given some hint of it?[4]

[1] C. H. Dodd (*Historical Tradition in the Fourth Gospel*, pp. 243 ff.) gives some attention to topographical details but regards these as evidence that the author has used an earlier tradition which he believed to be trustworthy.

[2] In a recent article S. Temple (*JBL*, LXXX, 1961, pp. 220–232) argues for an eyewitness core for the Gospel into which other material has been worked. In this case the eyewitness details would help to authenticate the tradition, but would be valueless as an indication of authorship.

[3] *Op. cit., ad loc.*

[4] Barrett (*op. cit.*, p. 104) explains the occurrence of such details as resulting from the author's sources or his desire to give verisimilitude to his work. But it is debatable whether John used sources (see pp. 278 ff.), and the appeal to the verisi-

Other small details, such as the following, leave the reader with the impression that the writer was personally present at the events: the barley loaves (vi. 9), the odour-filled house (xii. 3), Peter's beckoning action (xiii. 24), the reaction of the soldiers at the arrest of Jesus (xviii. 6), the weight of spices used in the embalming (xix. 39). In addition there are occasions when the writer purports to have remarkable knowledge of the reactions of the disciples (e.g. ii. 11 f., iv. 27, vi. 19, xii. 16, xiii. 22 f.) and of the Lord Himself (cf. ii. 11, 24, vi. 15, 61, xiii. 1).

More significant still is the number of times that John gives names to people mentioned anonymously in the parallel Synoptic records.[1] Thus Philip and Andrew are named in the narrative of the feeding of the multitude (vi. 7 f.), the Mary who anoints Jesus is shown to be the sister of Lazarus (xii. 3), the name of the high priest's servant whose ear Peter struck with his sword is given (xviii. 10). In addition, some are introduced into the narrative without parallels in the Synoptics, the most notable being Nathanael, Nicodemus and Lazarus. The least that can be deduced from these details is that the writer has based his narratives on good tradition;[2] the most, that the writer recalled the names of these people because he was personally acquainted with them. This latter suggestion seems no less probable than the former.

d. Comparisons with the Synoptic Gospels

This is not the place for a general discussion of Johannine-Synoptic relationships, which will be considered elsewhere. The present intention is simply to enquire whether the Synoptic Gospels throw any light on the authorship of the Fourth Gospel. It would at first seem highly unlikely, and yet certain approaches to the Fourth Gospel are so decidedly conditioned by its relationship to the Synoptic Gospels that

militude motive is invalid unless it can be shown that the author is the type of person who both psychologically and spiritually might be expected to resort to this method. But the Fourth Gospel does not suggest such a man. The problem arises, What amount of detail is a mark of genuineness in a work? Too much vagueness on the one hand, and too much detail on the other, have each at times been claimed to exclude an eyewitness author, so that such an author has a slender chance of his work being accepted as genuine.

[1] See earlier footnote, p. 226 n.4.
[2] Cf. A. J. B. Higgins, The Historicity of the Fourth Gospel (1960), p. 57.

no discussion of authorship would be complete without drawing attention to this matter.

(i) *Treatment of similar material.* The crucial problem is whether or not John's Gospel was dependent on the Synoptic Gospels. Many scholars consider that the author used both Mark and Luke (see later discussion) and if this opinion is correct it raises the problem whether an apostle would have used writings by non-apostles. It is widely assumed that no apostolic eyewitness would have depended on second-hand accounts, and full consideration must be given to this assumption (cf. the discussion on Matthew's Gospel, p. 39). But are its basic premises correct? To begin with it may be disputed whether John has used either of these Gospels, since the small amount of detail in which they run parallel is so slight that it may well be accounted for by oral tradition. If this be so the problem has no relevance for the solution of the authorship question of this Gospel. But even if it be admitted that it reflects both Mark and Luke, it is not entirely apparent why this could not have happened in any apostolic writing. Few scholars would dispute that the Fourth Gospel presupposes that the readers are acquainted with the Synoptic tradition. To cite one example, the apostles are abruptly introduced as 'the twelve' without further definition, and it is clearly assumed that the readers will know who they were. The scanty inclusion of snippits from Mark and Luke (if this is what the author did) could not be construed as too undignified for an apostle. Indeed, it may have been designed to jog the readers' memory of what they already knew.

(ii) *Introduction of unique material.* It is this material which leads at once to the heart of the Johannine problem. Criticism has tended to be dominated by the deviations and innovations of John as compared with the Synoptic Gospels and to have assumed that the latter must be regarded as a historical yardstick against which the former must be measured. The consequence has been that many scholars have dismissed the Fourth Gospel as unhistorical, and with such an assumption apostolic authorship was unthinkable, and the possibility of an eyewitness source ruled out. Differences in the account of John the Baptist, the cleansing of the temple, the chronology of our Lord's ministry, the presentation of miracles and the method of our Lord's teaching, to name the most prominent, were all reckoned to prove John's non-historicity. Such evidence was considered quite sufficient to set aside all the previously stated evidence which suggests an eyewitness, and therefore authentic, account. As will be noted later, critical opinions regarding John's historicity are showing a marked inclination to assign more historical value to this Gospel and this trend, if it continues, will make the objection now being considered less weighty.

It may, in fact, be maintained with considerable credibility that John's innovations are more an evidence for than against apostolic authorship. If the three Synoptics were already in circulation and were accepted as authentic accounts, it would need an author of no mean authority to introduce a Gospel differing from them so greatly in form and substance as does the Fourth Gospel. The only intelligible hypothesis is that an apostle was directly responsible for it, either as author or as main witness. If it has already been decided on other grounds that no apostle had anything to do with it, the production and reception of the Gospel remains an enigma. The best that can be supposed is that the churches generally assumed that an apostle was author (see discussion below on the external history of the Gospel). More details of alternative suggestions will be given when dealing with various hypotheses regarding authorship, but it should be noted here that uniqueness of material cannot be regarded as conflicting with the Gospel's own eyewitness claims and impressions. This is not to ignore the very real character of the Johannine problem, but merely to point out that it has little bearing on authorship except for those who altogether deny the historicity of the book.

e. Hellenistic thought

The extent of the Hellenistic background will be considered later, but those who find strong affinities in this Gospel with the higher religious concepts of the contemporary Hellenistic world[1] find difficulty in attributing such a Gospel to a Galilaean Jewish fisherman. If the background assumption is correct the difficulty must be conceded. But the extent of the difficulty will depend on several factors. The assessment of the author's indebtedness to Hellenism has been variously estimated, but the school of thought which could find almost nothing else but Hellenism would naturally find it impossible to ascribe the Gospel either to the apostle John or to any Palestinian Jew.[2] But this school of

---

[1] Cf. the approach of C. H. Dodd, *The Interpretation of the Fourth Gospel* (1953).
[2] F. C. Grant (*The Gospels, their origin and growth*, 1957, p. 175) is a strong representative of this position.

thought has lost considerable ground in recent years and most scholars would be prepared to grant, at most, only a measure of Hellenistic influence, and some would agree to very little, if any. The real problem is whether the apostle John would have been acquainted with Hellenistic thought. Hellenistic influence was certainly widespread in Palestine,[1] and the possibility of a Palestinian work showing such influence must be conceded. But if John is regarded as an uneducated Galilaean peasant, it may be argued that one would not normally expect such a man to produce such a Gospel.

But it is by no means certain that John was as uneducated as some have supposed. Zebedee appears to have been in a position to hire servants and it is not impossible that John and James may have been better educated than their fellow apostles. Admittedly this cannot be proved, but neither can it be disproved, at least unless Acts iv. 13 (ἀγράμματοι and ἰδιῶται) is assumed to disprove it. But a not improbable interpretation is that these terms were used contemptuously of those unschooled in rabbinic lore.

This whole matter of Hellenism and the author problem in John further depends on the degree to which the major thought-concepts are allowed to Jesus or are considered to be interpretations by the author. If, of course, our Lord is given credit for expressing His message in a form which could be adaptable to the universal mission, the existence of concepts which would be appreciated by Gentiles is no surprise in an apostolic writing. Nevertheless some consider it improbable that Jesus was in touch with such thought-forms. The Qumran discoveries have at least opened up the probability that the Johannine type of thought, from a literary point of view, was more widespread than is often supposed.[2]

[1] Cf. Barrett, *The Gospel according to St. John* (1956), p. 32; W. D. Davies, *Paul and Rabbinic Judaism* (1948), pp. 1–16; S. Liebermann, *Hellenism in Jewish Palestine* (1950).

[2] F. C. Grant (*op. cit.*) protests that the small amount of parallels with the Qumran literature do not compare with what he calls 'the vast array of parallels' with the Hellenistic literature. Yet the Qumran parallels are, at least, more contemporary with our Lord's time than much of the Hellenistic literature cited in support (as, for instance, in the Hermetic tracts). A. M. Hunter views the Qumran parallels as much more favourable to a Palestinian and probably apostolic authorship, especially when this is linked with linguistic considerations (Aramaicized Greek) and accurate Palestinian topography (*ET*, LXXI, 1959–60, pp. 164–167). On the other hand C. H. Dodd finds the main difficulty for apostolic authorship in the combination of rabbinic and Hellenistic motives at a deep level (*Historical Tradition in the Fourth Gospel*, p. 16).

f. Other considerations

It has sometimes been maintained as evidence against authorship by a Palestinian Jew that the writer always uses the description 'Jews' of those opposed to our Lord, in a manner which suggests that he is dissociated from the Jewish people and must therefore be a Gentile.[1] Too much stress cannot, however, be placed on this usage, for it may be an indication that the readers were Gentile, but not the author. If this were so we should expect the term used to be that with which Gentiles were most familiar.[2] It is probable that the term 'Jew' is used more especially in contradistinction from 'Christians', rather than from 'Gentiles', in the same sense in which it occurs in Revelation iii. 9. That the use of the term 'Jew' need not indicate a non-Jewish author is shown by Paul's usage in 1 Corinthians x. 32. It may in fact be maintained that only a Christian Jew would have felt as strongly as this author does the bitter hostility of his own people against his Lord and Master,[3] and the feeling would have been all the deeper had the author witnessed it with his own eyes.

Another factor is the author's alleged acquaintance with rabbinic methods of argument, which is then thought to be improbable in a working Galilaean fisherman. Would he have had opportunity to acquaint himself with current themes of discussion and become steeped in the Torah?[4] At first it may seem that this would not have been possible. But the force of the argument depends upon a certain view of John's position. Since it is possible to maintain that Zebedee was a master fisherman in a fair way of business, in view of the references to his hired servants, it follows that John may not have been so unac-

---

[1] For a critique of this view, cf. H. R. Reynolds, *HDB*, III (1899), p. 702. R. M. Grant (*A Historical Introduction to the New Testament*, 1963, p. 155) points out that the Qumran sectaries criticized the 'orthodox' Jews. Bultmann (*Das Evangelium des Johannes (KEK)*[13], p. 59) discusses the fact that the Jews are sometimes differentiated from ὁ ὄχλος. He considers that Ἰουδαῖοι is therefore used to denote the Jews in their essential characteristics, represented by the authorities. The speech-usage tells us nothing about the origin of the Evangelist (whether Jewish or not).

[2] Cf. A. P. Peabody, in E. Abbott, A. P. Peabody and J. B. Lightfoot, *The Fourth Gospel* (1892), p. 112.

[3] Cf. V. Taylor (*The Gospels*, p. 98) who, while admitting a polemic against unbelieving Jews, nevertheless denies any racial hatred and in fact suggests that only a Jew could feel as this author does.

[4] Cf. Dodd, *op. cit.*, p. 15.

quainted with Jewish rhetoric. Moreover, if John is the disciple known
to the high priest (xviii. 15) he may not have been out of touch with
rabbinical methods of discussion. Moreover, it is not impossible to
suppose that our Lord Himself had some acquaintance with contemporary Jewish trends and fashioned some of His teaching accordingly.

g. External evidence

It is always difficult to assess the evidence of the second-century Church
Fathers on the New Testament books, for a critic's estimate will be
invariably influenced by his general presuppositions. Thus some will
place more emphasis than others on negative evidence, rather than
positive, and others will be inclined to give credence only to the first
of a sequence of witnesses, dismissing the rest as mere echoes of the
first and therefore weakening the whole cumulative testimony. Although a completely unprejudiced approach is probably not possible,
an attempt will be made here to give a brief survey of the facts.

(i) *Evidence for the apostolic authorship of the Gospel.* There is no writer
who names the author of the Gospel until Irenaeus, who not only
makes clear that the author was John the Lord's disciple but also that
he published the Gospel at Ephesus and remained in that city until
Trajan's time.[1] Moreover, Eusebius reports that Irenaeus' authority
was Polycarp, who was claimed to have learned the truth from the
apostles.[2] It is in this context that the story is reported of John's encounter with Cerinthus at Ephesus. Another reference to Polycarp is
found in Irenaeus' letter to Florinus, in which he reminds his boyhood
friend of their early acquaintance with Polycarp and of the latter's
reminiscences of his conversations with John and others who had seen
the Lord.[3] There can be no doubt, therefore, that Irenaeus accepted
John the apostle as author of the Gospel and believed it to have been
published at Ephesus on the basis of Polycarp's testimony.

A similar witness is found in Polycrates, who was bishop of Ephesus
(AD 189–198) and who wrote in a letter to Victor of Rome that John,
who had been a witness and a teacher, now sleeps at Ephesus. Nevertheless in this case nothing is said about him publishing a Gospel.

The evidence of Irenaeus has been subjected to searching criticism

---

[1] Cf. *Adv. Haer.* ii. 22. 5, iii. 3. 4 cited in Eusebius, *HE*, iii. 23. 3 f. Cf. also
Adv. Haer. iii. 1. 1 cited in Eusebius *HE*, v. 8. 4.
[2] *HE*, iv. 14. 3–8.   [3] Eusebius, *HE*, v. 20. 4–8.

and many scholars have not been disposed to grant its validity. Their reluctance to do so springs mainly from the fact that Irenaeus' evidence conflicts with their critical conclusions. If on other grounds it is concluded that John could not have written the Gospel, then clearly Irenaeus must be wrong. Once we suspect that his tradition is inaccurate, it would not be difficult to suggest a plausible reason for the rise of the inaccurate tradition. Irenaeus' memory from boyhood times plays tricks with him, for the John of Polycarp's acquaintance was not John the apostle but another John. It was a case of mistaken identity.[1]

Now this theory is neat and sounds plausible, but is it valid? It supposes that Irenaeus had no other source of information than Polycarp, a supposition which is highly improbable. He frequently refers to an anonymous Presbyter (who was not a direct hearer of the apostles, according to Harnack), who is generally supposed to have been his predecessor at Vienne and Lyons, Pothinus, a man born well before the end of the first century (he died in AD 177 when over ninety years old.)[2] Moreover, Irenaeus was in close touch with Rome. Would he have held to a tradition which was not confirmed by the traditions of other important churches, especially in view of the fact that he had himself lived previously in the East?[3]

[1] J. N. Sanders (*The Fourth Gospel in the Early Church*, 1943, pp. 38, 39) went further and suggested that it was the pride of the Ephesian Christians which raised their John to the apostolate, and their anxiety for apostolic support in the Quartodeciman controversy which attributed to him the Fourth Gospel. But Sanders seems to have overlooked the futility of the Ephesian Christians attributing the Gospel to the apostle John unless their protagonists in the controversy acknowledged his authorship.
B. W. Bacon (*ZNTW*, 26, 1927, pp. 187–202; 31, 1932, pp. 132–150) attributed Irenaeus' testimony with regard to an Ephesian John not only to inaccuracy but to deliberate intention. He accepted an elder John but placed him in Jerusalem.
[2] H. P. V. Nunn (*The Fourth Gospel*, 1946, p. 19) pointed out that Irenaeus had seen some of his friends tortured to death for the sake of their beliefs and suggested that this must have affected the care with which he would accept Gospels which claimed to support those beliefs.
[3] James Drummond (*An Inquiry into the Character and Authorship of the Fourth Gospel*, 1903, p. 348) remarked, 'Critics speak of Irenaeus as though he had fallen out of the moon, paid two or three visits to Polycarp's lecture-room, and never known anyone else . . . he must have had numerous links with the early part of the century.' W. Bauer, on the other hand, suggested that suspicions arise over Irenaeus' evidence, because according to Eusebius' report Irenaeus stated that Papias was a disciple of John (*Das Johannesevangelium*[2], 1925, p. 235). But even if this be granted as an inaccuracy, it need not impugn the whole of Irenaeus'

Our confidence in Irenaeus' testimony is supported by the recognition that all subsequent to him assume the apostolic authorship of the Gospel without question (Tertullian, Clement of Alexandria, Origen). If they were merely repeating Irenaeus' opinion, they must have considered that opinion of sufficient value to repeat without suspicion. In addition there is the important evidence of the Muratorian Canon, contemporary with the time of Irenaeus, which describes the origin of the Gospel as proceeding from John after a vision given to Andrew that John should write and his associates should revise. In spite of the fact that this statement must be received with reserve, in view of what is generally thought to be the improbability of Andrew surviving until the late date to which the Gospel is assigned[1] (although it should be noted that there is no independent evidence of Andrew's later history), there is no reason to dispute that the general connection of John with the production of the Gospel was commonly accepted at that time in Rome. Another line of evidence which may be cited, but whose value is difficult to assess, is the anti-Marcionite Prologue. The text is corrupt, but it witnesses to the apostolic authorship (*Johannes euangelista unus ex discipulis dei*) of the Gospel and states that it was produced in Asia. Both these witnesses, however, suggest that others were associated with John in the actual production of the Gospel, and this must be borne in mind in deciding its origin.

It may be assumed with certainty that the tradition of Johannine authorship was considerably older than the time of Irenaeus, but why, it may be asked, does not Polycarp mention John in his letter to the Philippian church? He mentions Paul by name, but not John, whom he is supposed to have known. But this presents no difficulty unless more weight is to be attached to the argument from silence than it will reasonably bear. There was obvious point in Polycarp mentioning Paul in writing to a Pauline church, but there is no compelling reason why he must have mentioned John. One thing is clear and this is that Polycarp cannot be cited as evidence against the existence of the Gospel, or against the apostolic authorship. His silence may seem strange, but Polycarp's mind must not be assessed by comparison with what the

testimony. It is strange that Bauer is inclined to accept the witness of a much later and less reliable witness such as Philip of Side regarding John's early martyrdom. Cf. also C. K. Barrett (*The Gospel according to St. John*, 1956, pp. 86, 87), who equally distrusts Irenaeus' evidence.

[1] Cf. J. H. Bernard, *St. John*, I (*ICC*, 1928), p. lvi.

modern scholar would have done. Common sense suggests that arguments from silence could produce very misleading results,[1] and yet the criticism of the Fourth Gospel has suffered more from such methods than any other part of the New Testament. This will be further illustrated when the early use and authority of the Gospel is considered (see below).

(ii) *Evidence for John's early martyrdom and the tradition of Ephesian residence.* The preceding evidence has been considered in some detail because a misunderstanding of it has exercised a deep influence on Johannine criticism, but the evidence for John's early martyrdom may be dealt with more summarily in view of its slightness. It may be summarized as follows:

1. The martyrdom is deduced from Mark x. 39. Since both James and John are promised that they will drink the same cup as our Lord, it is claimed that John must have suffered the same fate as James. It is supposed that if this had not happened Mark would have altered his text.

2. Two late writers, an epitomist of Philip of Side (fifth century)[2] and George Hamartolus (ninth century)[3] report statements purported to have been made by Papias to the effect that John as well as James was killed by the Jews. In the case of Hamartolus the statement is followed by a citation of Mark x. 39.

3. A Syrian martyrology of AD 411[4] commemorates John and James on the same day (27 December) and describes them as 'apostles in Jerusalem'.

4. The Carthaginian Calendar (*c.* AD 505),[5] which has a similar entry for 27 December, links John the Baptist with James, but many scholars regard this as an error for John the apostle and claim this as evidence for his early death.

5. A homily of Aphraates (21)[6] states that apart from Stephen,

---

[1] W. Sanday (*The Criticism of the Fourth Gospel*, 1905, pp. 32 ff.) has some trenchant criticisms of this method of argument, approvingly citing Drummond's exposures. The latter writer has a telling example from Theophilus of Antioch, who does not mention the names of any Gospel writers except John and does not even mention the name of Christ (*op. cit.*, pp. 157 f.). He could not have been ignorant of these facts, but for some reason chose not to mention them.

[2] Cf. C. de Boor, *TU*, v, ii (1888), p. 170.   [3] *Chronicle*, iii. 134. 1.

[4] Cf. H. Lietzmann, *Die drei ältesten Martyrologien* (Kleine Texte, 2), 1911, pp. 7 f.

[5] Cf. Lietzmann, *op. cit.*, pp. 5 f.

[6] Cited by Feine-Behm, *Einleitung*, p. 105.

Peter and Paul there were only two martyr apostles, John and James.

The cumulative effect of this evidence is very small, while the individual links in the chain become even weaker on examination.[1]

Mark x. 39 is capable of other interpretations than as a prediction of martyrdom; and the *vaticinium ex eventu* approach to exegesis is open to grave suspicion since it supposes that all the Gospel writers were editors who took upon themselves the responsibility of adjusting their material to their own understanding of the events and had no intention of recording what was actually said. The deduction of martyrdom from this passage, which amounts to no more than a prediction of suffering, necessitates presuppositions regarding John's early death.

The evidence of Philip's epitomist and of George Hamartolus cannot be taken seriously since neither of them was noted for accuracy as a historian. Moreover, as C. K. Barrett[2] points out, both Irenaeus and Eusebius knew of Papias' writings but neither refers to this statement about John's martyrdom. It is further questionable whether Papias would have used the late Greek title 'The Theologian' for John, as Philip's report says that he did, while George himself clearly did not take the Papias report seriously, since he also speaks of the apostle John's peaceful end.

The rest of the evidence may be dismissed, for in all probability the martyrologies and Aphraates are confusing John the apostle with John the Baptist. The notion of John's early martyrdom may therefore be regarded as purely legendary. Galatians ii. 9, which must be dated after James' martyrdom in AD 44, shows John as one of the pillar-apostles, while Acts xii. 2, which records James' death, contains no hint of John's. In addition to appealing to evidence of such flimsy character, the advocates of the theory are obliged to juggle with these conflicting considerations and the best that can be done is to suppose that John Mark was one of the 'pillar-apostles' and to suggest that later tradition caused an omission from Acts xii. 2, both without any supporting evidence.

But is the Ephesian residence of John equally legendary? Some scholars consider that it is, but largely on negative grounds. There is no mention of John's connection with Ephesus in the New Testament,

---

[1] C. K. Barrett (*op. cit.*, p. 87), who admits that an early martyrdom of John would solve some problems, pointedly remarks that we cannot martyr the apostle for our critical convenience.

[2] *Op. cit., ad loc.*

unless the exile of the John of the Apocalypse be claimed as evidence of an Asiatic sphere, since Patmos is off the Ephesian coast. But this will carry weight only for those who regard John the apostle as author of the Apocalypse,[1] which many consider disputable. Moreover, it is thought strange that the author of Acts allowed Paul to address the Ephesian elders without referring to John, if by the time Acts was written John was resident in Ephesus. This is another *vaticinium ex eventu* approach, which would be entirely invalidated if Acts was published before John took up residence in Asia, which is not at all impossible. There is perhaps more point in the argument from Ignatius' omission of any reference to the apostle in his address to the Ephesian church, especially as this was so soon after John's reputed residence there. Barrett[2] places much weight on this consideration, disputing that it is a common argument from silence. The argument certainly supposes that Ignatius *must* have referred to John had he had any connection with Ephesus, but it is difficult to see on what conclusive grounds this view can be maintained. Ignatius does refer to several members of the church by name, including the bishop Onesimus, but he seems more concerned about securing the church's present devotion and loyalty to Onesimus than about its previous history—which is understandable since he wrote this on his way to martyrdom!

The same kind of argument from silence is made from the omission of any reference to John's place of residence in the writings of Polycarp, Papias or Justin.[3] The fact that Irenaeus is the first specific witness for Ephesus (apart from the legendary *Acts of John*) need not mean that his source of knowledge was unreliable. It need mean no more than our ignorance of the transmission of the tradition. Nevertheless, Irenaeus may be wrong and John may have had no connection with Ephesus at all. But if so, there is no knowing what happened to him after he withdrew from Jerusalem, nor where he was when the Fourth Gospel was produced. There is no other more reputable tradition.[4]

[1] Cf. the author's *New Testament Introduction: Hebrews to Revelation*, pp. 254 ff.

[2] *The Gospel according to St. John* (1956), p. 87.

[3] Justin is an indirect witness, however, since he states that 'A certain man among us, by name John, one of the apostles of Christ, prophesied in a revelation which was made to him' (*Dialogue*, 81). The dialogue, according to Eusebius, took place at Ephesus.

[4] T. W. Manson (*Studies in the Gospels and Epistles*, 1962, pp. 118 ff.) was dubious about the Ephesus tradition, but suggested that the Fourth Gospel shows traces of an earlier Antiochene provenance. But there is no external evidence for this, and

h. Various propositions regarding authorship

There have been three main types of theory regarding authorship, but within each there have been many variations and the main proposals will now be summarized.

(i) *The apostle John.* This, as has been seen, is the traditional view, which has much support for it in the internal evidence. Indeed, it may be said that there is no evidence which conclusively disproves it, in spite of much opposition to it. This view would, on the whole, seem to account for more facts than any other, even if it is not without its difficulties.

A modification of the view is that John the apostle was the witness and some other was the author. A parallel to this solution may be found in the traditional relationship between Peter and Mark in the production of the Second Gospel.[1] There is no fundamental objection to this approach, but it does involve a rather broad interpretation of the γράψας of John xxi. 24, in the sense of writing by means of another. There are nevertheless other New Testament parallels for this. It would not be out of keeping with the external evidence provided the apostle himself was assigned the main responsibility in the production of the Gospel. Under this theory the assistant or amanuensis would remain anonymous and the apostle would take the credit for the Gospel. In this respect it would differ from the Peter-Mark relationship and would suggest that John had more of a personal hand in the writing than Peter had in the case of Mark's Gospel.

A further modification, which seems less likely, is that a disciple of John wrote down the memoirs of the apostle after his death. According to this theory, the substance of the Gospel is John's but not the writing.

(ii) *John of Jerusalem.* The existence of a John of Jerusalem who had entrée into the high priest's house was first proposed by H. Delff.[2] In his view the John of the tradition was this Jerusalem John who later

Manson's evidence is mainly inferential. Cf. K. Aland's comments on the place of origin of the Gospel, *ZNTW*, 46 (1955), pp. 114–116; he argues for Asia Minor on the grounds of the use of John by the Montanists. Some scholars prefer Syria as the place of provenance of the Gospel, but most of these dispute Johannine authorship (cf. those mentioned by Feine-Behm-Kümmel, *Einleitung*, p. 173).

[1] A view recently adopted by R. V. G. Tasker, *The Gospel according to St. John* (*TNT*, 1960), p. 11. Cf. also V. Taylor, *The Gospels*, p 106.

[2] *Die Geschichte des Rabbi Jesus von Nazareth* (1889).

became influential among the Asiatic churches. He was trained in rabbinism and was present at the last supper. Yet apart from the advantage in this theory of the association of a personal eyewitness with the production of the Gospel, it has little to be said for it. Moreover, no external evidence of any kind exists for such a person.[1]

(iii) *Non-Johannine theories.* Several hypotheses have been suggested which simply ignore the name of John altogether. The logic of this general position is that if the internal considerations are believed to make apostolic authorship impossible, the external evidence must clearly be wrong. If it is, there is no reason to retain the name John at all. All that needs to be done is to suggest some theory for the rise of the tradition. Later apostolic ascription is the obvious answer. Thus J. N. Sanders[2] connected this ascription with the need for apostolic support in the Quartodeciman dispute, a view considerably weakened by the fact that John's Gospel would have been of little value in that dispute in any case, and by the futility of claiming any work as apostolic unless it was generally accepted as such.

Others have advocated a more direct theory of pseudonymity, in which all the eyewitness details are regarded as a skilful device to create the impression of apostolic authorship. But if so, why did the author not mention John's name, which would have been so much more effective and more in harmony with general pseudepigraphical practice? Moreover, such a theory demands some explanation as to how the work ever became generally accepted, but this provides an insuperable difficulty. Unless the Gospel were at once assumed to be genuinely apostolic it would have had increasing difficulty in creating that impression as time went on. There are no known cases of works recognized as pseudonymous ever later losing their pseudonymous ascription. If the writer designed to make his book seem truly apostolic he must have succeded in a manner wholly without parallel among the pseudepigrapha.

There has been some support for the view that this Gospel must be attributed to a group rather than to a single witness. It becomes in that

---

[1] Another unlikely candidate for authorship whose name was John is Mark, as proposed by P. Parker (*JBL*, LXXIX, 1960, pp. 97–110). But in his earlier article (*JBL*, LXXV, 1956, pp. 303–314), Parker argues for a second edition of the Gospel issued fairly late and it is difficult to see how this can be reconciled with his Mark suggestion.

[2] *The Fourth Gospel in the Early Church* (1943), pp. 38, 39.

case the product of a school. A parallel to this has already been seen in Stendahl's theory for the production of Matthew (see pp. 25 f.). There may be something to be said for this type of theory but when it comes to authorship it must be a question of a single individual, although the epilogue would lend support to the view that others were associated with him.

Some comments on various redactional theories will be made later, but it should be noted here that advocates of such theories naturally think more of a redactor than of an author. Such editorial theories may appear to have a considerable advantage in that any material not in harmony with what is thought to have been the mind of the original writer may be readily transferred to the redactor and its evidential value at once nullified. But the validity of this type of criticism must be seriously challenged.

(iv) *'John the Elder'*. A famous statement of Papias has given rise to a widespread conviction among many scholars that there was another John who had associations with Ephesus and had some connection with the production of the Fourth Gospel. This has led to what might be called the confusion theory for interpreting the external evidence. John the Elder became mixed up in the tradition with John the apostle. By this method Irenaeus' evidence is easily discounted by assuming that he was really referring to John the Elder. But before such a theory can claim credence the existence of this elder must be established beyond dispute. The evidence is as follows.

Papias is quoted by Eusebius[1] as stating in his *Dominican Expositions*, 'And again, if anyone came who had been a follower of the Elders, I used to enquire about the sayings of the Elders—what Andrew, or Peter, or Philip, or Thomas, or James, or John, or Matthew, or any other of the Lord's disciples, said (εἶπεν) and what Aristion and the Elder John, the Disciples of the Lord, say (λέγουσιν). For I did not think that I could get so much profit from the contents of books as from the utterances of a living and abiding voice.' The problem is one of interpretation, for Papias' words are not unambiguous. It is possible, for instance, to construe this statement, as C. K. Barrett[2] does, as indicating a chain of three groups between the time of our Lord and Papias; the apostles, the elders and other disciples. If this interpretation is correct it at once disposes of Irenaeus' assumption that Papias was a

---

[1] *He*, iii. 39.4.   [2] *The Gospel according to St. John* (1956), pp. 88 ff.

hearer of the apostle John and a companion of Polycarp. But this interpretation is open to challenge. The crucial question is what Papias means by the elders—are they to be distinguished from or identified with the Lord's disciples who are named? Barrett is convinced that the 'sayings of the elders' consisted of reports of what the named disciples (i.e. apostles) had already said, and that Papias only heard these elders' recollections through the medium of their followers. But if Papias is describing the apostles as 'elders' an entirely different interpretation results, for now it is from followers of the apostles that Papias sought his information, and this would be much closer to the evidence from Irenaeus. It is admittedly strange that Papias uses the word 'elders' (πρεσβύτεροι) if he meant to describe the apostles, but it is equally strange that he calls one of the elders a disciple of the Lord (i.e. the Elder John) and that one of the Lord's disciples is not even graced with this title. All would agree that Papias has expressed himself badly, but on the theory that he intends to distinguish between John the apostle and a John the Elder there are more difficulties than are generally realized. The main snag is Papias' description of both Aristion and John as οἱ τοῦ κυρίου μαθηταί which would appear to mean personal followers of the Lord and therefore indicate more than a synonym for 'Christians'. Aristion is not mentioned in the New Testament, but that need not, of course, exclude the possibility that he was a disciple of the Lord who survived until towards the end of the century. It must surely be admitted that it becomes slightly more conceivable if at least one of them (the Elder John) can be identified with one otherwise known. Moreover, under the theory being discussed, if personal disciples of the Lord were still testifying at the time of Papias' enquiries, why did not Papias enquire about the sayings of the Lord rather than the sayings of the elders? There seems no satisfactory answer.[1]

It is difficult under the three-link construction to understand Papias' description of the end result as 'A living and abiding voice'. But if by this he means the direct testimony of personal disciples of the Lord, his words become more intelligible. Moreover, he is clearly acquainted with books, among which must surely be included the Synoptic Gospels, at least Matthew and Mark, on whose authorship he comments

---

[1] B. W. Bacon (*ZNTW*, 26, 1927, pp. 197, 198) admitted the difficulty of the Greek phrase, but disposed of it by textual emendation, based on the Syriac. But textual emendations of this kind are never a satisfactory method of dealing with difficulties of interpretation.

elsewhere. But it is significant that Papias places the non-literary apostles before the literary ones, suggesting that he may have paid more attention to the oral teaching of the former because their testimony had not been reduced to writing. It seems that on the whole a more intelligible understanding of Papias' words is obtained if it be assumed that the two Johns are to be identified and that Papias is distinguishing between what John had said in the past and what at the time of his enquiry he was still saying. At the same time the possibility that there may have been two Johns cannot be excluded. It is supported by Eusebius' interpretation of Papias' words,[1] but since he wished to attribute the Apocalypse to a different John from the author of the Gospel his interpretation may not have been impartial. There is, in any case, no other historical evidence for the existence of this shadowy figure, unless it be the introduction to 2 and 3 John where the author introduces himself as the 'elder'.

One concluding comment is necessary. If it be granted that an Elder John did exist, Papias gives no information regarding his domicile, nor does he give any hint of his literary prowess. In fact, even if this elder's feet can be firmly planted in history on Papias' ambiguous evidence, there is no reason to believe that his pen could have produced the Fourth Gospel. The only tenuous connection is that he happened to possess a name identical with that to which the Fourth Gospel was traditionally ascribed, which facilitates the appeal to a 'confusion theory'. But if the later Christian Church thus mixed up apostles and elders might not Papias have done the same, which might well destroy the *raison d'être* for John the Elder's existence?[2]

On the assumption that John the Elder was a real historical figure many scholars have adopted the view that John the apostle was the witness and John the Elder was the author. This solution is something of a compromise, but it involves the assumption that two Johns belonged to the same circle and that the Gospel was their joint effort, a possible but not very probable proposition.

(v) *Evidence for the early use and authority of the Gospel.* It has already been shown that by the time of Irenaeus the Gospel was accepted as

[1] *HE*, iii. 39. 6. Eusebius also cites Dionysius' hearsay comment about there being two tombs bearing the name of John in Ephesus (*HE*, vii. 25. 16).

[2] It is not without strong reason that B. W. Bacon concluded that the Elder at Ephesus theory was 'a higher critical mare's nest'. (*Hibbert Journal*, 1931, p. 321.)

apostolic. It remains to enquire into its history before this date, but the investigator is here hampered by lack of information.[1] It was possibly known to Ignatius, although it is difficult to be certain. The language and theological ideas in several places show kinship with the Gospel which would support the opinion that Ignatius knew the Gospel. Polycarp nowhere cites it, although he appears to cite from the First Epistle. One or two passages in the *Epistle of Barnabas* could reflect knowledge of the Gospel, and the same applies to the *Shepherd of Hermas*, but literary dependence is difficult to establish.[2]

There is difference of opinion about Justin's knowledge of the Fourth Gospel. Certainly the theological ideas of Justin would seem to find roots in the Gospel and in one or two places it is highly probable that Justin directly cites it. Bernard's[3] conclusion was that 'Justin, then, used the Fourth Gospel a little before 150 AD and at one point (*Apol.* 61) quotes it as authoritative for a saying of Jesus'. J. N. Sanders[4] admitted that Justin used the Gospel, but thought that he did not regard it as Scripture or as apostolic. Barrett[5] is rather more cautious, denying that the evidence proves that Justin knew the Gospel, but agreeing that it gives some plausibility to that hypothesis. Much more telling evidence for Justin's knowledge of the Fourth Gospel is the fact that his pupil Tatian used it in his *Diatessaron* on an equal footing with the Synoptics.[6] It should also be noted that the first writer to produce a commentary on this Gospel was the Gnostic Heracleon. Indeed, this

---

[1] The paucity of positive evidence has led some scholars to maintain that the Gospel must be dated only a short time before the earliest definite traces of acquaintance. Thus P. W. Schmiedel (*Enc. Bib.*, 1914, col. 2550) placed it not earlier than AD 170. But this principle of criticism was proved false by the discovery of earlier papyrus fragments.

[2] Cf. J. H. Bernard (*op. cit.*, pp. lxxiff.) for the detailed evidence for these Apostolic Fathers. F. M. Braun (*NTS*, 4, 1958, pp. 119–124), suggests that the author of the *Epistle of Barnabas* had heard echoes of the Johannine preaching. On the relation of Clement of Rome to John's Gospel, cf. M. E. Boismard (*RB*, LV, 1948, pp. 376–387). He thinks Clement shows evidence of Johannine impressions but not citations.

[3] *Op. cit.*, p. lxxvi.

[4] *The Fourth Gospel in the Early Church* (1943), p. 31.

[5] *The Gospel according to St. John* (1956), p. 94.

[6] The force of this evidence is often disregarded. H. P. V. Nunn (*The Fourth Gospel*, 1946, p. 17), who considered that the *Diatessaron* evidence was an insuperable obstacle to those who would argue that Justin was unacquainted with the Fourth Gospel, is strongly critical of Sanders for ignoring it altogether.

Gospel seems to have enjoyed wide usage among the Gnostics. It is possible that this led to Irenaeus' use of the Gospel to demonstrate its essentially non-Gnostic character.[1]

In addition to the patristic evidence there are two fragments of papyrus which contain either the text of the Gospel itself (as the Rylands Papyrus 457)[2] or reminiscences of it (as the Egerton Papyrus 2),[3] both dated at least in the first half of the second century, possibly as early as about AD 130. Although these are no evidence for authorship, they do show that the Gospel circulated at an early date.[4]

Another line of evidence which is claimed to have a bearing on authorship is the alleged opposition to the Fourth Gospel in the second century. Appeal is made to the Alogi who are mentioned by Epiphanius[5] as having rejected the Gospel and as actually ascribing it to Cerinthus. Whether these Alogi represent a group or only one man, Gaius of Rome (as has been argued),[6] is not certain, but it is reasonably clear that their opinions were not widely held. In all probability they rejected the Gospel merely because they did not like its Logos doctrine. This Gaius, mentioned by Eusebius,[7] was anti-Montanist and might also have felt that the teaching on the Holy Spirit in John favoured Montanism. In addition, the publication by Hippolytus of a *Defence of the Gospel according to St. John and the Apocalypse* points to a prevalent opposition towards the Gospel, at least in Rome. Irenaeus also refers to people who rejected the Gospel. Now all these allusions may refer to one man, Gaius, with his immediate followers, and if so the opposition need not be taken seriously. Some scholars give more weight to this opposition by appealing to the evidence of the Muratorian Canon, which is said to go to some lengths in establishing the Gospel. This opposition is considered by J. N. Sanders[8] as evidence

---

[1] Cf. W. von Loewenich, *Das Johannesverständnis im zweiten Jahrhundert* (1932).

[2] Cf. C. H. Roberts, *An Unpublished Fragment of the Fourth Gospel* (1935).

[3] Cf. C. H. Dodd, *BJRL*, xx (1936), pp. 56–92 (reproduced in his *New Testament Studies*, pp. 12–52).

[4] T. W. Manson maintained, in view of this evidence, that if Justin did not quote the Gospel it was not because no copies were available (*Studies in the Gospels and Epistles*, 1962, p. 112).

[5] ii. 31.

[6] Cf. the discussion of V. H. Stanton (*The Gospels as Historical Documents*, 1923, p. 239) who criticizes Rendel Harris' advocacy of the theory that Gaius was associated with the Alogi.

[7] *HE*, iii. 28.   [8] *Op. cit.*, p. 38.

that the Gospel had to *fight* for recognition, which he then thought was inconceivable if it were the work of an apostle. But the evidence cited is inadequate as a proof that the Gospel gained its place only after a struggle. Had the opposition come from the general membership of some influential church the position might have been different. But it is inadvisable to place too much weight on the opinions of a small group such as Gaius and his companions.

III. PURPOSE

As with every other aspect of the Gospel, this problem has been fully discussed, but with widely differing conclusions. In this case, however, the author himself furnishes his readers with so specific a statement of his purpose that this must form the starting-place for any discussion. Yet it has not always done so. Many scholars are more intrigued with John's beginning than with his conclusion, as a result of which John xx. 31 is passed by with less than just attention, and theories of purpose are proposed which are entirely out of harmony with this statement.

a. The author's own statement

John says, 'these are written that you may believe that Jesus is the Christ, the Son of God, and that believing you may have life in his name' (Jn. xx. 31, rsv). It is clear from this statement that the primary aim was to encourage faith.[1] That must mean that the work was designed as an evangelistic instrument.[2]

It was, in fact, essentially a 'Gospel'. But John does not leave the readers in any doubt as to what the *content* of their faith was to be. It was not merely a general faith but a particular view of Jesus which John sought to inculcate, a view of Him under two distinct, yet closely

---

[1] Three important MSS, Sinaiticus, Vaticanus and Koredethi read the present tense instead of the aorist (πιστεύσητε). This reading would mean that the Gospel would confirm existing faith. Cf. Barrett, *op. cit.*, p. 479. C. H. Dodd (*The Interpretation of the Fourth Gospel*, p. 9) suggests that quite apart from the grammatical consideration the whole presentation of the Gospel supports an evangelistic aim.

[2] This purpose has been compared with the purpose of a dramatist who selects his material with an eye to persuading his public (cf. C. M. Connick, *JBL*, LXVII, 1948, pp. 159–169). C. F. D. Moule (*The Birth of the New Testament*, 1962, p. 94) points out that John's purpose is extremely individualistic and answers the question, What must *I* do to be saved? (Cf. also the same author's article in E. Stauffer's *Festschrift, Donum Gratulatorium*, 1962, pp. 171–190 (also published in *Nov. Test.*, 5, Fasc. 2–3), on the Individualism of the Fourth Gospel.)

connected ascriptions—the Christ and the Son of God. The former is more than a title, as W. C. van Unnik[1] has convincingly shown. It must mean 'the anointed One', i.e. 'the Anointed King', an ascription which could have its fullest relevance only to Jewish people, since the concept was not familiar to the Gentile world. A right understanding of this must have a profound bearing on discussions of the author's purpose. Whatever parallels with current Hellenistic thought are found, the author does not appear to have had a predominant Hellenistic circle of readers in mind when pursuing his purpose. But the other description is generally emphasized by those preferring a Hellenizing purpose, because it is thought that 'Son of God' is capable, as 'Christ' is not, of a Hellenistic interpretation.[2] Yet John's own combination of the two ascriptions must be maintained.

The author's preceding statement that Jesus did many signs not included in the book, but which were attested by eyewitnesses, gives further insight into his purpose. He was clearly selective, for he was acquainted with a mass of traditions which it was beyond the scope of his book to include (cf. xxi. 25). He apparently chose out only those 'signs' which would serve his immediate purpose, which should put us on our guard about placing too much emphasis on John's omissions. He was a writer with one dominant purpose and it must be expected that his handling of his material will support this purpose.

It is significant that only in this Gospel is the title 'Messiah' preserved in its transliterated form. The earliest encounter of Jesus with the disciples leads them to use this title to describe Him (i. 41), and it is evident that John intends his readers to understand this in a thoroughly Jewish sense (cf. i. 45, 49). The portrait of Jesus in John is therefore messianic at its commencement. At the other end of the ministry this theme is still dominant, for the messianic character of the entry into Jerusalem can hardly be disputed (xii. 12–19). Similarly our Lord admits His Kingship before Pilate (xviii. 33–37). He is also condemned and crucified as King of the Jews (xix. 3, 12–15, 19, 20), and it is not without point that John alone records Pilate's rejection of the chief priests' request for the wording over the cross to be modified. In the account of the feeding of the multitude, John alone tells us that the

---

[1] 'The purpose of St. John's Gospel', *Studia Evangelica* (1959), pp. 382–411.
[2] C. E. F. Scott, *The Fourth Gospel, its Purpose and Theology*[2] (1908), pp.182 ff.; G. H. C. Macgregor, *The Gospel of John* (MC, 1928), p. 367. R. Bultmann, in his *Theology of the New Testament*, does not discuss the implication of Jn. xx. 31.

people sought to make Jesus King but that Jesus withdrew Himself (vi. 15), no doubt because their conception of messianic Kingship differed radically from His.

A particular application of the view that John wrote not only for unbelievers but for Jews is seen in the theory of K. Bornhäuser[1] that the Gospel was intended as a missionary document for Israel. He considered that only Israelites would have fully comprehended this Gospel. The omission of the Christian ordinances from John's Gospel would also be in harmony with this view, since these ordinances could not be appreciated by unbelievers.[2]

b. An ancient account of John's purpose

One of the earliest attempts to analyse the author's aim was made by Clement of Alexandria and since his comments have had an influence on modern assessments of the Gospel, it is as well to give his statement in full. 'Last of all John perceiving that the bodily (or external) facts had been set forth in the (other) Gospels, at the instance of his disciples and with the inspiration of the Spirit composed a spiritual Gospel.'[3] This at once raises the problem of the relationship of John to the Synoptists, as far as it affects John's purpose. Two facts seem to be involved in Clement's evidence, first that John followed the Synoptists and was fully acquainted with the contents of their Gospels and, second, that John's Gospel was of a more spiritual character than the others, although here it is clearly necessary to define what Clement meant by 'spiritual'. Sanday[4] defined it as 'one that sought to bring out the divine side of its subject'. In other words, Clement believed that John's Gospel was supplementary to the Synoptic Gospels and was different in kind from them.[5] Moreover, he says that he received this tradition from the 'early presbyters', which shows that it represents an ancient and probably widely held viewpoint. Because of this it merits serious attention. Whether John actually used any of the Synoptic material or whether he drew what parallels there are from oral tradition is still a debated point,

---

[1] *Das Johannesevangelium eine Missionsschrift für Israel* (1928).

[2] Cf. *ibid.*, pp. 158–167.

[3] *Hypotyposes*, cited in Eusebius, *HE*, vi. 14. 7.

[4] *The Criticism of the Fourth Gospel* (1905), p. 71.

[5] A different explanation of Clement's statement is given by R. M. Grant (*JBL*, LXIX, 1950, pp. 305–322), who considers that by 'spiritual' he meant 'gnostic' and that he conceived John's purpose to have been the presentation of the secret teaching of Jesus. But such a use of 'gnostic' is likely to be misleading.

but there is much to be said for the latter (see later discussion of this problem). Nevertheless, if the evidence is insufficient to prove literary dependence on the Synoptists, there are enough indications to show that the author assumed that his readers would be acquainted with the contents of the other Gospels. Only under such a hypothesis can his choice of material be intelligently understood. Thus the omission of several significant Synoptic narratives occasions no surprise, neither does the abrupt introduction of material which presupposes knowledge of Synoptic tradition.

At the same time the large amount of didactic material in John's Gospel is well characterized as 'spiritual', for not only does John pay much attention to the Lord's teaching on the Holy Spirit, but the various discourses bring out the inner meaning of His teaching and even of some of His miracles. Some caution, however, is necessary lest the spiritual character of John's Gospel be emphasized to such an extent that the Synoptics are supposed to be wholly unspiritual.

c. The theory that John aimed to supersede the Synoptic Gospels

This view, advocated by H. Windisch,[1] has not found much support for the obvious reason that, taken alone, the Gospel would give an incomplete and inadequate account of the ministry of Jesus. It needs the Synoptics to make it intelligible and it is therefore inconceivable that any writer should imagine that this Gospel would have ousted any of the Synoptic Gospels, which were presumably well established by this time. This theory may therefore be dismissed without further discussion.[2]

d. The theory that the Gospel was a polemic against unbelieving Jews

The rather hostile manner in which the author refers to the Jews is claimed to support this theory. Indeed, the Jews throughout the Gospel seem to be opposed to Jesus, and although this attitude of hostility is plainly present in the Synoptic Gospels, in these latter the main offenders are the scribes and Pharisees and sometimes the Sadducees, as

[1] *Johannes und die Synoptiker* (1926), pp. 87 f. The theory was approved by Walter Bauer in an article surveying Johannine research in *TR*, n.f., 1 (1929), pp. 135–160.

[2] W. F. Howard (*The Fourth Gospel in Recent Criticism*[2], 1955, ed. C. K. Barrett, p. 135) justly considers the theory too artificial, although he considers that John sometimes corrects the Synoptic Gospels (he cites, for example, the timing of the anointing at Bethany and the dating of the last supper).

compared with the Johannine principle of referring to the nation as a whole.[1] It has already been noted that some have considered this as evidence enough that the author could not have been a Jew, but it has also been said that only a Jew could feel as deeply as John the bitter hostility of his own people toward Jesus.[2] Thus while there may be some truth in the theory that this anti-Jewish polemic formed part of the aim of the Gospel, it could have been only a subsidiary part.[3]

e. The view that John was combating Gnosticism

This approach is naturally closely tied to a near second-century dating for the Gospel (or even later), when the movements generally classed as Gnosticism were flourishing. The particular form of Gnosticism which John is claimed to be combating is Docetism, which maintained that Christ could never have been contaminated by the world which was essentially evil. This meant that Christ did not really become flesh. It may have seemed as if He did, but any contact with matter would have defiled Him. Hence, He could not suffer. It was not He who was nailed to the cross. His purpose was revelatory not redemptive. It is not difficult to see that the Fourth Gospel would have been a very useful instrument in combating this kind of error, for much stress is laid on the truly human character of the incarnation and passion. Our Lord is depicted as being weary and thirsty (iv. 6, 7), as weeping at Lazarus' grave (xi. 35), as admitting a real thirst on the cross (xix. 28),

---

[1] G. H. C. Macgregor(*JBL*, LXIX, 1930, pp. 150–159) maintained that the Gospel reflects the conflict between Judaism and apostolic Christianity. The references to the Jews are therefore a 'reading back'.

[2] Cf. p. 232 n.3. Cf. also Lord Charnwood, *According to St. John* (1925).

[3] V. Taylor (*The Gospels*, p. 98) suggests that the writer may have had in mind the antagonism to which his readers were exposed from Jewish opponents, but it is not clear in what way this Gospel would have been especially designed to help them. They might have derived encouragement from our Lord's attitude in face of Jewish opposition, but the same encouragement is available for all who are meeting hostility, whether from Jews or not. Nevertheless, if on other grounds Jewish-Christian readers are indicated, the suggestion might have some weight. R. M. Grant (*JBL*, LXIX, 1950, pp. 305–322) maintains that John's purpose was to reinterpret the career of Jesus by attacking Judaism. J. A. T. Robinson (*NTS*, 6, 1960, pp. 117–131) takes a different view, maintaining that the Gospel belongs to Hellenistic Judaism. It is not therefore a polemic against non-Christian Jews, but is an appeal to Diaspora Judaism not to refuse the Christ. C. F. D. Moule (*The Birth of the New Testament*, pp. 94, 95) sees John's purpose as a retelling of genuine Dominical tradition (as in Jn. ix) in the light of prevailing Jewish conflicts,

as possessing a real body out of which could flow blood and water (xix. 34). The anti-Docetism of John is even more evident in the First Epistle, and especially in the Second. Yet even if the Evangelist's representation effectively refutes the Docetic error, this need not mean that this was integral to the author's purpose. It is going too far to claim with R. H. Strachan[1] that a polemic against this error was one of the main purposes of the Gospel, but this is not to say that the author did not bear in mind the rising influence of Gnostic thought.

F. C. Grant[2] supposes that the author belonged to a circle devoted to early Christian Gnostic mysticism, as if he was rewriting the life of Christ using the language of contemporary Gnostic mysticism. However, Grant admits that the wonder is that this Gospel contains so few 'Gnostic or quasi-Gnostic elements'. A somewhat similar view was held by E. F. Scott,[3] who found a double reaction to Gnosticism in this Gospel, for, coupled with a studied avoidance of Gnostic terms such as γνῶσις, σοφία and πίστις, to exclude any possible confusion between the author's presentation and that of the heretical systems, he maintains that there is some sympathy with the doctrines of Gnosticism. He finds this in the writer's emphasis on the ideal value of the life of Christ, on the Gnostic antithesis between the lower and higher worlds, and on the importance of the act of 'knowing' in the religious life. He suggests that this double approach was possible because the relationship between Gnosticism and Christianity was as yet loosely defined. He posits, in fact, an age for the production of the Gospel between the first opposition to Gnosticism (as in Paul's Epistle to the Colossians) and the later all-out struggle to uproot it. But it must remain a problem for Scott's proposition that a church possessing the Colossian Epistle could have found sympathy for a movement whose beginnings Paul and the writer of the Epistle to the Hebrews had so strongly opposed. Another theory is that of Bultmann,[4] who understands the Gospel as a presentation of Christianity in terms of the Gnostic redeemer myth, but this is much more radical in character. He points out certain similarities between the Gospel and Gnostic mythological ideas and makes much of the view

[1] The Fourth Gospel[3] (1941), pp. 44 f.
[2] The Gospels, their origin and growth, pp. 163 ff.
[3] The Fourth Gospel, pp. 86–103.
[4] His commentary is presented from this point of view. Cf. also Theology of the New Testament, II (1955). Bultmann's basic theory for this Gospel was strongly criticized by E. Percy, Untersuchungen über den Ursprung der johanneischen Theologie (1939).

that Christ is essentially the Revealer. This interpretation of the purpose of the Gospel is dominated by Bultmann's general philosophical approach to Christianity and it is not surprising, therefore, that he himself finds some sympathy with certain aspects of Gnosticism which he finds echoed in this Gospel.

f. The theory that John was presenting a Hellenized Christianity

This is a view that has long been popular with the comparative religions school of thought. The Gospel is regarded as addressed to the contemporary Greek non-Christian world to persuade them to adopt Christianity, and to do this the life of Christ is expressed in religious terms which would be readily intelligible to them. This opinion finds its classic expression in the work of C. H. Dodd.[1] By marshalling an impressive array of parallels with the Hermetic literature, Philo of Alexandria, and Gnosticism (he considers Mandaism, but does not favour this as background for the Gospel), Dodd claims that the Gospel shows particular affinities with Philo and the *Hermetica*, and transforms ideas which are held in common with these contemporary religious movements (see discussion on the background of the Gospel, pp. 294 ff.). The existence of parallels in thought might not in itself throw any light on the purpose of the Gospel, especially as in all cases there are vital differences between the Johannine use of parallel terms and the use in contemporary movements. The use of Logos is a case in point, for John and Philo are poles apart in their fundamental conceptions. All this Dodd, of course, admits. The real crux is whether he is right in maintaining that the Gospel must be interpreted against a Hellenistic background.[2] There is less inclination than formerly to

---

[1] *The Interpretation of the Fourth Gospel* (1953). Cf. p. 9.

[2] It should be noted that whereas Dodd puts the main emphasis upon Hellenistic parallels he does not neglect Semitic parallels. Indeed he regards the Gospel as the best example among the literature of this period of the interpenetration of Greek and Semitic thought (cf. his book, *The Authority of the Bible*, 1938, p. 200). Moreover, he considers rabbinism as a parallel milieu with Hellenism in the interpretation of the Gospel (cf. *The Interpretation of the Fourth Gospel*, pp. 3 ff.). In his most recent book, *Historical Tradition in the Fourth Gospel*, Dodd argues for a considerable core of Palestinian tradition although he still maintains the Hellenistic flavouring. S. G. F. Brandon (*The Fall of Jerusalem and the Christian Church*[2], 1957) holds much the same viewpoint but from very different presuppositions, for he advocates that John shows the co-mingling of Jerusalemite Christianity with Paul and Hellenic Christianity, which in his view were previously strongly antagonistic (cf. also H. C. Snape, *HTR*, 47, 1954, pp. 1–14).

place such stress on Hellenistic influences on New Testament literature, but the Fourth Gospel is perhaps the strongest fortress of that view. It has received some recent knocks through the Dead Sea discoveries,[1] since certain parallels in the Qumran literature with the Johannine literature suggest that some of the terms which were previously confidently regarded as of Greek origin were in fact found in a Jewish milieu just prior to and contemporary with the rise of Christianity. Nevertheless, there have been some scholars who have declined to regard the Qumran evidence as damaging to a Hellenistic origin.[2] F. C. Grant, for example, points out that there are far more parallels in Hellenistic religious literature than in the Qumran literature and therefore on grounds of quantity the Hellenists defeat the Essenes. Another champion for the older view, H. M. Teeple[3] takes a different line, and maintains that there are many features in the Scrolls absent from John, many also in John absent from the Scrolls, and many partial parallels where similar terms are used in different ways. All this, according to him, shows that the origin of the Fourth Gospel cannot be found in the kind of milieu at Qumran. To back up this opinion he then shows that almost all the parallels claimed between John and the Scrolls can be more closely illustrated by comparison between the Scrolls and the Old Testament and/or the Apocrypha and pseudepigrapha. Moreover, he asserts that other New Testament books, which cannot claim a Palestinian origin, show as many parallels with the Scrolls as John. In fact, Teeple maintains that where John's parallels differ from Qumran thought they differ towards Hellenism and away from primitive Jewish thought.[4] Such careful comparisons as this author has made will be valuable in putting scholars on their guard against claiming too much from Qumran, but there are some presuppositions in Teeple's method of approach which considerably

[1] Particularly by W. F. Albright in his essay on 'Recent Discoveries in Palestine and the Gospel of St. John', in *The Background of the New Testament and its Eschatology* (ed. W. D. Davies and D. Daube, 1956), pp. 153–171. Cf. also F. M. Cross, Jr. (*The Ancient Library of Qumran and Modern Biblical Studies*, 1958, pp. 161, 162), who maintains that the evidence shows that John preserved primitive and authentic Jerusalem tradition, and J. A. T. Robinson's article, 'The New Look on the Fourth Gospel', in *Studia Evangelica*, pp. 338–350.

[2] For instance F. C. Grant, *op. cit.*, p. 175. Cf. also M. Burrows, *More Light on the Dead Sea Scrolls* (1958), p. 129.

[3] 'Qumran and the Origin of the Fourth Gospel', *Nov. Test.*, 4 (1960), pp. 6–25. *Ibid.*, p. 24.

NEW TESTAMENT INTRODUCTION

weaken the force of his conclusions. He takes it for granted, for instance, that in this Gospel we are dealing with the author's background of thought and not Christ's. Those more disposed to place greater confidence in the teaching of the Lord as being sufficiently comprehensive to appeal to men of all backgrounds will be less inclined to see the force of Teeple's arguments. Moreover, to argue from what is present in Qumran sources but absent from John misses the whole point of the uniqueness of Christianity. No-one who appeals to the Dead Sea Scrolls to support a Jewish milieu for John would ever imagine that John (or more precisely Jesus) would take over the tenets of Qumran lock, stock and barrel, as Teeple's argument supposes. The question of interdependence between John and Qumran is really irrelevant in the search for origins, since all that needs to be claimed is that the Scrolls show the currency of certain concepts, such as light and truth, which many earlier scholars considered to be essentially Greek. It may be true that John is more Hellenistic than the Scrolls, but this may be due to the breadth of our Lord's own mind rather than to the Hellenism of a Gentile mind imposed upon His teaching.

In spite of all the amassing of Hellenistic parallels, it is still possible for the Gospel to be read intelligibly against an essentially Jewish background and since this fits in with the author's own claims, it should not be jettisoned in favour of a view which virtually makes the Evangelist a greater genius than Christ Himself. This is not to deny that some interpretation of our Lord's teaching was necessary, but it is a plea to regard with strong suspicion any theory which finds it necessary to treat a whole Gospel as interpretation without paying attention to the historic facts. More will be said on this subject when the Evangelist's sources are discussed, but the general view under consideration must be regarded with the utmost reserve. It is tenable in a satisfying form only in so far as it derives its impulse from the genuine teaching of Jesus.

g. The suggestion that John was correcting a Baptist cult

It is known that in Ephesus there were groups of followers of John the Baptist who were imperfectly instructed in the tenets of Christianity (cf. Acts xix. 1–7). This kind of movement may well have been more widespread and it is an attractive hypothesis that this Gospel may have been partially designed to counteract an allegiance to John the Baptist which should have been given to Christ. The author goes to some lengths to demonstrate that Jesus was superior to John. Indeed,

John's sole function is to witness to Christ. In fact, he states categorically that he himself must decrease while Christ must increase (iii. 30). Moreover, Jesus Himself, while admitting John's greatness, shows that He has greater testimony than John's (v. 33 f.). All this must be granted,[1] but would not the Synoptic Gospels perform the same function with their inclusion of John's definite statement that Christ was mightier than he (cf. Mt. iii. 11; Mk. i. 7; Lk. iii. 16)? Admittedly the Fourth Gospel omits the narrative of the baptism of Jesus, but in the three Synoptic accounts John makes a clear distinction between his own baptism and that of Jesus.[2] Nevertheless, the existence of such a sect may have influenced the author in his choice of material in the opening portions of his Gospel.[3]

h. The idea that John pursued an ecclesiastical polemic

This is less evident, but has been seriously maintained by those who find in this Gospel sacramental teaching.[4] It is maintained that the omission of the Lord's supper was to offset a wrong approach to it in some of the churches of the writer's acquaintance. In its place he gives teaching regarding the inner meaning of the institution (vi).[5] It is further thought that the teaching of the new birth was to bring out the spiritual significance of the rite of baptism (cf. iii. 5).[6]

[1] For advocates of this view, cf. W. Baldensperger (*Die Prolog des vierten Evangeliums*, 1898), who found traces of this anti-Baptist polemic throughout the Gospel. Cf. Howard, *The Fourth Gospel in Recent Criticism*[2] (1955), ed. C. K. Barrett, pp. 57, 58, for comments on Baldensperger's view. This view was favoured by Strachan, *The Fourth Gospel*[3] (1941), pp. 109, 110 and W. Bauer, *Das Johannesevangelium*[2] (1925), pp. 14 ff. The latter cites Mandaean literature in honour of John.

[2] For a discussion of the Synoptic and Johannine references to John the Baptist, cf. J. A. T. Robinson's article on 'Elijah, John and Jesus', *NTS*, 4 (1958), pp. 263–281.

[3] Robinson (*op. cit.*, p. 279 n.2) questions the alleged existence of this sect and suggests the need for a thorough re-examination.

[4] For a full treatment of this view, cf. W. F. Howard, *Christianity according to St. John* (1943), pp. 143–150. Howard considered that over against all the pagan interpretations of the sacraments 'there stood the witness of the life of the Church and its sacramental tendency' (cf. p. 149).

[5] J. Jeremias (*The Eucharistic Words of Jesus*, Eng. Tr. 1955, pp. 72–87) takes a quite different line and maintains that the author consciously omitted the account to avoid disclosing the sacred formula to the heathen (i.e. as part of the Church's *disciplina arcani*).

[6] Some scholars have claimed many other veiled allusions to the sacraments in John's Gospel. O. Cullmann, for instance, finds such allusions in i. 29, 36, in the

Certainly this Gospel would correct any wrong sacramental tendencies, if such there were, when it was written, but it is rather precarious to infer this kind of sacramentalism from John's omission to mention the ordinances. Nonetheless, there are ecclesiastical interests in this Gospel which should not be overlooked. The allegories of the sheepfold and of the vine both contribute to the teaching of this Gospel about the Church, as does the high-priestly prayer of chapter xvii.

i. The view that John aimed to correct the Church's eschatology

It has been proposed (e.g. by C. K. Barrett)[1] that owing to the extended delay in the *parousia* it was necessary to provide an interpretation of primitive apocalyptic hopes. This, it is suggested, was provided by John. Such a theory might gain some apparent support from the kind of eschatological teaching contained in the Gospel. There is an absence of the apocalyptic kind of teaching found in the Synoptic Gospels. Instead there is what C. H. Dodd[2] calls 'realized eschatology'. The idea of an imminent return has receded and it is, therefore, proposed that John presents an eschatology which is a present reality rather than just a future hope. Yet the weakness of this general viewpoint is that too strong an antithesis is drawn between futuristic and realized eschatology. The latter is not the creation of the Church to explain away an unexpected delay. The two aspects are directly traceable to the teaching of Christ. Moreover, allusions to futuristic eschatology are found in John (cf. v. 25–29) alongside the 'realized' type of escha-

feeding of the multitude, in the allegory of the vine, in the miracle at Cana, in the feet-washing, in the blood and water from Christ's wounds, among others (cf. *Early Christian Worship*, Eng. Tr. 1953, pp. 37 ff.). For others tending towards the same direction, cf. C. K. Barrett, *The Gospel according to St. John* (1956), pp. 69–71, and W. Bauer, *op. cit.*, pp. 95 ff. See Sir F. C. Hoskyns and F. N. Davey's *The Fourth Gospel*[2] (1947), pp. 363 f., on the early lectionaries' interpretation of the miracles of the healing of the paralytic and of the blind man as baptismal miracles. Some admit the presence of sacramental allusions but consider these to be editorial (cf. E. Lohse, 'Wort und Sakrament in Johannesevangelium', *NTS*, 7, 1961, pp. 110–125, who attributes xix. 34b, iii. 5 and vi. 51b–58 to the editor of the Gospel; cf. J. Jeremias, *ZNTW*, 44, 1952–53, pp. 256, 257, and the critique of his article by G. Bornkamm, *ZNTW*, 47, 1956, pp. 161–169, and cf. also W. Michaelis, *Die Sakramente im Joh.*, 1946).

[1] *Op. cit.*, pp. 115, 116.
[2] *The Apostolic Preaching and its Developments*[2] (1944), pp. 65 ff.

tology. An adequate exegesis demands that both should be retained.[1]

i. The suggestion that John aimed to preserve a tradition suitable for liturgical use

If the theory that behind this Gospel lies a Jewish triennial lectionary is correct (see pp. 286 f.), it may follow that the author was aiming to present the discourses and narratives in a form which would appeal to Jewish Christians who were well familiar with the lectionary. Such a scheme, if the theory is correct, would provide sermon material suitable for the different Jewish festivals.[2]

Another suggestion of a somewhat similar character is that John's Gospel incorporates various prose-hymns which were intended to be sung chorally in the Church's worship.[3] These hymns which had been developed as a result of long meditation on Christ and His teaching have been incorporated, according to this theory, with an eye on the liturgical needs of the Church.

While in both these theories it is not impossible that the Gospel readily found adaptation for liturgical needs, it is not easy to believe that this was part of the original purpose. If the style shows affinities with poetic methods, for instance, there is no immediate justification for maintaining that material in hymnic form was editorially attributed to Jesus. It could equally well be true that Jesus Himself used poetic forms[4] and that this is the explanation of the inclusion of such material. At most, a liturgical purpose cannot be considered as more than subsidiary.

IV. DATE

As is so often the case with New Testament books, the dating of this Gospel is not possible with any precision. Various suggestions have been

---

[1] For a recent study of John's eschatology cf. L. van Hartingsveld's *Die Eschatologie des Johannesevangeliums* (1962).

[2] Cf. A. Guilding, *The Fourth Gospel and Jewish Worship* (1960), p. 57.

[3] Cf. W. H. Raney, *The Relation of the Fourth Gospel to the Christian Cultus* (1933). The passages which this writer isolates as showing the characteristics of hymnic structures are i. 1–18, iii. 14–21, 31–36, x. 1–18 and the discourses in xiv–xvi and the prayer of xvii. These, he thinks, were intended to be chanted by a choir. Other passages (v. 19–47, vi. 32–58, viii. 12–20, 21–30, 31–58, x. 25–38, xii. 20–36, 44–50, xiii. 12–30, 31b–35) consisting of narratives were probably intoned by a reader.

[4] Cf. C. F. Burney, *The Poetry of our Lord* (1925).

proposed, ranging from before the fall of Jerusalem to as late as the last quarter of the second century. The more extreme theories have been rejected and the majority of scholars are inclined to accept a date somewhere between AD 90 and 110. The following are the main considerations which enter into the question of date.

a. The external evidence for the early use of the Gospel

Various early evidences for the circulation of the Gospel during the first half of the second century have already been mentioned. The earliest certain evidence is that of the Rylands Papyrus 457, which is recognized by Sir F. Kenyon[1] as an early second-century manuscript. Whether this papyrus was used by orthodox Christians or by Gnostics,[2] it is proof of the existence of the Gospel at that early date. The discovery of this fragment, together with the Egerton Papyrus 2, has effectively silenced the earlier radical dating of the Gospel late in the second century.[3]

The question of whether Ignatius knew this Gospel has already been

---

[1] *The Text of the Greek Bible*[2] (1949), p. 75.

[2] Cf. C. K. Barrett, *op. cit.*, p. 106.

[3] Although there is still some debate regarding the relation of Egerton Papyrus 2 to John's Gospel, there are good grounds for maintaining its use of John's Gospel (cf. C. H. Dodd, *Historical Tradition in the Fourth Gospel*, p. 328 n.2, who admits borrowing in at least fragment 1 of the papyrus. Cf. also C. K. Barrett's comment, *op. cit.*, p. 92). Baur and the Tübingen school had dated John in the last quarter of the second century by virtually ignoring altogether the external evidence. Subsequently various scholars dated the Gospel about AD 135, as for instance P. Schmiedel (art. 'John, Son of Zebedee', in *Encyclopaedia Biblica*, 1914, col. 2551), who placed it in the period after Bar-Cochba's rebellion in AD 135, which was assumed to be alluded to in Jn. v. 43. This position was at first supported by E. Meyer (*Ursprung und Anfänge des Christentums*, I, 1921, pp. 310–340) but abandoned in Vol. III of the same work published two years later (p. 650). The idea is now regarded as 'a curiosity of criticism' (to cite Vincent Taylor, *The Gospels*, p. 84 n.2). So is the suggestion of H. Delafosse (*Le Quatrième Evangile*, 1925) that the Gospel was Marcionite (*c.* AD 135) and was later worked over by an orthodox writer (*c.* AD 170). (Cf. Howard's comment, *The Fourth Gospel in Recent Criticism*, p. 89.)

A more recent theory of a later editing of John's Gospel about AD 135 has been advanced by P. N. Harrison (*Polycarp's Two Epistles to the Philippians*, 1936, pp. 255–266, 302–310) on the grounds that the earlier part of Polycarp's epistle shows no knowledge of John, and since he dates this part *c.* AD 135, the Gospel, he considers, must be placed after this. But this is an argument based on silence and is too precarious to be regarded as an adequate basis for dating.

raised (p. 244), but many scholars deny that he did.[1] Some, however, consider that he quoted it rather loosely, and used its terminology in a new sense.[2] If it could be shown with any certainty that Ignatius knew the Gospel it would establish a *terminus ad quem* of AD 110 for the Gospel, and would furnish a strong ground for claiming a date some while earlier than this.[3] However, since this Ignatius evidence is disputed, other grounds for an early date will need to be considered.

b. The historical situation

This has already been discussed in the section on Purpose and there is no necessity to repeat the details here. Most of those who see some allusions to Gnosticism in this Gospel are nevertheless agreed that there is no evidence of developed Gnosticism here.[4] It is, therefore, assumed that the Gospel must have arisen before the period of the more highly organized Gnostic sects. If Docetism is sometimes in mind this would suggest a period when this tendency was exerting an influence, and it is known to have done this at the turn of the century, especially in Asia. There is rather more definite allusion to Docetic views in 1 John than in the Gospel,[5] and if both works were published at roughly the same time the evidence of 1 John would need to be taken into account in dating the Gospel. But the date of the Epistle cannot be conclusively

[1] E.g. J. N. Sanders (*The Fourth Gospel in the Early Church*, 1943, pp. 12 ff.) admitted that a common theological tradition lies behind both writers, but was not prepared to agree that Ignatius knew the Gospel.

[2] Cf. C. Maurer, *Ignatius von Antiochien und das Johannesevangelium* (1949). Cf. also the discussion of F. M. Braun, *Jean le Théologien* (1959), pp. 262–282.

[3] Even some scholars who do not admit the Ignatius evidence suggest a date round about AD 100–110, as for instance Sanders, *op. cit.*, p. 45, and C. H. Dodd, *BJRL*, xx (1936), pp. 56–92 (reproduced in his *New Testament Studies*, pp. 12–52). In his latest book, *Historical Tradition in the Fourth Gospel*, p. 424, Dodd considers a date about AD 100, and rather before than after, to be reasonable.

[4] For instance, J. Réville, *Le Quatrième Evangile, son Origine et sa Valeur historique* (1901), and A. Loisy, *Le Quatrième Evangile, deuxième édition refondue: Les Epîtres dites de Jean* (1921), both dated the Gospel before AD 125 on these grounds. Cf. also E. F. Scott (*The Fourth Gospel, its Purpose and Theology*[2], 1908, p. 103), who expresses the opinion that John wrote during the 'period of truce' before the great conflict with Gnosticism began.

[5] E. R. Goodenough (*JBL*, LXIV, 1945, pp. 164, 165) argues that 1 John does not deal with Docetism and need not be dated late. For a discussion on the date of the Epistle, see the present author's *New Testament Introduction: Hebrews to Revelation*, pp. 205, 206.

determined, and even if it could it is not indisputable that the Gospel must have been contemporary.

c. Relationship to the Synoptic Gospels

It goes without saying that if John used the Synoptics, or even if he was acquainted with them but did not use them, his Gospel must be dated later than the latest Synoptic Gospel. Those who date Matthew c. AD 80–85 are therefore unable to date John before about AD 90–95. On the other hand John shows no certain signs of acquaintance with Matthew. Moreover, a similar late dating for Luke is open to challenge, and if an early date for Luke is maintained (see p. 109) the *terminus a quo* for John would be more difficult to fix. And it would be still less conclusive if the view is held that John did not use the Synoptic Gospels. On the whole the relation to the Synoptics supplies little ground for the dating of this Gospel. Nevertheless, the general assumption that John is later than the other Gospels,[1] and the testimony of Clement of Alexandria in confirmation of this, have exerted considerable influence in dating the Gospel just before the turn of the century.

d. The effect on dating of decisions regarding authorship

If John the apostle was author of the Gospel, it could not have been published later than AD 100 at the outside limit, and hardly as late as this. The testimony of Irenaeus that John lived until Trajan's reign could place the Gospel during the last decades of the first century. Similar restrictions on dating would be imposed if John the Elder were author, if Papias' description of him as 'a disciple of the Lord' is taken seriously. Naturally, if no eyewitness had anything to do with the production of the book, there is no means of arriving at the *terminus a quo*, as is evident from the wide variety of opinions (and their wide chronological range) held by the earlier Johannine critics.

e. A theory for a dating before AD 70

Not many scholars have ventured to date the Gospel as early as pre-AD 70 and yet there are considerations in support of such a theory which have not received the attention which they deserve. V. Burch[2]

---

[1] R. M. Grant, in his recent book, *A Historical Introduction to the New Testament* 1963), p. 155, disputes that on literary or historical grounds it can be proved that John is either earlier or later than the Synoptic Gospels. This is a significant breakaway from the general assumption.

[2] *The Structure and Message of St. John's Gospel* (1928).

in his book on this Gospel, proposed an author and an editor and maintained that John's original contents and structure must be dated near to the date of the crucifixion and its final editing before AD 70.[1] This is an astonishing theory, which if true would make the core of John's Gospel the earliest material in the New Testament. It depends for its validity on Burch's treatment of the structure of the Gospel, and not all would accept this in its entirety. Nevertheless, it is likely that, if John was the author, he wrote some of this Gospel long before the book was published. Indeed, there is something to be said for the view that John made notes of our Lord's discourses shortly after hearing them. Most scholars reject such a notion as highly improbable, but a careful examination of the discourses lends it more support than is generally recognized. They are recorded in such a way as to give the impression that the writer is reporting what he has actually heard.[2] They must either represent very early tradition or else be an example of superb artistry.

Several scholars who feel that the external evidence excludes an early date for publication draw a distinction between the Johannine catechesis and the actual production of the Gospel, the former being early, the latter late.[3] There is no fundamental objection to this hypothesis, especially if John did not use the Synoptics. Moreover, doctrinal considerations, which have for so long been regarded as pointing to a time of full development for Johannine theology, have more recently tended to support an earlier rather than a later date, as for instance affinities with Qumran[4] and arguments for an early ecclesiasticism.[5]

Various forms of this theory of an early origin for John have been proposed. Some, for example, suggest that at an early date the writer

[1] *Ibid.*, pp. 225 ff.

[2] A recent writer, H. E. Edwards (*The disciple who wrote these things*, 1953), has devoted his attention to a study of this aspect.

[3] In addition to Burch mentioned above, reference may be made to C. Spicq's *L'Epître aux Hébreux* (1952), pp. 109–138, in which he discusses the author of Hebrews' relation to the Johannine catechesis and concludes that the former knew and was influenced by the latter. Cf. also C. H. Dodd's arguments for a distinction between Johannine tradition before AD 70 and the later publication of the Gospel (*Historical Tradition in the Fourth Gospel*).

[4] See earlier discussion, pp. 252 ff. Recently both A. M. Hunter (*ET*, LXXI, 1959–60, pp. 164–167) and C. L. Mitton (*ET*, LXXIII, 1961–62, pp. 19–22) have been favourable to an earlier date for John than AD 100. Hunter suggests AD 80 or even a decade earlier.

[5] Cf. E. R. Goodenough, *JBL*, LXIV (1945), pp. 145–182 (especially pp. 166 ff.).

recorded the *ipsissima verba* of John the teacher, and this personal oral instruction was formulated well before AD 70.[1] Others suggest that the Johannine Gospel depends on a Johannine catechesis which was independent of the Synoptic traditions and was worked up into its present state by a later editor.[2] Whatever be the merits of these varied hypotheses, they are significant because they all assume a much greater historical veracity for the material than the alternative hypotheses do. This is in line with the increasing tendency to give more credence than formerly to the Johannine traditions. This will be touched upon when dealing with historicity, but it is clear that the earlier the date that can be attached to the Johannine material the greater will its claim to reliability tend to be.

V. RELATION TO THE SYNOPTIC GOSPELS

Many of the crucial problems concerning John's Gospel arise from its relationship to the Synoptic Gospels. If John's Gospel existed on its own it would undoubtedly raise many problems in its own right, and the same would be true of the Synoptics apart from John. Whatever view of their relationship is held, it cannot be denied that each is necessary to make the other intelligible.[3] In so far as John's Gospel is generally regarded as being subsequent to the others (see discussion on dating), there is special significance in observing that John answers many of the problems raised by the others, a factor which will become clearer as we proceed.

---

[1] This is the opinion of H. E. Edwards, who connects up the production of the Gospel with the flight of the Christians to Pella (*op. cit.*, pp. 129, 130). C. C. Tarelli ('Clement of Rome and the Fourth Gospel', *JTS*, XLVIII, 1947, pp. 208, 209) reckoned that John was *published* before AD 70. Cf. P. Gardner-Smith's opinion that John may be as old as Mark (*St. John and the Synoptic Gospels*, 1938, pp. 93 ff.). R. M. Grant (*op. cit.*, pp. 159 f.) dates this Gospel just after AD 70 on the grounds that the author was aiming to present Christian faith to bewildered Jewish sectarians, and if these were connected with the Dead Sea Community the period may have been soon after AD 68 when it was destroyed.

[2] Zahn (*INT*, III, 1909, p. 347) cites H. H. Wendt (*Lehre Jesus*, I, 1886, pp. 215–342) as maintaining this view.

[3] H. S. Holland, in his book *The Fourth Gospel* (1923), bases his main argument for the character of John's Gospel on the observation that the Synoptic Gospels leave unsolved many problems to which John provides the answer. In other words the Synoptic Gospels required another Gospel to be written to make them intelligible.

a. Comparison of the Gospel material

Whereas the differences are at once apparent, the similarities between John and the Synoptic Gospels are not so obvious. Yet it is as well to approach the differences by means of the similarities.

(i) *Similarities.* All the records include narratives and comments about John the Baptist, the call of the disciples, the feeding of the five thousand, the sea trip of the disciples, the confession of Peter, the entry to Jerusalem, the last meal and various sections of the passion narrative.[1] In addition there are common narratives about the cleansing of the temple and an anointing of Jesus, but both placed in a different setting. These similarities may also be supplemented by a number of isolated words of Jesus and others.[2] Yet the whole of this common material contains very little verbal agreement. There are a few other allusions which are hardly sufficiently close to be called similarities, such as the placing of resurrection appearances by both Luke and John in Jerusalem, the possible connection between the feet-washing incident in John and the words of Luke xxii. 27, and the parallel fishing episodes of John xxi. 1 ff. and Luke v. 1 ff.

In common with the Synoptists John records samples of both healing and nature miracles of our Lord, although he treats them differently. Moreover, although John concentrates on the Jerusalem ministry, he records some Galilaean material in common with the Synoptists. But when this has been said we come to the end of the similarities. The differences are much more numerous.

(ii) *Differences.* It will be valuable to classify these differences in order to clarify this very complicated problem. The first class of difference is due to material in the Synoptic Gospels which John does not record. It is necessary here only to state the main omissions,[3] although there are very many more of a minor character. John does not record the virgin birth, the baptism, temptation or transfiguration of Jesus, the cure of any demoniacs or lepers, the parables, the institution of the Lord's supper, the agony in the garden, the cry of dereliction or the ascension. This is a considerable list and demands some explanation. If we may assume that the readers were acquainted with the Synoptic Gospels a

---

[1] These are the most important parallels (cf. Feine-Behm, *Einleitung*, p. 111).

[2] For details, cf. C. K. Barrett, *The Gospel according to St. John* (1956), pp. 34 ff.

[3] These are conveniently and concisely discussed by E. B. Redlich, *An Introduction to the Fourth Gospel* (1939), pp. 56 ff.

ready answer may be that the author has presupposed this and has seen no reason to repeat material that was already widely known. Yet many scholars feel that this explanation is inadequate and suggest that theological reasons prompted the omissions. Any theory which involves intentional suppressions must be regarded as highly improbable, for these are hardly intelligible if the readers were already acquainted with the Synoptic Gospels.[1] The theory of C. K. Barrett,[2] however, has perhaps more to be said for it, although it is not without considerable difficulties. He maintains that John has taken many of these events which are detachable from their Synoptic contexts, has stripped them of their 'historical individuality' and has built them into the 'theological framework of his gospel'. In this way he attempts to explain John's omission of the virgin birth. But this type of theory presupposes that neither John nor the Synoptists has preserved true history, which prejudges the whole matter. It would be nearer the truth to say that any omissions by John were dictated by his assuming his readers' acquaintance with the events, and by his specific purpose, which certainly took into account theological considerations, as xx. 31 shows. In this case John vi is not to be regarded as a substitute for the institution of the Lord's supper,[3] but as a complement to the Synoptic accounts, describing the Lord's preparation of the minds of His disciples for the significance of the ordinance.[4]

A second category of differences consists of the additional material in John's Gospel. This comprises a large proportion of the whole and includes certain incidents of considerable importance. The main material consists of the early Judaean ministry including the miracle at Cana, the encounters of Jesus with Nicodemus and the Samaritan woman, the healing of the cripple and the blind man in Jerusalem, the raising of Lazarus, the washing of the disciples' feet, the farewell discourses and

[1] Redlich (op. cit., p. 57) rightly points out that such an intention would have defeated the author's main object in inculcating belief in Jesus Christ.

[2] Op. cit., p. 42.

[3] Most scholars agree that Jn. vi is the Johannine account of the institution of the Eucharist. Cf. A. Correll, Consummatum Est (1958), pp. 63 ff., for a brief statement of various views. He maintains that John omitted the narrative of the institution because he considered that the Eucharist was impossible before Jesus' death. See pp. 255 f. for a different view.

[4] For this interpretation of Jn. vi, cf. B. F. Westcott, The Gospel according to St. John (1887), p. 113. Also A. Plummer, The Gospel according to St. John (1900), pp. 152–154.

parts of the passion narrative. John's Prologue (i. 1–18) is also unique. All this singular material requires as much explanation as do the Johannine omissions of Synoptic material. Why is so much new material introduced? If John is designed to supplement the Synoptic Gospels the answer will be ready to hand. But the problem has been raised whether John's unique material has the same authentic character as the Synoptic Gospels. Further comments will be made later regarding John's historicity, but special mention is required here of the problem of Lazarus, in view of its close connection with the Lord's arrest. In the Synoptics the arrest is precipitated by the cleansing of the temple, whereas in John that event is related much earlier, and the raising of Lazarus seems to take its place.[1] Yet to regard this as a discrepancy on John's part is to misunderstand the whole situation. The Lazarus event certainly stirred up the hatred of the chief priests and Pharisees, and spurred them on to seek the Lord's arrest, but they needed a more concrete charge to present to a Roman court than one based on a miracle.[2] The cleansing of the temple seemed to them to provide a sufficient cause to institute proceedings against Jesus. The contradiction is therefore only apparent.[3] As for the other events, most of them have similar parallels in the Synoptics. The multiplication of wine at Cana, for instance, is of the same type as the multiplication of the bread and fish by the Sea of Galilee.

A third category is the difference in presentation. There is less narrative and more discourse, and the introduction is more philosophical than that of the Synoptics. The Johannine portrait of Jesus differs from that of the others in presenting Him almost in the role of a Jewish Rabbi, using rabbinical methods of argument and lacking the more popular approach so prominent in the others. It may well be asked whether the two pictures are not incompatible. The discourses present

---

[1] As the reason for the Synoptists' omission of the Lazarus incident, it has sometimes been suggested that Lazarus may still have been alive when they were produced, in which case no mention would have been made of him then for reasons of discretion. But it is more probable that an explanation is to be found in the respective authors' purposes. J. N. Sanders (*NTS*, 1, 1954, p. 34) did not consider the silence of the Synoptists to be insuperable since other raisings are reported.

[2] Cf. B. Redlich (*op. cit.*, pp. 60 ff.), who argued that the raising of Lazarus was the *occasion* but not the *cause* of our Lord's arrest.

[3] Cf. A. J. B. Higgins, *The Historicity of the Fourth Gospel* (1960), p. 48.

a problem which must be faced. It has often been argued that the absence of Synoptic-type parables in John and of Johannine-type discourses in the Synoptics presents a contradiction. But this has been partially due to a misunderstanding. It is not true to say that John's account is altogether lacking in parabolic teaching. While the precise forms of the Synoptic parables may not be so clearly evident, there are passages in John in which sayings approximating to the Synoptic forms are discernible. C. H. Dodd,[1] for instance, has isolated seven such passages which he calls Johannine parabolic forms. Moreover the allegorical style of John x and xv is not so far removed from the parabolic style of the Synoptics. It is not difficult to regard one as a development from the other. In addition, John contains a considerable number of aphoristic sayings which are comparable to the type found in the other Gospels.[2]

The connected discourses present a more difficult problem since the Synoptic Christ does not engage in the same type of discourse as the Johannine Christ, and many scholars therefore regard the two presentations of Christ the Teacher as incompatible. The only recourse in this event is to treat the Johannine discourses as no more than a literary creation of the author himself or else as having been already reduced to this form in his sources. Owing to its somewhat homiletical character, C. K. Barrett[3] suggested that much of the discourse material was originally delivered in the form of sermons by the Evangelist. Some have posited a discourse source, while others have attributed the form of teaching to the author's own skill. All these theories are prompted by the dissimilarity with the Synoptic teaching material. But can the difficulty not be explained in a way which renders it unnecessary to suppose that Jesus could not have taught in the manner which John describes?

One consideration which may explain some of the phenomena is that almost all the discourses in John were delivered to the more educated people, mostly in Jerusalem, whereas the Synoptic audiences were more often the common people of Galilee. That a difference of audience would cause any skilled teacher to adapt his

[1] *Historical Tradition in the Fourth Gospel*, pp. 366–387.

[2] This was pointed out by J. Drummond (*An Inquiry into the Character and Authorship of the Fourth Gospel*, 1903, pp. 17 ff.), whose detailed list is conveniently summarized by Howard, *The Fourth Gospel in Recent Criticism*, p. 306.

[3] *The Gospel according to St. John* (1956), pp. 17, 20, 113 ff.

method can hardly be questioned.[1] But there are some passages for which this explanation would not seem to be valid, notably John vi, in which a discourse on the bread is delivered in Galilee in the same form and style as those in Jerusalem. But even here it should be noted that the discourse as a whole was not delivered in the open air but in the synagogue (vi. 59), and it is significant that the protagonists in the discussion are specifically described as Jews (vi. 41, 52), a term used characteristically by John of those who were particularly hostile to Jesus and who were representative of Judaism. It is, of course, true that John vi begins with a description of the feeding of the multitudes and leads on to the discussion about the heavenly bread, but it is evident that the discussion must have been restricted to a small number of people. It is quite clear that Jesus is not addressing the multitudes, and there is no reason therefore to suppose that He could not have addressed His audience on this occasion in the manner which John records. If the Synoptic presentation is the sole authentic tradition of Jesus the Teacher, the Johannine discourses must be admitted as a serious problem. But if Jesus could not have taught as the Johannine Christ taught, where did the idea arise that He did? It is inconceivable that such an unfamiliar picture could have received authentication if there were not already some basis for it in the tradition. Barrett's theory might seem in part to meet the difficulty if the Evangelist's sermons had conditioned his readers to expect Jesus to teach in the manner in which they had been accustomed to hear His teaching presented. But this theory could not account for the dialogue type of discourse, although it might apply to the farewell discourses (xiv–xvii), but even here the setting in the upper room restricts the applicability of the teaching, and makes it difficult to imagine that it could have been delivered from sermon material.

The difference between the Synoptic and Johannine teaching material must not be minimized, but is it not possible to find a solution in the versatility of Jesus as a teacher,[2] rather than in the acceptance of one

---

[1] Cf. Meinertz, *Einleitung*, p. 233.

[2] Even a Jewish scholar such as I. Abrahams (*Studies in Pharisaism and the Gospels*, I, 1917, p. 12) considered that John's discourses enshrine a genuine aspect of Jesus' teaching omitted from the Synoptics. Cf. also F. C. Burkitt, *The Gospel History and its Transmission*, pp. 239 ff.; Drummond, *op. cit.*, pp. 35 ff. W. H. Raney (*The Relation of the Fourth Gospel to the Christian Cultus*, 1933, pp. 71 ff.) maintains that most of the long discourse materials in John were Christian prose-hymns and if this theory is correct it would furnish an explanation of the different forms of our Lord's teaching in John and the Synoptics. He draws a distinction between

picture as authentic and the rejection of the other? Those who adopt the latter course (and the majority of scholars tend to do so) must frankly face the implications that they may be presupposing as the originator of the Johannine discourses one who was greater than Jesus Himself. If the great Johannine discourses are in no way related to the *ipsissima verba* of Jesus[1] they must have been the production of a greater reflective genius. But it is reasonable to suppose that the genius of Jesus' teaching method was capable of the Johannine discourses as well as of the Synoptic parables and aphorisms. This being so, the particular contribution of the author lay in a greater and more sympathetic understanding of this method of teaching than is found in the other Gospel writers.

The fourth category of differences consists of historical and chronological problems. The most notable differences are in the dating of the cleansing of the temple, the duration of the ministry, and the dating of the last supper. The first difficulty may be obviated by postulating two cleansings,[2] although this suggestion is usually dismissed, almost without consideration, as highly improbable.[3] On the other hand it cannot be argued conclusively that a double cleansing was impossible. If it happened once it could in theory happen twice, if similar conditions were repeated. It would not be the first time that such a double act of reformation proved necessary. The view that the temple police would not have allowed it to happen twice is not altogether convincing, for during the passion week the Lord's enemies were on the watch for Him in any case, but seem to have been powerless to stop Him. When they ultimately arrested Him they had to do it secretly for fear of the people. The whole act was done with such moral authority that it may

what he calls the continuous prose-hymns of John and the isolated poetic statements in the Synoptics. (Cf. his critique of C. F. Burney's evidence, *ibid.*, pp. 69, 70.) But a teacher capable of one would be equally capable of the other. Another theory particularly relating to the dialogue form in John's Gospel is that of C. H. Dodd (*BJRL*, xxxvii, 1954–55, pp. 54–67), who finds in them traces of the influence of current Hellenistic religious and philosophical models. According to him the Evangelist must be viewed as a literary craftsman who was himself responsible for the peculiarities of the Johannine discourses.

[1] Cf. R. H. Strachan's discussion, *The Fourth Gospel*[3] (1941), pp. 15–26.

[2] For a recent advocacy of a double cleansing, cf. R. V. G. Tasker, *The Gospel according to St. John* (1960), p. 61.

[3] The approach of C. K. Barrett is typical (cf. *op. cit.*, p. 163). He accepts John's dependence on Mark, which makes a double cleansing lacking in *literary* support.

even be questioned whether Jesus could have gone near the temple without doing it. Nevertheless, if there was one cleansing only, it needs to be decided whether the Synoptic or the Johannine timing of it is correct, and to suggest a reason for the variation between them. The majority of scholars maintain the Synoptic positioning of the incident because it leads naturally to the arrest and it is then supposed that John placed it early for symbolic reasons.[1] It is not conceivable that John was correcting the Synoptic narratives at this point, for his own passion story presupposes some such event to account for the arrest.[2] This consideration has led one scholar[3] to maintain a rearrangement of John with ii. 13b–25 placed after the raising of Lazarus, a reshuffling which would certainly resolve the difficulty if it could be substantiated.

The seeming variation in the duration of the ministry poses less of a problem than is often imagined. It is generally supposed that the Synoptists require only one year, whereas John requires almost three. But the chronological indications in the Synoptics are too vague to settle the question of the duration and there are in fact many incidental details which suggest a much longer period than one year.[4] Moreover, there are some obvious gaps in the Synoptic narratives, particularly in relation to the Judaean ministry. It is not impossible to regard both Synoptic and Johannine accounts as complementary in this matter. The one point of chronology in the midst of the ministry, common to all the Gospels, is the feeding of the five thousand, which John dates just before a Jewish Passover (Jn. vi. 4).[5] This dating is confirmed by the incidental comment of Mark that the grass was green (Mk. vi. 39),

[1] Cf. Higgins, *The Historicity of the Fourth Gospel* (1960), p. 44. Barrett (*op. cit.*, p. 163) attributes the change of position to theological rather than chronological motives. Cf. also J. H. Bernard (*St. John*, I, pp. 86 ff.) in support of the Synoptic dating. But C. J. Cadoux (*JTS*, xx, 1919, pp. 311 ff.) preferred the Johannine setting. T. W. Manson ('The Cleansing of the Temple', *BJRL*, xxxIII, 1951, pp. 271 ff.) dates the cleansing in Mark about six months before the passion narrative proper begins.

[2] See previous discussion on the Lazarus incident, p. 265.

[3] T. Cottam, *The Fourth Gospel Rearranged* (1952), pp. 47 ff.

[4] Redlich (*An Introduction to the Fourth Gospel*, 1939, pp. 68 ff.) sets these out concisely.

[5] If the theory is allowed that chapters v and vi should be reversed (see discussion on pp. 288 ff.), this will affect the duration of the ministry in John. Cf. E. F. Sutcliffe's advocacy of a two-year ministry, based on such a dislocation, *A Two Year Public Ministry* (1938), especially pp. 84 ff.

which shows that the season was April.[1] There was moreover another harvest season before this (i.e. one year earlier) when the disciples plucked the ears of corn (Mt. xii. i; Mk. ii. 23; Lk. vi. i). Another year must have elapsed after the feeding of the five thousand before the final Passover season at which Jesus was crucified. In addition John mentions another earlier Passover (ii. 13) during the early Judaean ministry. The major difference, therefore, is one of impression rather than of fact, owing mainly to the omission of the Judaean ministry from the Synoptics and their lack of data concerning the Jewish festivals.

The date of the last supper is a well-known crux, in which the Synoptic and Johannine records appear to differ in their account of its relation to the Jewish Passover. The former seem to identify the two, whereas John states clearly that the last supper was partaken before the Passover (xiii. 1). The whole problem is difficult and cannot be disposed of in the short space available in an introductory study. Yet the nature of the problem must be indicated and its suggested solutions briefly noted. The main factors may be summarized as follows:

1. The Synoptic Gospels are definite that the Sanhedrin determined not to arrest Jesus on the feast day (Mk. xiv. 2), which must mean that their plan was to arrest Him *before* the Passover. Now this is what John's narrative specifically implies.

2. Nevertheless Mark xiv. 12 makes equally clear that the place for the Passover was prepared on the same day as the sacrificing of the Passover lambs, which would seem to date the last meal on the same evening as the Passover.

3. Some details of the narrative relate to matters such as the carrying of arms, the buying of linen clothes and spices, and the hurried meeting of the Sanhedrin,[2] which would have been prohibited on a feast day. When the soldiers hurriedly remove the body of Jesus it is because of the scruples of the Jews regarding their holy days, which suggests that the crucifixion did not take place on a festival day. It is sometimes also claimed that the detail about Simon Cyrene returning from the country might indicate that he was returning home from work. This method of argument may, however, be questioned and the evidence cannot be pressed.[3]

---

[1] Cf. Higgins, *op. cit.*, pp. 30, 31.

[2] Cf. V. Taylor, *The Gospel according to St. Mark*, p. 666.

[3] A. J. B. Higgins (*The Lord's Supper in the New Testament*, 1952, pp. 17 ff.), who favours the Synoptic account in preference to the Johannine, minimizes

4. When Paul speaks of Christ our Passover (1 Cor. v. 7) he may have had in mind an actual tradition that Jesus was crucified at the same time as the Passover lambs were being slain, which would agree with John's account.

A variety of solutions has been proposed. Those who dispute the authenticity of the Fourth Gospel narrative as a whole take up the view that John is wrong and the Synoptics are right.[1] With the recent greater inclination to give more credence to the historicity of John's Gospel, the tendency to accept its testimony regarding the supper has gathered weight. In this case John's Gospel is regarded as a correction of the Synoptic dating. These two opposing points of view are based on the principle of either/or. Yet the last word has not been said, for a third possibility is a both/and solution, in which both John and the Synoptics may possibly be right. It is difficult to maintain that John was correcting the Synoptics on this matter unless some adequate explanation is forthcoming of the strength of the contrary tradition. It is better, therefore, if at all possible, to search for a solution which maintains the validity of both. Recently such a solution has been proposed by Mlle A. Jaubert.[2]

It is not possible to discuss all the details, but the general idea is that there were two calendars which fixed the Passover by different methods; in one it always fell on the same day of the week (i.e. Wednesday), and in the other it was adjustable in accordance with lunar calculations. The evidence for the former, which is the more unusual, is found in the Book of Jubilees. Since this calendar is now believed to

the strength of the objections listed above. Cf. the same author's article on 'The Origins of the Eucharist', NTS, 1 (1954–55), pp. 200–209. Higgins' own view is that John has antedated the chronology for theological reasons. The objections are even more strongly challenged by J. Jeremias, The Eucharistic Words of Jesus (1955), pp. 49–57.

[1] The negative criticism of the nineteenth century, which strongly called in question the Johannine historicity, inevitably left in its wake a bias against the veracity of any element of Johannine testimony. For a résumé of the earlier critical approach to John, cf. H. W. Watkins' Bampton Lectures, Modern Criticism considered in its relation to the Fourth Gospel (1890). For an account of the gradual change of attitude in the twentieth century, cf. W. F. Howard's The Fourth Gospel in Recent Criticism, pp. 128 ff., pp. 164 ff.

[2] 'La date de la dernière Cène', RHR, 146 (1954), pp. 140–173; La Date de la Cène (1957); 'Jésus et le calendrier de Qumrân', NTS, 7 (1960), pp. 1–30.

have been used in the Qumran community,[1] there is the possibility that at the time of the passion of our Lord the Essenes were observing the Passover before the Pharisaic observance in Jerusalem. If this is a valid inference it is further possible that the Synoptic accounts might be understood against the background of this calendar, whereas the Johannine narrative might be related to the Jerusalem calendar. There is some evidence that special regulations applied to Galilee[2] and it may be that the same calendar as in the Book of Jubilees was observed there, in which case it would be easy to see why Jesus and His disciples would have kept the Passover before the official feast in Jerusalem. M. Black, in fact, even wonders whether the Passover observed by our Lord was regarded in Jerusalem as illegal.[3] No solution to the problem is wholly without difficulties,[4] but this theory of divergent calendars seems to point the way to a possible answer.[5]

Another idea closely akin to this, but which does not bring in the Essenes, is to suppose that John reflects Sadducean custom in his Passover chronology, whereas the Synoptic narratives reflect the Pharisaic.[6]

[1] This was pointed out by D. Barthélemy, *VT*, 3 (1953), pp. 250–264, and is supported by J. T. Milik, *Ten Years of Discovery in the Wilderness of Judaea* (1959), pp. 107–113. Cf. also J. Morgenstern, *VT*, 5 (1955), pp. 34–76. On the significance of the Qumran evidence on this question, cf. J. Blinzler, *ZNTW*, 49 (1958), pp. 238–251; J. Jeremias, *JTS*, n.s., x (1959), pp. 131–133.

[2] M. Black (*The Scrolls and Christian Origins*, 1961, p. 200) cites the Babylonian Talmud, *Pes.* iv. 5 ff. Cf. the discussion by B. Gärtner, *John 6 and the Jewish Passover* (1959).

[3] *Op. cit.*, p. 201. Cf. also E. Stauffer, *Jesus and His Story*, pp. 94, 95, who maintains that Jesus, accused of heresy, would not be allowed to partake of an official Passover meal.

[4] A. J. B. Higgins (*The Historicity of the Fourth Gospel*, pp. 61, 62) is critical of Mlle Jaubert's theory on two main grounds. First, the occurrence in the same week of the Essene Passover and the Jerusalem Passover could happen only every thirty years, and he thinks this coincidence is therefore suppositional, in addition to the fact that no evidence remains that Jesus observed the Essene calendar. Secondly, the evidence cited by Mlle Jaubert of an early Christian practice of celebrating the last supper on a Tuesday evening, Higgins regards as worthless because it arose out of an arbitrary fixing of Christian feast days. Another critic whose opinion cannot be ignored is J. Jeremias, who considers that the author is more persuasive than convincing (*JTS*, x, 1959, pp. 131 ff.).

[5] In his article on 'The Date and Significance of the Last Supper', *SJT*, 14 (1961), pp. 256–269, A. Gilmore prefers an open verdict, but is not unsympathetic towards Mlle Jaubert's views.

[6] This proposal is discussed by R. P. Martin in the *Theological Students' Fellowship Bulletin*, 29 (1961), pp. 4–8.

According to the former custom the 'Omer' was offered on the day following the sabbath after the Passover (i.e. Nisan 16), whereas the Pharisees interpreted Leviticus xxiii. 11 as meaning the day following the Passover (i.e. Nisan 15). Some scholars have claimed that John belonged to the Sadducean party[1] and that this accounts for his narrative reflecting the Sadducean tradition. It may well be, therefore, that the last meal was not the regular Passover meal, but came to be interpreted in that way.

It will be seen, therefore, that the historical and chronological differences may well be capable of an interpretation which does not involve contradictions or corrections, and this will clearly affect any theory of relationship.

b. Explanation of the relationship

Windisch[2] pointed out that there are four possible explanations. John may be either supplementary to, independent of, interpretative of, or a substitute for, the Synoptists. The first of these has most to be said for it and is most generally accepted. It is supported by several considerations. The large amount of material in John, which is absent from the Synoptics, would be well accounted for if John were filling in the gaps. Moreover, John often avoids unnecessary duplication, so that it would seem he assumes his readers will be acquainted with the Synoptic records. Since the Gospel as a whole, with its concentration upon the ministry in Judaea and Jerusalem and its greater quantity of discourse material, was evidently conceived on a different pattern from that of the Synoptics, it is reasonable to suppose that it was composed with the others in mind. It should be noted that this view is tenable even if it be maintained that John did not use the Synoptic Gospels as a source. But it does, of course, presuppose some knowledge of the content of those Gospels by both the author and his readers.

The second possibility, that of independence,[3] is difficult to maintain

[1] Cf. E. Stauffer, *New Testament Theology* (1955), pp. 40 f.; F. C. Burkitt, *The Gospel History and its Transmission* (1906), pp. 248 ff.

[2] *Johannes und die Synoptiker* (1926).

[3] In his recent article comparing the Johannine and Synoptic passion narratives, P. Borgen (*NTS*, 5, 1959, pp. 246–259) maintains that John follows a tradition independent of the Synoptics, although that tradition had become fused with Synoptic tradition before coming into the hands of the Evangelist. Yet as Higgins (*op. cit.*, p. 21) points out, it is strange that the Synoptics show no evidence of fusion with the Johannine tradition.

in view of the factors mentioned above. It is extremely difficult, for instance, to see why John should omit all direct reference to the ordinances if he were ignorant of the other Gospels. Furthermore it is difficult to conceive of any historical situation at a relatively late date in which the Synoptic Gospels were unknown. It is significant that this problem has led some advocates of the independence theory to postulate an early date for John.[1]

The third possibility, that of interpretation, has many advocates. It has been particularly favoured by the Hellenistic school of Johannine scholars,[2] who treat the whole Gospel as an interpretation of Jesus and His teaching especially designed for Gentile readers. Although this school of thought is not now as strong as it was, it still appears to many scholars as the best solution of the Johannine problem.[3] It is built, nevertheless, on an assumption, i.e. that the content of the Gospel is not intended to give an objective historical account. If this assumption should prove incorrect, the main support for the theory collapses with it. Moreover, if John were seriously attempting to 'interpret' the other Gospels, it is difficult to see why he includes so few parallels to them. There are, therefore, some major problems attached to this view. At the same time, there is clearly some element of interpretation, as, for example, in the Prologue.

The fourth suggestion, held by Windisch himself, is that John aimed to replace the Synoptics. But this has already been pointed out as highly improbable. There is, in fact, no evidence which leads us to suppose

---

[1] Cf. E. R. Goodenough, *JBL*, LXIV (1945), pp. 145–182; cf. also H. E. Edwards, *The disciple who wrote these things* (1953). J. A. T. Robinson ('The Place of the Fourth Gospel', in *The Roads Converge*, ed. P. Gardner-Smith, 1963, pp. 49–74) argues that the Johannine tradition is pre-AD 70. *N.B.* R. Gyllenberg maintained that the beginning of the Johannine tradition was as old as that of the Synoptists (*Neutestamentliche Studien für R. Bultmann*, ed. W. Eltester, 1954, pp. 144–147). He deduces this from a form-critical point of view.

[2] Cf. E. F. Scott, *The Fourth Gospel, its Purpose and Theology*[2] (1908), pp. 53 ff. J. Grill (*Untersuchungen über die Entstehung des vierten Evangeliums*, I, 1902, II, 1923) is one of the more extreme advocates of Hellenizing influences. But for a more moderate view see also C. H. Dodd, *The Interpretation of the Fourth Gospel*. R. Bultmann in *Eucharistion*, II (1923), pp. 1–26; *idem*, *ZNTW*, 24 (1925), pp. 100–146, and W. Bauer, *Das Johannesevangelium*[2] (1925), both make much of Mandaean parallels. Cf. also B. W. Bacon's *The Gospel of the Hellenists* (1933).

[3] R. H. Lightfoot (*St. John's Gospel: a Commentary*, 1956, pp. 33 ff.) held to John's interpretative purpose, although he was much more moderate in his approach to John's historicity than Bultmann and Bauer.

that John ever supplanted any of the other Gospels in any section of the Church. In fact, as has already been shown, the earliest Gospel to attain widespread distribution was Matthew's Gospel, not John's, and it would be necessary to suppose, on Windisch's theory, that the author was entirely unsuccessful in his quest.

VI. STRUCTURE

There are several problems which arise from a study of the Johannine structure: its comparison with the Synoptic structure, the question of literary sources and editorial processes, and the unity of the Gospel. There has been discussion of all or most of these problems through the whole period of critical enquiry. As a reaction to the sceptical attitude of the more destructive school of critics, many of the source-critical theories were attempts to salvage something of value from the Fourth Gospel while jettisoning the other material. It is small wonder that a large number of divergent theories resulted.[1]

a. The unity of the Gospel

It is of first importance to discover whether or not the book as it has been transmitted was the work of one author or of more than one, for it is useless to discuss the structure until this matter has been settled. Some would treat the Prologue (i. 1–18) as apart from the rest.[2] Others maintain the separateness of chapter xxi.[3] Many theories of disparate material in the body of the Gospel have also circulated.[4] Since there are so many divergences in the different theories it is impossible to give details. In fact, what is more important is to give some indication of the principles on which such theories have been variously based.

One idea which has led to theories of different sources used in the structure of John is that the discourse sections must be separated from

---

[1] A convenient summary of these may be found in Howard, *The Fourth Gospel in Recent Criticism*, pp. 297 ff.

[2] See pp. 284 f.

[3] L. Vaganay, *RB*, xlv (1936), pp. 512 ff.; M. E. Boismard, *RB*, liv (1947), pp. 473–501. The latter suggests as author of this chapter a disciple of John who has been influenced by his oral teaching, thus accounting for the similarities and differences which he detects in this chapter compared with the rest. For a recent defence of chapter xxi, cf. Cassian, *NTS*, 3 (1957), pp. 133–136.

[4] See p. 276.

the narrative portions.[1] But the narrative portions so often merge almost imperceptibly into the discourse material (as for example in Jn. iii) that it is impossible to draw any clear line of demarcation between them. One source consisting entirely or even mainly of Johannine discourse material is most improbable, since in most cases the narrative sections are the setting for the discourses which follow.

Another criterion which some scholars have used is that of alleged discrepancies and contradictions, which are reckoned to point to different strata. Many of the older liberal critics[2] argued along this line, but the alleged 'discrepancies' and 'contradictions' were not impossible to obviate by some other quite satisfactory interpretation. In other words, this process was largely governed by the presuppositions with which individual critics approached the Gospel.

A third method of approach is to suppose an author and a redactor and to attempt to discern what portions of the book might be attributed to the latter. There is a large conjectural element here also, for it is often impossible to differentiate between the various types of style which are alleged to be present. One such theory was that of B. W. Bacon,[3] who attributed chapter xxi to the redactor, together with various other portions which were connected in some way with the Appendix (he includes, for instance, the account of Peter's denial). But Bacon's analysis was dominated by his theory regarding the purpose of the redactor, i.e. to harmonize the Asiatic and Roman traditions. Another theory is Bultmann's,[4] which postulates an ecclesiastical redactor, who has added some passages and phrases to bring the Gospel into line with the Synoptic tradition and ecclesiastical theology (sacra-

---

[1] As, for example, by H. H. Wendt (cited by Howard, *op. cit.*, p. 96). E. Renan (*Vie de Jésus*, 1863) questioned the discourses rather than the narratives, which he preferred to those of the Synoptics (cf. p. xxx). Recently a similar view has been advocated by E. Schweizer, *Ego Eimi* (1939), p. 106 (cited by Barrett, *op. cit.*, p. 8).

[2] For a review of older theories, cf. H. W. Watkins, *Modern Criticism considered in its relation to the Fourth Gospel* (1890), pp. 169 ff.

[3] *The Fourth Gospel in Research and Debate*[2] (1918), pp. 481 ff.

[4] Cf. *RGG*, III[3] (1959), pp. 842 ff. R. H. Strachan (*The Fourth Evangelist, Dramatist or Historian?*, 1925, pp. 84 ff.) maintained a theory that the ideal plan of the Gospel was governed by symbolic considerations and that a redactor superimposed some chronological sequence to bring it into line with what he conceived a Gospel should be. But the extent of symbolism may be questioned, and in any case it is a matter of opinion whether or not one author may be responsible for these two different plans, assuming that two plans can positively be deciphered.

ments and eschatology). But the same conjectural basis is evident here.[1]

A rather more reliable criterion, although fraught with considerable dangers, is that of literary and stylistic comparisons. If there were passages which differed in a marked way from the style of the main portions of the Gospel, this might be some indication of the use of separate sources, or of the hand of a redactor, but stylistic changes within the Gospel are hard to substantiate, even in chapter xxi. The general impression of unity is, in fact, borne out by stylistic considerations. The Johannine grammatical peculiarities are fairly evenly distributed throughout the Gospel.[2] On the whole, therefore, it may be said that stylistic criteria favour the unity of the Gospel.

Yet another method of discrimination has quite recently been used— that of statistics. It has been maintained that by statistical investigation an original form of the Gospel can be differentiated from the existing enlarged copy. The pioneers in this field are G. H. C. Macgregor and A. Q. Morton,[3] the latter claiming to supply statistical justification of the theories of the former. Certain passages are observed to have longer paragraphs than others, and these are regarded as belonging to a hand different from that responsible for the remainder of the Gospel. Statistical methods are also used to support theories of widespread textual dislocations. But, as Morton himself admits,[4] paragraph study is not a conclusive guide. It can only assist in source analysis. Thus Macgregor claims that the J_2 panels (as these writers call the additional material) are introduced at exactly equal intervals, thus giving an indication of the almost mathematical bent of the editor's mind. He further claims that the evidence shows that there are numerous derangements in the text which he suspects are due to the processes of conflating J_1 and J_2.[5] By means of comparisons between the length of paragraphs, sentences and even words in each of these parts, Morton concludes

---

[1] Cf. also the theory of E. Hirsch (*Studien zum vierten Evangelium*, 1936), who proposed an original form of the Gospel which was written by an unknown Antiochian and was later adapted for the general use of the Asiatic churches. But cf. the criticisms of E. Ruckstuhl, *Die literarische Einheit des Johannesevangeliums* (1951), pp. 13 ff. Both Hirsch and Bultmann base their theories on style-critical methods (cf. Hirsch's discussion on style criticism, *ZNTW*, 43, 1950–51, pp. 129–143), but in general it is difficult to free style criticism from the investigator's personal inclinations. For Bultmann's sources theory for this Gospel, see p. 281.

[2] Cf. Howard, *op. cit.*, p. 107.   [3] *The Structure of the Fourth Gospel* (1961).

[4] *Ibid.*, p. 47.   [5] *Ibid.*, p. 56.

that there are real and substantial differences.[1] It is not at once obvious that the method used is justifiable, for no confirming parallels are cited to support the assumption that differences in length (in word, or sentence or paragraph) are indicative of difference of authorship. Until such confirmation is forthcoming, to maintain that it is illogical to argue for the unity of the material is unconvincing.

A critical study of the style of John's Gospel has in fact convinced E. Schweizer[2] of its essential unity. He finds similar characteristics in all its parts and concludes that no theory but uniform authorship is adequate to explain these stylistic facts.

Various theories based on the idea of partition and redaction have been advanced. It is not possible to give more than a general impression of these—details can be sought elsewhere.[3] Some of these theories assume a basic document which has been subjected to various later modifications. Either the basic document has been supplemented from the Synoptic Gospels and the combined material furnished with editorial comments, or the latter process alone has been used extensively. Other hypotheses presuppose that the basic document did not materially differ from the finished product, except in the case of a few small editorial comments. The main problem with all these theories is the lack of agreement between different exponents about the extent and delineation of the redactional material, which at least suggests that the method of determination is ultimately unsatisfactory. Moreover, since it is possible to make an intelligible interpretation of the Gospel without recourse to theories of interpolation or redaction, it would seem reasonable to require an indisputable basis for such theories before they can lay claim to credibility. No such claim could fairly be made for any of those theories so far produced, and in the absence of this the unity of the Gospel may legitimately be maintained.

b. The problem of literary sources

The major question is whether or not the author has used any of the Synoptic Gospels. Since both tradition and literary analysis suggest

[1] *Ibid.*, pp. 86–92.
[2] *Ego Eimi* (1939). For a full discussion of Schweizer's viewpoint, cf. E. Ruckstuhl, *op. cit.*, pp. 180 ff.
[3] Cf. Howard's useful summary, *The Fourth Gospel in Recent Criticism*, pp. 297 ff.

that John's Gospel came after the Synoptics, there is at once a likeli-
hood that the author was aware of their existence. But does this
involve his use of Mark as a source? Two opposing answers have
been given.

The view that John has used Mark is widely held and is based on the
following considerations. Portions of John's Gospel are claimed to be
so closely paralleled in Mark as to require a theory of literary dependence. The most notable passages are the anointing at Bethany (Jn. xii.
1–8; Mk. xiv. 3–9), the cure of the impotent man at Bethesda (Jn. v. 8;
Mk. ii. 9), and the feeding of the five thousand (Jn. vi. 1–21; Mk. vi.
30–52), which are all said to reveal verbal similarities. With regard to
the first, J. H. Bernard[1] claimed that these similarities are too close to
be explained by a common oral tradition. However, when the total
number of verbal agreements is reckoned up they amount to a very
small proportion of the common material, and would hardly justify
the definite rejection of the possibility of a common source. This is
particularly so if eyewitness reminiscences lie behind both accounts.
Bernard referred to a number of other traces, largely of incidental
character, of John having used Mark.

C. K. Barrett,[2] who strongly maintains John's use of Mark,
places emphasis upon the fact that several narrative portions which
show some verbal contact follow the same sequence in John as
they do in Mark. This factor must clearly be given full weight,
but the support for the theory would be much stronger if the verbal agreements were more substantial. Nevertheless, this approach
to the relationship between John and Mark is supported by many
scholars.[3]

In addition there are claims that John has used Luke, of which the
most weighty instances usually cited are the anointing (cf. Lk. vii.
38), the prediction of the denial (Jn. xiii. 38; Lk. xxii. 34), the reference to the unused tomb (Jn. xix. 41; Lk. xxiii. 53) and details in the

---

[1] St. John, I, pp. xcvi, xcvii.

[2] The Gospel according to St. John (1956), pp. 34, 35. He cites a list of ten narrative sections occurring in the same order in John and Mark.

[3] For details, cf. Feine-Behm-Kümmel, Einleitung, p. 137. Cf. E. K. Lee,
NTS, 3 (1956), pp. 50–58. In the passion narratives there are many incidental
similarities between Mark and John, but there are also many differences of language and detail. S. I. Buse (NTS, 4, 1958, pp. 215–219) has suggested that the
Fourth Evangelist was acquainted not with Mark but with one of his passion
sources (Vincent Taylor's B source).

resurrection accounts[1] (cf. Jn. xx. 12, Lk. xxiv. 4; Jn. xx. 6, 7, 19, 20, Lk. xxiv. 12, 36). Again this evidence is sparse in quantity and could demonstrate literary dependence only if it were altogether unlikely that the data could have been obtained from another source.[2] There has been little support for the view that John shows literary dependence on Matthew.[3]

The contrary view that John did not use the Synoptic Gospels at all has been championed by P. Gardner-Smith,[4] who not only complained about the paucity of evidence for literary dependence but also its inconclusive nature. According to him the parallels are capable of being explained without recourse to the theory that John used the Synoptics as sources. Moreover, Gardner-Smith pointed out that the differences in the common material are more significant than the similarities. As a result of this careful study there has been less inclination to assume John's use of either Mark or Luke.[5]

[1] Cf. B. Lindars' examination of the sources of John's resurrection narratives (*NTS*, 7, 1961, pp. 142–147). He considers that these narratives cannot be traced to any one of the Synoptic Gospels, but rather depend on the traditions behind them. For a recent examination of all the relevant material and an advocacy of John's use of Luke's Gospel, cf. J. A. Bailey, *The Traditions common to the Gospels of Luke and John* (1963). This author supposes, nevertheless, that many traditions came to both Luke and John independently, sometimes written, sometimes oral.

[2] A different view of the relation between Luke and John is advocated by M. E. Boismard (*RB*, LXIX, 1962, pp. 185–211), who suggests an editing of John by Luke, at least in Jn. iv. 46b–53 and xx. 24–29. On the anointing cf. the article of K. Weiss (*ZNTW*, 46, 1955, pp. 241–245), who argues that the Western Text in Lk. vii. 46 was original and that John had misunderstood Luke's version of the anointing. Another view is that John combined Mk. xiv. 3 ff. (= Mt. xxvi. 6 ff.) with Lk. vii. 36 ff. (cf. Feine-Behm-Kümmel, *Einleitung*, p. 138). W. Grundmann (*Das Evangelium nach Lukas*, pp. 17–22) denies literary dependence between Luke and John, but prefers to think of a common tradition.

[3] Cf. H. F. D. Sparks (*JTS*, n.s., III, 1952, pp. 58–61). But Gardner-Smith criticizes this point of view (*JTS*, n.s., IV, 1953, pp. 31–35).

[4] *St. John and the Synoptic Gospels* (1938). Cf., for similar views, F. C. Grant, *JBL*, LVI (1937), pp. 290–307. At an earlier date J. Schniewind (*Die Parallelperikopen bei Lukas und Johannes*, 1914) had strongly maintained that John did not use Luke. Bultmann thinks that John was independent of Luke, but used Mark, Q and L (*ThLZ*, 80, 1955, cols. 521–526). P. Parker (*NTS*, 9, 1963, pp. 317–336) suggests that Luke and John must have been associated in mission work.

[5] Cf. C. H. Dodd's article in *NTS*, 2 (1955), pp. 75, 76, on the Johannine *Herrnworte*, and his *Historical Tradition in the Fourth Gospel*. He argues for an independent tradition. For further recent discussions see S. Mendner, *ZNTW*, 47 (1956), pp. 93–112; J. N. Sanders, *NTS*, 1 (1954–55), pp. 29 ff.; D. M. Smith,

It should be noted that not all the arguments used by Gardner-Smith can be considered valid, for he argues that several of the parallels between John and the Synoptic Gospels cannot be due to literary dependence, because if they were it would mean that John would be flatly contradicting his source Mark. But the argument would not apply if such contradiction is not first of all assumed.[1] In other words the basis of some, at least, of Gardner-Smith's hypothesis is the irreconcilability of John and the Synoptics. Nevertheless, if this basis be rejected, it may still be reasonably maintained that the similarities and differences in the Gospels are more likely to have arisen during the oral period or through the different sources of evidence available (e.g. from eyewitness accounts[2]) than from the use of written sources.

Whatever conclusions are reached about this matter, it can safely be said that John did not use Mark as a framework. It is in fact John's distinctive framework which has distinguished his Gospel most notably from the Synoptics.

A complicated theory of John's literary sources is held by R. Bultmann,[3] who suggests two main sources, a revelation discourses source (*Offenbarungsreden*) and a signs source. In addition, the author possibly had a third source for the passion narrative which Bultmann believes was independent of the Synoptic Gospels. He arrives at his sources by an examination of stylistic phenomena and rhythmic patterns, as a result of which he claims to be able to distinguish not only the separate sources but also the redactional elements. The revelation discourses were based on Gnostic materials and originally existed in Aramaic. In spite of the great learning with which the theory has been presented it has not commended itself to many scholars. Bultmann's pupil, H.

Jnr., *JBL*, LXXXII, 1963, pp. 58–64 (who disputes dependence) and E. D. Freed, *JBL*, LXXX (1961), pp. 329–338 (who maintains it). It has been argued that the common belief that John was the end-product of primitive Christian development was responsible for the literary dependence theory (cf. E. R. Goodenough, *JBL*, LXIV, 1945, pp. 145–182).

On the other hand, a recent article by C. Goodwin (*JBL*, LXXIII, 1954, pp. 61–75) has argued from John's use of the Old Testament that it may be expected that he would use his sources with even greater freedom. He thinks this might mean that he may have used the other Synoptics when verbal parallels are slight.

[1] Examples may be found in P. Gardner-Smith, *op. cit.*, pp. 8, 16, 23, 48.

[2] Michaelis (*Einleitung*, p. 106) considers that the author relied on eyewitness sources.

[3] Cf. his *Das Evangelium des Johannes* and his article in *RGG*, III[3] (1959), pp. 842 ff.

Becker,[1] developed the idea of the Gnostic origin of the revelation discourses, but other pupils of Bultmann have been more sceptical of this proposition.[2]

Stylistic phenomena are not a reliable indication of Johannine sources as E. Ruckstuhl[3] has cogently pointed out in his criticism of Bultmann's theory. He maintains that the stylistic features that Bultmann used as criteria for distinguishing between his two major sources occur in both. In fact, Ruckstuhl claims that style criticism must lead to the denial of written sources altogether. Although not all Bultmann's critics would go as far as this, most agree that the stylistic unity of John's Gospel is a difficulty for his theory. B. Noack,[4] however, argues for oral traditions behind the Gospel, maintaining that a purely narrative document like Bultmann's signs source is without precedent. He maintains further that the Evangelist's citations of the Old Testament appear to be from memory, and this would lead to the assumption that it was not his habit to cite sources meticulously. A major weakness in Bultmann's method is in his dealing with the editorial comments of the Evangelist. When these betray stylistic peculiarities similar to those of the sources, he resorts to the theory that here the editor is affected by the style of his sources, but this brings the whole method under suspicion.[5] Moreover, to maintain his rhythm criterion Bultmann is obliged to conjecture an Aramaic origin of the discourses which then leaves him free to attribute all non-rhythmic features to a prosaic redactor. But this method of dealing with difficulties is unconvincing.[6] E. Käsemann[7] has criticized Bultmann on other grounds, particularly disagreeing with the idea of a Gnostic source being used by a Christian Evangelist. In fact, by challenging Bultmann's theological interpretation, Käsemann questions the necessity for his source theory.

[1] *Die Reden des Johannesevangeliums und der Stil der gnostischen Offenbarungsreden* (1956).

[2] Cf., for instance, Käsemann: see below.

[3] *Die literarische Einheit des Johannesevangeliums* (1951), pp. 20–179. On the unity of the Gospel, W. Grossouw (*Nov. Test.*, 1, 1956, pp. 35–46) points out that in spite of his literary theories, Bultmann treats the Gospel as a unity in his *Theologie* (except for sacramental theology and eschatology).

[4] *Zur johanneischen Tradition, Beiträge zur Kritik an der literarkritischen Analyse des vierten Evangeliums* (1954), pp. 9–42.

[5] Cf. Noack, *op. cit.*, pp. 31 ff.

[6] Cf. R. H. Fuller's criticism, *The New Testament in Current Study* (1962), p. 113.

[7] Cf. his article, 'Neutestamentliche Fragen von heute', *ZTK*, 54 (1957), pp. 15 f.

A modified theory of Johannine origins has been put forward by
W. Wilkens[1] who suggests that the author as it were made his own
sources, and has written his Gospel in three stages or editions. In this
way he attempts to account for the differences as well as the stylistic
unity. However, the attempt to distinguish the stages must inevitably
be difficult and to a large extent conjectural. It is unlikely for this reason
that any general agreement will be reached along such lines. Another
scholar who concentrates on the earlier stages of the Johannine material
is S. Schulz[2] who, although claiming to find some Gnostic reinter-
pretations of originally Jewish elements, and therefore showing some
points of contact with Bultmann's position, nevertheless rejects the
idea of written sources.[3]

More recently C. H. Dodd has investigated the possibility of isolating
what he calls the pre-canonical tradition behind this Gospel, which he
considers must have existed in an oral form.[4] This he suggests is much
closer to the Synoptic tradition than the rest of the Gospel, but is nevertheless independent of the Synoptic Gospels. He has summarized the
contents of this traditional material in the following way.[5] (1) A full
account of the work of John the Baptist, particularly as a reformer
within Judaism; (2) testimonies of John the Baptist to Jesus (although
Dodd does not date this element in the tradition so early); (3) an account of the early ministry of Jesus and the relationship between Jesus
and John during this period; (4) an account of Jesus the Healer, although
this was little used by the Evangelist; (5) a considerable amount of
topographical information; (6) probably a fuller account of the Gali-

---

[1] *Die Entstehungsgeschichte des vierten Evangeliums* (1958).

[2] *Untersuchungen zur Menschensohnchristologie im Johannesevangelium, zugleich
ein Beitrag zur Methodengeschichte der Auslegung des 4 Evangeliums* (1957). The same
author has a second book *Komposition und Herkunft der johanneischen Reden* (1960).

[3] For another advocacy of written sources approached from a different point of
view from that of Bultmann, cf. C. Broome (*JBL*, LXIII, 1944, pp. 107–121) who
maintained John's use of written sources, but supposed that only the shorter
logia sources were reproduced *verbatim*, the longer passages being more freely
edited. Several recent articles have dealt with source criticism in John. Cf. H. M.
Teeple's article on Methodology (*JBL*, LXXXI, 1962, pp. 279–286); D. M.
Smith's article in *NTS*, 10 (1964), pp. 336–351, mainly on Bultmann and his
critics; J. M. Robinson, *JBL*, LXXVIII (1959), pp. 242 ff.; C. K. Barrett, *ThLZ*, 84
(1959), cols. 828 f.; E. Haenchen, *ZTK*, 56 (1959), pp. 15–54.

[4] His book, *Historical Tradition in the Fourth Gospel* (1963), is wholly devoted to
this investigation.

[5] A useful summary is given, *ibid.*, pp. 429, 430.

laean ministry than the author has used; (7) a detailed passion narrative; (8) a body of traditional teaching material, including sayings, parables and dialogues. Dodd's investigations, which are carried out in a detailed and penetrating manner, are significant for various reasons. Having rejected the theory of literary dependence on the Synoptic Gospels, he has made a serious attempt to explain the presence in John of Synoptic-like material and in doing so has shown this material to be much more extensive than has often been supposed. It follows from this that, if Dodd is correct, much of the Johannine tradition rests on oral material which circulated before the production of the Synoptic Gospels and was contemporaneous with the oral sources of the latter. Such a conclusion could not fail to contribute towards a greater appreciation of the validity of the Johannine tradition and would help to combat any theory which erected insuperable barriers between John and the Synoptics.

c. The Johannine framework

The Gospel has a distinctive introduction which is unparalleled in the Synoptic Gospels. This Prologue is most significant because of its theological character and because of the importance it attaches to the manifestation of John the Baptist. Our present purpose is to consider how far the Prologue was intended to be an integral part of the Gospel. Again this has led to a variety of answers.

It has been supposed that the Prologue must be regarded as detached from the rest of the Gospel, as if the author introduced Christ's incarnation in Hellenistic terminology to capture the attention of his contemporaries.[1] Another view is that the author has incorporated a hymn on the Logos and has sought to integrate this with his purpose for the Gospel as a whole.[2] Both of these views assume that the interpretation of the Prologue furnishes the key to the understanding of the author's purpose. But it is possible to conceive that the author's main aim in the Prologue was to lead into his historical account of the life and teaching

---

[1] W. Baldensperger, *Der Prolog des vierten Evangeliums* (1898), cited by Howard, *The Fourth Gospel in Recent Criticism*, p. 57. It should be noted that Baldensperger did not regard the references to John the Baptist as intrusions into the Logos material, but as an essential part of the author's purpose. For a contrary view, cf. P. Gaechter, *ZkT*, 78 (1936), pp. 99–111.

[2] Cf. C. Cryer, *ET*, xxxii (1921), pp. 440 ff.; J. H. Bernard, *St. John*, i, p. xxx. Feine-Behm-Kümmel (*Einleitung*, p. 148) cite E. Käsemann and R. Schnackenburg as recent advocates for a pre-Johannine Christian hymn behind the Prologue.

of Jesus. This latter view is proposed by C. H. Dodd,[1] who regards the Logos doctrine as appropriate for leading 'a public nurtured in the higher religion of Hellenism' to 'the central purport of the Gospel, through which he (i.e. the writer) may lead them to the historical actuality of its story'. Some scholars firmly reject the view that the Prologue is Hellenistic and maintain on the contrary a Jewish origin. Both Rendel Harris[2] and C. F. Burney[3] argued strongly for this position. It is reasonable, therefore, to regard the Prologue as an integral part of the author's purpose in introducing his historical account.[4]

It is when the main body of the Gospel material is examined that it is difficult to discover the author's method of arrangement. The structure seems to be very loose. Dodd[5] connects i. 19–51 with the Prologue and considers the theme of the passage to be testimony, which leads up to what he calls the book of signs (ii–xii). This book consists of seven episodes and a conclusion. Each episode consists of both narrative and discourse related to a dominant theme.[6] There are many variations in the pattern on which the different episodes are constructed, but Dodd maintains that the episodes are so arranged as to be linked together. He has affixed titles to his episodes in the following manner: the new beginning (ii. 1–iv. 42); the life-giving Word (iv. 46–v. 47); Bread of life (vi); light and life: manifestation and rejection (vii–viii); judgment by the light (ix. 1–x. 21, x. 22–39); the victory of life over death (xi. 1–53); life through death: the meaning of the cross (xii. 1–36). This book of signs is then followed by the book of the passion (xiii–xxi). Such a scheme is a serious attempt to do justice to the structure of the book and draws particular attention to the Johannine emphasis on 'signs'. Other scholars have been content with a much looser understanding of the structure. J. H. Bernard,[7] for instance, divides the main portion of the Gospel into two parts, the first embracing the ministry in Galilee, Jerusalem and Samaria (Jn. i. 19–iv, vi), and the second

[1] The Interpretation of the Fourth Gospel (1953), p. 296.
[2] The Origin of the Prologue of St. John's Gospel (1917).
[3] The Aramaic Origin of the Fourth Gospel (1922). The same conclusion was arrived at by D. Plooij, Studies in the Testimony Book (1932), p. 27. Cf. also T. W. Manson, On Paul and John (1963), p. 148, and M. Black, An Aramaic Approach to the Gospels and Acts[2] (1954), pp. 207–209.
[4] J. A. T. Robinson maintains that the original Gospel opened with a historical account of John the Baptist and that this was later superimposed with the Logos material (NTS, 9, 1963, pp. 120–129).
[5] Op. cit., pp. 292 ff.   [6] Ibid., p. 384.   [7] Op. cit., pp. xxx ff.

dealing only with the ministry in Jerusalem (v, vii–xii. 50), but he makes no attempt to systematize the material within these sections. Similarly C. K. Barrett[1] finds the material in the section i. 19–xii very disparate, but he does find a discernible movement of thought which links together the various units.

Bultmann[2] divides the book into two main parts: the revelation of the glory before the world (ii–xii) and the revelation of the glory before the Church (xiii–xx). In the first part he finds four main sections: the encounter with the Revealer (ii. 23–iv. 42); the revelation as decision (iv. 43–vi. 59, vii. 15–24, viii. 13–20); the Revealer in conflict with the world (most of vii–x); the secret victory of the Revealer over the world (x. 40–xii. 33, viii. 30–40, vi. 60–71). In the second part is contained the farewell of the Revealer (xiii–xvii) and the passion and Easter narratives (xviii–xx). It will be seen that Bultmann achieves some unity of theme by means of rearrangement. Moreover, his dominant idea of a Revealer is influenced by his philosophical and theological position. Nevertheless, his two major divisions are suggestive.[3]

Some have attempted to find in John a sevenfold structure pervading the whole,[4] but this seems to be artificial in character. Others have proposed a kind of Jewish liturgical structure based on the feasts.[5] But it is difficult to believe that this framework formed the main basis for the Johannine structure. Another hypothesis somewhat akin to this is the view that behind the Gospel is to be discerned a Jewish lectionary and that the structure of the Gospel has been determined by this lectionary, with the result that the materials were arranged to form a commentary on the Old Testament passages set in the calendar.[6] This is an interesting theory, although it is again difficult to imagine that the finished product grew up in this way. If it did, the author

---

[1] *The Gospel according to St. John* (1956), pp. 11 ff.

[2] *Das Evangelium des Johannes*, cf. pp. 5–7.

[3] This is followed by I. H. Marshall (*NBD*, p. 645), although without Bultmann's rearrangement or presuppositions.

[4] Cf. E. Lohmeyer's view, *ZNTW*, 27 (1928), pp. 11–36. A. Feuillet cites J. Rabenech, *Einführung in die Evangelien* (1921), for a similar theory (Robert-Feuillet's *Introduction*, II, p. 623).

[5] Cf. D. Mollat in the Jerusalem Bible (cited in Robert-Feuillet, *op. cit.*, p. 623).

[6] Cf. A. Guilding, *The Fourth Gospel and Jewish Worship* (1960). For a brief critique of this theory, cf. J. R. Porter's article 'The Pentateuch and the Triennial Lectionary Cycle: An Examination of a Recent Theory', in *Promise and Fulfilment, Essays presented to S. H. Hooke* (ed. F. F. Bruce, 1963), pp. 163–174. Also L. Morris, *The New Testament and the Jewish Lectionaries* (1964).

certainly used considerable skill in imposing an essential unity on the material. At the same time there are many interesting parallels and the idea that John's Gospel was arranged with a view to providing a Christian lectionary over a period of three and a half years is intriguing. It is not easy, however, to see that any validity can in this case be placed on John's historical sequence.[1]

Mention must also be made of theories which propose a typological motive as an element in the Johannine structure. Several writers[2] have found typological parallels between various Old Testament passages and Johannine material, notably from the book of Exodus. But even where the parallels are confined to Exodus different schemes have been proposed and the question naturally arises whether any importance can be attached to theories of this sort. For instance, a theory[3] which sees parallels between the Mosaic miracles of Exodus ii. 23–xii. 51 and the Johannine signs presents a fascinating prospect, but stretches credulity when detailed comparisons are made. It is hard enough to believe that the author himself had such parallels in mind and almost inconceivable that any of his original readers would have suspected it.

VII. THEORIES OF DISLOCATION

In spite of the fact that this Gospel gives a general impression of unity, some scholars consider that there is evidence of dislocation. In some cases the connecting links which join adjacent sections are very loose and have therefore given rise to the hypothesis that the original text has suffered some mechanical disarrangements in course of transmission. The suggestion is not entirely impossible, especially if the autograph was in codex form, although there is no certain evidence to show whether codices were used quite as early as this.[4] The major objection

[1] A. Guilding maintains that the author is more interested in lectionary time than in historical time. This, she thinks, accounts for the different chronology of the cleansing of the temple (cf. *op. cit.*, pp. 4, 186 ff.).

The view that this Gospel was designed for liturgical use was maintained by A. Schlatter, *The Church in the New Testament Period* (1955), p. 300.

[2] Cf. H. Sahlin, *Zur Typologie des Johannesevangeliums* (1950); J. J. Enz, *JBL*, LXXVI (1957), pp. 208–215; B. P. W. S. Hunt, *Some Johannine Problems* (1958); T. F. Glasson, *Moses in the Fourth Gospel* (1963).

[3] Cf. R. H. Smith, *JBL*, LXXXI (1962), pp. 329–342.

[4] On the development of the codex form of manuscript, cf. Sir F. Kenyon's *The Story of the Bible* (1936), pp. 27 ff. More recently C. H. Roberts has published an important article on 'The Codex' (*The Proceedings of the British Academy*, XXXII, 1954), in which he shows that during the second century the codex seems

to this kind of hypothesis is the great number of different theories proposed, which considerably lessens the credibility of the idea as a whole.[1]
It is possible to give only the main passages involved, but these will
give sufficient indication of the type of data on which the theories are
based.

1. iii. 22–30. It is suggested that this passage would fit better if
placed between ii. 12 and ii. 13, on the grounds that in its present position it interrupts the Nicodemus discourse.[2]

2. v and vi. These chapters are thought to be better if transposed,
as in chapters iv and vi Jesus is in Galilee, whereas in chapter v He is in
Jerusalem.

3. vii. 15–24 is regarded as a continuation of the controversy
at the close of chapter v, and it is claimed that when this passage is
brought forward, vii. 25 ff. follows naturally on vii. 1–14.

4. x. 19–29 is similarly thought to continue the earlier controversy
of chapter ix, hence x. 30 ff. would then follow x. 1–18. It is claimed
that x. 1–18 would follow naturally after x. 19–29.

5. xiii–xvi. A rearrangement of these chapters so that xv and xvi
precede xiv is thought necessary in view of xiv. 31 which appears to be
the conclusion of the discourses.

6. xviii. 13–24 is said to contain confusion in its account of the trial.
Some rearrangement is supported by the Sinaitic Syriac text of the
Gospel, which has the following order, xviii. 12, 13, 24, 14, 15, 19–23,
16–18, 25 f.[3]

to have been used more widely for Christian purposes than for secular purposes
which suggests that this form may have originated among the Christians at a very
early date. It is not inconceivable, therefore, that the original, or else a very early
copy of John, may have been in such a form.

[1] Moffatt gives several suggestions (*ILNT*, p. 554). Bernard provides a very
full discussion of these proposed dislocations and favours all those cited and more
beside (*St. John*, I, pp. xvi ff.). Other exponents who may be mentioned are J. M.
Thomson, *Exp.*, VIII, ix (1915), pp. 421 ff.; Warburton Lewis, *Disarrangements in
the Fourth Gospel* (1910); G. H. C. Macgregor, *The Gospel of John* (*MC*, 1928);
F. R. Hoare, *The Original Order and Chapters of St. John's Gospel* (1944); T. Cottam,
The Fourth Gospel Rearranged (1952).

[2] A different approach to the Nicodemus incident is that of S. Mendner (*JBL*,
LXXVII, 1958, pp. 293–323) who thinks that portions of chapter iii belonged originally after vii. 51 and were dislocated after AD 135.

[3] For a theory based on the changes of order in the Syriac but differing slightly
in detail by placing verse 15 after and not before verses 19–23, cf. W. R. Church,
JBL, LXIX (1950), pp. 375–383.

Although some of these suggested rearrangements may possibly improve the connection of thought, there are some important considerations against such theories generally.

1. Amended arrangements can be justified only if the existing arrangement is incapable of intelligent interpretation and that can hardly be said of many, if any, of the above proposals. Indeed, it may be suggested that in some cases the rearrangements cause more dislocation to the connection of thought than the original alleged dislocations.[1]

2. Only for the last rearrangement suggested above can any textual evidence be produced. This must inevitably lessen the credibility of the hypotheses, even if it does not actually rule them out. It is possible to suppose that the dislocations happened in the original copy or else in a very early copy before the existing textual evidence arose. It is difficult however to maintain that disarrangements happened in an original autograph without the writer or his closest associates noticing.[2] It has further been noted in support of this kind of dislocation theory that Tatian placed the cleansing of the temple and the Nicodemus episode after vii. 31 in his *Diatessaron*, but this can hardly be taken as evidence for the order of the original text of John.[3]

3. The suggested rearrangements rest on the assumption that the author was meticulous about chronological and topographical order, but there is little evidence that he was. For instance, he often uses the vague μετὰ τοῦτο (or ταῦτα), by which he implies no more than a

---

[1] C. K. Barrett (*The Gospel according to St. John*, 1956, p. 183) strongly maintains the unity of chapter iii as it stands. In his opinion iii. 31–36 carries on the sense of iii. 22–30, in which case there is no need to reverse them. Bernard (*op. cit.*, p. xxiv) admits that to place this section before the cleansing of the temple and the 'signs' at Jerusalem would be unnatural, but he treats this section as a dislocation by placing it after iii. 36, a view supported by C. J. Cadoux, *JTS*, xx (1919), p. 317. This is rather less difficult and shows a better connection with chapter iv.

[2] Cf. Barrett, *op. cit.*, pp. 19, 20. It is little more convincing to maintain, as W. H. Raney does (*The Relation of the Fourth Gospel to the Christian Cultus*, 1933, pp. 75 ff.), that some of these dislocated sections consist of prose-hymns which were written on detachable hymn-sheets for choral purposes and which became deranged when replaced. It would be more reasonable to suppose with T. Cottam (*op. cit.*, pp. 77 ff.) that the author left his work in draft form on separate papyrus sheets and that after his death someone prepared them for publication and in doing so deranged the order.

[3] Cf. B. Redlich, *An Introduction to the Fourth Gospel* (1939), p. 104.

general idea of sequence. At the same time it would be a mistake to suppose that John was entirely disinterested in chronology, for both at the beginning and the end of the Gospel he includes a sequence of days, and in several incidents he mentions the hours when events happened. The point is that what appears disjointed to the modern scholar may not have appeared so to John.[1]

4. It is claimed by Barrett[2] that John's theological thought does not always move in straight lines, by which he means that he changes his point of view in course of dealing with the same subject, thus enlarging the whole theme. Whereas this may be true of some of the discourses, in which case the method of exposition could be that of Jesus and not John, it should be noted that the suggested dislocations affect narratives more than discourses (except in the case of the rearrangement of whole chapters). Nevertheless, the whole Gospel as it stands contains a fair impression of continuity which may well represent John's original conception.[3]

5. The *pericope adulterae* (vii. 53–viii. 11), which not only looks out of keeping with its immediate context but is treated as such in some strata of the textual tradition, is sometimes claimed as justification for the theory that other sections may be displaced. This would be further strengthened by the consideration sometimes brought forward that some, at least, of the rearranged sections mentioned above are similar in length to this *pericope*, while others are in multiples of it.[4] This line of argument, if true, cannot be lightly dismissed, but its validity needs to be tested and its credibility carefully weighed. The suggestion that vii. 53–viii. 11 can be used as a standard of measurement is highly dubious, for comparison with the number of lines for this passage and those mentioned above shows that this passage contains

---

[1] J. Moffatt (*ILNT*, p. 552) admitted the danger of making the assumption that John's mind was as logical or chronological as his critics', but he nevertheless favoured widespread dislocations, although he attributed these to copyists or later editors.

[2] *Op. cit.*, p. 20.

[3] See discussion on the unity of the Gospel, pp. 275 ff.

[4] First suggested by F. Spitta, *Zur Geschichte und Literatur des Urchristentums* (1893), I, p. 157. Cf. Warburton Lewis (*Disarrangements in the Fourth Gospel*, 1910, p. 15), who argued that xv and xvi were exactly six times the length of vii. 15–24, and the similar methods of A. C. Clark, *The Primitive Text of the Gospels and the Acts* (1914), pp. vi, 68 ff.; *idem*, *JTS*, XVI (1915), pp. 225 ff.; H. S. Cronin, *JTS*, XIII (1912), pp. 563–571.

more lines (16½ of Souter's text) than, for instance, vii. 15–24 (14½ lines) or iii. 22–30 (14 lines). On the other hand, Bernard works out the number of letters in each of six of his suggested dislocations and makes them all come very approximately to multiples of 750 letters, which he supposes was an average per leaf of papyrus. Unfortunately Bernard does not include in his calculations his two most impressive dislocations, chapters vi and xiv, but nevertheless his evidence is suggestive. It is known from Oxyrhynchus Papyrus P⁵, which preserves the outermost leaf but one of John's Gospel, that an equivalent of about fourteen lines of Souter's text would have occupied each page, which would confirm Bernard's estimate of about 750 letters *per page*. But in considering dislocations it is necessary to take into account more than *one* page. In fact, in a codex book *four* pages (*recto* and *verso* on a folded sheet) would be involved, as P⁵ demonstrates.[1] But the above dislocations could not be made to fit neatly into such a scheme. It might be more conceivable if smaller quires were used (i.e. of 8 to 12 leaves, of which there are some early examples), but the problem still arises of more than one page being involved for each dislocation.[2]

On the whole there appear to be too many doubtful assumptions in this type of theory to make it convincing, and since the text is at least intelligible as it stands it is preferable to leave it as it is.

VIII. LANGUAGE AND STYLE

The author of this Gospel writes in a form of Greek which is stamped with his own individuality. The range of his vocabulary is severely limited and yet the effect that he produces is dignified and compelling. He is given to repetition of words and phrases, which nevertheless is

[1] If, of course, the *verso* was not used only two pages of the codex would be involved. Cf. the argument of W. G. Wilson (*JTS*, I, 1949, pp. 59, 60) that none of the dislocations suggested would fit exactly into multiples of two full pages. He thought that disarrangement of pages in a codex was therefore improbable. It could not have happened on a scroll, since the papyri sheets were joined before, not after, they were written on.

[2] Taking the P⁵ fragment as a model of a sheet of the whole codex, it would be difficult, for instance, to make the chapter iii dislocation correspond with the chapter xviii dislocation, and unless they did the error could not have arisen through mechanical misplacement. At most, the theory would require that a scribe placed some of these sections accidentally on the *verso* instead of the *recto* side. But again it is difficult to conceive that this would have happened, and then entirely escaped detection.

never monotonous. He does not contrive to achieve elegance of expression by classical standards, but what he does achieve is a simple impressiveness of presentation. In spite of his simple style, his Greek never becomes inaccurate. C. K. Barrett[1] says, 'It is neither bad Greek nor (according to classical standards) good Greek.' J. H. Moulton[2] considered that the author 'was a man who, while cultured to the last degree, wrote Greek after the fashion of men of quite elementary attainment'. The same writer thought that the linguistic evidence indicated that Greek was not the author's mother tongue.[3] This will have some bearing on the question of the original language of the Gospel mentioned below.

It is worth noting that many of the theological words found frequently in John occur much less often in the Synoptic Gospels (e.g. such words as love, truth, life, light, witness, abide). Similarly, in the reverse direction, many of the expressions used frequently in the Synoptics are little used, or do not occur at all, in John (e.g. kingdom, people (λαός), call, pray or prayer).[4]

Perhaps the most characteristic feature of John's style is the widespread use of καί, instead of co-ordinating clauses, in joining sentences (*parataxis*). It is this feature more than any other which creates such an impression of simplicity in the Greek. The author is clearly more intent on imparting a message than on stylistic niceties.[5]

The presence of poetic forms in this Gospel has not escaped the notice of scholars. For instance, Rendel Harris[6] noted such a form in John vii. 37, 38, while C. F. Burney[7] devoted careful attention to poetic forms in John and found the same phenomenon in the teaching of Jesus in this Gospel as in the Synoptics. He found evidence of such poetic forms as synonymous-, antithetic-, synthetic-

---

[1] *Op. cit.*, p. 5.

[2] J. H. Moulton and W. F. Howard, *A Grammar of New Testament Greek*, II, p. 33.

[3] *Ibid.*, pp. 31, 32.

[4] For a list of the occurrences of these and other words in John and the Synoptics, see Barrett, *The Gospel according to St. John* (1956), pp. 5, 6.

[5] For a study of characteristic Johannine words or constructions which are rare in, or absent from, the rest of the New Testament, cf. E. Schweizer's study *Ego Eimi* (1939); J. Jeremias' article on 'Johanneischer Literarkritik', *Theologische Blätter* (1941), pp. 33–46, and E. Ruckstuhl, *Die literarische Einheit des Johannesevangeliums* (1951), pp. 180 ff.

[6] *Exp.*, VIII, XX (1920), p. 196.   [7] *The Poetry of our Lord* (1925).

and step-parallelism. This and other features influenced Burney in his theory of an Aramaic origin for this Gospel, which will be considered next.

The attempts to prove an Aramaic original for any of the Gospels cannot be said to have succeeded, although interest in this subject remains unabated. The two most thoroughgoing advocates of the Aramaic origin of John are C. F. Burney[1] and C. C. Torrey,[2] but most scholars agree that their evidence for an Aramaic written source from which our Greek Gospel was translated is improbable. W. F. Howard criticized Burney's arguments on the ground that he did not distinguish between Aramaic constructions found in the Gospel and not found in the contemporary colloquial Greek from those which were common to both. When the latter are eliminated the evidence looks far less impressive. If, of course, specific mistranslations are traceable this would be far stronger support for the theory. But Matthew Black,[3] who advocates Semitic influence on the writers of the Gospels, admits only a very few mistranslations. Even in these cases, it is not agreed that this is the only possible explanation for the Greek text.[4]

It would seem a fair conclusion that the author was not unacquainted with Semitic idioms, although he does not allow glaring Semitisms to intrude into his Greek. If the author were the apostle John some Semitic influence would naturally be expected. The main problem would then be whether a Galilaean such as John would have been able to avoid giving more evidence than he has of Aramaic influence. The answer is bound to be affected by other considerations, since no conclusive linguistic criterion exists. Barrett,[5] who does not regard the apostle as author, contents himself with suggesting that the writer treads 'the boundary between the Hellenic and the Semitic'.

[1] *The Aramaic Origin of the Fourth Gospel* (1922).
[2] *The Four Gospels* (1933). 'The Aramaic Origin of the Gospel of St. John', *HTR*, 16 (1923), pp. 305-344.
[3] *An Aramaic Approach to the Gospels and Acts* (1946), pp. 207, 208.
[4] M. Burrows (*JBL*, XLIX, 1930, pp. 95-139) was favourable to the view that an Aramaic original was translated into Greek by a redactor, a view not unfavourably considered by G. H. C. Macgregor, *The Gospel of John* (*MC*, 1928), p. lxvi. Burrow's article supported in the main the position of Burney and Torrey, although critical of details.
[5] *Op. cit.*, p. 11.

IX. THE BACKGROUND OF THE GOSPEL

In all New Testament books the background is important, and in none is it more so than this Gospel. The exegesis of the whole book has been considerably influenced by different opinions regarding the milieu of both writer and readers. It will be possible to give only the barest outline of the main elements which have been claimed to contribute to this milieu, and to indicate the probability or improbability of each.

a. Primitive Christianity

This Gospel cannot be regarded in isolation from early Christian history. It was produced within the context of that history and cannot be interpreted apart from the background of primitive theology. This goes without saying if the author was either an eyewitness or someone in touch with an eyewitness. We have already dealt with the impact of the Synoptic tradition, which from a literary point of view is not extensive. But how does the Johannine presentation of Christ relate to the Synoptic description? It would be a fair answer to state that there is no conflict between the two presentations, although the Johannine account is clearly different in emphasis. If the early character of the Johannine material is admitted, it may be that this material must be regarded as contemporary with primitive Christianity. In other words it represents a parallel genuine tradition. At all events, a close connection of this Gospel with the primitive tradition must be maintained.[1]

b. Paulinism

It has been claimed by some that the author of this Gospel was a Paulinist.[2] This type of theory assumes that Johannine theology is one stage further developed than Paul's teaching, just as the latter is a development of Jesus' teaching. Indeed it has been supposed that the Epistle to the Hebrews[3] falls between Paul and John in the line of development, and this would push John to the end position in Christian theology. Yet it is probably nearer the true position to maintain that Christian theology did not develop by this method, but that several co-lateral streams, of which Paul, Hebrews and John represent con-

[1] Cf. C. H. Dodd's conclusion in his *Historical Tradition in the Fourth Gospel*, pp. 423 ff.

[2] Cf. E. F. Scott (*The Fourth Gospel, its Purpose and Theology*[2], 1908, p. 46), who considers that John is everywhere indebted to Paul.

[3] Cf. R. H. Strachan, *The Historic Jesus in the New Testament* (1931).

temporary manifestations, developed at an early stage. Dodd[1] has urged caution in the use of Paul to interpret John. At the same time the two cannot be separated. Both present a vital aspect of Christian theology.

c. Judaism

It would be surprising if there were no points of contact between John and contemporary Judaism, though in assessing the evidence the investigator must carefully distinguish between influences derived from Old Testament sources and those belonging to rabbinism.[2] The main problem confronting the study of the latter is that much of the evidence comes from a later period, although it is confidently maintained that our extant sources preserve material contemporary with John, if not with Jesus. Many parallels may be cited which might at least show that Judaism may have contributed to the setting of the Gospel. Since Jesus was a Jew it would be extraordinary if this had not happened, but the points of difference between the teaching of Jesus as John reports it and the teaching of the Rabbis are more striking than the similarities. One scholar, H. Odeberg,[3] has suggested that this Gospel has sometimes a greater affinity with Jewish mysticism than with rabbinism, but again the wide differences between such mysticism and the Gospel cannot be overstressed.

Some comment must here be made on the relation of John to Essenism. Some of the features of the Qumran literature find echoes in John and, although some scholars have made exaggerated claims for the connection of John's Gospel with the Qumran type of approach, there can be no doubt that these recently discovered MSS have influenced the general approach to John's Gospel. It is no longer convincing to maintain that the Gospel is wholly Hellenistic in view of the fact that many of the abstract concepts which were characteristic of Greek thought are also found in the Qumran literature, e.g. light and truth. There is also a similar love of antitheses such as light versus darkness,

---

[1] *Op. cit.*, p. 5.

[2] Cf. *ibid.*, pp. 74–94, for a discussion of rabbinic Judaism as a background to John. Cf. also A. Schlatter, *Der Evangelist Johannes*[2] (1930) and the relevant sections in Strack-Billerbeck's *Kommentar* for studies in the Jewish background of this Gospel.

[3] *The Fourth Gospel interpreted in its Relation to Contemporaneous Religious Currents* (1929). Cf. W. F. Howard's brief comments in *The Fourth Gospel in Recent Criticism*, pp. 158, 159.

truth against error. Moreover, there are some remarkable parallels in language. R. E. Brown[1] considers that the author was acquainted with the Qumran thought and expression, although the evidence is not enough to suggest knowledge of the sectarian literature. O. Cullmann[2] has rightly pointed out that the differences are more significant than the similarities, particularly in relation to the Person of Christ.

d. Hermetic literature

It is only comparatively recently that attention has been turned to the Johannine parallels with the *Hermetica*, which was a body of philosophical and religious tractates attributed in Egypt to Hermes Trismegistus. The extant remains are very late, but these writings are believed to have originated in the second and third centuries AD. C. H. Dodd,[3] who has made a special study of this literature, considers that John shows a kinship with the *Hermetica*, but that there is no evidence of literary borrowing. Once again, when this connection of John with the kind of thought represented by the *Hermetica* is examined, it must at once be admitted that John's characteristic features are very different from the Hermetic literature. Dodd himself makes wide use of the *Hermetica* to illustrate the background of thought of the Gospel, but it may be questioned whether this kind of background was in the author's mind to the extent that he supposes. In fact there is closer linguistic affinity between John and the Septuagint than between John and the *Hermetica*.[4]

e. Philonism

The Alexandrian Philo may be cited as representative of Hellenistic Judaism, in which he was by far the most influential figure. The main point of contact between John and Philo relates to the Prologue, it being supposed that the Logos idea must be interpreted in the light of Philo's treatment. Such a viewpoint has recently lessened in influence

---

[1] Cf. his article in *The Scrolls and the New Testament* (ed. K. Stendahl), pp. 183–207. Cf. *idem*, in *Neotestamentica et Patristica*, pp. 111–122. Cf. also the works of F. C. Grant, M. Burrows and H. M. Teeple mentioned on p. 253 n.2, 3 and cf. F. M. Braun, *RB*, LXII (1955), pp. 5–44.

[2] Cf. his article in *The Scrolls and the New Testament*, p. 22.

[3] Cf. *The Bible and the Greeks* (1935), and his *The Interpretation of the Fourth Gospel*, pp. 10–53.

[4] Cf. the study by G. D. Kilpatrick on 'The Religious Background of the Fourth Gospel' in *Studies in the Fourth Gospel* (ed. F. L. Cross, 1957), pp. 36–44.

following the greater inclination to find the roots of the Logos idea in Hebraic thought. Nevertheless, since Philo was so influential in Hellenistic Judaism during the period of early Christian history, his mode of teaching cannot be ignored in outlining the background of the Gospel. In both Philo and John certain symbolism is used, as for instance the description of God as Light, as a Fountain and as a Shepherd.[1] As in the case of all the other elements in the non-Christian background the differences are more striking than the similarities. Whereas the differences belong to the essentials, the similarities are peripheral. The Logos of Philo becomes radically transformed in John's account. It becomes incarnate in Christ, an idea quite alien to Philo.

f. Other possible background features

Gnosticism sometimes speaks in language similar to John's, particularly in respect of dualistic conceptions and ideas of redemption. But it is important to note that recent studies have stressed the necessity of drawing a distinction between developed Gnosticism and the early Gnostic stage.[2] It is only the latter which could have any relevance to the Johannine literature, but the difficulties of determining the content of this incipient movement are not inconsiderable.[3] Most of the extant literature belongs to the later stage. Nevertheless, it is at least probable that John's Gospel was produced at a time when Gnostic ideas were becoming more dominant in pagan and Christian circles in Asia.[4] At the same time there is no evidence in the Gospels that the

[1] For details, cf. Dodd, *op. cit.*, pp. 54 ff. Parallels in thought do not, of course, involve literary dependence (cf. R. McL. Wilson, *Nov. Test.*, 1, 1956, pp. 225 ff.).

[2] Cf. R. McL. Wilson's study, *The Gnostic Problem* (1958).

[3] Bultmann, in his *Das Evangelium des Johannes* (KEK[13], 1953), is the most thoroughgoing commentator appealing to a Gnostic milieu for John's Gospel. Cf. also the work of H. Becker (*Die Reden des Johannesevangeliums und der Stil der gnostischen Offenbarungsreden*, 1956), who carries Bultmann's suggestions still further and actually attempts to reconstruct the Greek Gnostic source which he supposes John used. Cf. the review of this book by K. Grayston (*NTS*, 5, 1959, pp. 82–84), who shows the fallacy of Becker's method in using for his parallels materials which are much later than John's Gospel. The Gospel is, in fact, the middle term between the Wisdom Literature and Gnosticism.

[4] Cf. the recent articles of C. K. Barrett and J. Munck in *Current Issues in New Testament Interpretation* (ed. W. Klassen and G. F. Snyder, 1962), pp. 210–233, 234–238. The former speaks of a pre-Johannine Gnosticism whose language John appears to use, while the latter criticizes Bultmann's theory for John on the grounds that he has not critically evaluated the Gnostic material and has too readily assumed that this was a unity.

author is consciously selecting or adapting his material to meet this particular threat, unless it was the beginnings of Docetism.[1] It is of interest that the later Gnostics seem to have been particularly attracted to this Gospel,[2] but they did not derive their characteristic emphases from this source.

Mandaism is another movement which has been appealed to as a part of the Johannine background. But this idea cannot be substantiated. The data on Mandaism are too late to provide any certain idea of a pre-Christian cult as Reitzenstein[3] maintained. The Mandaean literature may therefore be disregarded as a contribution to the Johannine background. If there are parallels it is certain that the Fourth Gospel has contributed to the thought-forms of the later Mandaean movement and not *vice versa*. The appeal to Mandaean parallels has been made by both Bultmann[4] and Bauer,[5] but has found little favour among other scholars.[6]

X. HISTORICITY

Because of the unique character of John's Gospel more discussion has ranged around its historicity than over that of the Synoptic Gospels. In the section dealing with its relation to the Synoptics some indications were given of the various explanations of this relationship, and it was noted that in some hypotheses the unhistorical character of John was taken for granted. The problems of historicity are too wide to be dealt with here, but the main schools of thought will be indicated, to give a general idea of the issues involved.

---

[1] Already discussed under Purpose, pp. 250 ff.

[2] For a detailed treatment, cf. W. von Loewenich, *Das Johannesverständnis im zweiten Jahrhundert*, Beiheft *ZNTW*, 13 (1932).

[3] *Das iranische Erlösungsmysterium* (1921)—cited by Dodd, *The Interpretation of the Fourth Gospel*, p. 128.

[4] 'Der religionsgeschichtliche Hintergrund des Prologs zum Johannes-Evangelium', *Eucharistion*, II (1923), pp. 1–26, and *ZNTW*, 24 (1925), pp. 100–146.

[5] *Das Johannesevangelium* (*LHB*[2], 1925).

[6] C. H. Dodd (*op. cit.*, pp. 115–130) rejects the evidence as too late to be significant. Cf. W. G. Kümmel, *Das Neue Testament* (1958), pp. 449 ff. S. Schulz (*Komposition und Herkunft der johanneischen Reden*, 1960) considers that the background of some of the units of tradition in this Gospel (he concentrates on the Prologue and the ἐγώ εἰμί sayings) is mainly to be found in Jewish sectarianism and Mandaean Gnosticism. Cf. also his earlier book *Untersuchungen zur Menschensohnchristologie* (1957).

a. The symbolism school

This is an interpretation of the Johannine account which assumes that the author has presented his material in allegorical form with no intention that it should be regarded as history. Thus P. Schmiedel[1] regarded the six water-pots in the Cana incident as representing the week-days (law) which prepared for the sabbath (the gospel wedding feast). This kind of treatment necessarily makes nonsense of the history, and if it be maintained that the author's approach throughout is moulded according to this pattern, Johannine historicity is at once ruled out. However, not all who admit some allegorization in the Gospel would discount the historicity of the whole.[2]

b. The interpretation school

Because of the interaction between narrative and discourse in this Gospel, it would seem to be a more natural view of the historicity to suppose that the author's aim was not to treat his material as scientific history, but rather to interpret it. Consequently history and interpretation merge into one another. The result is what C. K. Barrett[3] calls 'an interpreted history' of Jesus. Such a theory is a serious attempt to preserve a genuine historic basis for the Gospel, and yet at the same time leaves open to the critic the possibility of attributing to the author's interpretative purpose some of the material which appears to him to be historically less valid. Hence Barrett calls the Gospel 'impressionistic rather than photographically accurate in detail'.[4]

c. The realism school

This third method of looking at the Gospel involves approaching it as true history. Certainly this is the most natural way of all to treat the book. It reads as if the author intended it to be received as real history,[5] an account of events which actually happened, and of discourses which actually took place. Where the Gospel runs parallel to the Synoptic Gospels it may be seen that it is consistent with their presentation of

[1] Art., 'Gospels', Encyclopaedia Biblica (1914), col. 1796.
[2] Cf. for instance C. K. Barrett on Jn. ii. 1–12 (The Gospel according to St. John, pp. 156–162). C. H. Dodd seems to place more emphasis on a symbolic type of interpretation (op. cit., pp. 84, 138), although he does not regard the Gospel generally as unhistorical.
[3] Op. cit., p. 117.   [4] Ibid., p. 118.
[5] Cf. A. C. Headlam, The Fourth Gospel as History (1948), pp. 11–31.

the history, a factor which must carry considerable weight for all except those who equally dispute the historical validity of the Synoptic accounts including Mark. If the historical reliability of these parts be granted, it raises a presumption in favour of the historicity of the remaining Johannine material. A. J. B. Higgins[1] has drawn attention to incidental confirmation of this view in the personal names used in the Johannine account, especially when these are compared with the Synoptic use.

Not all who are disposed to treat the Johannine material seriously as history would agree on the extent of the historicity. Many would not be prepared to regard all the details as historical, although they accept a general reliability in John's account. It is sometimes asserted that in certain features John's account is superior to the Synoptics,[2] which marks a more realistic approach to Johannine historicity than that of earlier critics. At the same time, once the basic historicity of the narratives is granted, it would seem reasonable to assume the historicity of the whole until historical improbabilities can be demonstrated. In other words, an interpretation of the relationship between John and the Synoptics which preserves the historicity of both, where that is possible, is to be preferred to any hypothesis which presupposes some unhistorical strata in one of them. This is not a plea for harmonization at all costs, but a plea for an examination of the possibility of harmonization as a first essential, instead of excluding it without serious consideration, as sometimes happens. In any such consideration it will be recognized that each Gospel has its own distinctive purpose both in the selection and in the employment of the historical material.

CONTENTS

I. THE PROLOGUE (i. 1–18)

The main theme is the incarnation of the Word.

The Word and the created order (i. 1–5). The Word as God's revelation of Himself (i. 6–18).

---

[1] *The Historicity of the Fourth Gospel*, pp. 53 ff.

[2] Cf. T. W. Manson's article 'The Life of Jesus: Some Tendencies in Present-day Research', in *The Background of the New Testament and its Eschatology* (ed. W. D. Davies and D. Daube, 1956), p. 219 n.2. Cf. also J. A. T. Robinson's article, 'The New Look on the Fourth Gospel', *Studia Evangelica*, pp. 338–350.

II. INTRODUCTORY EVENTS (i. 19–ii. 12)

The incarnate Word is introduced in typically Jewish scenes, covering one complete week.

The witness of John the Baptist (i. 19–34). The call of the first disciples (i. 35–51). The marriage at Cana—*Sign 1* (ii. 1–12).

III. THE PUBLIC MINISTRY (ii. 13–xii. 50)

a. Encounters (ii. 13–iv. 45)

This section gives some examples of the impact of Jesus on various groups.

The cleansing of the temple (ii. 13–22). The discussion with Nicodemus and the subsequent witnesses to the claims of Jesus (iii. 1–36). The dialogue with the Samaritan woman and its sequel (iv. 1–42). Warm reception by the Galilaeans (iv. 43–45).

b. Healings (iv. 46–v. 9)

The nobleman's son—*Sign 2* (iv. 46–54). The man at the pool of Bethesda—*Sign 3* (v. 1–9). Dispute over healing on the sabbath, and subsequent discourse (v. 10–47).

c. Further signs (vi. 1–vii. 1)

The feeding of the multitude—*Sign 4* (vi. 1–14). Jesus walking on the lake—*Sign 5* (vi. 15–21). Discourse on the bread of life (vi. 22–vii. 1).

d. Jesus at the Feast of Tabernacles (vii. 2–viii. 59)

Disputes about the Messiah, and official moves to arrest Jesus (vii. 2–52). The adulteress (vii. 53–viii. 11). Disputes over Jesus' claim to be the Light of the world, over His departure, over Abrahamic descent generally and Jesus' relation to Abraham in particular (viii. 12–59).

e. The healing of the man born blind (ix. 1–41)

The miracle—*Sign 6* (ix. 1–7). The reaction of neighbours, Pharisees and parents (ix. 8–23). The man's developing faith (ix. 24–41).

f. Discourse on the Shepherd (x. 1–42)

Jesus claims to be the good Shepherd and rouses conflicting reactions (x. 1–30). Growing hostility leads to Jesus' withdrawal beyond Jordan (x. 31–42).

g. The death and resurrection of Lazarus (xi. 1–46)

The report of his death (xi. 1–16). Discussion about resurrection and life (xi. 17–37). The miracle—*Sign 7* (xi. 38–44). The reaction of the authorities (xi. 45–57).

h. Further developments in and around Jerusalem (xii. 1–50)

The anointing at Bethany (xii. 1–8). The plot to kill Lazarus (xii. 9–11). The entry into Jerusalem (xii. 12–19). The quest of some Greeks for Jesus, and His statements to them (xii. 20–26). Divine attestation to Jesus, and His explanation of His approaching death (xii. 27–36a). The withdrawal of Jesus (xii. 36b–50).

IV. THE PASSION AND RESURRECTION NARRATIVES
(xiii. 1–xxi. 25)

a. The last supper (xiii. 1–xvii. 26)

The symbolic action of feet-washing and its meaning (xiii. 1–20). The betrayal predicted and Judas' hasty departure (xiii. 21–30). The glorification of Jesus, the establishment of a new commandment and the prediction of Peter's denial (xiii. 31–38).

The farewell discourses (xiv. 1–xvi. 33). Promises for the future (xiv. 1–4). Christ as Revealer (xiv. 5–15). Teaching about the Spirit (xiv. 16–26). The gift of peace (xiv. 27–31). The vine analogy (xv. 1–17). Statements about the believer's relation to the world (xv. 18–27). Warnings about persecutions (xvi. 1–4). Further teaching about the Spirit (xvi. 5–15). Jesus speaks of His death but expresses confidence in His ultimate victory (xvi. 16–33).

The prayer of consecration (xvii. 1–26): a prayer for the glorification of the Son and for the encouragement of believers.

b. The passion of Jesus (xviii. 1–xix. 42)

The arrest (xviii. 1–12). The examination before Annas and Caiaphas, and the denial of Peter (xviii. 13–27). Jesus before Pilate (xviii. 28–xix. 16). The crucifixion (xix. 17–37). The burial (xix. 38–42).

c. The resurrection narratives (xx. 1–xxi. 25).

The appearances in Jerusalem (xx. 1–31). The appearances in Galilee (xxi. 1–23). The final certification of the record (xxi. 24, 25).

CHAPTER NINE

THE ACTS OF THE APOSTLES

I. CHARACTERISTICS

The importance of this book cannot be exaggerated and it is no wonder that it has frequently been the focus of attention during the period of historical criticism (i.e. since 1800). Its importance must, however, be deduced first of all from the nature of its contents and only secondarily from the part it has played in critical discussions. Its main features may be summarized as follows.[1]

a. Its place in the New Testament

It is not without some significance that in the present canonical order Acts has been placed between the Gospels and Epistles, although it did not occupy this position in all the ancient canonical lists. It serves admirably as a link between the records of Jesus and the apostolic correspondence. In many ways the Epistles are not fully intelligible until they are read against the background of the book of Acts. The book shows effectively the main trends in the development of Christianity and presents in effect samples of the continuing work of Jesus. It therefore makes a vital contribution to the discussion of the relationship between the teaching of Jesus and the apostolic doctrine. As will be shown later, the value of its contribution has been variously estimated according to the view taken of its historicity, but the fact remains that it is the only extant historical account of the primitive Christian period outside the Epistles, from a Christian point of view.

b. Its view of history

The many references to the Holy Spirit in this book are a sufficient indication that the writer regards the development of Christian history as due to a superhuman control. He does not gloss over the difficulties which the Christian mission encountered, but he purposes to show that God was directing each movement of the history. As Christian influence spreads from Jerusalem to Rome there is no impression given

---

[1] For a brief survey of recent literature on Acts, see the writer's article in *Vox Evangelica* (ed. R. P. Martin), II (1963), pp. 33–49. Also E. Grässer, *TR*, n.f., 26 (1960), pp. 93–167, and W. C. Kümmel, *TR*, 22 (1954), pp. 194 ff.

that this progress is due ultimately to human achievement, not even to the dynamic and indefatigable labours of an apostle Paul. God was hedging His people round, preventing undesirable developments here and prompting to sustained evangelistic efforts there. In short, God was as active in the early Christian communities and in the messengers of the gospel as He had been in the movements and teachings of Jesus.

c. Its portrait of primitive communities

In spite of the fact that the author gives glimpses into church life during the first generation, there is no consecutive attempt to describe the conditions within the various churches, nor to give much information about early church orders or methods of worship. All that can justly be said is that Acts gives a valuable general impression of primitive church life. It is necessary to supplement its data with other material from the Epistles and even then there is much more that we could wish to know. The author of Acts has, however, clearly portrayed the spiritual and moral characteristics of the early Christians. The impression of unity is inescapable, in spite of the existence of differences of opinion. The account of the Council of Jerusalem in Acts xv shows the importance which not only the leaders but the rank and file members attached to presenting a united front. The early experiment in communal living, in spite of its ultimate cessation, bears eloquent testimony to the strong desire for unity. Even here the Acts presents in vivid contrast the failure of Ananias and Sapphira to enter into the true spirit of the other believers. The severe condemnation of their moral lapse is recorded in order to make clear the moral aspect of primitive community life. One of the most characteristic features of the book, however, is the element of joyfulness among these early Christians,[1] and this is a striking example of the continuation of a theme which had been notably stressed in the Gospel of Luke. Without the book of Acts our knowledge of the spiritual outlook of those believers would be immeasurably the poorer.

d. Its record of primitive theology

In a book which consists so largely of narratives and concentrates upon the missionary movements it is surprising to find so much indication of primitive doctrine. This is naturally mainly contained in the numer-

[1] Cf. P. G. S. Hopwood, *The Religious Experience of the Primitive Church* (1936).

ous speeches which present samples of the apostolic preaching. The
primitive character of this doctrine may be seen from a comparison
with the evidence of the primitive *kerygma* as found in various parts of
the Epistles. Those passages which are said to be traceable to the apostolic proclamation as distinct from the apostolic teaching (*didache*) bear
close resemblance to the content of the early speeches in Acts. C. H.
Dodd,[1] in his notable work on this subject, finds several passages in
Romans, 1 Corinthians, Galatians and Thessalonians which compare
with passages in the speeches of Acts ii, iii, iv, v, x and xiii. In this case
the book of Acts is a valuable source-book for the study of primitive
theology. Not all have followed Dodd in his clear-cut dissection between *kerygma* and *didache*, and it would probably be wiser to assume
that they were contemporary developments which often in fact overlapped.[2] At the same time the book does not narrate the genesis of
early creeds, and what information it gives is wholly of an incidental
and informal kind. The titles ascribed to our Lord are a valuable guide
to primitive Christology. Jesus is both Lord and Christ, God's Servant and His Son, Prince of Life and Saviour, the Righteous One and
Lord of all. This presents a rich if embryonic Christology,[3] but it
would be misleading to suppose that there were not other aspects
which the Acts speeches do not happen to mention. In other words,
the book of Acts presents us with samples of early Christian mission
preaching but gives no samples of didactic addresses to believers, unless Paul's speech to the Ephesian elders at Miletus comes under this
category (but it contains little didactic material). The importance of
the book of Acts is in its preservation of the main doctrinal themes
presented in apostolic preaching, even if there is no evidence of an
attempt to develop a systematized theology.

e. Its focus on Peter and Paul

It is one of the most striking features about Acts that it says so little
about the other apostles and so much about Peter and Paul. This is

[1] *The Apostolic Preaching and its Developments.*

[2] Cf. the detailed discussion of this in R. H. Mounce's book, *The Essential
Nature of New Testament Preaching* (1960), pp. 40 f., 60 ff. It should be noted that
it cannot be supposed that the *kerygma*, if recoverable, represents a stock outline
used by the early preachers, for a study of Acts speeches disposes of this idea. It is
rather a convenient survey of primitive Christology, cf. W. Baird, *JBL*, LXXVI
(1957), pp. 181-191.

[3] Cf. S. S. Smalley, *ET*, LXXIII (1961-62), pp. 35 ff.

G.A.—20

obviously intentional, but it is not easy to find a reason. It may have been because the author was acquainted with these two more than the others. Or it may have been that the chief apostle to the Gentiles was matched with the chief apostle to the Circumcision. There are some striking parallels in the two parts of the record, which have suggested to some that one part was written in imitation of the other. The effect of this phenomenon on criticism will be noted later, but for the present it is the facts which concern us.

In chapters i–xii the narrative moves from Jerusalem to Antioch, and in this section it is Peter who occupies the limelight. He takes the lead both before and after Pentecost. Although accompanied by John when they met the impotent man, it was Peter who commanded him in Christ's name to walk. It was he who twice led the defence before the Sanhedrin, and when deception was discovered within the Church it was he who voiced the condemnation against Ananias and Sapphira. His shadow was the means used to heal many sick people. Moreover, when he and John were sent from Jerusalem to Samaria, it was Peter who dealt with Simon the sorcerer. Dorcas was raised from the dead and the paralysed Aeneas was healed through his agency. And Cornelius was directed to send specifically for Simon Peter, who later found it necessary to explain his action before the Jerusalem church. The first part then ends with Peter's miraculous deliverance from prison.

Several of these features reoccur in the story of Paul. Both heal cripples (iii. 2–8, xiv. 8–12), both heal by strange means, Peter through his shadow, Paul with his clothes (v. 15, xix. 12), both have encounters with sorcerers (viii. 18, xiii. 6), both are concerned in restoration scenes (ix. 36, xx. 9), and both are miraculously released from prison (xii. 7, xvi. 26). The parallels are striking and draw attention to the fact that Paul was as much an apostle as Peter.

The personality of Paul is strongly portrayed. He is introduced dramatically at Stephen's death, and his ravages against the Church are faithfully mentioned. Many little details in the subsequent narrative bring him to life. The intensity of his gaze (xiii. 9, xiv. 9, xxiii. 1), the beckoning of his hand (xiii. 16, xxvi. 1), his kneeling at Miletus (xx. 36–38) and his rending of his clothes at Lystra (xiv. 14). The narrative at the end of Acts (from xx onwards) centres almost wholly on Paul and shows him moving on towards Rome inevitably but with courageous determination.

II. DATE

In a historical book such as Acts, which constitutes the main document on primitive Christianity, the date of production is clearly of considerable importance. As so often in problems of dating New Testament books, the prior decision regarding authorship will naturally affect the presuppositions with which the subject is approached. Moreover, in this case, the decision already reached regarding the date of the third Gospel will clearly have an influence on the date of Acts, since this book must be dated subsequent to Luke. Our present approach will be first to treat the subject of date in the light of the traditional position concerning authorship, and then to discuss alternatives. If, of course, the conclusions regarding date demand a period too late to make the traditional authorship possible, it would require a fresh consideration of the latter problem.

There are three main proposals: first, before AD 64, secondly AD 70–85 and thirdly a second-century date. They will be considered in this order.

a. Arguments for a date before AD 64

(i) *The absence of reference to important events which happened between AD 60 and 70.* The fall of Jerusalem is nowhere referred to and, although it is not decisive that Luke must have hinted at it if it had already occurred,[1] there is a strong presumption in favour of this opinion. It would have been difficult for him to avoid some allusion to it, although it must be recognized that the destiny of Jerusalem would not have appeared so tragic to the Christian Church as a whole as it would to the Jewish people. At the same time it is not without significance that Luke in his Gospel centres more attention on Jerusalem than do his fellow Synoptists.[2]

---

[1] E. M. Blaiklock (*The Acts of the Apostles*, 1959, p. 16) expresses a caution about placing too much weight upon this kind of evidence. 'Luke, an accomplished historian and a disciplined writer, need not have coloured his narrative of doings in Jerusalem by references to later events irrelevant to his theme.'

[2] Luke's so-called 'travel-narrative' (Lk. ix. 51–xviii. 14) has as its focal point the movement of Jesus towards Jerusalem, and the same interest in the holy city is seen in the author's choice of resurrection narratives, all of which are centred in Jerusalem.

Another event of importance was the persecution of the Church under the Emperor Nero.[1] This precipitated so great a crisis that it is difficult to imagine that the earliest Christian historian could have ignored it so completely if he wrote after the event. Although the geographical area affected was confined to Italy, it is still astonishing that Luke makes no mention of it in ending his story at Rome. The only other possibilities would be to suppose that Acts was written after such an interval that the grim details of the horror had faded from the author's mind, or else that he was unaware of it. It might just conceivably be agreed that the author would have no cause to mention it, in which case it could be discounted as a factor affecting dating, but probability is on the side of a date before it.

A further event of less widespread importance, but one which might well have interested Luke, was the martyrdom of James, the Lord's brother. In fact Luke mentions two early martyrs: James, son of Zebedee, and Stephen. Moreover, the description of James' position as president of the Jerusalem church and the care with which Luke describes his relationships with Paul show that the author regarded him as a key figure in primitive Christian history.

Yet all these three suggestions are arguments from silence and must be used with reserve.

(ii) *The absence of reference to the death of Paul.* The abrupt ending of Acts has for long been an enigma. The author leaves his readers with a description of Paul, a prisoner at Rome, but enjoying considerable liberty to preach and teach. Yet there is no indication about what happened to Paul after this. The reason for the abrupt ending is subject to various interpretations and these must be carefully examined in considering its effect upon the dating.

1. The author records all he knew. If, at the time of writing, Paul was still in his own hired house awaiting further developments, the abruptness is at once explained. There was nothing else to report.[2]

---

[1] Cf. R. B. Rackham, *The Acts of the Apostles*[14] (1951), pp. li f.

[2] Ancient support for such a view may be found in the comment in the Muratorian Canon, which states that Luke recorded those events which fell under his notice ('conprendit quae sub praesentia eius singula gerebantur'), but adds, somewhat apologetically, 'sicuti et semota passione Petri euidenter declarat, et profectione Pauli ab urbe ad Hispaniam proficiscentis'. But it is strange that this Canon makes no reference to the martyrdom of Paul. It should be noted that th ending of Acts may not have seemed so unsatisfactory to Luke as it does to many.

2. The author did not wish to mention the outcome of the trial. It is suggested that he knew of Paul's death, but that it was no part of his purpose to close with this.[1] Such a procedure would, in fact, draw too much attention to the man, whereas Luke's purpose was to describe rather the progress of the gospel. It has even been suggested that to conclude with Paul's death would hint at a parallel with the conclusion of the Gospel with its climax in the passion story and that it was to avoid this that Luke omits all reference to it.[2] But this latter motive would not be applicable if the Gospel and Acts were conceived as a continuous narrative, and in any case the author regarded the passion of Jesus as the beginning and not the end of the real work of Jesus in the world.[3] It is not sufficient, on the other hand, to propose a theory of the author's intention without supplying an adequate motive for the intention, and it may be questioned whether this condition has been fulfilled.

3. The author intended to write a third volume. On the analogy of the connection between the Gospel and Acts it has been proposed that Luke had in mind another volume which would have related the subsequent history of Paul and his associates, and this has had the support of some notable scholars.[4] It would, of course, get over the difficulty of the abrupt end of Acts, but such a desirable end is achieved only by the postulation of an entirely hypothetical volume which has left no trace in Christian history. The theory admittedly does not demand that

F. J. Foakes Jackson (*The Acts of the Apostles*, 1931, p. 236) even described the ending as 'highly artistic'. It certainly brings out, even at the end, the triumphant note in the ministry of Paul, an emphasis to which R. R. Williams (*The Acts of the Apostles*, 1953, pp. 24–33) calls attention in his analysis of the structure of the book as a whole. Cf. also J. A. Bengel, *Gnomon of the New Testament* (Eng. Tr. 1858), pp. 731, 732.

[1] This is the position adopted by E. Trocmé, Le '*Livre des Actes*' et l'*Histoire* (1957), p. 36.

[2] A. Jülicher in his *Einleitung*[7] (1931, ed. E. Fascher), p. 433, considers that there is no mention of the martyrdom of either Peter or Paul because there was no resurrection narrative corresponding to the passion story in the Gospels.

[3] J. C. O'Neill (*The Theology of Acts in its Historical Setting*, 1961, pp. 56 f.) finds significance in the fact that Luke does not end with Paul's martyrdom, although he regards Acts xx as a clear prophecy of it. According to him, Luke considered the place of the end of his history (Rome) to be more important than Paul's death. A similar emphasis on a place (Jerusalem) is found at the end of the Gospel.

[4] For instance F. Spitta, *Die Apostelgeschichte* (1891), pp. 318, 319; Sir W. M. Ramsay, *St. Paul the Traveller and Roman Citizen* (1920), pp. 27 ff.; T. Zahn, *NkZ*, 28 (1917), pp. 373–395; W. L. Knox, *The Acts of the Apostles* (1948), p. 59 n.1.

the proposed volume should have left any trace, for it does not demand that Luke actually wrote the third instalment.[1] It would suffice that the author intended to write it. But the Acts does not give the impression that it was written as part of a continuing series. The gospel has reached Rome and this forms a natural climax to the history of the primitive period. There is something to be said for the objection that it is difficult to imagine what a third volume would have contained in order to have reached the same spiritual stature as the two former volumes.[2] Moreover the great amount of space devoted to Paul's trials is unintelligible as an introduction to a further narrative of the same kind. In other words, it is easier to assume that Paul's trial was still in progress than that the author has in this way drawn his second book to a close in anticipating a third volume. While the suggestion cannot be ruled out, it cannot be said to be very convincing.

The silence of Acts regarding the death of Paul may, therefore, be said to raise a presumption in favour of an early date. But one objection to this conclusion needs to be noted. In Acts xx. 25 ('I know that ye all . . . shall see my face no more') some scholars find clear evidence that the author knew that martyrdom crowned Paul's Roman imprisonment.[3] But if this passage preserves the genuine tradition of Paul's address to the Ephesian elders, it is capable of being interpreted as a presentiment on Paul's part without necessitating the presumption that it must have been fulfilled. After all, Paul's plans, according to Romans, were to turn westwards towards Spain and he evidently at that time had no intention of revisiting Ephesus.[4] The Pastoral Epistles presuppose that he did,[5] but scholars who dispute an early date for Acts almost invariably regard the Pastorals as non-Pauline and for them this line of argument would naturally lack validity.

[1] Cf. E. M. Blaiklock, *op. cit.*, p. 195.
[2] Cf. the criticisms to this effect by Trocmé, *op. cit.*, p. 36.
[3] O'Neill (*op. cit.*, p. 56) goes so far as to maintain that the author included an allusion to Paul's martyrdom in Acts xx so that it might overshadow the latter part of the story without actually concluding with an account of the event itself. M. Dibelius (*Studies in the Acts of the Apostles*, 1956, p. 158 n. 46) thinks it certain that Acts xx. 25 presupposes that Paul has already been put to death.
[4] F. F. Bruce (*The Acts of the Apostles*[2], Greek Text, 1952, pp. 11, 12) denies that Acts xx. 25 shows the author's knowledge of Paul's martyrdom, and regards the statement as descriptive only of Paul's expectation.
[5] Cf. the author's *New Testament Introduction: The Pauline Epistles* (1961), pp. 203 ff., 210 ff. for a discussion of the evidence.

(iii) *The primitive character of the subject-matter.* It is significant that the major interests of the author of Acts are those prevalent in the earliest period of Church history, but which were not so relevant in later times. The Jewish-Gentile controversy is dominant and all other evidence apart from Acts suggests that this was a vital issue only in the period before the fall of Jerusalem. Even by the time of Paul's later letters it had ceased to be a burning issue. Moreover, the question of Gentile inclusion was taken for granted when once the universal character of the Christian Church had been established. Again, the preoccupation with food requirements in the report of the decisions of the Jerusalem Council points to an early stage of Christian development. Before the fall of Jerusalem all these factors were of vital significance.

(iv) *The primitive nature of the theology.* Supporting evidence of a more incidental character, but nevertheless highly significant, is found in the theological language. The whole book gives the impression of primitiveness. Such titles for Jesus as 'the Christ', 'the Servant of God', 'the Son of man', reflect primitive tradition. Equally primitive are the description of Christians as 'disciples', the use of λαός for the Jewish nation, and the reference to Sunday as the first day of the week.[1] Either the author writes early enough to be in direct, living touch with actual eyewitnesses, or he possesses such remarkable historical skill that he is able to reproduce with clear fidelity the primitive climate of thought. The former alternative is the more credible.

(v) *The attitude of the State towards the Church.* Luke is at pains to demonstrate the impartiality of the imperial officials regarding Christianity. In no case is it the Roman officials who persecute the Church. The local government at Ephesus is represented as distinctly helpful towards Paul and his companions, while the cause of persecution against the Church is in every case the intrigues of the Jews. This is precisely what might be expected before Nero's persecution in AD 64,[2] but

[1] Cf. the discussion of F. F. Bruce, *op. cit.*, pp. 12, 13; O'Neill, who on other grounds dates Acts late, denies the primitive meaning of the use of Χριστός and κύριος in Acts, although admitting that they are used in a purely primitive way (*op. cit.*, p. 119). The same goes for ὁ παῖς τοῦ θεοῦ (*ibid.*, pp. 133 ff.) which quickly dropped out of Christian vocabulary. But on O'Neill's presuppositions no other assessment is really possible, for primitive traces in a so-called late document must be considered insertions designed to create the impression of primitiveness.

[2] This is strongly maintained by Rackham, *The Acts of the Apostles*[14] (1951), p. lii.

subsequent to that date the imperial officials would be more suspicious of Christianity and less inclined to treat it under the general concession to Judaism as a *religio licita*. The concluding word in Acts (ἀκωλύτως) is significant in this respect, for it forms a fitting climax to Luke's design to show the unhindered progress of the gospel.[1]

(vi) *The relation of Acts to the Pauline Epistles.* It is universally admitted that the author of Acts shows little or no acquaintance with Paul's Epistles and it may reasonably be claimed as a consequence that Acts must have been published before the collection of the *Corpus Paulinum*, or at least before this collection had had much general circulation. There are differences of opinion as to when the collection was made, but this circumstance favours as early a date as possible for Acts.[2] Those who consider that the collection was actually prompted by the publication of Acts assume a period, subsequent to Paul's death, during which he was neglected, and this automatically excludes an early date for Acts, but the whole theory is open to serious challenge.[3]

b. Arguments for a date between AD 70 and 85

The major reason for preferring this to the earlier date is the author's use of Mark. It has already been shown that the dating of Luke generally takes as its starting-point the date of Mark as AD 60–65 and assumes that Luke has adjusted the vague reference in Mark xiii to 'the abomination of desolation', to the more specific 'compassed with armies' through his knowledge of the details of the siege. In other words, Luke is supposed to have written after AD 70. In that case Acts

---

[1] Cf. F. Stagg, *The Book of Acts. The Early Struggle for an unhindered Gospel* (1955). E. Haenchen (*Die Apostelgeschichte*, p. 656) discusses the possibility that ἀκωλύτως may have been an attempt to conciliate the Roman authorities even in spite of the Neronian persecutions, but this is less probable than the alternative view that places the statement in a milieu before these persecutions.

[2] This factor will clearly be assessed differently by different scholars. G. H. C. Macgregor (*The Acts of the Apostles*, IB, 1954, p. 11), who dated Acts AD 80–85, nevertheless considered that the absence of use of Paul's letters not only favoured an early date, but favoured Lucan authorship, and this view is widely shared. But if the collection of Paul's letters is dated earlier than this (cf. discussion in my *New Testament Introduction: The Pauline Epistles*, 1961, pp. 265 ff.), it would require an earlier date for Acts, unless it could be maintained that Luke had no interest in Paul as a letter-writer.

[3] For a discussion of the theory see my *New Testament Introduction: The Pauline Epistles*, pp. 259 ff.

would clearly need to be dated later still.[1] Reasons have already been given why this widely accepted dating of Luke may be challenged, and if the Gospel is dated as early as AD 60 (see discussion on p. 109) this would suggest an early date for Acts and would be in keeping with the argument already given for a date before AD 64. It is a doubtful method of dating early books to use a particular interpretation of the one available datum and then to build a superstructure of other books upon it. It will be clear that if a predictive element in the ministry of Jesus is allowed the whole basis of this generally held dating collapses.

It should nevertheless be noted that not all who accept the traditional authorship of Luke date the book before the fall of Jerusalem. If Luke is the author and it is deemed necessary to date the Gospel after AD 70, the upper limit for the dating of Acts is restricted only by the probability of Luke's life-span, which is very difficult to estimate. It would certainly not be impossible for Luke to have written Acts any time up to about AD 85 but it could hardly have been much later. A date between AD 70 and 85 is, therefore, preferred by the majority of scholars.

E. J. Goodspeed[2] produced a list of additional reasons for a date as late as AD 90 for Luke-Acts, which were mainly inferences from the contents. Late features, according to him, can be seen in certain literary characteristics, in the infancy interest, in the resurrection interest, in the doctrine of the Spirit, primitive miracles, cessation of the Jewish controversy, interest in psalmody, church organization, primitive glossalalia, the inferences from xx. 25, 38 that Paul is dead, Paul's heroic stature, the emergence of the sects, lack of acquaintance with Paul's letters and the historical background of a successful Gentile mission. Quite apart from the questionable character of some of Goodspeed's inferences (e.g. that Paul is dead from Acts xx. 25, 38), it is by no means clear that any of the points he mentions requires a date any later than the early sixties. In any case he accepts the Lucan authorship and supposes that the author collected his material long before his book was actually published.

---

[1] It may be of interest to note that one or two scholars have maintained that Acts was published before Luke. C. S. C. Williams (*ET*, LXIV, 1952–53, pp. 283 ff.) argues that Acts followed Proto-Luke in production but preceded the publication of the Gospel, while H. G. Russell (*HTR*, 48, 1958, pp. 167–174) suggests that Acts influenced the production of the Gospel.

[2] *Introduction to the New Testament* (1937), pp. 191 ff.

c. Arguments for a second-century date

Earlier critics of the Tübingen school popularized a second-century dating for Acts because their reconstruction of the history demanded it. The reconciliation tendency of the author to patch up the Petrine-Pauline clash required a considerable time interval to develop. But the subjective character of this kind of criticism has assured its doom and the dismissal of the historical reconstruction of this school of thought has caused a general disinclination towards a second-century dating. But there are still some arguments which are advanced in support of this dating.

(i) *The relation of Acts to Josephus.* The fact that both Acts (in the speech of Gamaliel, v. 36) and Josephus refer to a rising under a Jew named Theudas has given rise to the theory that the author of Acts consulted Josephus' *Antiquities*[1] while writing his history. If this deduction is correct Acts must be dated after AD 94.[2] An alleged contradiction between Josephus and the Gospel has already been cited in discussing the dating of Luke (see p. 106), and a similar contradiction is suggested here. Acts places the rising of Theudas before the rising of Judas the Galilaean, but the latter happened in the time of Augustus, while Josephus dates the former at a period subsequent to Gamaliel's speech. There are two possible explanations. Either one of these reports must be wrong, or else the Theudas mentioned by Luke was not the Theudas mentioned by Josephus. Most scholars prefer the former alternative and generally presume that the historian in error must be Luke. But the author of Acts almost certainly did not consult Josephus, for had he done so he would surely not have made so obvious a blunder. Moreover, it is no more self-evident that Acts must be wrong and Josephus correct than *vice versa*.[3] It is, of course, possible that two rebellions were instigated by men named Theudas, since this was a

---

[1] *Antiquities*, xx. 5 (Whiston's edition).

[2] This theory was maintained by F. C. Burkitt (*The Gospel History and its Transmission*[3], 1911, pp. 105–110), following the arguments of Krenkel's *Josephus und Lucas* (1894). It has had considerable influence. Its traces are even found among some who maintain Lucan authorship. R. R. Williams, in his Torch Commentary on Acts, suggests that Luke may have had no exact report of Gamaliel's speech and that the error crept in through careless editing of the text with the aid of Josephus' works (*op. cit.*, pp. 64, 65).

[3] F. F. Bruce (*The Acts of the Apostles*[2], 1952, p. 25) comments, 'There is nothing here to suggest literary dependence; as for discrepancies, Luke is as likely to be right as Josephus,'

fairly common name, but such a theory is none too convincing without corroborating evidence.

(ii) *The relation of Acts to second-century writers.* Some scholars have gone much farther than Josephus and have found affinities between Acts and the second-century Church Fathers. It has recently been maintained that Justin shared the same theological outlook as Acts although he makes no literary use of the book.[1] But theological affinities are a precarious method of assessing dating, for the theory that Acts and Justin's works were both produced about the same time is certainly not the only explanation of the relationship, nor is it even the most reasonable, for it raises far more problems than it solves.[2] It may be assumed that Acts was linked with the third Gospel almost from its inception, in which case it would be inconceivable for Marcion to have been acquainted with Luke and not Acts. But it would have been equally improbable for Marcion to have chosen as his one Gospel a book which was clearly not of ancient standing. All the evidence points to an arbitrary rejection of Acts by Marcion on the same grounds as those on which he rejected the remaining Gospels.[3]

A second-century dating of Acts which gained such favour among earlier critics is not likely to be reinstituted by any argument based on theological affinities, in view of the strong traditional testimony against such a theory. Moreover, it is difficult to imagine that the strong impression Acts gives of recording factual details, particularly in the latter part dealing with Paul's activities, is the work of a second-century writer.[4] It is far less credible to regard the book as the product of a writer's historical imagination than it is to regard it as the record of one who was in close proximity to the events he relates—which would be the case with a first-century dating.

[1] Cf. J. C. O'Neill, *The Theology of Acts*, pp. 10 ff. In an appendix, O'Neill claims to establish that Justin did not know Luke's Gospel either (pp. 28–53). But H. F. D. Sparks(*JTS*, n.s., XIV, 1963, pp. 462–466) strongly criticizes his method.

[2] Cf. Feine-Behm-Kümmel, *Einleitung*, pp. 124, 125.

[3] O'Neill gets over the difficulty by maintaining that Marcion's copy of Luke was a form of the canonical Gospel corrected against what he supposed were older sources(*op. cit.*, pp. 19 ff.). O'Neill's conclusion is that Luke-Acts need not have been issued until about ten years before Marcion's Canon (i.e. *c.* AD 130). Contrast the view expressed by H. J. Cadbury and the editors in Jackson-Lake's *Beginnings of Christianity*, II, p. 358, that it is extremely unlikely that Luke would ever have been canonized had it not been generally known before the time of Marcion.

[4] Cf. Sparks, *op. cit.*, p. 461.

III. PURPOSE

Since the book of Acts is a continuation of the third Gospel, it is reasonable to suppose that the purpose which is there clearly stated in the preface will obtain for this part of the work as well. It has been shown (see pp. 87 ff.) that Luke's primary purpose was historical and this must be considered as the major aim of Acts, whatever subsidiary motives may have contributed towards its production.

a. A narrative of history

Leaving aside for the present the much-debated question of the historical value of Acts, we may assume that Luke intended his work to be regarded as historical, but not in the sense of a dry chronicle of events. The author, by reason of the wide range of his subject, has been forced to be selective. There is much that we would like to know of which Luke says nothing. The history before the narrative of Paul's life and work is somewhat scrappy and gives the impression that the author's purpose is to get to Paul as soon as possible. Even when dealing with Paul he omits certain features, for example Paul's visit to Arabia after his conversion and the journeys of Timothy and Erastus between Macedonia, Athens and Corinth.[1] The author clearly had a different approach towards his historical record than have modern historians because, quite apart from the assumption that ancient historians had little conception of exact scientific writing, Luke was more than a historian. He was in a real way a part of the history itself. He was describing events which had made a deep impression upon his mind. He could not detach himself, even had he wanted to, from the thrill of the divine happenings which he had heard about or had seen with his own eyes.

There is an implication in Luke's preface that others before him had felt the urge to commit to writing the events which lay behind the early Christian movement, and it may be that Luke considered unsatisfactory such attempts as he had seen. This latter presupposition is not, however, conclusively demanded by the evidence.[2] It could be that the author possessed a dominant urge to produce a record of the facts irrespective of the work of his predecessors.

[1] See my New Testament Introduction: The Pauline Epistles, pp. 184. Feine-Behm-Kümmel (op. cit., p. 103) appeal to the omissions in Acts as evidence that Acts is not a historical work.

[2] Cf. H. J. Cadbury, The Making of Luke-Acts (1927), p. 303.

b. A Gospel of the Spirit

Since Luke-Acts must be considered as a whole, and since the first part possesses the character of a Gospel, the second part must be viewed in the light of this fact.[1] For the author the important thing is the recognition of a divine activity behind the events, hence his great emphasis on the work of the Holy Spirit.[2] The Church comes into being through the baptism of the Spirit (ii. 38). Fullness of the Spirit was the evidence of true Christianity (ii. 4, vi. 3, viii. 17, x. 44, xix. 6). It was the Spirit who directed the mission work of the primitive Church, seen for instance in the action of the Antiochene church (xiii. 2) and in the prohibitions which prevented Paul and his party from entering Bithynia (xvi. 7). It is not inappropriate that this book has been called the Acts of the Holy Spirit and it is significant that several times the record of events is described as the continued activity of Jesus. In His name the lame man is healed (iii. 6, iv. 10), in His name the apostles preached (v. 40). Both Stephen and Saul see a heavenly vision of Jesus (vii. 55, ix. 5). This is but an illustration of what Luke says in his preface that in his former book he wrote what Jesus *began* to do and teach (Acts i. 1), which shows that his present purpose is to describe the continuation of that work.[3]

c. An apology

The two former propositions would not explain the particular selection of material which Luke has made and consequently many scholars have proposed an apologetic purpose. There is much to be said for this,

[1] This has recently been stressed by Trocmé (*Le 'Livre des Actes' et l'Histoire*, 1957, pp. 42 ff.), who maintains that the new form of historical narrative was preserved only because it was attached to an already acknowledged Gospel form.

[2] In his article on 'The Construction and Purpose of the Acts of the Apostles' (*StTh*, 12, 1958, p. 55) A. Ehrhardt claims, 'For the whole purpose of the Book of Acts ... is no less than to be the Gospel of the Holy Spirit.' This approach was stressed by many older exegetes, but it is good to find some modern authors who are prepared to find in this the key to the understanding of Luke's purpose.

[3] As Rackham (*The Acts of the Apostles*[14], 1951, p. xxxviii) states, 'These twenty-eight chapters are but *the beginning* (i. 1, xi. 15): we are still living under the dispensation of the Spirit.' By this he explains the lack of a conclusion. Cf. W. C. van Unnik's view that Acts was designed to be a confirmation of the Gospel for those who had had no personal acquaintance with Christ in the flesh (*Nov. Test.*, 4, 1960, pp. 26–59).

although not all the forms in which the theory is presented are accept-
able. The earlier Tübingen critics saw Acts as a compromise between
Petrinism and Paulinism, in which case the author was dominated by a
very definite 'tendency'. But this kind of criticism is now discounted.[1]
The apologetic purpose is seen in two directions: the approach to the
Jews and the approach to the Roman authorities.

    The author appears to go out of his way to show the close connec-
tion between Christianity and its antecedents in Judaism. The Christians, and particularly Paul himself, still observe Jewish ceremonial
requirements: Timothy is circumcised and Paul takes a vow, while
James, both at the Council of Jerusalem and on the occasion of his later
meeting with Paul, draws attention to the relationship between Jewish
practices and Christian procedure. The appeal to the Old Testament as
predicting events which were happening in the Christian Church
would influence Jewish readers in the direction of a favourable view
of the Church. But it is in its approach to official relationships with the
Roman Empire that Acts becomes most clearly apologetic. In every
case the author brings out the impartiality of the Roman officials. The
attitude of Gallio may be viewed as typical. He cared for none of the
religious questions which formed the basis of Jewish charges against
Paul. The fact is that he would not have understood them. Another
proconsul, Sergius Paulus, is seen to be most favourable towards the
gospel. The city secretary at Ephesus was conciliatory, and the Asiarchs
(probably here officials appointed to maintain order at religious festivals) are seen as helpful to Paul. Is all this an attempt to exonerate Rome
from implication in the constant harassing of the Christian Church?
Throughout it is the Jews who are the instigators, and throughout the
Roman authorities do not take their charges seriously. Both Agrippa
and Festus agreed that Paul might have been freed if he had not
appealed to Caesar (xxvi. 32).[2]

    It is an attractive idea that the author wished to show that Christian-
ity was politically harmless in order that the authorities might be pre-

---

[1] The idea of the Tübingen critics that Gnosticism is the key to the understanding of Acts is not altogether rejected, for C. K. Barrett regards Acts as an apology
addressed to the Church showing Paul's anti-Gnostic orthodoxy (*Luke the Historian in Recent Study*, 1961, p. 63).

[2] It should be noted that Festus had the power to acquit Paul in spite of the appeal,
but it would have been politically inexpedient for him to have done so. Cf.
Sherwin-White, *Roman Society and Roman Law in the New Testament* (1963), p. 65.

pared to extend to it the same toleration as they gave to Judaism.[1] Yet it must not be supposed that Luke takes up a position of compromise in order to persuade the authorities to regard Christianity under the umbrella of Judaism. Had such been his purpose he would surely have omitted to mention the constant hostility of the Jews towards Christian mission preaching. To throw all the onus for the disturbance on to the Jews would be a strange way of convincing anybody that Christianity was still to be regarded as a branch of Judaism, quite apart from the obvious dangers of such a compromise for the subsequent history of the Church.

d. A defence brief for Paul's trial

This suggestion is closely linked to the apologetic motive, but is tied to a particular occasion.[2] The idea is that Paul's trial is still in progress and Luke has prepared for Theophilus a full explanation of the rise and character of Christianity for the purpose of correcting misunderstandings. It is assumed under this view that Theophilus was a person of high rank who would have influence with the emperor. Streeter[3] suggested that he was Flavius Clemens. But the identity of Theophilus is mere conjecture and it is purely hypothetical that such a book as Acts would have allayed the suspicions of so infamous a character as Nero.[4] Moreover, Luke's preface suggests that Theophilus had already been instructed in the Christian faith and it would appear to have been at least part of Luke's purpose to instruct him more fully.[5] Although

[1] M. Schneckenberger (*Ueber den Zweck der Apostelgeschichte*, 1841, pp. 244 ff.) first argued for this view (cited by Trocmé, *op. cit.*, p. 52). For a modern presentation, cf. B. S. Easton's essay on 'The Purpose of Acts' in *Early Christianity* (ed. F. C. Grant, 1954), pp. 41 ff.

In his book *Roman Hellenism and the New Testament* (1962), pp. 172–178, F. C. Grant maintains that the term *religio licita* was not used until the third century of the Christian era. He considers that in Roman eyes *religio* was so bound up with the State that a rival *religio* would have been regarded as intolerable. All that Christianity could hope for would be toleration, not recognition.

[2] Cf. D. Plooij, *Exp.*, VIII, viii (1914), pp. 511–523; VIII, xiii (1917), pp. 108–124; A. Wikenhauser, *Die Apostelgeschichte und ihr Geschichtswert* (1921), pp. 30–34; H. Sahlin, *Der Messias und das Gottesvolk* (1945, Acta Seminarii Neotestamentici Upsaliensis, XII, pp. 30–56. The latter regards part of Acts as part of Proto-Luke which has been later edited as a defence for Paul (cf. Michaelis' criticisms, *Einleitung*, p. 137).

[3] *The Four Gospels*, pp. 533 ff.

[4] C. K. Barrett (*op. cit.*, p. 63) calls such an idea 'absurd'.

[5] H. J. Cadbury (*op. cit.*, p. 315) prefers to understand Luke's preface as indicating Luke's intention to correct a misunderstanding of Christianity.

this theory cannot be disproved, it lacks strong historical probability.[1]

e. A theological document

Many scholars have placed the emphasis on Luke's theological interests.
The movement of Christianity from Jerusalem to Rome had more than
geographical interest[2] for the author. It had theological significance. It
revealed the triumph of Christianity in a hostile world.[3] Thus the
arrival of Paul in Rome was a fitting conclusion to the history.

   Some scholars have taken this point of view much further and have
seen in Luke a historian who is wholly dominated by a theological
purpose. His narrative is treated not so much as a record of facts as an
interpretation. Thus Dibelius[4] maintained, 'The whole work aims not
so much at letting the readers know what really happened as at helping
them to understand what all this means, the invasion of the world of
hellenistic culture by the Christian Church.' In similar vein J. C.
O'Neill[5] considers that both Jerusalem and Rome have for the author
tremendous theological importance. Haenchen[6] maintains a similar
theory, but sees Acts as an edifying piece of literature, in which the
author uses literary means to make the events memorable to his readers,
and for this purpose uses what material he possesses with considerable
freedom. While it is probable that not enough weight has been attached to theological motives, the approach of these scholars impinges

---

   [1] Feine-Behm-Kümmel (*Einleitung*, p. 103) dismiss this view as false because
an early date for Acts is unacceptable. But if that obstacle is removed and Acts
is dated early (as argued above, pp. 307 ff.) this objection is invalid. A great
obstacle to the theory is the absence from Acts of any reference to the trial in
Rome.

   [2] Several scholars have maintained that Luke's main purpose was geographical,
to record the planting of the gospel in the imperial city. (Cf. E. Jacquier, *Les
Actes des Apôtres*[2], 1926, p. cii; T. Zahn, *Die Apostelgeschichte*, 1919–21, pp. 14,
15.) This view is criticized by Trocmé (*op. cit.*, pp. 83 ff.) on the grounds that
Christianity had reached Rome before Paul, and in any case there was no need
to demonstrate by this means the triumph of universalism since this is clear from
Acts xv.

   [3] This is well brought out in the analysis of the book by R. R. Williams under
the caption, 'Nothing can stop the Gospel' (*The Acts of the Apostles*, 1953, pp.
24–33).

   [4] *Studies in the Acts of the Apostles* (1956), p. 133.

   [5] *The Theology of Acts*, pp. 58 ff.   [6] Cf. *Die Apostelgeschichte*, pp. 93–99.

on the historicity of Acts, and this raises a problem which will merit further consideration.

IV. HISTORICITY

This book has been a constant battleground for critical scholars obsessed with the problem of Luke's veracity. The era has now passed when the historicity of Acts can with any plausibility be wholly discredited, but nevertheless many scholars find difficulty in some of Luke's details. A brief indication of these difficulties will be given in the following discussion.

a. Luke's political knowledge

Sir William Ramsay has done much to reinstate Luke as a serious historian and this is largely due to archaeological researches. The author of Acts was acquainted with all the different political arrangements in those provinces which enter into the narration of Paul's missionary journeys. This is a remarkable testimony to Luke's accurate knowledge in view of the several changes in administration of parts of the empire effected during the period covered by his history. The following details will give some indication of the extent of this knowledge. At the time when Paul was in Cyprus a proconsul was in charge, and although there had been many changes within a brief period Luke used the correct title when describing Sergius Paulus. Philippi is accurately described as a Roman colony, whose officials are called στρατηγοί, apparently representing the senior magistrates according to the Roman pattern of duoviri iuri dicundo.[1] At Thessalonica the unusual politarchs, for which no parallels were known to exist in imperial organization, are now vouched for by inscriptions. At Malta the ruler is correctly styled the primus or chief man, while at Ephesus there are correct references to the local government organization, with Asiarchs[2] controlling

[1] Cf. A. N. Sherwin-White, Roman Society and Roman Law in the New Testament (1963), pp. 92, 93. This author rejects the older view that στρατηγοί represents the Latin praetores, on the grounds that this term was already becoming archaic by 63 BC.

[2] Sherwin-White points out that this title was used of presidents (and perhaps ex-presidents) of the Council of Asia, but was also used of administrators of the imperial cult, or of the city deputies who formed the Council (ibid., p. 90). In some provinces the corresponding title (e.g. Lyciarch, Pontarch, Bithyniarch) was restricted to one holder, the president. Luke's use of the plural, therefore, shows specific knowledge of the different set-up in Asia.

G.A.—21

religious affairs, the Secretary (or Chief Clerk)[1] wielding considerable influence, and the proconsular authorities being regarded as the final court of appeal.

In addition to these, Luke shows detailed knowledge of the rights and privileges of Roman citizens. Especially is this evident in the reluctance of the apostle Paul to invoke his privileges, for not only was it true that in the New Testament period provincials who possessed Roman citizenship claimed also citizenship of their own cities, but it was also difficult for wandering peoples to prove their Roman citizenship by appeal to the official registers in their own home areas. It would not always have been to Paul's advantage to invoke his privileges, although in the case of his appeal to Caesar it was clearly to escape from the hostility of the Jews. In Luke's various references to Roman legal procedures, he shows himself to be well informed. In fact, there is no instance where Luke has introduced an anachronism, which is a striking testimony to the general reliability of his narrative.[2] Moreover, the description of the Gentile world which forms the background of Paul's mission perfectly fits into what is known of city life in the Graeco–Roman world. Nevertheless many other considerations have been held to dispute this conclusion.

b. The relationship with Paul's Epistles

This problem has been the subject of a mass of literature and it will be impossible to give more than the main features which have caused difficulties in the minds of many scholars.

(i) *Paul and the church of Jerusalem.* The fact that in Acts Paul appears to visit Jerusalem three times (ix. 20 ff., xi. 30, xv. 2), compared with the two occasions (Gal. i. 16 ff., ii) which Paul himself mentions for the same period (if Galatians is dated *after* the Council of Jerusalem), has led to the assumption that Luke is incorrect. But the validity of this

---

[1] The official title was Clerk of the People. He was the chief administrative official of the city and there is evidence for such an official in Ephesus and other Asiatic cities during the New Testament period. There was a lesser official called the Clerk of the Council, but the Acts story, which describes the γραμματεύς as addressing the people, is clearly referring to the more important office (cf. Sherwin-White, *op. cit.*, pp. 86, 87).

[2] On the whole subject of Luke's reliability in this respect, cf. Sherwin-White *op. cit.*, *passim*. It is well demonstrated that the dramatic date of the Acts narrative belongs to the Julio-Claudian period of Roman administration, which strikingly supports the contention that the author had access to first-hand information.

assumption depends on far too many dubious propositions. It requires us to suppose that Paul is stating *all* the occasions when he visited Jerusalem, whereas he may well be citing only the occasions when he had personal contact with the apostles, and this would appear to exclude xi. 30. Nevertheless, some scholars have proposed to treat the visits of xi. 30 and xv as duplicate accounts of the same event, which would, of course, impugn the accuracy of Luke's information.[1] But it is highly improbable that the author would have become muddle-headed over such an important and significant event as this.[2] Moreover, such a theory is not demanded by the evidence.[3]

(ii) *Paul and the Jewish law.* The Acts twice describes Paul as supporting Jewish ritual observances, once when recommending the circumcision of Timothy and again when he submitted to James' suggestion regarding the vow and its accompanying shaving of the head. Such deference to Jewish scruples is, however, reckoned by some to be alien to the attitude of Paul in his Epistles, where he not only resists the perpetuation of circumcision, but also proclaims Christian freedom from bondage to the law. Is this a real contradiction or is it merely apparent? When Paul's own dictum (in 1 Corinthians) that the strong must be prepared to consider the effect of their actions on the weak is taken into account, his own willingness to take a Jewish vow is not inexplicable. It was not a matter which had a vital effect on his Christian position. His attitude towards circumcision was rather different. In the Epistles Paul makes clear his decided opposition to circumcision being regarded as a *sine qua non* for Gentile believers, but there is no reason to suppose that Paul intended to oppose circumcision as a Jewish practice (cf. Rom. ii. 25). The circumcision of Timothy, whose mother was Jewish, would merely regularize his racial affinities, but the circumcision of a Gentile

---

[1] Cf. A. C. McGiffert, *A History of Christianity in the Apostolic Age* (1897), p. 171; K. Lake in *The Beginnings of Christianity*, v, pp. 195 ff. More recently E. Hirsch, *ZNTW*, 29 (1930), pp. 63–76; J. R. Porter, *JTS*, XLVIII (1947), pp. 169 ff.

[2] H. Windisch, although inclined to regard Acts xi and xv as duplicate accounts, nevertheless admitted that it 'is strange that "Luke" was ignorant of these matters; nevertheless it is not impossible that he might have given an incorrect version of the matter' (*The Beginnings of Christianity*, II, p. 319).

[3] For a full discussion of this problem see the writer's *New Testament Introduction: The Pauline Epistles*, pp. 80 ff. In view of the difficulties of the traditional view, J. N. Sanders speculated about a new reconstruction of the course of events in which he maintained two Jerusalem visits before AD 44, and suggested that Paul was not present at the Council (*NTS*, 2, 1955, pp. 133–143).

Christian, with no Jewish background whatever, would give the impression that circumcision was an essential part of Christianity, which would then have been constituted a sect of Judaism. There is no essential contradiction over this question. It has sometimes been supposed on the strength of Galatians ii. 3 that Paul had at the Council of Jerusalem opposed the demand that Titus should be circumcised.[1] But since Titus was a Greek he was in a different position from Timothy.

(iii) *Paul and the Council decrees.* According to the Acts, certain decrees were proposed and agreed to by Paul which involved the enforcement of certain ritual prohibitions on the Gentile converts. The generally accepted text contains four such prohibitions: idolatrous pollutions, unchastity, things strangled and blood (Acts xv. 20). The last two relate to dietary regulations. The 'Western' text omits the third taboo and the list in that case becomes a moral catechism, assuming 'blood' to be an equivalent for murder. But it seems quite unnecessary to urge Gentile Christians to abstain from murder. The common text makes more sense, although it would appear to enjoin a Jewish food law on Gentile converts and would raise a difficulty as to whether Paul would ever have agreed to that. Moreover, in Galatians ii, Paul not only does not mention the decrees, but expressly says that no obligations were laid upon him but to remember the poor (verses 6, 10). While this at first sight looks like a discrepancy, there are considerations which should cause us to think carefully before reaching this conclusion. Paul, in Galatians, is referring to his own position, not that of all the Gentile converts. He is speaking in self-defence.

It is significant that the decrees were addressed only to the Gentiles in the churches of Antioch, Syria and Cilicia (Acts xv. 23). At the same time, Acts xvi. 4 states clearly that Paul delivered the decrees to the South Galatian churches, which suggests that he regarded them as generally applicable. In any case there are no strong reasons for supposing that Paul *must* quote them in Galatians, since he may have preferred direct arguments to support his claims. Furthermore if Galatians was written before the Council of Jerusalem the decrees were not by then agreed upon.

The incident at Antioch in which Paul resisted Peter's action is thought to be strange following the agreements at the Council, and consequently the veracity of the Acts account is called in question.[2]

[1] Cf. H. Windisch, *op. cit.*, p. 320.   [2] *Ibid.*, p. 326.

But this discrepancy is more apparent than real, for Paul makes it clear that Peter had acted inconsistently, and this cannot be said to be impossible although it is certainly unexpected. But it is equally strange that Paul should charge Barnabas with insincerity. The difficulty is, of course, lessened if the dissimulation occurred before the Council, although Peter's earlier Caesarean experience should have prepared him to resist the pressure of the Jewish rigorists.

(iv) *Luke's portrait of Paul.* When considering the question of authorship it was pointed out that a comparison between the Paul presented in Acts and the Paul who reveals himself in his letters has led some scholars to find discrepancies. E. Haenchen[1] places emphasis on three differences.

1. Acts presents Paul as a wonder-worker who can heal through communicating his power through a handkerchief, or who can raise the dead Eutychus, or can shake off a deadly serpent unharmed. But the apostle makes reference to working wonders in 2 Corinthians xii. 12, which Haenchen does not regard as very exceptional, since in any case Paul did not base the evidence for his apostleship on such external factors. There is a difficulty here only if it is assumed that Luke records the miraculous as an evidence of Paul's apostleship, but he nowhere says this, and the interpretation may be challenged.

2. Whereas in Acts Paul is portrayed as a convincing speaker to a variety of different audiences, whether to Jews or Greeks, government officials or philosophers, in the Epistles Paul himself disclaims any rhetorical power and even includes his opponents' estimate of him as of no account as a speaker (cf. 2 Cor. x. 10). Haenchen sees this contradiction as having arisen from a later assumption that Paul the great missionary must have been Paul the great speaker, although in fact it was not so. But it is noteworthy that Acts nowhere describes Paul in such terms as Apollos is described ('an eloquent man', Acts xviii. 24), although on Haenchen's theory this might well have been expected. Moreover, on many of the occasions in Acts his so-called eloquence was far from persuasive, for it frequently resulted in open hostility and on at least one occasion in ridicule. It is very doubtful, therefore, whether much weight should be attached to this supposed discrepancy.

3. Although in the Epistles Paul strongly affirms his equality with the Jerusalem apostles, Acts gives no hint that Paul had any need to do

[1] *Die Apostelgeschichte*, pp. 100 ff.

this. His apostolic status seems to have been assumed at an early point in the narrative. But it is precisely because it is assumed, that the supposed discrepancy loses weight. Luke portrays Paul's apostolic mission to the Gentiles as a continuation of the earlier activities of Peter and others in Judaea and Samaria. To him apostolic status was incidental to his main purpose in describing the spread of the gospel. Paul's own battle for equality of status had as its setting the internal conditions of the primitive churches, but Acts says very little about these.

None of these problems requires the conclusion that Luke's history is unreliable, for a reasonable solution is possible in each case. An additional consideration which is not unfavourable to Luke's reliability is the primitiveness of the conditions in the early Church reflected in his account.[1] Whatever value is placed on alleged parallels between Acts and the Qumran literature,[2] they draw attention to some points of contact and may suggest a similar general milieu. It should be noted that the differences[3] between Qumran and the primitive Christian community are greater than the similarities, which again emphasizes Luke's knowledge of the distinctive Christian features of the Jewish-Christian community.[4]

c. The speeches in Acts

The assessment of the Acts speeches forms an important factor in determining the historicity of the book, and some indication must therefore be given of the various ways of approaching the author's method. Peter, Stephen and Paul are the main orators and to these are attributed various types of speeches. F. F. Bruce[5] has divided these speeches into

---

[1] Bo Reicke, in his *Glaube und Leben der Urgemeinde* (1957), maintains the genuinely early character of the traditions incorporated into Acts i-vii.

[2] Cf. S. E. Johnson's suggestions in *The Scrolls and the New Testament* (ed. K. Stendahl, 1958), pp. 129 ff. He found parallels in the reception of the Spirit as pledge of eternal life, the idea of communal life and of religious poverty, the organization into a Council of twelve, the distinction between the members and the leaders, the common meal and the method of biblical citation and interpretation.

[3] For example, the absence from Acts of a novitiate, of probation, or of classification of members into trades, or of communal works.

[4] O. Cullmann considers that the Hellenists of Acts vi were connected with the kind of Judaism represented by the Qumran texts (*JBL*, LXXIV, 1955, pp. 213-226, reproduced in Stendahl's collection, *op. cit.*, pp. 18 ff.). But against this, cf. P. Winter, *ThLZ*, 82 (1957), col. 835.

[5] *The Speeches in the Acts of the Apostles* (1944), p. 5.

four groups: evangelistic, deliberative, apologetic and hortatory. The form of each is determined by its respective occasion and purpose. But the major question regarding them all is whether they reproduce the content of the words spoken or whether they are inventions of Luke in order to represent what he considered would have been said. To answer this question it will be necessary to consider various propositions.

(i) *The approach of ancient historiography.* The classical statement on this is that of Thucydides, who carefully described his method. He admitted that he could not always recall the speeches word for word, so that he had formed the habit of making the speakers speak in a way which seemed to him to be demanded by the occasion, though he concluded, 'of course adhering as closely as possible to the general sense of what was actually said'.[1] It is often supposed that this means that Thucydides invented most of his speeches, although occasionally conforming them to actual reports.[2] Yet Thucydides seems to be arguing for the substantial historicity of his speeches, for otherwise he would not have been at such pains to stress that some of the speeches he had himself heard, while others he received from various sources. Basically truth lies behind the record. Thucydides' successors did not maintain his high notion of the historian's task and many of them produced historical works in the manner of dramatic or rhetorical exercises. But to which of these categories does Luke belong? M. Dibelius was quite emphatic that Luke invented his speeches and supported this contention by an appeal to their general similarities, irrespective of the identity of the speakers. But this conclusion has been as strongly challenged by others, notably Foakes Jackson,[3] Sir William Ramsay[4] and B. Gärtner.[5]

---

[1] *History of the Peloponnesian War,* i. 22. 1.

[2] For a discussion of Thucydides' statement, cf. H. Patzer, *Das Problem der Geschichtsschreibung des Thukydides und die thukydideische Frage* (1937), pp. 44 ff.; A. W. Gomme, *A Historical Commentary on Thucydides* (1945), I, pp. 140, 141; M. Dibelius, *Studies in the Acts of the Apostles* (1956), pp. 140 ff.; B. Gärtner, *The Areopagus Speech and Natural Revelation* (1955), pp. 13 f. Gomme thinks that Thucydides put the speeches in his own style, but this does not mean that the content was his own. The fact that different interpretations can be put on Thucydides' words should lead to some caution in building too much upon them. It cannot be cited as the main evidence in support of a literary process of inventiveness.

[3] *The Acts of the Apostles* (1931), p. xvi.

[4] *St. Paul the Traveller and Roman Citizen* (1920), p. 27.

[5] *Op. cit.,* pp. 26 ff.

Gärtner rightly pleads for greater emphasis upon the Jewish historical tradition to counterbalance the Greek tradition in the background of Luke's writings. In other words it is by no means obvious that Luke's historical method must be interpreted on the basis of Greek principles, if indeed there were principles which can in any sense be regarded as generally adopted among Greek historians.[1]

(ii) *The approach of Luke in his Gospel.* Although no canonical parallels exist by which the Acts speeches may be gauged, the method used in the Gospel can be compared with the other Synoptic accounts and a comparative estimate of Luke's reliability can be formed. It has already been seen that Luke exercised great care over his choice of sources and that he has faithfully reproduced his material (see comments on Luke's preface, p. 202). Especially is this seen in his treatment of the discourse material in Luke xxi, if it is established that he used Mark xiii. Although there are minor changes, there is no evidence that Luke has invented material not found in his sources.[2] Indeed, the Gospel as a whole shows no evidence of such a tendency, and in view of this it is a fair assumption that he would not have resorted to it in the continuation in Acts.

(iii) *The primitive character of the theology of the speeches.* It has been emphasized, particularly by C. H. Dodd,[3] that the early speeches of Acts contain the primitive *kerygma*. They are, therefore, a true representation of an early pre-Pauline theology and this can only reasonably be accounted for on the assumption that Luke incorporates a genuine tradition in his speeches. Those who dispute Luke's historicity, however, claim that the theology is of a later type.[4] Yet if Luke was the author the theology cannot be very developed, particularly if the book of Acts was published before the death of Paul (see discussion above, pp. 307 ff.).

[1] R. M. Grant (*A Historical Introduction to the New Testament*, 1963, p. 141), in urging caution against regarding Thucydides as the only model of ancient historians, remarks that Polybius (second century BC) was severely critical of speech invention and regarded the historian's task as recording what was actually said.

[2] Cf. F. C. Burkitt's opinion in his article on 'Luke's use of Mark' in *The Beginnings of Christianity* (ed. Foakes Jackson and Lake), II, pp. 106 ff.

[3] *The Apostolic Preaching and its Developments*[2] (1944), pp. 7 ff.

[4] Thus J. C. O'Neill (*The Theology of Acts*, 1961) maintains that Luke is dominated by the theology of the first half of the second century (see especially pp. 166 ff.).

(iv) *The relation of the content of the speeches to the ipsissima verba*. Even if the tradition which is incorporated in the speeches is substantially historically correct, does this mean that Luke has preserved the precise words which were spoken? The majority of those who would maintain the reliability of Luke's record would not be prepared to maintain that he has preserved the *ipsissima verba*.[1] The content is historically true, but the words are Luke's own. The same kind of approach has already been met in dealing with the Fourth Gospel, but it has yet to be proved that the words could not bear any relationship to what was actually spoken. Each speech is so exactly adapted to its historical situation[2] that it would have been an example of consummate art on Luke's part to provide so perfectly suitable a framework for the words. It is not true, as some have maintained, that all the Acts speakers speak alike,[3] for the various types of speeches are admirably suited to their respective audiences,[4] the *Areopagitica* in Acts xvii. 22 ff. furnishing a conspicuous example.[5] There seems to be no substantial reason for rejecting the view that Luke has preserved personal reminiscences, either his own or those of others, of the speeches that he has chosen to incorporate into his own history. Recent emphasis on form criticism has led some to deny even the possibility of this, since no *Sitz im Leben* can be envisaged in which the speeches could have been preserved for twenty to thirty years.[6] But it is not altogether impossible that some written transcripts

[1] Cf. the recent approach of B. Gärtner (*The Areopagus Speech and Natural Revelation*, p. 33) who attributes the 'outer form' of the speeches to Luke, although considering that Luke gives reliable specimens of the apostolic message.

[2] Foakes Jackson (*The Acts of the Apostles*, p. xvi), for instance, considered that the speeches were 'wonderfully varied as to their character, and as a rule admirably suited to the occasion on which they were delivered'.

[3] So M. Dibelius, *A Fresh Approach to the New Testament and Early Christian Literature* (1936), p. 262. In a recent study, E. Schweizer (*ThZ*, XIII, 1957, pp. 1–11) claims that a basic pattern lies behind all the Acts speeches and that it is necessary to combine the individual speeches to obtain a total picture. J. T. Townsend (*ATR*, XLII, 1960, pp. 150 ff.) also considers that the speeches must be treated as a whole, which, if true, would lessen the connection of each speech with its specific situation.

[4] Cf. F. F. Bruce, *The Acts of the Apostles*[2] (1952), pp. 18 ff.; F. J. Foakes Jackson, *op. cit.*, p. xiv. For a study of the particular emphasis in Stephen's speech, cf. M. Simon, *St. Stephen and the Hellenists in the Primitive Church* (1958); A. F. J. Klijn, *NTS*, 4 (1958), pp. 25–31.

[5] N. B. Stonehouse, *Paul before the Areopagus and other New Testament Studies* (1957), pp. 1–40. For authors adopting a contrary opinion, cf. p. 101 n.3.

[6] Cf. C. F. Evans, *JTS*, n.s., VII (1956), pp. 25 ff.

may have existed.[1] It may have been Luke's intention to give samples of different kinds of mission preaching, and if this were so the samples would lose in weight if they were Luke's own compositions. On the other hand, the manner in which they are introduced gives the impression that they are an integral part of the narrative.[2]

V. SOURCES

It was inevitable that source criticism, which had found so fruitful a field for its conjectures in the Synoptic Gospels, should turn its attention to the book of Acts. It had strong grounds for doing so, since the reliability of a historical work depends on the reliability of its sources. But the desirability of isolating sources did not guarantee that such a quest was possible. Certainly criticism left no stone unturned in the attempt, as the great number of widely differing hypotheses amply testifies. But their very diversity suggests a basic weakness of approach and it will be profitable, before outlining the various types of theories, to discuss first the factors which affect the different critics' approach to the whole subject. Lack of agreement on sources springs generally from a basic difference in presuppositions regarding a number of closely related problems.

a. Factors affecting the source criticism of Acts

(i) *Unity of authorship*. Is the book a unity or not? If the answer is in the affirmative, the question of sources can be approached from only two possible points of view. Either the unity of the book stems from the mind of one author who has not only left the imprint of his own mind upon the book, but has also himself been the main collector of the materials; or it stems from the mind of an author who has imposed upon separate materials his own unifying influence in both content and style. Those who maintain unity of authorship, therefore, tend to classify themselves in one of two categories: those who deny sources altogether or those who adopt an author-editor hypothesis as distinct from a compiler hypothesis.

---

[1] E. M. Blaiklock (*The Acts of the Apostles*, 1959, p. 17) suggested that Paul's speeches existed in manuscript form. Against this view, cf. Feine-Behm-Kümmel, *Einleitung*, p. 109.

[2] For the substantial historicity of the early speeches in Acts, cf. L. Goppelt's study, *Die apostolische und nachapostolische Zeit* (1962), pp. 24 f.

Those who deny the unity of the book will naturally advocate some kind of source theory to account for the supposed differences which have led them to deny the unity. In these cases the source hypotheses become strictly a corollary of previously formed opinions regarding the unity. The sources need not, of course, be written, but they must have left their mark on the author, who in turn must be regarded either as none too skilful in his use of information which has come to him, or else as having left his work unfinished. Since it has already been shown, however, that there are strong grounds for maintaining the unity of the book, these latter theories have a considerable initial disadvantage.

(ii) *The identity of the author.* In the previous discussion on authorship it was shown that a reasonable case may be made out for the view that the author was a companion of Paul and that the traditional ascription to Luke was in all probability correct. Those scholars who do not accept this identification fall into two groups: some admit that behind at least part of the book there is the personal witness of one or more of Paul's travelling companions (Luke, Silas, Timothy), while others deny altogether that any eyewitness accounts are behind it. Clearly there will be far fewer problems for those who accept Lucan authorship than for those who do not, since it may reasonably be maintained that Luke would have had access to a number of eyewitnesses for those parts of the story where he was not personally present. This is particularly evident for the major section of the book dealing with Paul's experiences. But acceptance of Lucan authorship does not, of course, eliminate the possibility of the use of written sources and this must be borne in mind.

On the other hand, those who adopt an anonymous authorship for Acts have less to guide them in their proposals regarding sources, and may very well depend too much on their own guesses. Theories proceeding from such presuppositions obviously demand most careful scrutiny before any weight is attached to them. This is particularly evident in the case of theories depending on a late date (e.g. second century), for these must necessarily place less credence on the author's sources of information than other theories.

(iii) *The interpretation of Luke's preface.* This has already been discussed in the chapter on Luke's Gospel (see p. 92) and it is a fair inference that the principles which apply to the Gospel will apply equally to Acts.

Yet there is a distinction which is not unimportant in the discussion of sources. Whereas in the case of the Gospel other parallel accounts are known, which at least opens up the possibility that Luke was acquainted with them, in the case of Acts no similar record exists. This means that more stress must be placed on the author's own researches. Cadbury,[1] in fact, maintains that Luke is perhaps intending to include himself in the category of eyewitnesses. While this cannot, of course, be applied to the Gospel, the preface clearly does not exclude the possibility that Luke was a witness of some of the events related in Acts. If this is a true interpretation it will clearly have a bearing on the problem of sources. But some scholars have interpreted the preface to mean that the generation of eyewitnesses is now passed.[2] Yet since the author expressly claims to have followed carefully the events he records, it is most intelligible to suppose that he belongs to the same period. It is also most intelligible to suppose that he uses the first person when he wishes to indicate his own presence at the events he records (see discussion on the we-sections, pp. 95 f.).

(iv) *Criteria used for distinguishing sources.* As is apparent in the criticism of the Gospels, different criteria seem to have been employed at different periods and the success or failure of the criticism is made or marred by the validity of the supporting evidence used. In the Acts, a *linguistic* criterion has been used for various purposes. Some have traced an Aramaic origin for the first part of Acts or at least for portions of this first part; others have claimed a different Greek style for certain parts (e.g. the we-sections); while still others have as strongly maintained the linguistic unity of the whole. In face of these different conclusions from the same criterion it is obviously impossible to place much weight upon it. It is at best a precarious method of locating sources.

Another is the *historical* criterion, which proves almost as unsatisfactory. If two of the same type of event are recorded in any book and there happen to be certain similarities in the records, it is at once assumed by some scholars that they are duplicates and that, therefore, one is less historical than the other. A notable example is Harnack's opinion that the account of the gift of the Holy Spirit in Acts ii is less authentic than that in Acts iv, which led him to attribute them to

---

[1] *Exp.*, VIII, xxiv (1942), pp. 411–416. Cf. also *Beginnings*, v, pp. 497, 498. See also p. 95 n.3.

[2] Cf. A. Loisy (*Evangile selon Luc*, 1924, p. 75) and all who date Acts in the second century.

different sources. But since these accounts may more intelligibly be understood as complementary than as being duplicates, Harnack's basis of criticism is considerably weakened. No satisfactory approach is possible unless it is assumed as a first principle that the account must be treated as it stands unless in this case it is unintelligible. Appeal to doublets, contradictions and the like has littered the history of criticism with far too many hypotheses which are indefensible on sound principles of criticism.

No more successful has been the *theological* criterion whereby different strata have also been distinguished, as for instance the use of the expression Servant (or Son) of God in the first part of Acts in contradistinction from its context. Or again, the differences in content of the Pauline speeches and the Pauline Epistles have been claimed to indicate an author out of touch with Pauline theology. But such principles of criticism are based on a confusion between an author, his sources and his mental environment. As a companion of Paul was not obliged to reflect Pauline thought in imitation of Paul's Epistles, so the theological content of his narrative is an unreliable guide to his probable sources.

(v) *The influence of form criticism.* It is not surprising that the form-historical method which has had such an effect on the criticism of the Synoptic Gospels should equally be applied to the problem of the Acts sources and should similarly have had the effect of drawing attention away from source criticism. But classification of forms is more limited in Acts and has been confined mostly to itineraries and speeches. Its most notable advocate has been Dibelius[1] (see below), whose influence is apparent in much recent criticism. The method has had a notable

[1] Cf. his series of essays, *Studies in the Acts of the Apostles* (1956). In his first essay, 'Style Criticism of the Book of Acts', pp. 1–25, Dibelius examines the various narrative materials, classifying them into legend, tale or anecdote. While he claims by this to be assessing only the story-teller's method, yet in actual fact he is also assessing the authenticity of the material. Innumerable details are regarded as the author's own composition, which in itself indicates Dibelius' historical assessment of the value of the material. The story about the eunuch and the conversion of Cornelius are both, for instance, classed as legends, which have been influenced in their narration by the author's literary purpose. In some cases the original form of the story was actually non-Christian, examples of which are found in the account of the sons of Sceva (xix. 14–16) and in the story of the death of Herod (xii. 20–23). These examples will suffice to show the way in which form criticism deals with historical material.

effect in concentrating interest on the historical situation rather than on the fruitless attempt to establish a multiplicity of written sources. Although it has sometimes led to 'historical' verdicts which are far from historical, its positive effect has been in lessening dependence on source criticism. Its greatest weakness has been to assume that the early Christians were not interested in their own earlier history, with the consequence that Luke's data have become suspect. But this assumption is sufficiently disposed of by appeal to the historical situation underlying Paul's Epistles.[1]

(vi) *The explanation of the we-sections.* In any conjectures which might be proposed to account for the origin of Luke's information, the passages where the author uses the first person (the we-sections) are the natural starting-point. These passages[2] are introduced without explanation into narratives in the third person. There have been various theories to explain this phenomenon.

1. The most obvious reason for the first person is that the author wishes to indicate that in these passages he was himself present among the travelling companions of Paul. This interpretation would mean that the author merely changes from the third to the first person, almost unconsciously, because he is at these points producing a first-hand account. It may be called a literary device to differentiate between primary and secondary sources of information. This view is supported by the uniformity of style and language with the rest of the book and the use of the first person singular in i. 1.

2. Somewhat akin to the foregoing is the view that the we-sections form the whole or part of the author's own personal diary or travel jottings which contained information regarding places visited, people contacted and notable events witnessed. In that case he would have quoted the relevant portions, retaining the first person as in the original entry. That this view is less natural than the former is evident from the

---

[1] J. Jervell (*StTh*, 16, 1962, pp. 25–41) criticizes the position adopted by both Dibelius and Haenchen by drawing attention to occasions when Paul refers to the knowledge of other churches among various Christian groups (e.g. Rom. i. 8; 2 Cor. iii. 1–3; 1 Thes. i. 8; 2 Cor. viii. 1). Jervell maintains that this formed a part of God's Word to unbelievers. At least it shows that in Paul's time efforts were made to spread news from church to church of the 'faith' of various groups of believers.

[2] For details, see p. 95. There is no need, of course, to limit the we-sections too narrowly to those passages where the first person actually occurs (cf. Michaelis, *Einleitung*, p. 133).

fact that it presupposes an extraordinarily mechanical use of his own 'diary' on the part of the author, a process which is out of character with his literary method, not only in the rest of Acts but also in the Gospel. On the other hand certain parallels might be cited to illustrate this procedure from other ancient writers. Yet the fact remains that it is difficult to believe that any author would incorporate jottings, in all their stylistic peculiarities, which in their original form were probably never intended to be published without adaptation.

3. Another view is that the author has used someone else's diary or travel notes and has consequently retained the first person when he has incorporated this material. But it is even less natural to suppose that another author would have retained the 'we' form, particularly without giving any indication of the identity of the person speaking. If the author of the personal diary is the author of the whole, this procedure is at least intelligible in spite of its difficulties. But if he is a different man it is not easy to see any reason for his method.

4. The only other possibility is to suppose that the first person is no indication of an eyewitness, but is introduced intentionally by the author to give the impression of verisimilitude to his record. In this view it would be a purely fictional device.[1] But this raises far more problems than it solves, for it would be difficult to account for the relatively little use made of such a device. Why is it limited to the concluding part of the book if it rests on no historical basis? Moreover a greater impression of verisimilitude would surely have been created by a fiction writer if a name had been indicated in connection with the we-sections, after the manner in which apocryphal writings generally make indisputably clear which apostle is speaking when the first person is used.

Any source theories which proceed from these we-sections must reckon with the probabilities and the difficulties of these various interpretations. These general remarks will enable the following theories to be considered in their right perspective and will be a useful guide in assessing them.

b. Various types of theories

(i) *Personal information.* Those who maintain that Luke is the author of Acts have ready to hand a most likely hypothesis regarding the origin

---

[1] Cf. Haenchen, *Die Apostelgeschichte*, pp. 76–78.

of his information, at least for the major part of the book.[1] Since *ex hypothesi* the author was among Paul's travelling companions, he would have immediate access to all the necessary information recorded in ix. 1–31, xi. 25–30, xii. 25–xxviii. 31. For the rest of the book the source of information can only be conjectured, but there are some reasonable suggestions which may very well be right. It is certain that Luke knew Mark, for both were with Paul when he wrote his Colossian Epistle (Col. iv. 10, 14), and from him he may have received much useful information regarding the early days of the Church in Jerusalem. As there is in Acts xii. 12 mention of a prayer-meeting at the house of Mark's mother, it is justifiable to suppose that his home was a regular *rendezvous* not only for the Christians generally but also for the apostles. There could have been few happenings before the Council at Jerusalem (Acts xv) of which Mark had no first-hand knowledge.

If, as some suppose, Luke's home was at Antioch he would, moreover, have had access to a group of eyewitnesses who could have told him much about the history of Antiochene Christianity, and it is significant that Luke says a great deal about happenings at Antioch, so much so that some scholars have suggested a special Antiochene written source (see below). Then there were Philip and his daughters at Caesarea, who entertained Luke with Paul (according to Acts xxi. 8) and from whom he could have obtained much information regarding the events recorded in Acts vi. 1–viii. 3, for Philip was associated with Stephen in administration and ministry. About the same time Luke lodged with a Cypriot named Mnason who is described as an early[2] disciple (Acts xxi. 16). In addition to all these there was Mark's uncle Barnabas who was well known at Antioch, and if Luke was a native there, would be well known to him, but in any case Paul would have been able to tell Luke about Barnabas' part in early Christian history. By direct contact with all these Christians named above, with the rest of Paul's close circle of friends, such as Silas, Titus, Timothy,

---

[1] Among those who have strongly favoured this theory may be mentioned F. H. Chase, *The Credibility of the Book of the Acts of the Apostles* (1902), pp. 19 ff.; R. B. Rackham, *The Acts of the Apostles* (1901), pp. xli ff.; F. F. Bruce, *The Acts of the Apostles* (Greek Text)[2] (1952), pp. 21 ff. J. V. Bartlet (*The Acts*, CB, 1901, p. 22) mentions that after several years' careful study of Acts he abandoned the idea of written sources and resorted to the theory that Luke made notes from eyewitnesses.

[2] The word ἀρχαῖος means 'original', suggesting that Mnason was one of the earliest disciples.

Tychicus, and with a great number of unnamed eyewitnesses,[1] Luke could have obtained all the data he needed for his history.

In spite of the reasonable character of these conjectures many scholars have rejected them in favour of written sources. Those who reject the Lucan authorship of the whole book have no alternative, if they are to maintain any basic historical material in the narrative. Yet there is no need to exclude personal reminiscences from theories of written sources, if these are granted to be based on authentic material. On the other hand, some of the advocates of the following theories admit Lucan authorship, but are not satisfied with a purely oral theory of sources.

(ii) *A combination of written and oral sources.* Since the subject-matter of the book of Acts divides naturally into two parts, focused respectively on the two great personalities of Peter and Paul, it is not surprising that theories have been proposed which combine a written source for the first part with an oral or personal source for the second.[2] B. Weiss[3] noted that the first part was more Hebraistic than the second part and therefore proposed that this first part was derived from a Jewish-Christian history of the primitive Church up to the Council of Jerusalem. This idea of an original Hebrew or Aramaic source has received an impetus through the work of C. C. Torrey,[4] who considered that

[1] A recent Roman Catholic writer, A. Hastings (*Prophet and Witness in Jerusalem*, 1958, pp. 26 ff.), suggests that among these eyewitnesses were Simeon of Cyrene (whom he identifies with Simeon the Black in Acts xiii. 1) and Joanna, the wife of Chuza, Herod's steward, from whom he suggests that Luke may have obtained information about Herod (some of which is not recorded in the other Synoptic Gospels). W. Michaelis (*Einleitung*, pp. 131 f.) suggested that some of the eyewitnesses may have made written notes, or even that some churches may have preserved written notes of their past history. This would approximate to some of the theories of written sources considered below. It is not altogether improbable that Luke had access to the original letter (or copy) mentioned in Acts xv. 23 ff.

[2] E. Barnikol ('Das Fehlen der Taufe in den Quellenschriften der Apostelgeschichte und in den Urgemeinden der Hebräer und Hellenisten', in *Wissenschaftliche Zeitschrift der Martin-Luther-Universität Halle-Wittenberg*, VI, 4, 1957, pp. 593–610) holds that Luke uses two sources, a Peter-Philip source and a we-source, but that he adapted both to his own views, especially on baptism.

[3] *Manual Introduction to the New Testament* (Eng. Tr.), II, 1888, pp. 332 ff.

[4] *The Composition and Date of Acts* (*Harvard Theological Studies*, I, 1916). Cf. also idem, *Documents of the Primitive Church* (1941), pp. 112–148; *ZNTW*, 44 (1952–53), pp. 205–223. This view is supported by W. J. Wilson, *HTR*, 11

many of the difficulties in Acts i–xv are solved if they are regarded as mistranslations of Semitisms. This view has been contested,[1] although it has gained some support in a modified form.[2]

Closely linked with this type of theory is the view that the first part of Acts was originally a continuation of Mark's Gospel written by Mark but taken over and adapted by Luke.[3] Or else that Luke was in possession of the Gospel when writing Acts and either consciously or unconsciously assimilated the apostles' actions to those of Jesus.[4] The main difficulty of any theory which rests on the supposition of greater Aramaic influence in one part than in another is the general stylistic and linguistic unity of the whole. If, of course, Luke fashioned his sources and conformed them to his own style, the phenomenon may be admissible. At the same time M. Black does not think the Aramaisms are sufficient to prove an Aramaic source,[5] although he admits the possibility in the speeches of Peter and Stephen.

(iii) *A combination of duplicate sources*. The main advocate for the theory that in the first part of Acts two parallel sources were used was A.

(1918), pp. 74–99, 322–335 and more recently and more tentatively by M. Black, *An Aramaic Approach to the Gospels and Acts* (1946), p. 207. Cf. also G. Kittel, *Die Probleme des palästinnischen Spätjudentums und das Urchristentum* (1926), pp. 56–58.

[1] Cf. the criticisms and modifications of F. J. Foakes Jackson, *HTR*, 10 (1917), pp. 325–361; F. C. Burkitt, *JTS*, xx (1919), pp. 320–329; H. J. Cadbury, *AJTh*, 34 (1920), pp. 436–450 and E. J. Goodspeed, *JBL*, xxxix (1920), pp. 83–101. It has been pointed out by H. F. D. Sparks that the influence of the lxx on Luke should be set against the Semitisms (*JTS*, xliv, 1943, pp. 129–138; *idem*, n.s., i, 1950, pp. 16–28; *idem*, Bulletin of *Studiorum Novi Testamenti Societas*, ii, 1951, pp. 33–42). Cf. also A. W. Argyle, *JTS*, n.s., iv (1953), pp. 213 f.

[2] W. L. Knox (*Some Hellenistic Elements in Primitive Christianity*, 1944, p. 7; *idem*, *The Acts of the Apostles*, 1948, pp. 18 f.) restricted the possible Aramaic source to i. 2–v. 16. J. de Zwaan (*The Beginnings of Christianity*, ii, pp. 44 ff.) similarly with the addition of ix. 31–xi. 18. C. H. Dodd (*The Apostolic Preaching and its Developments²*, 1944, p. 20) agrees with these modifications.

[3] Cf. L. Dieu, *RB*, xxix (1920), pp. 555–569; xxx (1921), pp. 86–96. Cf. also F. C. Burkitt, *Christian Beginnings* (1924), p. 83. A. E. Haefner has recently revived this type of theory and has professed to find a bridge between Mk. xvi. 8 and Acts iii. 1 ff. (which he considers a continuation of Mark, cf. Harnack's views) in Acts i. 13, 14 (*JBL*, lxxvii, 1958, pp. 67–71). But his arguments are highly conjectural.

[4] So C. S. C. Williams, *ET*, lxiv (1952–53), pp. 283 f.; *idem*, *The Acts of the Apostles* (1957), pp. 12, 13.

[5] *Op. cit.*, p. 207. Some of Luke's oral traditions may, of course, have been transmitted to him in an Aramaic form (cf. Michaelis, *Einleitung*, p. 133).

Harnack.[1] The following is a summary of his proposals, A and B standing for the two distinct sources: i, ii (B), iii. 1–v. 16 (A), v. 17–42 (B), vi. 1–viii. 4 (a Jerusalem-Antiochene source), viii. 5–40 (A), ix. 1–30 (Paul's conversion source), ix. 31–xi. 18 (A), xi. 19–30 (a Jerusalem-Antiochene source), xii. 1–23 (A), xii. 25–xv. 35 (a Jerusalem-Antiochene source). The basis of Harnack's differentiation between these sources was mainly on supposed differences of narratives, inaccuracies and even contradictions. Thus he found much material in his B source which he thought was a doublet from his A source (e.g. the accounts of the outpouring of the Spirit in Acts ii and iv) and he therefore concluded that the B material was historically useless. Most of the A source was derived from good Jerusalem tradition, although some parts seem connected with Caesarea (e.g. viii. 8–40, ix. 29–xi. 18 and xii. 1–24).

Harnack's theory, with various modifications, has had a wide vogue among scholars who have shared his presuppositions,[2] but with the recent diminution of attention paid to minute problems of sources, and a lessening also of inclination to attribute every apparent difference to a different written source, its influence has definitely waned. Its basis has been strongly criticized by J. Jeremias[3] on the grounds that the doublets are capable of an alternative explanation, which is true of most cases of alleged duplicate narratives in biblical criticism. Accord-

---

[1] *Die Apostelgeschichte* (1908), pp. 131–188. This type of theory was first proposed by F. Spitta, *Die Apostelgeschichte, ihre Quellen und deren geschichtlicher Wert* (1891).

[2] Cf. F. J. Foakes Jackson and K. Lake, *The Beginnings of Christianity*, II (1922), pp. 137–157. Cf. also M. Goguel, *Introduction au Nouveau Testament*, III (1922), pp. 172 ff. More recently, H. W. Beyer (*Die Apostelgeschichte*[9], 1959, pp. 15 ff. and pp. 28 ff.) still shows the influence of Harnack's theory, and it forms the basis of A. Q. Morton and G. H. C. Macgregor's mathematical hypothesis of the structure of the Acts. Cf. *The Structure of Luke and Acts* (1964), pp. 34 ff. Cf. J. Dupont (*Les Sources du Livre des Actes*, 1960, pp. 40 ff.) for information on Harnack's influence.

[3] *ZNTW*, 36 (1937), pp. 205–221. With regard to the two accounts of the apostles' appearance before the Sanhedrin in Acts iv. 5–22, v. 21b–41, Jeremias suggests that the first was for legal warning which was necessary before legal action could be taken. The idea was hinted at by K. Bornhäuser, *Studien zur Apostelgeschichte* (1934), p. 58, and has since been favoured by W. G. Kümmel (*TR*, 14, 1942, p. 169), but has been rejected by Bo Reicke, *Glaube und Leben der Urgemeinde* (1957), pp. 108–110, and E. Haenchen, *Die Apostelgeschichte*, pp. 209 ff., on the ground that the warning would have been given privately before two witnesses.

ing to Jeremias the accounts are complementary and not repetitive. It is a sound principle of criticism, which has been too little observed, that where an explanation based on the text as it stands is possible, that is to be preferred to conjectures based on alleged contradictions. By this canon Harnack's theory must be considered unjustified.

(iv) *A combination of complementary sources.* Not all who believe that more than one source lies behind the first part of Acts adhere to Harnack's theory, either in its contents or in its principles of criticism. Setting aside the idea of duplicate sources, some scholars have nevertheless found several sources which have been amalgamated to form the first part of the book. The main theories of this type to be noted are those of L. Cerfaux and E. Trocmé. The former[1] conceives of a basic descriptive document comprising ii. 41–v. 40, to which are added several other groups of tradition, some Galilaean, some Caesarean and one described as a 'Hellenistic dossier'; some are written, some oral.[2]

Trocmé[3] expounds a theory very similar, with chapters iii–v regarded as based on a homogeneous document, which Luke has adapted and expanded. In addition, other documents were used, one for the geographical material in chapter ii, another for the discourses, another, a Hellenistic source, for vi. 1–7 and so on. Luke, according to this theory, had at his disposal a number of sources, many of them small traditional fragments, which he has welded into a whole. Once again the multiplication of written sources tends to lessen the credibility of the theories.[4] Nevertheless, if such theories as these are true, they can only enhance our admiration for the literary skill of Luke in editing them into such an apparent unity.

(v) *The Antiochene source theory.* Most of the theories already considered have in different ways acknowledged indebtedness to Antioch as a source of information regarding the primitive Church. But some

---

[1] *ETL*, 13 (1936), pp. 667–691 (reproduced in *Recueil Lucien Cerfaux*, 1954, pp. 63–91).

[2] In his later work Cerfaux himself is far less confident about the possibility of fixing the limits of written sources other than the we-sections. Cf. *ETL*, 16 (1939), pp. 5–31, reproduced in *Recueil Lucien Cerfaux*, Tome II (1954), pp. 125–156; *idem*, in Robert-Feuillet's *Introduction* (1959), pp. 349 ff.

[3] *Le 'Livre des Actes' et L'Histoire*, pp. 154–214.

[4] P. Benoit (*Biblica*, XL, 1959, pp. 778–792) speaks of a criss-crossing of Palestinian, Pauline and Antiochene traditions, but the difficulties of unravelling these with any certainty will at once be apparent.

scholars have made an Antiochene written source the main feature of their theories. Many have advocated it,[1] but there is no necessity to mention more than the two most recent advocates. J. Jeremias[2] begins with Acts vi. 1 and decides that certain portions are superimposed. When these are eliminated what is left is an Antiochene source comprising vi. 1–viii. 4, ix. 1–30, xi. 19–30, xii. 25–xiv. 28, xv. 35 ff. But the case for a homogeneous source is not given a convincing basis by a rather arbitrary elimination of all heterogeneous elements. Moreover, it is difficult to believe that a source began at vi. 1 without some indication of the previous history of the Jerusalem church.[3] One of the very doubtful consequences of Jeremias' theory is the placing of the apostolic Council before the first missionary journey.

R. Bultmann[4] acknowledges indebtedness to both Harnack and Jeremias but differs from both in the constitution of his Antiochene source, supposing that the source is prolonged into chapter xvi, perhaps to xxviii, but is partial only in xiii and xiv. At the same time he seems to envisage two documents, both of which were connected with the Antiochene church and were, perhaps, found in its archives. This theory presupposes that the Antiochene church had composed a kind of chronicle of their earlier history, a not impossible procedure in spite of Haenchen's[5] objection that the Christians would not have thought of writing for a future generation.

(vi) *The 'itinerary' theory.* Largely owing to the influence of form criticism there has arisen a school of thought which does not consider it possible to locate sources for the first part of Acts. In this part the attention is focused on small units in which the tradition circulated before becoming fixed in the Acts narrative. Interest in sources is

[1] E.g. H. H. Wendt, *ZNTW*, 24 (1925), pp. 293–305. He had expressed the idea in his *Die Apostelgeschichte*[8] (1899) before Harnack's work appeared. Cf. also J. Weiss, 'Das Judenchristentum in der Apostelgeschichte und das sogennante Apostelkonzil', *TSK*, 3 (1893), pp. 480–540. For an English advocate, compare J. A. Findlay, *The Acts of the Apostles*[2] (1936), pp. 50 f.

[2] *ZNTW*, 36 (1937), pp. 205–221.

[3] W. Grundmann saw this difficulty and suggested that the source must have begun with such an account (*ZNTW*, 38, 1939, pp. 45–73). But in this case, Luke must have used an inferior substitute in his account of the earlier history, which is improbable.

[4] 'Zur Frage nach den Quellen der Apostelgeschichte' in *New Testament Essays: Studies in Memory of T. W. Manson* (ed. A. J. B. Higgins, 1959), pp. 68–80.

[5] *Op. cit.*, pp. 75, 76.

therefore concentrated on the second part particularly (xiii. 4–xiv. 28, xvi. 1–xxi. 26), where Paul's journeys are then traced to an 'itinerary source'. This is the position of Dibelius.[1] The idea of an itinerary source is not new, since the 'we-sections' would naturally suggest this possibility, particularly if the author of Acts is not considered to be a companion of Paul. But Dibelius does not tie his source to the we-passages, and explains the latter as a simple device by which Luke indicates his presence with Paul. In this way Dibelius' view seems somewhat akin to the first theory mentioned, that of personal information, but the fundamental difference is that Dibelius does not consider the occurrence of the 'we' to be an indication of the source of Luke's account. It is important to him, nevertheless, to isolate the source, and he does this by maintaining that some non-edificatory material has been used and that certain incoherences are apparent, both of which, he thinks, point to a source rather than to personal reminiscences or local traditions.[2] In an attempt to explain the usefulness of an 'itinerary document', Dibelius suggests that it might have served a useful purpose if the same journey had to be repeated.[3] But the unconvincing character of this suggestion gives the measure of the difficulty of finding an adequate motive, for it is inconceivable that Paul would have needed an 'itinerary' to remind him where he had been, especially in the case of places where he had established churches.

It will be seen that the only justification for this theory is the claim that it accounts for a series of insignificant details and supposed discrepancies. But if Luke is the author, as Dibelius himself strongly held,[4] it is difficult to see what advantage is gained by attributing these to Luke's editorial processes rather than to his personal recollections. At least, the discrepancies are a matter of interpretation[5] and may be

[1] Dibelius expressed his opinions in a number of essays from 1923 to 1947 and these were conveniently collected in his *Aufsätze zur Apostelgeschichte* (1951), Eng. Tr. by Mary Ling, *Studies in the Acts of the Apostles* (1956). The references are to the English edition (cf. pp. 104 ff.). Cf. also Dibelius' article in *TR*, n.f., 3 (1931), pp. 233–241 on the form-historical problem in the Acts of the Apostles.

[2] Cf. the reasons stated and the conclusions drawn in his latest essay, *Studies in the Acts of the Apostles*, pp. 196 ff.

[3] *Ibid.*, p. 199.   [4] Cf., for example, *ibid.*, pp. 135 ff.

[5] To consider one instance cited by Dibelius, Acts xiv. 8–18 is said to be an insertion, because verses 6 and 7 have already mentioned the apostle at Lystra and Derbe, whereas verse 8 returns to an incident at Lystra (*ibid.*, p. 198). But verses 6, 7 give a general summary of the whole work in Lycaonia. Could not Luke have paused then to cite the most striking incidents during this part of the

otherwise explained, and the mention of insignificant details is of the very warp and woof of personal narrative.[1]

(vii) *The fiction theory.* In varying degrees many hypotheses have attributed the whole or part of Acts to the literary ingenuity of a fiction writer. It has already been remarked that the we-sections are supposed by some scholars to be a fictitious device. But the idea that the whole itinerary is a fiction is not without recent advocates. The most notable is G. Schille,[2] who conceives that the sections which give information regarding Paul's journeys, consisting of four geographical blocks (xiii–xiv, xvi–xviii, xix–xx and xxi ff.), are simply a literary fiction. The narratives are, moreover, said to be strewn with errors which prove that the author had no source at his disposal. Schille concedes that Luke may have possessed some traditions, but the itinerary imposed upon them is his own composition. In fact, in disposing of Dibelius' itinerary theory, Schille seems to land himself in scepticism regarding the historicity of Acts, for he suggests that the itinerary in Acts is more in line with the missionary policy reflected in the *Didache* than with that of the apostolic age, not recognizing that the *Didache*, with its advice to stay only a day or so at one place, does not deal with the problem of the longer time needed for the establishment of churches.

(viii) *The theories of successive redactions.* In common with other New Testament books, Acts has been subjected to a series of redactional hypotheses. Many of those already mentioned depend on redactional processes, but a type of theory not so far included is that of H. Sahlin[3] which conceives of the process of publication for Luke-Acts in three stages: (1) a Jewish-Christian writing comprising Luke i. 5–Acts xv. 41,

---

journey, which happened at Lystra? Another example is the omission of any reference to the earthquake at Philippi after the conversion of the gaoler in Acts xvi. 35 ff., but the account is obviously much abridged and the earthquake motive would not have added anything to the story of Paul's release.

[1] A. D. Nock (*Gnomon*, xxv, 1953, pp. 597 ff.), while adhering in general to an 'itinerary' hypothesis, has criticized Dibelius on the grounds that the passages without edificatory purpose are inserted for literary reasons to give the reader time to relax from the main action of the narrative.

[2] *ThLZ*, 84 (1959), cols. 165–174. For a criticism of Schille's views, cf. J. Dupont, *Les Sources du Livre des Actes* (1960), p. 149. Cf. also E. Haenchen, *op. cit.*, pp. 14*, 15*.

[3] *Der Messias und das Gottesvolk. Studien zur proto-lukanischen Theologie*, pp. 11–18. Cf. also P. H. Menoud, 'Remarques sur les textes de l'ascension dans Luc-Actes', *Neutestamentliche Studien für R. Bultmann* (1954), pp. 148–156.

part Hebrew and part Aramaic; (2) a Greek revision and adaptation of this for Paul's trial, perhaps by Luke himself; (3) a later editorial process which divided it into two by the addition of a conclusion to Luke and an introduction to Acts. That there may have been stages in the preparation of the manuscript cannot be denied, but any theory based on redactional processes is bound to be very largely conjectural. In this case, the difficulty of conceiving a scroll of sufficient length to accommodate Luke-Acts is against the theory. It is more natural to suppose that the whole work was originally in two parts on separate scrolls of similar length.[1]

From this brief survey two facts stand out. Attempts to isolate the sources which Luke has used have not been successful, and it is questionable whether any further progress in this direction is likely to be made. This means that the idea of assuming Luke's personal knowledge of the events, either from his own observations or from direct eyewitnesses, is as credible as any, and much more credible than most, of the alternative suggestions.

VI. THE TEXT

One of the most interesting problems in textual criticism concerns the original form of the book of Acts. A discussion of the problem lies beyond the scope of this Introduction[2] and no more than the briefest explanation can be included here. The 'Western'[3] Text of Acts differs so considerably from the other early texts that it has posed the question of whether there were in fact two editions. It was F. Blass[4] who suggested that Luke himself prepared two editions, but his views on this have not won much support.[5] A. C. Clark[6] was pre-

---

[1] Cf. Feine-Behm-Kümmel, *Einleitung*, p. 99.

[2] For a useful survey of literature on this subject, cf. E. Trocmé, *Le 'Livre des Actes' et l'Histoire*, pp. 20–37. Cf. also C. S. C. Williams' Study, *Alterations to the Text of the Synoptic Gospels and Acts, 1951*, pp. 54–82.

[3] The chief witness for this text is a fifth-century MS, Codex Bezae (D).

[4] Fr. Blass, 'Die Textüberlieferung in der Apostelgeschichte', *TSK*, 67 (1894), pp. 86–119. Zahn argued for the same view in *Die Urausgabe der Apostelgeschichte des Lukas* (1916), pp. 1–10.

[5] Haenchen suggests a common author is highly improbable since the two texts often contradict one another (*Die Apostelgeschichte*, p. 48). F. Kenyon's criticism (*The Text of the Greek Bible²*, 1949, pp. 232, 233) mainly concerns the difficulty of finding an adequate motive for many of the alterations.

[6] *The Primitive Text of the Gospels and Acts* (1914). Idem, *The Acts of the Apostles* (1933), pp. xlix ff., 374–376.

pared to argue that the 'Western Text' is more original than the generally accepted text, which he considered to be an edited form. But this idea has gained even less support.[1] The opposite view, that the 'Western Text' forms a deviation from the original text, is much more probable.

A mediating proposal, which amounts to a modification of Blass's theory, is that Luke made several drafts in the successive processes of revision and that some of the earlier drafts may have been circulated and may have formed the basis of the 'Western Text', while the more authoritative form of text became the basis of the 'Alexandrian' and other types of texts.[2] It is possible that the author himself never quite finished the work of editing.

The opinion of such an authority as Sir Frederick Kenyon[3] is that, unless future discoveries supply further data which enable the critic to reach a solution to the problem of the text, 'the problem must be solved according to the intrinsic probabilities of the methods of insertion or excision'. Since the 'Western Text' of Acts is longer than the Alexandrian Text, Kenyon feels that probability is against the insertions of the former, and this is where the matter must perhaps rest for the present.

Attempts to explain the history of the 'Western Text' by an appeal to the processes of translation from an Aramaic document have been made, notably by C. C. Torrey[4] who maintained that an Aramaic version of the original Greek text was produced with the special intention of commending Luke-Acts to Jewish readers. Torrey held that many of the modifications in the Western Text may be explained as insertions to make the text more acceptable to such readers.[5]

VII. LANGUAGE

In the sections dealing with sources and with textual tradition mention was made of the theory of an Aramaic source used for the early part of Acts. C. C. Torrey's theory (see pp. 337 f.) has not won general support. It has been criticized on the grounds that many of Torrey's

---

[1] Cf. Kenyon's criticisms, *op. cit.*, pp. 234 ff. J. H. Ropes, *The Beginnings of Christianity* (1926), III, pp. ccxv–ccxlvi, maintained that the 'Western Text' was a later edited text.

[2] Cf. R. B. Rackham, *op. cit.*, p. xxvi.　　　　[3] *Op. cit.*, p. 236.

[4] *Documents of the Primitive Church* (1941), pp. 112–148.　　[5] *Ibid.*, pp. 127 ff.

Aramaisms can be shown to be Septuagintalisms.[1] There can be no doubt that Luke was very well acquainted with the Septuagint, but apart from this the *Koiné* Greek tended to be charged with Semitisms in the eastern district.[2]

One of the peculiarities of Luke to which attention has recently been drawn is his tendency towards certain rhythmic qualities of language, particularly to a love for doubling. R. Morgenthaler[3] has compiled a mass of impressive lists of instances in which Luke has doubled isolated words, full sentences, and whole sections, while this doubling even affects the conception of the entire work. It is built up on the principle of pairs. There is no doubt that Morgenthaler has overdone his examples, for which he has been criticized,[4] but when due allowance has been made for his too confident claims enough evidence still remains to demonstrate without question Luke's love of doubling. This is part of his artistic equipment.

Luke's style is good but not particularly literary. It is rather of a good conversational type. It would have been readily understood by any readers of general intelligence. It was, therefore, admirably adapted to his purpose.

[1] Cf. H. F. D. Sparks, 'The Semitisms of Acts', *JTS*, n.s., 1 (1950), pp. 16–28. Also E. Jacquier (*Les Actes des Apôtres*[2], 1926, p. cxvii), who called Luke's language 'sacred prose'.

[2] Cf. the comments on this by L. Cerfaux, 'Les Actes des Apôtres' in Robert-Feuillet's *Introduction*, II, p. 372.

[3] *Die lukanische Geschichtsschreibung als Zeugnis* (1949). This work is in two volumes, of which the first deals with the form and the second with the content of Luke-Acts. The idea of Luke's rhythmic style was earlier suggested by A. Loisy, *Les Actes des Apôtres* (1925), p. 302.

[4] Cf. the comments of W. G. Kümmel in *TR*, n.f., 22 (1954), pp. 197 ff. Others who have criticized the theory are E. Käsemann, *Verkündigung und Forschungen* (1950–51), pp. 219 ff.; H. Conzelmann, *ThZ*, IX (1953), pp. 304 ff., and C. K. Barrett, *Luke the Historian in Recent Study* (1961), pp. 36 ff. But Trocmé (*op. cit.*, p. 17) considers that Morgenthaler's theory is worthy of consideration.

CONTENTS

I. PROLOGUE (i. 1–5)
In this prologue Luke connects this book with his former book.

II. INITIAL EVENTS (i. 6–26)
The ascension (i. 6–12). The disciples gather in the upper room and elect a successor to Judas Iscariot (i. 13–26).

III. THE BIRTH OF THE CHURCH IN JERUSALEM (ii. 1–v. 42)
The day of Pentecost (ii. 1–47): the Spirit's descent; Peter's sermon; the first believers. A lame man healed in the temple; the arrest and return of Peter and John (iii. 1–iv. 31). An experiment in community living; contrast in giving between Barnabas and Ananias and Sapphira (iv. 32–v. 11). Healings and a further clash with the authorities (v. 12–42).

IV. THE BEGINNING OF PERSECUTION (vi. 1–ix. 31)
The work, trial and martyrdom of Stephen, followed by general persecution (vi. 1–viii. 3). The work of Philip in Samaria; his leading of the Ethiopian to Christ (viii. 4–40). The conversion of Saul; his return to Jerusalem; general prosperity of the church (ix. 1–31).

V. THE SPREAD OF CHRISTIANITY TO THE GENTILES (ix. 32–xii. 25)
Peter's healing of Aeneas at Lydda and raising of Dorcas at Joppa (ix. 32–43). The conversion of Cornelius; Peter's defence before the Jerusalem Christians, and their acceptance of the inclusion of the Gentiles (x. 1–xi. 18). Developments at Antioch; Barnabas is sent from Jerusalem and Saul brought from Tarsus; famine relief is organized (xi. 19–30). Persecution under Herod: James is killed; Peter's arrest and escape; the death of Herod, and progress in the Church (xii. 1–25).

VI. THE FIRST MISSIONARY JOURNEY (xiii. 1–xv. 41)
The setting apart of Barnabas and Saul (xiii. 1–3). The work in Cyprus; Sergius Paulus converted; the resistance of Elymas (xiii. 4–12). The work in Pisidian Antioch (xiii. 13–52). The work in other cities—

Iconium, Lystra, Derbe—and return to Antioch (xiv. 1–28). The Jerusalem Council (xv. 1–29). The letter delivered to the church at Antioch; plans for a return visit to the churches established on the first journey, and disagreement over Mark (xv. 30–41).

VII. THE SECOND MISSIONARY JOURNEY (xvi. 1–xviii. 23)

Timothy joins Paul on the return visit to Lystra (xvi. 1–5). Fresh horizons: work in Europe—the call to Macedonia and journey to Philippi (xvi. 6–12). Work in Philippi (xvi. 13–40). Work in Thessalonica and Berea (xvii. 1–14). Paul at Athens (xvii. 15–34).Work in Corinth (xviii. 1–17). A brief visit to Palestine and Antioch (xviii. 18–23).

VIII. THE THIRD MISSIONARY JOURNEY (xviii. 24–xx. 6)

Extensive work in Ephesus (xviii. 24–xix. 20). Second visit planned to Macedonia and Greece (xix. 21, 22). The riot at Ephesus and Paul's departure (xix. 23–xx. 1). Further work in Macedonia and Greece (xx. 2–6).

IX. JOURNEY TO JERUSALEM (xx. 7–xxi. 17)

At Troas: the incident over Eutychus (xx. 7–12). Paul's journey to Miletus, and his address to the Ephesian elders there (xx. 13–38). Brief visit to Tyre (xxi. 1–6). Events at Caesarea: Agabus' prophecy (xxi. 7–14). Arrival at Jerusalem (xxi. 15–17).

X. PAUL IN JERUSALEM (xxi. 18–xxiii. 35)

Events leading to his arrest and appearance before the Sanhedrin (xxi. 18–xxii. 29). Paul before the Sanhedrin (xxii. 30–xxiii. 10). Paul sent to Felix by Lysias (xxiii. 11–35).

XI. PAUL BEFORE FELIX, FESTUS AND AGRIPPA AT CAESAREA (xxiv. 1–xxvi. 32)

Accusation and defence before Felix (xxiv. 1–27). Investigation by Festus (xxv. 1–12). Hearing before Agrippa (xxv. 13–xxvi. 32).

XII. THE JOURNEY TO ROME (xxvii. 1–xxviii. 31)

The account of the voyage and the shipwreck (xxvii. 1–44). Hospitality at Malta, where Paul escapes death from a viper and performs many healings (xxviii. 1–10). Paul arrives in Rome and remains under house arrest, preaching and teaching (xxviii. 11–31).

GENERAL BIBLIOGRAPHY

Abbott, E. A., Peabody, A. P. and Lightfoot, J. B. *The Fourth Gospel*, 1892.

Abbott, E. A. *Corrections of Mark*, 1901.

Abbott, E. A. *Johannine Vocabulary*, 1905.

Abbott, E. A. *Johannine Grammar*, 1906.

Abrahams, I. *Studies in Pharisaism and the Gospels*, I, 1917.

Adeney, W. F. *St. Luke (CB)*,[2] 1922.

Aland, K., Eltester, W. and Klostermann, E., editors, *Studia Evangelica*, 1959.

Albertz, M. *Die synoptischen Streitgespräche*, 1921.

Albertz, M. *Die Botschaft des Neuen Testament*, I, 1947, II, 1952.

Alexander, J. A. *A commentary on the Gospel of Mark*, r.p. 1960.

Alford, H. *Greek Testament*,[6] 1868.

Allen, W. C. *The Gospel according to St. Mark*, 1915.

Allen, W. C. *The Gospel according to St. Matthew (ICC)*, 1907.

Allen, W. C. and Grensted, L. W. *Introduction to the Books of the New Testament*, 1918.

Arndt, W. F. *The Gospel according to St. Luke*, 1956.

Askwith, E. H. *The Historical Value of the Fourth Gospel*, 1910.

Bacon, B. W. *Introduction to the New Testament*, 1900.

Bacon, B. W. *Is Mark a Roman Gospel?*, 1919.

Bacon, B. W. *The Fourth Gospel in Research and Debate*,[2] 1918.

Bacon, B. W. *The Gospel of Mark: its Composition and Date*, 1925.

Bacon, B. W. *Studies in Matthew*, 1930.

Bacon, B. W. *The Gospel of the Hellenists*, 1933.

Bailey, J. A. *The Traditions common to the Gospels of Luke and John*, 1963.

Baillie, D. M. *God was in Christ*,[2] 1955.

Baldensperger, W. *Die Prolog des vierten Evangeliums*, 1898.

Balmforth, H. *The Gospel according to St. Luke (Clar B)*, 1930.

Barr, A. *A Diagram of Synoptic Relationships*, 1938.

Barrett, C. K. *The Holy Spirit and the Gospel Tradition*, 1947.

Barrett, C. K. *The Gospel according to St. John*, 1956.

Barrett, C. K. *Luke the Historian in Recent Study*, 1961.

Bartlet, J. V. *The Acts (CB)*, 1901.

Bartlet, J. V. *St. Mark (CB)*, 1922.

Bartsch, H. W., editor, *Kerygma und Mythos*, 1948–55.

Bauer, W. *Das Johannesevangelium (LHB)*,[2] 1925.

Beare, F. W. *The Earliest Records of Jesus*, 1962.

Beasley-Murray, G. R. *Jesus and the Future*, 1954.

Beasley-Murray, G. R. *Preaching the Gospel from the Gospels*, 1956.

Beasley-Murray, G. R. *A Commentary on Mark Thirteen*, 1957.

Becker, H. *Die Reden des Johannesevangeliums und der Stil der gnostischen Offen-barungsreden*, 1956.

Behler, G.-M. *Les Paroles d'adieux du Seigneur*, 1960.

Bernard, J. H. *The Gospel according to St. John* (*ICC*), 1928.

Beyer, H. W. *Die Apostelgeschichte* (*NTD*),[9] 1959.

Black, M. *An Aramaic Approach to the Gospels and Acts*,[2] 1954.

Black, M. *The Scrolls and Christian Origins*, 1961.

Blackman, E. C. *Marcion and his Influence*, 1948.

Blaiklock, E. M. *The Acts of the Apostles* (*TNT*), 1959.

Blair, E. P. *Jesus in the Gospel of Matthew*, 1960.

Blass, F. *Philology of the Gospels*, 1898.

Blunt, A. W. F. *The Acts of the Apostles* (*Clar B*), 1923.

Blunt, A. W. F. *The Gospel according to St. Mark* (*Clar B*), 1929.

Boman, T. *Hebrew Thought compared with Greek*, 1960.

Boobyer, G. H. *St. Mark and the Transfiguration Story*, 1942.

Bornhäuser, K. *Das Johannesevangelium eine Missionsschrift für Israel*, 1928.

Bornhäuser, K. *Studien zum Sondergut des Lukas*, 1934.

Bornhäuser, K. *Studien zur Apostelgeschichte*, 1934.

Bornkamm, G. *Jesus of Nazareth*, 1960 (Eng. Tr. from German edition, 1956).

Bornkamm, G., Barth, G. and Held, H. J. *Tradition and Interpretation in Matthew*, 1963 (Eng. Tr. from German edition, 1960).

Box, G. H. *St. Matthew* (*CB*), 1922.

Brandon, S. G. F. *The Fall of Jerusalem and the Christian Church*,[2] 1957.

Branscombe, B. H. *The Gospel of Mark* (*MC*), 1937.

Braun, F.-M. *Jean le Théologien* (*EB*), 1959.

Briggs, C. A. *The Messiah of the Gospels*, 1895.

Browning, W. R. F. *The Gospel according to St. Luke* (*TC*), 1960.

Bruce, A. B. *The Synoptic Gospels* (*EGT*), 1907.

Bruce, F. F. *The Speeches in the Acts of the Apostles*, 1944.

Bruce, F. F. *The Spreading Flame*, 1958.

Bruce, F. F. *The Acts of the Apostles* (Greek text),[2] 1952.

Bruce, F. F. *Commentary on the Book of Acts* (*NLC*), 1954.

Bruce, F. F., editor, *Promise and Fulfilment, Essays presented to S. H. Hooke*, 1963.

Bultmann, R. *Primitive Christianity in its Contemporary Setting*, 1956.

Bultmann, R. *Theology of the New Testament* (Eng. Tr.), I, 1952, II, 1955.

Bultmann, R. *Das Evangelium des Johannes* (*KEK*),[13] 1953.

Bultmann, R. *The History of the Synoptic Tradition* (Eng. Tr. by J. Marsh), 1963, from the 3rd German edition, 1958.

Bultmann, R. and Kundsin, K. *Form Criticism* (Eng. Tr. by F. C. Grant),[2] 1962.

Bundy, W. E. *Jesus and the First Three Gospels*, 1955.
Burch, V. *The Structure and Message of St. John's Gospel*, 1928.
Burgon, J. W. *The Last Twelve Verses of the Gospel according to St. Mark vindicated against recent objectors and established*, 1871.
Burkill, T. A. *The Injunctions to Silence in Mark's Gospel*, 1956.
Burkill, T. A. *The notion of miracle with special reference to St. Mark's Gospel*, 1959.
Burkill, T. A. *Mysterious Revelation: An examination of the Philosophy of Mark's Gospel*, 1963.
Burkitt, F. C. *The Gospel History and its Transmission*,[3] 1911.
Burkitt, F. C. *The Earliest Sources for the Life of Jesus*,[2] 1922.
Burkitt, F. C. *Christian Beginnings*, 1924.
Burney, C. F. *The Aramaic Origin of the Fourth Gospel*, 1922.
Burney, C. F. *The Poetry of our Lord*, 1925.
Burton, H. *The Gospel according to St. Luke (Exp. Bib.)*, 1909.
Bussmann, W. *Synoptische Studien*, I, 1925, II, 1929, III, 1931.
Butler, B. C. *The Originality of Matthew*, 1951.

Cadbury, H. J. *The Style and Literary Method of Luke (HTS)*, 1919, 1920.
Cadbury, H. J. *The Book of Acts in history*, 1955.
Cadbury, H. J. *The Making of Luke-Acts*,[2] 1958.
Cadoux, A. T. *The Sources of the Second Gospel*, 1935.
Caird, G. B. *Saint Luke (PelC)*, 1963.
Campenhausen, H. von, *Kirchliches Amt und geistliche Vollmacht*, 1953.
Carpenter, S. C. *Christianity according to St. Luke*, 1919.
Carrington, P. *The Primitive Christian Calendar*, 1952.
Carrington, P. *According to Mark*, 1960.
Carter, C. W. and Earle, R. *The Acts of the Apostles*, 1959.
Cerfaux, L. *Recueil Lucien Cerfaux*, 1954.
Cerfaux, L. and Dupont, J. *Les Actes des Apôtres*,[2] 1958.
Chadwick, G. A. *The Gospel according to St. Mark (Exp. Bib.)*,[6] 1896.
Chapman, J. *Matthew, Mark and Luke*, 1937.
Charnwood, Lord *According to St. John*, 1925.
Chase, F. H. *The Credibility of the Book of the Acts of the Apostles*, 1902.
Clark, A. C. *The Primitive Text of the Gospels and the Acts*, 1914.
Clark, A. C. *The Acts of the Apostles*, 1933.
Clogg, F. B. *Introduction to the New Testament*,[3] 1948.
Cole, A. *The Gospel according to St. Mark (TNT)*, 1961.
Colwell, E. C. *The Greek of the Fourth Gospel*, 1931.
Conzelmann, H. *Die Apostelgeschichte (LHB)*, 1963.
Conzelmann, H. *The Theology of St. Luke (Eng. Tr.)*, 1960.
Correll, A. *Consummatum Est*, 1958.
Cottam, T. *The Fourth Gospel Rearranged*, 1952.

Cox, G. E. P. *The Gospel according to St. Matthew* (*TC*), 1952.
Cranfield, C. E. B. *The Gospel according to St. Mark* (*CGT*, n.s.), 1959.
Creed, J. M. *The Gospel according to St. Luke*, 1930.
Cross, F. L., editor, *Studies in the Fourth Gospel*, 1957.
Cross, F. M. *The Ancient Library of Qumran and Modern Biblical Studies*, 1958.
Crum, J. M. C. *The Original Jerusalem Gospel*, 1927.
Crum, J. M. C. *St. Mark's Gospel*, 1936.
Cullmann, O. *Early Christian Worship* (Eng. Tr.), 1953.
Cullmann, O. *Christology of the New Testament*,[2] 1963.
Cullmann, O. *Peter: Disciple, Apostle, and Martyr*,[2] 1962.
Curtis, W. A. *Jesus Christ the Teacher*, 1943.

Dalman, G. *The Words of Jesus*, 1902.
Daube, D. *The New Testament and Rabbinic Judaism*, 1955.
Davey, J. E. *The Jesus of St. John*, 1958.
Davies, J. G. *He ascended into Heaven*, 1958.
Davies, W. D. *Christian Origins and Judaism*, 1962.
Davies, W. D. *Paul and Rabbinic Judaism*, 1948.
Davies, W. D. and Daube, D., editors, *The Background of the New Testament and its Eschatology*, 1956.
Delafosse, H. *Le Quatrième Evangile*, 1925.
Delff, H. *Die Geschichte des Rabbi Jesus von Nazareth*, 1889.
Dibelius, M. *Jungfrauensohn und Krippenkind*, 1932.
Dibelius, M. *From Tradition to Gospel* (Eng. Tr.),[2] 1934.
Dibelius, M. *Gospel Criticism and Christology*, 1935.
Dibelius, M. *A Fresh Approach to the New Testament and Early Christian Literature*, 1936.
Dibelius, M. *Studies in the Acts of the Apostles* (Eng. Tr.), 1956.
Dodd, C. H. *The Bible and the Greeks*, 1935.
Dodd, C. H. *History and the Gospel*, 1938.
Dodd, C. H. *The Apostolic Preaching and its Developments*,[2] 1944.
Dodd, C. H. *The Johannine Epistles* (*MC*), 1946.
Dodd, C. H. *According to the Scriptures*, 1952.
Dodd, C. H. *New Testament Studies*, 1953.
Dodd, C. H. *The Interpretation of the Fourth Gospel*, 1953.
Dodd, C. H. *Historical Tradition in the Fourth Gospel*, 1963.
Dodd, C. H. *The Authority of the Bible*, 1938.
Dods, M. *The Gospel according to St. John* (*Exp. Bib.*),[2] 1894.
Dods, M. *The Gospel of St. John* (*EGT*), 1907.
Doeve, J. W. *Jewish Hermeneutics in the Synoptic Gospels and Acts*, 1954.
Drummond, J. *An Inquiry into the Character and Authorship of the Fourth Gospel*, 1903.

Duncan, G. S. *Jesus, Son of Man*, 1948.
Dupont, J. *Les Sources du Livre des Actes*, 1960.
Dupont-Sommer, A. *The Essene Writings from Qumran*, 1961.

Earle, R. *The Gospel according to Mark*, 1957.
Easton, B. S. *The Gospel according to St. Luke*, 1926.
Easton, B. S. *The Gospel before the Gospels*, 1928.
Easton, B. S. *Early Christianity: the Purpose of Acts and other papers* (editor, F. C. Grant), 1954.
Edwards, D. *The Virgin Birth in History and Faith*, 1941.
Edwards, H. E. *The disciple who wrote these things*, 1953.
Edwards, R. A. *The Gospel according to St. John*, 1954.
Eichhorn, J. G. *Historische-kritische Einleitung in das Neue Testament*, 1812.
Eisler, R. *The Enigma of the Fourth Gospel*, 1938.
Elliott-Binns, L. E. *Galilean Christianity*, 1956.
Eltester, W., editor, *Neutestamentliche Studien für R. Bultmann*, 1954.
Eltester, W., editor, *Judentum, Urchristentum, Kirche (Festschrift für J. Jeremias)*, 1960.

Farrer, A. *The Glass of Vision*, 1948.
Farrer, A. *A Study in St. Mark*, 1951.
Farrer, A. *St. Matthew and St. Mark*, 1954.
Fascher, E. *Die formgeschichtliche Methode*, 1924.
Feine, P.- Behm, J. *Einleitung in das Neue Testament*,[11] 1956.
Feine, P.- Behm, J.- Kümmel, W. G. *Einleitung in das Neue Testament*,[12] 1963.
Fenton, J. C. *Saint Matthew (PelC)*, 1963.
Filson, F. V. *The Gospel according to St. Matthew (BC)*, 1960.
Filson, F. V. *Three Crucial Decades: Studies in the Book of Acts*, 1963.
Findlay, J. A. *Jesus in the First Gospel*, 1925.
Findlay, J. A. *The First Gospel and the Book of Testimonies*, 1933.
Findlay, J. A. *The Acts of the Apostles*,[4] 1952.
Flew, R. N. *Jesus and His Church*, 1956.
Fuller, R. H. *The New Testament in Current Study*, 1962.
Furneaux, W. M. *The Acts of the Apostles: A Commentary for English readers*, 1912.

Gardner, H. *The Limits of Literary Criticism*, 1956.
Gardner-Smith, P. *The Christ of the Gospels*, 1938.
Gardner-Smith, P. *St. John and the Synoptic Gospels*, 1938.
Gardner-Smith, P., editor, *The Roads Converge*, 1963.
Gärtner, B. *The Areopagus Speech and Natural Revelation* (Eng. Tr. from *Acta Seminarii Neotestamentici Upsaliensis*, xxi), 1955.
Gärtner, B. *John 6 and the Jewish Passover*, 1959.

Garvie, A. E. *The Beloved Disciple*, 1922.

Geldenhuys, J. N. *Commentary on the Gospel of Luke (NLC)*, 1950.

Gerhardsson, B. *Memory and Manuscript*, 1961.

Gibson, J. M. *The Gospel according to St. Matthew (Exp. Bib.)*, 1890.

Gieseler, J. K. L. *Historisch-kritischer Versuch über die Entstehung und die frühesten Schicksale der schriftlichen Evangelien*, 1818.

Gilmour, S. M. *The Gospel according to St. Luke (IB)*, 1952.

Glasson, T. F. *Moses in the Fourth Gospel*, 1963.

Godet, F. *Introduction to the New Testament: The Collection of the Four Gospels and the Gospel of St. Matthew*, 1899.

Goguel, M. *La naissance du christianisme*, 1946.

Goguel, M. *Introduction au Nouveau Testament*, III, 1922.

Gomme, A. W. *A Historical Commentary on Thucydides*, 1945.

Goodspeed, E. J. *Introduction to the New Testament*, 1937.

Goodspeed, E. J. *Matthew, Apostle and Evangelist*, 1959.

Goppelt, L. *Die apostolische und nachapostolische Zeit*, 1962.

Gould, E. P. *The Gospel according to St. Mark (ICC)*, 1896.

Goulder, M. D. *Type and History in Acts*, 1964.

Grant, F. C. *The Earliest Gospel*, 1943.

Grant, F. C. *The Gospel according to St. Mark (IB)*, 1951.

Grant, F. C. *The Gospels, their origin and growth*, 1957.

Grant, F. C. *Roman Hellenism and the New Testament*, 1962.

Grant, R. M. *The Earliest Lives of Jesus*, 1961.

Grant, R. M. *A Historical Introduction to the New Testament*, 1963.

Green, F. W. *The Gospel according to St. Matthew (Clar B)*, 1936.

Griesbach, J. J. *Commentatio qua Marci evangelium totum e Matthaei et Lucae commentariis decerptum esse demonstratur*, 1789.

Grill, J. *Untersuchungen über die Entstehung des vierten Evangeliums*, I, 1902, II, 1923.

Grobel, K. *Formgeschichte und synoptische Quellenanalyse*, 1937.

Grundmann, W. *Das Evangelium nach Lukas*,[2] 1961.

Guilding, A. *The Fourth Gospel and Jewish Worship*, 1960.

Guthrie, D. *New Testament Introduction: The Pauline Epistles*, 1961.

Guthrie, D. *New Testament Introduction: Hebrews to Revelation*, 1962.

Guy, H. A. *The Acts of the Apostles*, 1953.

Guy, H. A. *The Origin of the Gospel of Mark*, 1954.

Hackett, H. B. *A Commentary on the Original Text of the Acts of the Apostles*, 1877.

Haenchen, E. *Die Apostelgeschichte neu übersetzt und erklärt (KEK)*,[13] 1961.

Harnack, A. *The Sayings of Jesus* (Eng. Tr.), 1908.

Harnack, A. *Die Chronologie der altchristlichen Literatur bis Eusebius*, 1897.

Harnack, A. *Luke the Physician* (Eng. Tr.), 1907.

Harnack, A. *The Date of Acts and the Synoptic Gospels* (Eng. Tr.), 1911.

Harnack, A. *The Acts of the Apostles* (Eng. Tr.), 1908.

Harris, J. R. *Testimonies*, I, 1916.

Harris, J. R. *The Origin of the Prologue of St. John's Gospel*, 1917.

Harrison, P. N. *Polycarp's Two Epistles to the Philippians*, 1936.

Hartingsveld, L. van *Die Eschatologie des Johannesevangeliums*, 1962.

Hastings, A. *Prophet and Witness in Jerusalem. A Study of the Teaching of St. Luke*, 1958.

Hawkins, Sir J. C. *Horae Synopticae*,[2] 1909.

Headlam, A. C. *The Life and Teaching of Jesus the Christ*, 1923.

Headlam, A. C. *The Fourth Gospel as History*, 1948.

Heard, R. *An Introduction to the New Testament*, 1950.

Hebert, G. *The Christ of Faith and the Jesus of History*, 1962.

Henderson, I. *Myth in the New Testament*, 1952.

Hendriksen, W. *Exposition of the Gospel according to John*, 1953.

Henshaw, T. *The Foundation of the Christian Church*, 1946.

Henshaw, T. *New Testament Literature*, 1952.

Herder, G. *Von der Regel der Zustimmung unserer Evangelien*, 1797.

Heuschen, J., editor, *La Formation des Evangiles*, 1957.

Higgins, A. J. B. *The Lord's Supper in the New Testament*, 1952.

Higgins, A. J. B. *The Reliability of the Gospels*, 1952.

Higgins, A. J. B. *The Historicity of the Fourth Gospel*, 1960.

Higgins, A. J. B., editor, *New Testament Essays: Studies in Memory of T. W. Manson*, 1959.

Hirsch, E. *Studien zum vierten Evangelium*, 1936.

Hirsch, E. *Frühgeschichte des Evangeliums*,[2] 1951.

Hoare, F. R. *The Original Order and Chapters of St. John's Gospel*, 1944.

Hobart, W. K. *The Medical Language of St. Luke*, 1882.

Holland, H. S. *The Fourth Gospel*, 1923.

Holtzmann, H. J. *Einleitung in das Neue Testament*, 1885.

Hooke, S. H. *Alpha and Omega*, 1961.

Hooker, M. D. *Jesus and the Servant*, 1958.

Hopwood, P. G. S. *The Religious Experience of the Primitive Church*, 1936.

Hort, A. F. *The Gospel according to St. Mark* (Greek Text), 1914.

Hoskyns, Sir E. C. and Davey, F. N. *The Riddle of the New Testament*,[3] 1947.

Hoskyns, Sir E. C. and Davey, F. N. *The Fourth Gospel*,[2] 1947.

Howard, W. F. *Christianity according to St. John*, 1943.

Howard, W. F. *The Gospel according to St. John (IB)*, 1952.

Howard, W. F. *The Fourth Gospel in Recent Criticism* (edited by C. K. Barrett),[2] 1955.

Huck, A.-Lietzmann, H. *Synopsis of the First Three Gospels* (edited F. L. Cross),[9] 1949.

Hughes, P. E. *Scripture and Myth*, 1956.
Hunt, B. P. W. S. *Primitive Gospel Sources*, 1951.
Hunt, B. P. W. S. *Some Johannine Problems*, 1958.
Hunter, A. M. *The Gospel according to St. Mark* (*TC*), 1949.
Hunter, A. M. *Interpreting the New Testament, 1900–1950*, 1951.
Hunter, A. M. *Introducing New Testament Theology*, 1957.
Hunter, A. M. *Introducing the New Testament*,[2] 1957.
Hunter, A. M. *Paul and his Predecessors*,[2] 1961.

Jackson, F. J. F. *The Acts of the Apostles* (*MC*), 1931.
Jackson, F. J. F. and Lake, K., editors, *The Beginnings of Christianity*, 1920–33.
Jacquier, E. *Le Nouveau Testament dans l'Eglise Chrétienne*, 1911.
Jacquier, E. *Les Actes des Apôtres* (*EB*),[2] 1926.
Jameson, H. G. *The Origin of the Synoptic Gospels*, 1922.
Jaubert, A. *La Date de la Cène*, 1957.
Jeremias, J. *Die Wiederentdeckung von Bethesda*, 1949.
Jeremias, J. *The Parables of Jesus*[2] (Eng. Tr.), 1963.
Jeremias, J. *The Eucharistic Words of Jesus*, 1955.
Jeremias, J. *Unknown Sayings of Jesus*, 1957.
Jeremias, J. *Jesus' Promise to the Nations*, 1958.
Johnson, S. E. *The Gospel according to St. Matthew* (*IB*), 1951.
Johnson, S. E. *The Gospel according to St. Mark* (*BC*), 1960.
Jones, M. *St. Paul the Orator*, 1910.
Jones, M. *The New Testament in the Twentieth Century*, 1924.
Jülicher, A.-Fascher, E. *Einleitung in das Neue Testament*,[7] 1931.

Käsemann, E. *Verkündigung und Forschungen*, 1950–51.
Käsemann, E. *Exegetische Versüche und Besinnungen*, I, 1960.
Kenyon, Sir F. *The Story of the Bible*, 1936.
Kenyon, Sir F. *The Bible and Modern Scholarship*, 1948.
Kenyon, Sir F. *The Text of the Greek Bible*,[2] 1949.
Kilpatrick, G. D. *The Origins of the Gospel according to St. Matthew*, 1946.
Kittel, G. *Die Probleme des palästinnischen Spätjudentums und das Urchristentum*, 1926.
Klassen, W. and Snyder, G. F., editors, *Current Issues in New Testament Interpretation*, 1962.
Klostermann, E. *Das Matthäusevangelium* (*LHB*),[2] 1927.
Klostermann, E. *Das Markusevangelium* (*LHB*),[4] 1950.
Klostermann, E. *Das Lukasevangelium* (*LHB*),[4] 1950.
Knopf, R. *Die Apostelgeschichte*, 1906.
Knowling, R. J. *The Acts of the Apostles* (*EGT*), 1900.
Knox, J. *Marcion and the New Testament*, 1942.

Knox, J. *Chapters in a Life of Paul*, 1954.

Knox, J. *The Early Church and the Coming Great Church*, 1957.

Knox, J. *The Death of Christ: The Cross in New Testament History*, 1959.

Knox, W. L. *Some Hellenistic Elements in Primitive Christianity* (Schweich Lectures), 1944.

Knox, W. L. *The Acts of the Apostles*, 1948.

Knox, W. L. *Sources of the Synoptic Gospels*, I, 1953, II, 1957.

Köster, H. *Synoptische Überlieferung bei den apostolischen Vätern*, 1957.

Kragerud, A. *Der Lieblingsjünger im Joh.*, 1959.

Krenkel, M. *Josephus und Lucas*, 1894.

Kümmel, W. G. *Das Neue Testament*, 1958.

Kundsin, K. *Topologische Überlieferungsstücke im Joh.*, 1925.

Lagrange, M.-J. *L'Evangile de Jésus-Christ* (EB), 1954.

Lagrange, M.-J. *Evangile selon St. Matthieu* (EB),[7] 1948.

Lagrange, M.-J. *Evangile selon St. Marc* (EB),[4] 1929.

Lagrange, M.-J. *Evangile selon St. Luc* (EB),[8] 1948.

Lagrange, M.-J. *Evangile selon St. Jean* (EB),[5] 1936.

Lake, K. and S. *An Introduction to the New Testament*, 1938.

Lamont, D. *Studies in the Johannine Writings*, 1956.

Laurentin, R. *Structure et Théologie de Luc*, I–II (EB), 1957.

Leaney, A. R. C. *The Gospel according to St. Luke* (BC), 1958.

Lee, E. K. *The Religious Thought of St. John*, 1950.

Léon-Dufour, X. *Concordance of the Synoptic Gospels in seven colours*, 1956.

Lessing, G. E. *Neue Hypothese über die Evangelisten als bloss menschliche Geschichtsschreiber*, 1778.

Lewis, F. W. *Disarrangements in the Fourth Gospel*, 1910.

Liebermann, S. *Hellenism in Jewish Palestine*, 1950.

Lietzmann, H. *The Beginnings of the Christian Church*, 1937.

Lietzmann, H. *Die drei ältesten Martyrologien* (Kleine Texte, 2), 1911.

Lightfoot, R. H. *History and Interpretation in the Gospels*, 1935.

Lightfoot, R. H. *Locality and Doctrine in the Gospels*, 1938.

Lightfoot, R. H. *The Gospel Message of St. Mark*, 1950.

Lightfoot, R. H. *St. John's Gospel: a Commentary*, 1956.

Lindars, B. *New Testament Apologetic*, 1961.

Loewenich, W. von *Das Johannesverständnis im zweiten Jahrhundert* (Beiheft ZNTW, 13), 1932.

Lohmeyer, E. *Galiläa und Jerusalem*, 1936.

Lohmeyer, E.-Schmauch, W. *Das Evangelium des Matthäus* (KEK), 1956.

Lohmeyer, E.-Sass, G. *Das Evangelium des Markus* (KEK),[12] 1953.

Lohse, E. *Mark's Witness to Jesus Christ*, 1955.

Loisy, A. *Les Evangiles synoptiques*, 1907–08.

Loisy, A. *Evangile selon Luc*, 1924.

Loisy, A. *Les Actes des Apôtres*,[2] 1925.

Loisy, A. *Le Quatrième Evangile, deuxième édition refondue: Les Epîtres dites de Jean*, 1921.

Luce, H. K. *St. Luke* (*CGT*), 1949.

Lumby, J. R. *The Acts of the Apostles* (*CGT*), 1899.

Lüthi, W. *Die Apostelgeschichte ausgelegt für die Gemeinde*, 1958.

Macgregor, G. H. C. *The Gospel of John* (*MC*), 1928.

Macgregor, G. H. C. and Ferris, T. P. *The Acts of the Apostles* (*IB*), 1954.

Macgregor, G. H. C. and Morton, A. Q. *The Structure of the Fourth Gospel*, 1961.

Macgregor, G. H. C. and Morton, A. Q. *The Structure of Luke and Acts*, 1964.

Macgregor, G. H. C. and Purdy, A. C. *Jew and Greek: Tutors unto Christ*,[2] 1959.

Major, H. D. A., Manson, T. W. and Wright, C. T. *The Mission and Message of Jesus*, 1937.

Manson, T. W. *The Teaching of Jesus*,[2] 1935.

Manson, T. W. *The Sayings of Jesus*, 1949.

Manson, T. W. *The Beginnings of the Gospel*, 1950.

Manson, T. W. *Studies in the Gospels and Epistles*, 1962.

Manson, T. W. *On Paul and John*, 1963.

Manson, W. *Jesus the Messiah*, 1943.

Manson, W. *The Gospel of Luke* (*MC*), 1930.

Marlé, R. *R. Bultmann et l'interprétation du N.T.*, 1956.

Marshall, L. H. *Formgeschichte and its limitations*, 1942.

Martin, R. P., editor, *Vox Evangelica*, II, 1963.

Marxsen, W. *Der Evangelist Markus*,[2] 1959.

Massaux, E. *Influence de l'Evangile de St. Matthieu sur la littérature chrétienne avant St. Irenée*, 1950.

Maurer, C. *Ignatius von Antiochien und das Johannesevangelium*, 1949.

McClymont, J. A. *St. John* (*CB*),[2] 1922.

McGiffert, A. C. *A History of Christianity in the Apostolic Age*, 1897.

McNeile, A. H.-Williams, C. S. C. *Introduction to the New Testament*,[2] 1953.

McNeile, A. H. *The Gospel according to St. Matthew*, 1915.

Meinertz, M. *Einleitung in das Neue Testament*,[5] 1950.

Menoud, P. H. *L'Evangile de Jean d'après les recherches récents*,[2] 1947.

Menzies, A. *The Earliest Gospel*, 1901.

Meyer, E. *Ursprung und Anfänge des Christentums*, 1921–23.

Michaelis, W. *Die Sakramente im Joh.*, 1946.

Michaelis, W. *Einleitung in das Neue Testament*[3] (with *Ergänzungsheft*), 1961.

Milik, J. T. *Ten Years of Discovery in the Wilderness of Judaea*, 1959.

Milligan, G. *New Testament Documents*, 1913.

Mitton, C. L. *The Gospel according to St. Mark* (EC), 1957.

Moffatt, J. *Introduction to the Literature of the New Testament,*[3] 1918.

Montefiore, C. G. *The Synoptic Gospels,*[2] 1927.

Montefiore, C. G. *Rabbinic Literature and Gospel Teachings,* 1930.

Montefiore, H. and Turner, H. E. W. *Thomas and the Evangelists,* 1962.

Morgenthaler, R. *Die lukanische Geschichtsschreibung als Zeugnis,* 1949.

Morgenthaler, R. *Statistik des neutestamentlichen Wortschatzes,* 1958.

Morris, L. *The New Testament and the Jewish Lectionaries,* 1964.

Moule, C. F. D. *The Birth of the New Testament,* 1962.

Moulton, J. H. and Howard, W. F. *A Grammar of New Testament Greek,* II, 1929.

Mounce, R. H. *The Essential Nature of New Testament Preaching,* 1960.

Mowinckel, S. *He that Cometh,* 1956.

Nairne, A. *The Faith of the New Testament,* 1920.

Nepper-Christensen, P. *Das Matthäusevangelium—ein judenchristliches Evangelium?,* 1958.

Neufeld, V. H. *The Earliest Christian Confession,* 1963.

Nicklin, T. *Gospel Gleanings,* 1950.

Nineham, D. E. *Saint Mark* (PelC), 1963.

Nineham, D. E., editor, *Studies in the Gospels,* 1955.

Noack, B. *Zur johanneischen Tradition,* 1954.

Norden, E. *Agnostos Theos,* 1913.

Nunn, H. P. V. *The Fourth Gospel,* 1946.

Nunn, H. P. V. *The Son of Zebedee,* 1927.

Nunn, H. P. V. *The Authorship of the Fourth Gospel,* 1952.

Odeberg, H. *The Fourth Gospel interpreted in its Relation to Contemporaneous Religious Currents,* 1929.

Ogg, G. *The Chronology of the Public Ministry of Jesus,* 1940.

O'Neill, J. C. *The Theology of Acts in its Historical Setting,* 1961.

Oxford Society, *The New Testament in the Apostolic Fathers,* 1905.

Parker, P. *The Gospel before Mark,* 1953.

Patten, C. S. *Sources of the Synoptic Gospels,* 1915.

Patzer, H. *Das Problem der Geschichtsschreibung des Thukydides und die thukydideische Frage,* 1937.

Peake, A. S. *A Critical Introduction to the New Testament,* 1909.

Percy, E. *Untersuchungen über den Ursprung der johanneischen Theologie,* 1939.

Percy, E. *Die Botschaft Jesu,* 1953.

Plooij, D. *Studies in the Testimony Book,* 1932.

Plummer, A. *The Gospel according to St. John* (CGT), 1900.

Plummer, A. *Commentary on St. Luke (ICC)*, 1896.

Preuschen, E. *Die Apostelgeschichte (LHB)*, 1912.

Price, J. L. *Interpreting the New Testament*, 1961.

Quasten, J. *Patrology*, I, 1950.

Rackham, R. B. *The Acts of the Apostles (WC)*,[14] 1951.

Ragg, L. *St. Luke (WC)*, 1922.

Ramsay, Sir W. M. *Was Christ born at Bethlehem?*, 1898.

Ramsay, Sir W. M. *The Church in the Roman Empire*,[6] 1900.

Ramsay, Sir W. M. *Luke the Physician*, 1908.

Ramsay, Sir W. M. *The First Christian Century*, 1911.

Ramsay, Sir W. M. *The Bearing of Recent Discoveries on the Trustworthiness of the New Testament*, 1915.

Ramsay, Sir W. M. *St. Paul the Traveller and Roman Citizen*, 1920.

Raney, W. H. *The Relation of the Fourth Gospel to the Christian Cultus*, 1933.

Rawlinson, A. E. J. *The Gospel according to St. Mark (WC)*,[7] 1949.

Redlich, E. B. *The Student's Introduction to the Synoptic Gospels*, 1936.

Redlich, E. B. *An Introduction to the Fourth Gospel*, 1939.

Redlich, E. B. *Form Criticism*, 1939.

Rehkopf, F. *Die lukanische Sonderquelle*, 1959.

Reicke, B. *Glaube und Leben der Urgemeinde (AbThANT)*, 1957.

Reitzenstein, R. *Das iranische Erlösungsmysterium*, 1921.

Renan, E. *Vie de Jésus*, 1863.

Renan, E. *Les Evangiles*, 1877.

Rengstorf, K. H. *Das Evangelium nach Lukas (NTD)*,[8] 1958.

Reuss, E. *History of the Sacred Scriptures of the New Testament*, 1884.

Réville, J. *Le quatrième Evangile, son Origine et sa Valeur historique*, 1901.

Richardson, A. *The Gospels in the Making*, 1938.

Richardson, A. *The Miracle-stories of the Gospels*, 1941.

Richardson, A. *The Gospel according to St. John (TC)*, 1959.

Riddle, D. W. and Hutson, H. H. *New Testament Life and Literature*, 1946.

Ristow, H. and Matthiae, K., editors, *Der historische Jesus und der kerygmatische Christus*, 1962.

Robert, A.-Feuillet, A. *Introduction à la Bible*, II, 1959.

Roberts, C. H. *An Unpublished Fragment of the Fourth Gospel*, 1935.

Robinson, J. M. *The Problem of History in Mark*, 1957.

Robinson, J. M. *A New Quest of the Historical Jesus*, 1959.

Robinson, T. H. *St. Mark's Life of Jesus*, 1922.

Robinson, T. H. *The Gospel of Matthew (MC)*, 1928.

Roller, O. *Münzen, Geld und Vermögensverhältnisse in den Evangelien*, 1929.

Ropes, J. H. *The Synoptic Gospels*, 1934 (r.p. 1960).

Ropes, J. H. *The Apostolic Age in the Light of Modern Criticism*, 1906.
Ruckstuhl, E. *Die literarische Einheit des Johannesevangeliums*, 1951.

Sahlin, H. *Der Messias und das Gottesvolk*, 1945.
Sahlin, H. *Studien zum dritten Kapitel des Lukasevangeliums*, 1949.
Sahlin, H. *Zur Typologie des Johannesevangeliums*, 1950.
Salmon, G. *Introduction to the New Testament*,[6] 1892.
Sanday, W. *The Criticism of the Fourth Gospel*, 1905.
Sanday, W., editor, *Oxford Studies in the Synoptic Problem*, 1911.
Sanders, J. N. *The Fourth Gospel in the Early Church*, 1943.
Sanders, J. N. *The Foundations of the Christian Faith*, 1950.
Schlatter, A. *Die Kirche des Matthäus*, 1929.
Schlatter, A. *Das Evangelium des Lukas*, 1931.
Schlatter, A. *Der Evangelist Johannes*, 1930.
Schlatter, A. *The Church in the New Testament Period* (Eng. Tr.), 1955.
Schleiermacher, F. *A critical Essay on the Gospel of St. Luke* (Eng. Tr.), 1825.
Schmidt, K. L. *Der Rahmen der Geschichte Jesu*, 1919.
Schneckenberger, M. *Ueber den Zweck der Apostelgeschichte*, 1841.
Schneemelcher, W., editor, *Das Problem der Sprache in Theologie und Kirche*, 1959.
Schniewind, J. *Die Parallelperikopen bei Lukas und Johannes*, 1914.
Schniewind, J. *Das Evangelium nach Matthäus (NTD)*,[9] 1960.
Schniewind, J. *Das Evangelium nach Markus (NTD)*,[8] 1958.
Schoeps, H. J. *Theologie und Geschichte des Judenchristentums*, 1949.
Schulz, S. *Untersuchungen zur Menschensohnchristologie*, 1957.
Schulz, S. *Komposition und Herkunft der johanneischen Reden*, 1960.
Schürmann, H. *Quellenkritische Untersuchung des lukanischen Abendmahlsberichtes*, 1953–57.
Schweizer, E. *Ego Eimi*, 1939.
Schweizer, E. *Church Order in the New Testament* (Eng. Tr.), 1961.
Scott, E. F. *The Literature of the New Testament*, 1932.
Scott, E. F. *The Fourth Gospel, its Purpose and Theology*,[2] 1908.
Scrivener, F. H. A. *A Plain Introduction to the Criticism of the New Testament* (edited E. Millar),[4] 1894.
Scroggie, W. G. *A Guide to the Gospels*, 1948.
Sherwin-White, A. N. *Roman Society and Roman Law in the New Testament*, 1963.
Sidebottom, E. M. *The Christ of the Fourth Gospel*, 1961.
Simon, M. *St. Stephen and the Hellenists in the Primitive Church*, 1958.
Simons, E. *Hat der dritte Evangelist den kanonischen Matthäus benutzt?*, 1880.
Sjöberg, E. *Der verborgene Menschensohn in den Evangelien*, 1955.
Smith, B. T. D. *St. Matthew (CGT)*, 1927.

Solages, B. de *A Greek Synopsis of the Gospels*, 1959.

Souter, A. *The Text and Canon of the New Testament*,[2] 1954.

Sparks, H. F. D. *The Formation of the New Testament*, 1952.

Sparks, H. F. D. *A Synopsis of the Gospels*, 1964.

Spitta, F. *Die Apostelgeschichte, ihre Quellen und deren geschichtlicher Wert*, 1891.

Spitta, F. *Zur Geschichte und Literatur des Urchristentums*, 1893.

Stagg, F. *The Book of Acts. The Early Struggle for an unhindered Gospel*, 1955.

Stanton, V. H. *The Gospels as Historical Documents*, 1923.

Stauffer, E. *New Testament Theology*, 1955.

Stauffer, E. *Jesus and His Story*, 1960.

Stauffer, E. *Festschrift, Donum Gratulatorium*, 1962.

Steinmann, A. *Die Apostelgeschichte übersetzt und erklärt*,[4] 1934.

Stendahl, K., editor, *The Scrolls and the New Testament*, 1958.

Stendahl, K. *The School of St. Matthew and its use of the Old Testament*, 1954.

Stevenson, J., editor, *A New Eusebius*, 1957.

Still, J. I. *St. Paul on Trial*, 1923.

Stokes, G. T. *The Book of the Acts of the Apostles (Exp. Bib.)*,[4] 1894.

Stonehouse, N. B. *The Witness of Matthew and Mark to Christ*, 1944.

Stonehouse, N. B. *The Witness of Luke to Christ*, 1951.

Stonehouse, N. B. *Paul before the Areopagus and other New Testament Studies*, 1957.

Stonehouse, N. B. *Origins of the Synoptic Gospels*, 1963.

Strachan, R. H. *The Fourth Evangelist, Dramatist or Historian?*, 1925.

Strachan, R. H. *The Fourth Gospel*,[3] 1941.

Strachan, R. H. *The Historic Jesus in the New Testament*, 1931.

Strack, H. L. and Billerbeck, P. *Kommentar zum Neue Testament aus Talmud und Midrasch*, 1922–61.

Strathmann, H. *Das Evangelium nach Johannes (NTD)*,[8] 1955.

Strecker, G. *Der Weg der Gerechtigkeit*, 1962.

Streeter, B. H. *The Primitive Church*, 1929.

Streeter, B. H. *The Four Gospels*, 1924.

Sutcliffe, E. F. *A Two Year Public Ministry*, 1938.

Swete, H. B. *The Gospel according to St. Mark*,[3] 1927.

Tasker, R. V. G. *The Nature and Purpose of the Gospels*, 1944.

Tasker, R. V. G. *The Gospel according to St. Matthew (TNT)*, 1961.

Tasker, R. V. G. *The Gospel according to St. John (TNT)*, 1960.

Taylor, R. O. P. *The Groundwork of the Gospels*, 1946.

Taylor, V. *Behind the Third Gospel*, 1926.

Taylor, V. *Formation of the Gospel Tradition*, 1935.

Taylor, V. *The Gospels*,[5] 1945.

Taylor, V. *The Gospel according to St. Mark*, 1953.

Taylor, V. *The Life and Ministry of Jesus*, 1954.
Temple, W. *Readings in St. John's Gospel*, 1943.
Tenney, M. C. *The Gospel of John (NLC)*,[2] 1954.
Tenney, M. C. *New Testament Survey*,[2] 1961.
Theron, D. J. *Evidence of Tradition*, 1957.
Thiessen, H. C. *Introduction to the New Testament*,[4] 1956.
Tödt, H. E. *Der Menschensohn in der synoptischen Überlieferung*, 1959.
Torrey, C. C. *The Four Gospels: A New Translation*, 1933.
Torrey, C. C. *Documents of the Primitive Church*, 1941.
Trilling, W. *Das wahre Israel*, 1959.
Trocmé, E. *Le 'Livre des Actes' et l'Histoire*, 1957.
Turner, C. H. *The Gospel according to St. Mark*, 1928.
Turner, H. E. W. *Jesus, Master and Lord*,[2] 1954.
Turner, H. E. W. *Historicity and the Gospels*, 1963.

Unnik, W. C. van, editor, *Neotestamentica et Patristica*, 1962.

Vaganay, L. *Le Problème synoptique*, 1954.

Ward, A. M. *The Gospel according to St. Matthew (EC)*, 1961.
Watkins, H. W. *Modern Criticism considered in its relation to the Fourth Gospel*, 1890.
Weiss, B. *Lukasevangelium (KEK)*,[9] 1901.
Weiss, B. *Manual Introduction to the New Testament* (Eng. Tr.), I, 1887, II, 1888.
Weiss, J. *Das älteste Evangelium*, 1903.
Weiss, J. *The History of Primitive Christianity* (Eng. Tr.), 1937.
Wellhausen, J. *Das Evangelium Matthaei*, 1904.
Wellhausen, J. *Das Evangelium Marci*, 1903.
Wellhausen, J. *Einleitung in die drei ersten Evangelien*,[2] 1911.
Wendling, E. *Ur-Markus*, 1905.
Wendt, H. H. *Die Apostelgeschichte*,[8] 1899.
Werner, M. *Der Einfluss paulinischer Theologie im Mk-Ev* (Beiheft ZNTW, 1), 1923.
Westcott, B. F. *The Gospel according to St. John*, 1887.
Westcott, B. F. *An Introduction to the Study of the Gospels*,[7] 1888.
Wetzel, G. *Die synoptischen Evangelien*, 1883.
Wikenhauser, A. *Die Apostelgeschichte und ihr Geschichtswert*, 1921.
Wikenhauser, A. *New Testament Introduction* (Eng. Tr.), 1958.
Wikenhauser, A. *Synoptische Studien für A. Wikenhauser*, 1935.
Wilckens, U. *Die Missionsreden der Apostelgeschichte*,[2] 1963.
Wiles, M. F. *The Spiritual Gospel*, 1960.
Wilkens, W. *Die Entstehungsgeschichte des vierten Evangeliums*, 1958.

Williams, A. L. *The Hebrew Christian Messiah*, 1916.
Williams, C. S. C. *The Acts of the Apostles (BC)*, 1957.
Williams, R. R. *The Acts of the Apostles (TC)*, 1953.
Wilson, R. McL. *The Gnostic Problem*, 1958.
Windisch, H. *Johannes und die Synoptiker*, 1926.
Wood, H. G. *Jesus in the Twentieth Century*, 1960.
Woolf, B. L. *The Background and Beginnings of the Gospel Story*, 1935.
Wrede, W. *Das Messiasgeheimnis in den Evangelien*, 1901 (r.p. Göttingen, 1963).
Wright, A. *The Composition of the Four Gospels*, 1890.
Wright, A. *Synopsis of the Gospels in Greek*, 1896.
Wright, A. *Some New Testament Problems*, 1898.
Wright, A. *St. Luke in Greek*, 1900.
Wright, G. E. and Fuller, R. H. *The Book of the Acts of God*, 1957.

Zahn, T. *Introduction to the New Testament* (Eng. Tr.), 1909.
Zahn, T. *Die Urausgabe der Apostelgeschichte des Lukas*, 1916.
Zahn, T. *Die Apostelgeschichte*, 1919–21.
Zahrnt, H. *The Historical Jesus* (Eng. Tr.), 1963.

CLASSIFIED BIBLIOGRAPHY

MATTHEW

Commentators: Allen (*ICC*) 1907, Box (*CB*) 1922, Bruce, A. B. (*EGT*) 1907, Cox (*TC*) 1952, Fenton (*PelC*) 1963, Filson (*BC*) 1960, Gibson (*Exp. Bib.*) 1890, Green (*Clar B*) 1936, Johnson (*IB*) 1951, Klostermann (*LHB*)[2] 1927, Lagrange (*EB*)[7] 1948, Lohmeyer-Schmauch (*KEK*) 1956, McNeile 1915, Robinson (*MC*) 1928, Schlatter 1929, Schniewind (*NTD*)[9] 1960, Smith (*CGT*) 1927, Tasker (*TNT*) 1961, Ward (*EC*) 1961, Wellhausen 1904.

Authors of Special Studies: Bacon 1930, Blair 1960, Bornkamm, Barth, G., Held 1963, Butler 1951, Farrer 1954, Findlay 1925, 1933, Goodspeed 1959, Kilpatrick 1946, Massaux 1950, Nepper-Christensen 1958, Stendahl 1954, Strecker 1962, Trilling 1959.

MARK

Commentators: Alexander r.p. 1960, Allen 1915, Bartlet (*CB*) 1922, Beasley-Murray 1957, Blunt (*Clar B*) 1929, Branscombe (*MC*) 1937, Bruce, A. B. (*EGT*) 1907, Carrington 1960, Chadwick (*Exp. Bib.*)[6] 1896, Cole (*TNT*) 1961, Cranfield (*CGT*, n.s.) 1959, Crum 1936, Earle 1957, Gould (*ICC*) 1896, Grant 1943, (*IB*) 1951, Hort 1914, Hunter (*TC*) 1949, Johnson (*BC*) 1960, Klostermann (*LHB*)[4] 1950, Lagrange (*EB*)[4] 1929, Lightfoot 1950, Lohmeyer-Sass (*KEK*)[12] 1953, Marxsen[2] 1959, Mitton (*EC*) 1957, Nineham (*PelC*) 1963, Rawlinson (*WC*)[7] 1949, Schniewind (*NTD*)[8] 1958, Swete[3] 1927, Taylor 1953, Turner 1928, Weiss, J. 1903, Wellhausen 1903.

Authors of Special Studies: Abbott 1901, Bacon 1919, 1925, Beasley-Murray 1957, Boobyer 1942, Burgon 1871, Burkill 1956, 1959, 1963, Cadoux 1935, Farrer 1951, 1954, Guy 1954, Lohse 1955, Menzies 1901, Robinson, J. M. 1957, Robinson, T. H. 1922, Wendling 1905, Werner 1923, Wrede 1901.

LUKE

Commentators: Adeney (*CB*)[2] 1922, Arndt 1956, Balmforth (*Clar B*) 1930, Browning (*TC*) 1960, Bruce, A. B. (*EGT*) 1907, Burton (*Exp. Bib.*) 1909, Caird (*PelC*) 1963, Creed 1930, Easton 1926, Geldenhuys (*NLC*) 1951, Gilmour (*IB*) 1952, Grundmann[2] 1961, Klostermann (*LHB*)[4] 1950, Lagrange (*EB*)[8] 1948, Leaney (*BC*) 1958, Loisy 1924, Luce (*CGT*) 1949, Manson, W. (*MC*) 1930, Plummer (*ICC*) 1896, Ragg (*WC*) 1922, Rengstorf (*NTD*)[8] 1958, Schlatter 1931, Weiss, B. (*KEK*)[9] 1901, Wright 1900.

Authors of Special Studies: Barrett 1961, Bornhäuser 1934, Cadbury (*HTS*) 1919, 1920,[2] 1958, Carpenter 1919, Conzelmann 1960, Harnack 1907, Hastings 1958, Hobart 1882, Krenkel 1894, Laurentin (*EB*) 1957, Morgenthaler 1949,

Ramsay 1908, Rehkopf 1959, Sahlin 1949, Schleiermacher 1825, Schürmann 1953–57, Stonehouse 1951, Taylor 1926.

JOHN

Commentators: Barrett 1956, Bauer (*LHB*)[2] 1925, Bernard (*ICC*) 1928, Bultmann (*KEK*)[13] 1953, Charnwood 1925, Dods (*Exp. Bib.*)[2] 1894, (*EGT*) 1907, Hendriksen 1953, Holland 1923, Hoskyns and Davey[2] 1947, Howard (*IB*) 1952, Lagrange (*EB*)[5] 1936, Lightfoot 1956, Loisy 1921, Macgregor (*MC*) 1928, McClymont (*CB*)[2] 1922, Plummer (*CGT*) 1900, Richardson (*TC*) 1959, Schlatter 1947, Strachan[3] 1941, Strathmann (*NTD*)[8] 1955, Tasker (*TNT*) 1960, Tenney (*NLC*)[2] 1954, Westcott 1887.

Authors of Special Studies: Abbott 1905, 1906, Askwith 1910, Bacon[2] 1918, 1933, Baldensperger 1898, Becker 1956, Bornhäuser 1928, Braun (*EB*) 1959, Burch 1928, Burney 1922, Colwell 1931, Correll 1958, Cottam 1952, Cross, ed. 1957, Davey 1958, Dodd 1953, 1963, Drummond 1903, Edwards, H. E. 1953, Edwards, R. A. 1954, Eisler 1938, Gärtner 1959, Garvie 1922, Glasson 1963, Grill 1902, 1923, Guilding 1960, Harris 1917, Hartingsveld 1962, Headlam 1948, Higgins 1960, Hirsch 1936, Hoare 1944, Howard 1943, 1955, Hunt 1958, Kragerud 1959, Kundsin 1925, Lamont 1956, Lee 1950, Lewis 1910, Loewenich 1932, Macgregor and Morton 1961, Manson, T. W. 1963, Maurer 1949, Menoud[2] 1947, Michaelis 1946, Noack 1954, Nunn 1927, 1946, 1952, Odeberg 1929, Percy 1939, Raney 1933, Redlich 1939, Réville 1901, Roberts 1935, Ruckstuhl 1951, Sahlin 1950, Sanday 1905, Sanders 1943, Schulz 1960, Schweizer 1939, Scott[2] 1908, Sidebottom 1961, Strachan 1925, Temple 1943, Watkins 1890, Wiles 1960, Wilkens 1958.

ACTS

Commentators: Bartlet (*CB*) 1901, Beyer (*NTD*)[9] 1959, Blaiklock (*TNT*) 1959, Blunt(*Clar B*) 1923, Bruce, F. F.[2] 1952, (*NLC*) 1954, Carter and Earle 1959, Cerfaux and Dupont[2] 1958, Conzelmann (*LHB*) 1963, Findlay[4] 1952, Furneaux 1912, Guy 1953, Hackett 1877, Haenchen (*KEK*)[13] 1961, Harnack 1908, Jackson (*MC*) 1931, Jacquier (*EB*)[2] 1926, Knopf 1906, Knowling (*EGT*) 1900, Knox 1948, Loisy 1920, Lumby (*CGT*) 1899, Lüthi 1958, Macgregor and Ferris (*IB*) 1954, Preuschen (*LHB*) 1912, Rackham (*WC*)[14] 1951, Reicke 1957, Steinmann[4] 1934, Stokes (*Exp. Bib.*)[4] 1894, Wendt 1899, Williams, C. S. C. (*BC*) 1957, Williams, R. R. (*TC*) 1953, Zahn 1919–21.

Authors of Special Studies: Bornhäuser 1934, Bruce 1943, Cadbury 1955,[2] 1958, Chase 1902, Clark 1933, Dibelius 1956, Dupont 1960, Easton 1954, Filson 1963, Gärtner 1955, Goulder 1964, Jackson and Lake 1920–33, Norden 1923, O'Neill 1961, Schneckenberger 1841, Simon 1958, Spitta 1891, Stagg 1955, Trocmé 1957, Wilckens[2] 1963, Zahn 1916.

GENERAL WORKS ON THE GOSPELS AND ACTS

Aland, Eltester and Klostermann, ed. 1959, Albertz 1947, 1952, Bailey 1963, Bartsch 1948–55, Beasley-Murray 1954, Black[2] 1954, 1961, Bornkamm 1960, Burkitt[3] 1911,[2] 1922, 1924, Clark 1914, Doeve 1954, Gardner-Smith 1938, Gerhardsson 1961, Gieseler 1818, Grant, F. C. 1957, Grant, R. M. 1961, Harnack 1908, 1911, Headlam 1923, Herder 1797, Higgins 1952, Hirsch[2] 1951, Lessing 1778, Lightfoot 1934, 1938, Meyer 1921–23, Morton and Macgregor 1964, Nicklin 1950, Nineham, ed. 1955, Percy 1953, Renan 1877, Richardson 1938, 1941, Schniewind 1914, Stanton 1923, Stauffer 1960, Streeter 1924, Sutcliffe 1938, Tasker 1944, Taylor, R. O. P. 1946, Taylor, V.[5] 1945, 1954, Torrey 1933, Turner[2] 1954, 1963, Westcott[7] 1888, Windisch 1926, Wood 1960, Woolf 1935, Wright 1890.

SYNOPTIC STUDIES

Abrahams 1917, Albertz 1921, Barr 1938, Beare 1962, Bultmann 1963, Bundy 1955, Bussmann 1925–31, Chapman 1937, Crum 1927, Griesbach 1789, Hawkins[2] 1909, Hunt 1951, Jameson 1922, Jeremias[2] 1963, Knox, W. L. 1953, 1957, Köster 1957, Léon-Dufour 1956, Loisy 1907–08, Major, Manson and Wright 1937, Manson[2] 1935, 1949, 1962, Montefiore[2] 1927, 1930, Parker 1953, Patten 1915, Plooij 1932, Redlich 1936, Ropes 1934, Sanday, ed. 1911, Simons 1880, Solages 1959, Stonehouse 1944, 1963, Vaganay 1954, Wellhausen[2] 1911, Wetzel 1883.

FORM CRITICISM

Bultmann and Kundsin[2] 1962, Dibelius[2] 1934, 1935, Easton 1928, Fascher 1924, Grobel 1937, Hebert 1962, Henderson 1952, Hughes 1956, Marlé 1956, Marshall 1942, Redlich 1939, Ristow and Matthiae, ed. 1962, Robinson, J. M. 1959, Schmidt 1919, Taylor 1935, Zahrnt 1963.

WORKS OF INTRODUCTION

Allen and Grensted 1918, Bacon 1900, Clogg[3] 1948, Dibelius 1936, Feine-Behm-Kümmel[12] 1963, Goodspeed 1937, Grant, R. M. 1963, Heard 1950, Henshaw 1952, Holtzmann 1885, Hoskyns and Davey[3] 1947, Hunter[2] 1957, Jacquier 1911, Jones 1924, Jülicher-Fascher[7] 1931, Lake, K. and S. 1938, McNeile-Williams[2] 1953, Meinertz[5] 1950, Michaelis[3] 1961, Milligan 1913, Moffatt[3] 1918, Peake 1909, Price 1961, Reuss 1884, Riddle and Hutson 1946, Robert-Feuillet 1959, Salmon[6] 1892, Scott, E. F. 1932, Sparks 1952, Tenney[2] 1961, Thiessen[4] 1956, Weiss, B. 1887, Wikenhauser 1958, Zahn 1909.

AUTHOR INDEX

Abbott, E. A., 128
Abrahams, I., 267
Aland, K., 239
Albertz, M., 124, 181
Albright, W. F., 226, 253
Alford, H., 42
Allen, W. C., 38, 58, 68, 71, 126, 143, 150, 158
Argyle, A. W., 338

Bacon, B. W., 27, 29, 32 f., 42, 69, 71, 234, 242 f., 274, 276
Bailey, J. A., 280
Baillie, D. M., 180
Baird, W., 305
Baldensperger, W., 255, 284
Barnikol, E., 337
Barr, A., 173
Barrett, C. K., 12, 138, 194, 217, 219, 225 ff., 231, 235, 237, 241, 244, 246, 256, 258, 263 f., 266-9, 276, 279, 283, 286, 289 f., 292 f., 297, 299, 318 f., 346
Barth, G., 29, 160, 188
Barthélemy, D., 272
Bartlet, J. V., 58, 168, 336
Bauer, W., 234 f., 249, 255 f., 274, 298
Beach, C., 68
Beasley-Murray, G. R., 23, 133
Becker, H., 282, 297
Bengel, J. A., 309
Benoit, P., 165, 166, 184 f., 340
Bernard, J. H., 217, 235, 244, 269, 279, 284 f., 288, 289, 291
Bertram, G., 181
Beyer, H. W., 104, 339
Birdsall, J. N., 15
Black, M., 36, 45, 52, 77, 138, 272, 285, 293, 338
Blackman, A. C., 15
Blaiklock, E. M., 104, 307, 310, 330

Blair, E. P., 23, 41
Blass, F., 74, 108, 344
Bleiben, T. E., 103
Blinzler, J., 272
Boismard, M. E., 244, 275, 280
Boor, C. de, 236
Borgen, P., 169, 273
Bornhäuser, K., 248, 339
Bornkamm, G., 21, 22, 26, 81, 142, 154, 160, 188 f., 256
Boslooper, T., 168
Bowman, J. W., 52
Box, G. H., 30, 167
Bradby, E. L., 143
Brandon, S. G. F., 69-72, 133, 252
Braun, F. M., 244, 259, 296
Briggs, C. A., 165
Broome, C., 283
Brown, J. P., 129, 143
Brown, R. E., 296
Bruce, F. F., 11, 69, 75, 94, 103, 310, 311, 314, 326, 329, 336
Bultmann, R., 22, 52, 59, 81, 92, 124, 169, 180 f., 183-8, 205, 217, 224, 226, 232, 247, 251 f., 274, 276, 277, 280 ff., 283, 286, 297 f., 341
Bundy, W. E., 90, 124, 153, 174
Burch, V., 260 f.
Burgon, J. W., 73
Burkill, T. A., 50, 77, 79
Burkitt, F. C., 35, 74, 128, 135, 141, 155 f., 168, 267, 314, 328, 338
Burney, C. F., 45, 137, 147, 257, 268, 285, 292 f.
Burrows, M., 253, 293, 296
Buse, I., 169, 279
Bussby, P., 138
Bussmann, W., 130, 137, 142
Butler, C., 131

Cadbury, H. J., 58, 87, 90, 93 ff., 97 f., 315 f., 319, 332, 338

Cadoux, C. J., 269, 289
Caird, C. B., 169 f., 172, 175
Calvin, J., 116
Cambier, J., 88
Campenhausen, H. von, 22
Carpenter, S. C., 98, 107
Carrington, P., 25, 62, 63, 120
Casey, R. P., 63
Cassian, Bp., 275
Cave, C. H., 158
Cerfaux, L., 132, 340, 346
Chapman, J., 68
Charles, R. H., 22
Charnwood, Lord, 250
Chase, F. H., 102, 336
Church, W. R., 288
Clark, A. C., 95, 290, 344
Clark, K. W., 21
Clark, W. L., 74
Clogg, F. B., 147
Colani, T., 132
Colson, F. H., 66, 90
Connick, C. M., 246
Conybeare, F. C., 72
Conzelmann, H., 88, 92, 95, 104, 133, 163, 188, 191, 346
Correll, A., 223, 264
Cottam, T., 269, 288 f.
Couchard, P. L., 76
Cranfield, C. E. B., 61, 75, 133
Creed, J. M., 73, 87, 89 f., 97, 103, 104, 107, 110, 167, 173 f.
Cronin, H. S., 290
Cross, F. L., 114
Cross, F. M., 253
Crum, J. M. C., 147
Cryer, C., 284
Cullmann, O., 22, 52, 255 f., 296, 326
Curtis, W. A., 200

Dalman, G., 52
Davey, F. N., 256
Davies, W. D., 62, 231
Daube, D., 158
Delafosse, H., 258
Delff, H., 239

Dibelius, M., 59, 67, 99–103, 124, 167, 181 ff., 187, 310, 320, 327, 329, 333 f., 342 f.
Dieu, L., 338
Dobschütz, E. von, 42
Dodd, C. H., 22, 23, 28, 43, 59 ff., 108, 156, 169, 187, 191, 199, 217, 219, 227, 230 ff., 245 f., 252, 256, 258, 259, 261, 266, 268, 274, 280, 283 ff., 294–9, 305, 328, 338
Doeve, J. W., 199
Drummond, J., 234, 236, 266 f.
Duncan, G. S., 52
Dupont, J., 100, 339, 343
Dupont-Sommer, A., 155

Easton, B. S., 124, 186, 319
Edwards, D., 168
Edwards, H. E., 261 f., 274
Ehrhardt, A., 317
Eichhorn, J. G., 116
Elliott-Binns, L. E., 77
Eltester, W., 101, 134, 158
Enz, J. J., 287
Evans, C. F., 78, 80, 104, 163, 329
Evans, O. E., 141

Farmer, W. R., 161, 182
Farrer, A., 63, 74, 120, 123, 137, 143, 145, 151, 206
Fascher, E., 144, 181
Feine, P., 168
Feine, P.—Behm, J., 38, 164 f., 236, 263
Feine, P.—Behm, J.—Kümmel, W. G., 29, 40, 68, 95, 99, 104, 126, 128, 146, 148, 155, 217, 224, 239, 279, 280, 284, 315 f., 320, 330, 344
Fenton, J. C., 29
Feuillet, A., 286
Filson, F. V., 30, 44, 103, 223
Findlay, J. A., 29, 156, 341
Flew, R. N., 22
Freed, E. D., 281
Fuchs, E., 81, 198
Fuller, R. H., 144, 183, 282

Gaechter, P., 41, 284
Gardner, H., 63
Gardner-Smith, P., 80, 139, 262, 274, 280 f.
Gärtner, B., 26, 102, 104, 272, 327, 329
Geldenhuys, N., 104, 107 f.
Gerhardsson, B., 120, 197 f., 200
Gieseler, J. K. L., 117 f.
Gilmore, A., 272
Gilmour, S. M., 89, 173
Glasson, T. F., 287
Godet, F., 33, 39
Goguel, M., 171, 339
Gomme, A. W., 327
Goodenough, E. R., 259, 261, 274, 281
Goodspeed, E. J., 90, 313, 338
Goodwin, C., 281
Goppelt, L., 330
Goulder, M. D. and Sanderson, M. L., 167
Grant, F. C., 59, 64 f., 67 f., 77, 124, 135, 160, 183, 186, 230 f., 251, 253, 280, 296, 319
Grant, R. M., 103, 108, 146, 148, 170 f., 224, 232, 248, 250, 260, 262, 328
Grässer, E., 303
Grayston, K., 297
Griesbach, J. J., 122
Grill, J., 274
Grobel, K., 201
Grossouw, W., 282
Grundmann, W., 104, 130, 142, 176, 280, 341
Guilding, A., 120, 257, 286 f.
Guthrie, D., 57, 96, 99, 217, 238, 259, 303, 310, 312, 316, 323
Guy, H. A., 60
Gyllenberg, R., 274

Haefner, A. E., 338
Haenchen, E., 26, 100 f., 103, 104, 188, 216, 283, 312, 320, 325, 334 f., 339, 341, 343 f.
Harnack, A., 67 f., 71, 97, 100, 109, 142, 166, 219, 332 f., 338 f., 341
Harris, J. R., 155 f., 199, 245, 285, 292

Harrison, P. N., 16, 258
Hartingsveld, L. van, 257
Hastings, A., 88, 337
Hawkins, Sir J. C., 110, 128, 130, 136 f., 142, 151, 168 f.
Headlam, A. C., 219, 299
Heard, R. G., 67 f.
Hebert, G., 24, 82
Held, G., 188
Henderson, I., 180
Henshaw, T., 205
Herder, G., 117
Higgins, A. J. B., 52, 160, 226, 228, 265, 269, 270 f., 272 f., 300
Hillyer, N., 20
Hirsch, E., 134, 277, 323
Hoare, F. R., 288
Hobart, W. K., 96
Holland, H. S., 262
Holtzmann, H. J., 67
Hommel, H., 101
Hooke, S. H., 206
Hooker, M. D., 52
Hopwood, P. G. S., 304
Hort, F. J. A., 76
Hoskyns, F. C. and Davey, F. N., 256
Howard, W. F., 44, 77, 225, 249, 255, 258, 266, 271, 275, 277 f., 284, 293, 295
Huck, A., 114
Hughes, P. E., 180
Hunt, B. P. W. S., 34, 199, 287
Hunter, A. M., 157, 231, 261

Jackson, F. J. F., 309, 315, 327, 329, 338 f.
Jacquier, E., 320, 346
Jameson, H. G., 122
Jaubert, A., 271 f.
Jeremias, J., 15, 21, 38, 52, 91, 134, 144, 193, 225, 255 f., 271 f., 292, 339, 341
Jervell, J., 334
Johnson, S. E., 39, 51, 56, 58, 64, 68, 135, 153, 326
Jülicher, A.—Fascher, E., 309

Karnetski, M., 77
Käsemann, E., 81, 224, 282, 284, 346
Kennard, J. S., 27
Kenyon, Sir F., 219, 258, 287, 344 f.
Kilpatrick, G. D., 24, 27, 29, 31 f., 35, 40 ff., 44, 51, 107, 149, 151 f., 157, 159, 172, 296
Kittel, G., 338
Klassen, W. and Snyder, G. F., 223, 297
Klein, G., 104
Klijn, A. F. J., 329
Klostermann, E., 133
Knox, J., 15, 20, 52, 104 f.
Knox, W. L., 52, 61, 74, 80, 95, 104, 117, 134, 138, 142, 157 f., 164 ff., 168, 309, 338
Köster, H., 16, 104
Kragerud, A., 224
Krenkel, M., 314
Kümmel, W. G., 95, 298, 303, 339, 346
Kundsin, K., 185, 226
Kürzinger, J., 33, 36 ff.

Lachmann, C., 123
Lagrange, M. J., 77
Lake, K., 323
Lake, K. and S., 54, 129, 141, 193
Laurentin, R., 165
Leaney, A. R. C., 92, 166
Lee, E. K., 279
Léon-Dufour, X., 139
Lessing, G. E., 116
Lewis, F. W., 288, 290
Liebermann, S., 231
Lietzmann, H., 114, 224, 236
Lightfoot, R. H., 66, 73 f., 77, 79, 81, 124, 274
Lindars, B., 92, 157, 280
Lockton, W., 122
Loewenich, W. von, 245, 298
Lohmeyer, E., 70, 73, 77, 79, 286
Lohse, E., 62, 88, 256
Loisy, A., 101, 259, 332, 346
Luce, H. K., 167

Macgregor, G. H. C., 171, 247, 250, 277 f., 288, 293, 312, 339
Machen, J. G., 167
MacNeill, H. L., 168
Manson, T. W., 32, 34, 50, 52, 63, 69, 75 f., 81 f., 107, 132, 135 f., 138, 148 f., 154, 163, 180, 238 f., 245, 269, 285, 300
Manson, W., 52, 89, 184
Marshall, I. H., 194, 286
Martin, R. P., 272, 303
Marxsen, W., 50, 58, 64, 188
Massaux, E., 19
Matthiae, K., 148
Maurer, C., 259
McCasland, S. V., 156
McCown, C. C., 74
McGiffert, A. C., 323
McNeile, A. H., 22, 70, 153, 158
McNeile, A. H.—Williams, C. S. C., 15, 155, 162, 164 f.
Mendner, S., 280, 288
Meinertz, M., 44, 71, 219, 267
Menoud, P. H., 95, 343
Meyer, E., 258
Michaelis, W., 27, 39 f., 42, 44, 58, 63, 88, 90, 98, 103, 134, 176, 220, 256, 281, 319, 334, 337 f.
Michel, O., 23
Milik, J. R., 272
Miller, E., 73
Mitton, C. L., 261
Moffatt, J., 123, 132, 288, 290
Mollat, D., 286
Montefiore, H., 125
Montefiore, H. and Turner, H. E. W., 16, 145
Morgenstern, H., 272
Morgenthaler, R., 91, 110, 346
Morris, L., 286
Morton, A. Q., 171, 277 f., 339
Moule, C. F. D., 23, 26, 38, 67, 246, 250
Moulton, J. H. and Howard, W. F., 44, 77, 166, 292
Mounce, R. H., 305
Mowinckel, S., 52, 214

Munck, J., 37, 297
Murray, J., 57

Nauck, W., 101
Nepper-Christensen, P., 21, 31, 37
Nestlé, E., 76, 137
Nicklin, T., 39, 62, 130
Nineham, D. E., 55, 60 f., 65, 67, 80, 124, 135, 184, 189 f.
Noack, B., 282
Nock, A. D., 343
Norden, E., 100 f.
Nunn, H. P. V., 234, 244

Odeberg, H., 295
Oepke, A., 22
O'Neill, J. C., 103 ff., 309, 310, 315, 320, 328
Osty, C. E., 169
Otley, R. R., 73

Parker, P., 35, 139, 240, 280
Patten, C. S., 142
Patzer, H., 327
Peabody, A. P., 232
Percy, E., 63, 251
Perry, A. M., 139, 168 f.
Petrie, C. S., 146, 174
Plooij, D., 155, 285, 319
Plummer, A., 165, 264
Porter, J. R., 286
Potter, R. D., 225
Prentice, W., 98

Quasten, J., 32
Quispel, G., 16

Rabenach, J., 286
Rackham, R. B., 308, 311, 317, 336, 345
Ramsay, Sir W. M., 97, 106, 309, 321, 327
Raney, W. H., 257, 267, 289
Rawlinson, A. E. J., 53, 74, 179
Redlich, E. B., 124, 153, 183, 187, 189, 219, 263 ff., 269, 289
Rehkopf, F., 173
Reicke, B., 103, 163, 326, 339

Reitzenstein, R., 298
Renan, E., 276
Rengstorf, K. H., 90, 97
Réville, J., 259
Reynolds, H. R., 232
Riesenfeld, H., 197
Rigg, H. A., 66, 69
Ristow, H. and Matthiae, K., 148
Robert, A.—Feuillet, A., 139, 286, 346
Roberts, C. H., 245, 287
Robinson, D. F., 132
Robinson, J. A. T., 250, 253, 255, 274, 285, 300
Robinson, J. M., 81, 283
Robinson, T. H., 50
Roller, O., 58
Ropes, J. H., 25, 31, 139, 345
Rosché, T. R., 146
Ruckstuhl, E., 277 f., 282, 292
Russell, H. G., 313

Sahlin, H., 88, 164, 176, 287, 319, 343
Salmon, G., 73
Sanday, W., 129, 168, 219, 236, 248
Sanders, J. N., 15, 67, 223, 234, 240, 244 f., 259, 265, 280, 323
Sanderson, M. L., 167
Sawyerr, H., 61
Schille, G., 25, 54, 343
Schlatter, A., 287, 295
Schleiermacher, F., 116 f.
Schmidt, K. L., 59, 92, 179
Schmiedel, P. W., 244, 258, 299
Schnackenburg, R., 284
Schneckenberger, M., 319
Schneider, J., 163
Schniewind, J., 27, 64, 71, 142, 144, 280
Schoeps, H. J., 21
Schulz, S., 283, 298
Schürmann, H., 91, 148, 173, 181
Schweizer, E., 22, 50, 52, 176, 276, 278, 292
Scott, E. F., 224, 247, 251, 259, 274, 294
Scrivener, F. H. A., 73
Sherwin-White, A. N., 56 f., 167, 318, 321 f.

Simon, M., 329
Simons, E., 123
Sjöberg, E., 52
Smalley, S. S., 305
Smith, C. W. F., 22
Smith, D. M., 280, 283
Smith, M., 198
Smith, R. H., 287
Snape, H. C., 252
Snyder, C. F., 223
Solages, B. de, 114, 137
Souter, A., 15, 16, 76
Sparks, H. F. D., 91, 105, 114, 280, 315, 338, 346
Spicq, C., 261
Spitta, F., 75, 165, 290, 309, 339
Stagg, F., 312
Stanton, V. H., 34, 123, 126, 132, 168, 245
Stauffer, E., 167, 272 f.
Stempvoort, P. A. van, 95
Stendahl, K., 25 f., 28, 41, 157 f., 326
Stephenson, A. M. G., 67
Stevenson, J., 15
Stonehouse, N. B., 31, 36, 74, 87, 102, 129, 329
Strachan, R. H., 222, 251, 255, 268, 276, 294
Strack, H. L.—Billerbeck, P., 295
Strecker, G., 21, 150, 156
Streeter, B. H., 22, 26 f., 43 f., 66, 70, 74, 109, 123 f., 128 ff., 132, 137, 142, 147 f., 150, 154, 158, 160, 162, 168, 319
Styler, G. M., 131
Sutcliffe, E. F., 269
Swete, H. B., 62, 66, 72 f., 76, 126

Tarelli, C. C., 262
Tasker, R. V. G., 24, 147, 219, 239, 268
Taylor, V., 22, 39 f., 43, 50 ff., 55, 57 f., 62 f., 64, 69, 70, 74, 76 f., 85, 91, 107, 109, 124, 128, 130, 132 ff., 137, 141 f., 145, 147 f., 151, 154, 159 f., 162, 166, 168 f., 171-6, 184, 187, 193 f., 201, 205, 232, 239, 250, 258, 270, 279

Teeple, H. M., 253 f., 283, 296
Temple, S., 133, 169, 227
Theron, D., 37, 66, 68
Thompson, P. J., 164
Thomson, J. M., 114, 288
Throckmorton, B. H., 134
Titus, E. L., 223
Tödt, H. E., 52
Torrey, C. C., 45, 69, 74, 77, 129, 164, 166, 293, 337, 345
Townsend, J. F., 329
Trilling, W., 23
Trocmé, E., 104, 309 f., 317, 320, 340, 344, 346
Turner, C. H., 60, 76, 129, 135
Turner, H. E. W., 16, 66, 135, 152, 184 ff., 205
Turner, N., 166
Tyson, J. B., 74

Unnik, W. C. van, 37, 247, 317

Vaganay, L., 45, 128, 131, 138, 275
Vielhauer, P., 102, 104, 164
Volkmar, G., 67

Walker, N., 132, 156
Watkins, H. W., 271, 276
Weiss, B., 168, 337
Weiss, J., 54, 168, 179, 341
Weiss, K., 280
Wellhausen, J., 58, 179 f.
Wendling, E., 134
Wendt, H. H., 262, 276, 341
Werner, M., 67
Westcott, B. F., 20, 118-21, 264
Wetzel, G., 119
Wikenhauser, A., 12, 102, 139, 144, 319
Wilckens, U., 102
Wilder, A. N., 95, 198
Wiles, M. F., 221
Wilkens, W., 283
Williams, C. S. C., 103, 313, 338
Williams, R. R., 104, 309, 314, 320
Wilson, R. McL., 143, 145, 165 f., 297

Wilson, W. G., 291
Wilson, W. J., 337
Windisch, H., 98, 100, 102, 249,
  273 f., 323 f.
Winter, P., 164 f., 326
Wood, H. G., 55, 64, 98, 131, 180,
  205

Wrede, W., 179 f.
Wright, A., 119

Zahn, T., 45, 66, 262, 309, 320,
  344
Zahrnt, H., 82
Zwaan, J. de, 338

SUBJECT INDEX

Abraham, 213

Acts, authorship: see Luke

Acts, characteristics: relation to other New Testament books, 303; view of history, 303; portrait of primitive communities, 304; record of primitive theology, 304; focus on Peter and Paul, 305 f.

Acts, date: arguments for a date before AD 64, 307 ff.; arguments for a date AD 70–85, 312 f.; arguments for a second-century date, 314 f.

Acts, historicity: Luke's political knowledge, 321 f.; relationship to Paul's Epistles, 322 ff.; the speeches in Acts, 326

Acts, purpose: a narrative of history, 316; a spiritual gospel, 317; an apology, 317 f.; a defence brief, 319; a theological document, 320

Acts, sources: factors affecting them, 330 ff.; various types of theory, personal information, 335 ff.; combination of written and oral sources, 337 f.; combination of duplicate sources, 338 ff.; combination of complementary sources, 340; Antiochene source, 340; itinerary theory, 341 ff.; fiction theory, 343; theories of successive redactions, 343 f.

Acts of John, 238

Agrippa II, 71

Alogi, 205, 245

Ancient historiography, 327

Anti-Marcionite Prologues, 57, 69 n. 2, 90, 93, 97 n. 5, 235

Aphraates, 236

Apologetics, 14, 24

Apophthegms, 183, 187

Aramaic, 36 f., 44 f., 76 f., 127, 165, 293, 337 f., 345 f.

Areopagitica, 101, 329

Aristion, 72

Basilides, 104

Bernice, 71

Caligula, 69

Canonicity, 15 ff., 204 f.

Carthaginian Calendar, 236

Catechesis, 14, 26, 206, 209 f., 262

Chrysostom, 58, 221

Claudius' edict, 72

Cleansing of the temple, 268 f.

Clement of Alexandria, 15, 65, 67 ff., 93, 235, 248, 260

Clement of Rome, 16, 244

Complexes in Mark's Gospel, 62

Connected sequences in the Gospels, 190

Contents of M, 152 f.

Contents of Q, 139 ff.

Corpus Paulinum, 312

Council decrees, 324

Criteria for distinguishing sources, 332 f.

Demythologization, 180

Diatessaron, 244

Didache, 43, 104

Dionysius of Alexandria, 243

Dioscorides, 97

Discourses: Matthew's Gospel, 27 ff.; John's Gospel, 266 ff.

Dislocation theories for John's Gospel, 287–291

Docetism, 250, 259 f., 298

Documentary hypothesis for the Synoptic Gospels, 123 f.

Duration of the ministry of Jesus, 269

Ebionites, 78
Editorship in New Testament criticism, 201 ff.
Egerton Papyrus (2), 245, 258
Epiphanius, 245
Eusebius, 72, 97, 108, 245
Evangelistic purpose of Mark, 53 f.
Exodus typology in John's Gospel, 287
External testimony, a right approach to this, 195 ff.

Fall of Jerusalem, 43 f., 69 ff., 106 ff., 312 f.
Form criticism: general criticisms, 189 ff.; limits, 191 f.; reasons for its rise, 178–181; theories of theological editing, 188 f.
Form criticism, types of theory: missionary preaching theory, 181 f.; Christian imagination theory, 183 ff.; theory of purely literary analysis, 186; theories of limited value, 187 f.
Form criticism, value of, 192 ff.
Formless stories, 187
Four source theory, 124 f.
Fragment theory for the Gospels, 116

Galatians and Acts, 322–325
Galen, 97
Galilee in Mark's Gospel, 77 ff.
George Hamartolus, 236 f.
Gnostic Redeemer myth, 251
Gnostics, 145, 244 f., 250 f., 258 f., 281 f., 297 f.
Gospel according to the Hebrews, 35
Gospel of Peter, 31
Gospel of Thomas, 145
Gospels, their literary form, 11, 12
Guess-work theories in Gospel criticism, 196

Habakkuk commentary (Qumran), 25
Heracleon, 244
Hermetic literature, 252, 296
Hippocrates, 97

Historicity in Mark, 79–82
Holy Spirit: in Gospel criticism, 206 f.; in John's Gospel, 213

Ignatius, 16, 43, 238, 244, 258 f.
Irenaeus, 15, 27, 36, 57, 65, 68 f., 75, 93, 233 f., 238, 260

Jerome, 65, 90
Jesus' power to predict, 44, 70
John and the Synoptic Gospels: differences through John's omissions, 263 f.; differences through John's additions, 264 f.; differences in presentation, 265 ff.; historical and chronological problems, 268 ff.; explanation of the relationship, 273
John, authorship: personal allusions, 217 ff.; the 'beloved disciple', 220 ff.; Palestinian background, 224 ff.; eyewitness details, 227 f.; comparisons with the Synoptic Gospels, 228 ff.; Hellenistic thought, 230 f.; other considerations, 232 f.; external evidence, 233 ff.; various propositions regarding authorship, 239–246
John, background: primitive Christianity, 294; Paulinism, 294 f.; Judaism, 295 f.; Hermetic literature, 296; Philonism, 296; Gnosticism, 297 f.; Mandaism, 298
John, characteristics: the place of the Old Testament, 212 f.; the Spirit, 213 f.; great themes, 214 f.; comparative lack of movement, 215; portrait of Jesus, 215 f.
John, dislocations, 287–291
John, early use of, 243 ff., 258 f.
John, historicity of, 298 ff.
John Mark, 67
John of Jerusalem, 239
John, purpose of: author's own statement, 246 ff.; an ancient account, 248 f.; supercession theory, 249; polemic theory, 249 f.; anti-Gnostic theory, 250 ff.; Hellen-

John, purpose of:—*cont.*
   ization theory, 252 ff.; anti-Baptist theory, 254 f.; ecclesiastical polemic idea, 255 f.; eschatological corrective theory, 256 f.; liturgical purpose, 257
John's early martyrdom, alleged evidence in support, 236
John's Ephesian residence, 237 f.
John's framework, 284
John, sources of, 278 ff.
John the Elder, 241 ff.
John, unity of the Gospel, 275–278
Josephus, 57, 106, 314
Justin, 11, 16, 67, 73, 103 f., 238, 244

Kerygma, 59, 80

Last supper, John's dating of, 270–273
Latinisms, 56, 58
Law, Paul's attitude to, 323
Lazarus as 'beloved disciple', 223
Legends, 182
Little Apocalypse (Mark), 132 f.
Liturgical influences, 14, 62 f., 257, 286 f.
Logia, 32–39
Logos doctrine, 216, 284 f.
Lucian, 12
Luke, authorship: preface, 92 f.; testimony of tradition, 93 f.; internal testimony, unity of authorship in Luke-Acts, 94 f.; author a companion of Paul, 95 ff.; objections to Lucan authorship: historical discrepancies, 98 f.; we-sections, 99 ff.; theological difficulties, 101 ff.; literary parallels, 103; conclusions of discussion on authorship, 103
Luke, canticles of, 165
Luke, characteristics: comprehensiveness, 84; universalism, 84; interest in people, 85 f.; prayer, 86 f.; the Holy Spirit, 87; joyfulness, 87
Luke, great omission of, 129 ff.

Luke, 'journey' narrative of, 92, 174
Luke, preface of, 13, 87 f., 92 f., 202 f., 331 f.
Luke, special material of: general contents, 161 ff.; nativity narratives 163 ff.; Proto-Luke, 168–176
Luke's portrait of Paul, 325
LXX influence in Luke's nativity narratives, 166 f.

Mandaism, 298
Marcion, 104 f., 315
Mark, authorship: identity of Mark, 65; connection with Peter, 65 ff.
Mark, beginning of, 75 f.
Mark, characteristics: Gospel of action, 49 f.; Gospel for the Gentiles, 50 f.; its candour, 51; its portrait of Jesus, 51 ff.
Mark, date: conflicting external testimony, 68 f.
Mark, ending of, 72–75
Mark, evidence for Gentile readers, 55 ff.; evidence for Roman origin, 57 ff.
Mark, framework of the Gospel, 59 ff.
Mark, passion narrative of, 133 f.
Mark, priority of: reasons in support, 126 ff.; problems arising, 128 ff.; alternative theories, 131 f.
Mark, sources of, 132–136
Mark's use of Q, 134 f.
Matthew, authorship: ancient tradition, 31 ff.; objections to the traditional view, 39 ff.; incidental supports, 42
Matthew, characteristics: conciseness, 19; messianic interest, 19 f.; particularism and universalism, 20 f.; ecclesiastical elements, 21 f.; eschatological elements, 22
Matthew, origin of: community idea, 24 f.; school idea, 25 f.
Matthew, place of origin, 26 f.
Matthew, priority of, 131 f.
Matthew's sayings collection (M): reasons for postulation, 151 f.; main

Matthew's sayings collection (M):—
cont.
characteristics, 152; probable con-
tents, 152 f.; value, 153 f.; date
and place of origin, 154
Matthew's special material: testimony
book, 154–157; birth narratives,
157 f.; other narratives, 159 f.
Medical language of Luke, 96 f.
Memory techniques among the Jews,
197 f.
Messianic secret, 55, 179
Montanism, 245
Moses, five books of, as a pattern
for Matthew, 29
Muratorian Canon, 93, 195, 235
Mutual dependence theory, 122
Myths, 182

Nathaniel as 'beloved disciple', 223
Nazarenes, 78, 116
Nero, Redivivus, 22
Novellen, 182
Numerical groupings in Matthew,
29 f.

Objections to the oral theory, 120 ff.
Old Testament testimonia, 199
Oral theory, 117–122, 197 ff.
Oral theory compared with form
criticism, 121 f.
Origen, 37, 65, 93, 221, 235
Original Gospel hypothesis, 116

Pantaenus, 37
Papias, 17, 27, 31 ff. (on Matthew),
57, 65 ff. (on Mark), 156, 241 ff.
(on the Elder John), 260
Paradigms, 182
Parousia, 13
Pella, 108, 262 n. 1
Pericope adulterae, 290 f.
Persecution, 70
Personal reminiscence in Gospel
development, 197 f.
Petrine tradition behind Mark, 135 f.
Philip of Side, 236 f.

Philo, 296 f.
Philostratus, 12
Poetic forms in John, 292
Polycarp, 16, 104, 233 ff., 238, 244,
258
Pre-canonical tradition in John, 283 f.
Prologue of John, 284 f.
Pronouncement sayings, 187
Proto-Luke, 168–176, 210: grounds
for the hypothesis, 169 ff.; criticisms
of hypothesis, 172 ff.; value of
hypothesis, 175 f.

Q, discussion of the hypothesis:
reasons for hypothesis, 136 ff.;
multiple theories, 137 f., 141; character of the document, 141; different
uses by Matthew and Luke, 142;
recension theory, 143; problems,
143 ff.; lack of parallel literary types,
145; probable purpose, 146 f.; value,
147 f.; date and place of origin, 148;
authorship, 148 f.; conclusion of
discussion, 149 f.
Q, the sayings source, 34, 67, 136–150
Quartodeciman dispute, 234 n.1, 240
Quirinius, 167
Qumran, 25, 231, 253 f., 261, 271 f.

Rabbinical methods of argument, 232
Rabbinical methods of teaching,
197 ff.
Realized eschatology, 256
Redeemer, Mark's references to Christ
as, 53
Revealer theory for John's Gospel,
286
Rylands' Papyrus (457), 245, 258

Selectivity in Gospel production,
207 f.
Semitisms in Luke, 109 f.
Shepherd of Hermas, 57
Simplification in Gospel criticism, 203
Sitz im Leben, 180 f., 185, 206, 329
Son of man concept, 52

Source criticism in John's Gospel, 278 f.
Speeches in Acts, 326 ff.
Spiritual character of John's Gospel, 248 f.
Stylistic criteria in Acts, 332
Stylistic phenomena in John, 281 f.
Suffering Servant, 52
Synoptic comparisons: divergences, 115; similarities, 114 f.
Syrian martyrology, 236

Tatian, 16, 116, 244
Tertullian, 15, 67, 93, 104, 235
Testimonia, 34 f., 154–157
Theological editing of forms, 188
Theological motives in Gospel production, 88, 92
Theophilus, 89 f.

Thucydides, 88, 327 f.
Title of Matthew's Gospel, 31
Tradition-bearers, 202 f.
Typology, 63 f.

Uniqueness of the subject of the Gospels, 205
Unit-traditions, 189 ff.
Unity of John's Gospel, 275–278
Ur-Markus, 128 f., 132, 134

Valentinus, 104
Victor of Capua, 16

We-sections in Acts, 93, 95 f., 99 ff., 334 f.
Western Text of Acts, 344 f.
Written notes, probable early use of, 200